PUNIC WARS
&
CULTURE WARS

CHRISTIAN ESSAYS ON HISTORY
AND TEACHING

*To Bob,
God's blessings on seeing Him
in history.
Ben House*

Ben House

Foreword by
Dr. George Grant

Covenant Media Press
© 2008

Ben House,
Punic Wars & Culture Wars: Christian Essays on History and Teaching

© 2008 by Ben House

Published by Covenant Media Press
Nacogdoches, TX
www.cmfnow.com

All rights reserved. No part of this publication may be reproduced, stored in a retrieval system, or transmittred in any form by any means, electronic, mechanical, photocopy, recording, or otherwise, without prior permission of the author, except as provided by USA copyright law.

ISBN: 978-0-9678317-8-7

Contents

Acknowledgements vii
Foreword to House Wars, Punic and Otherwise xi

1. The Importance of Being Irrelevant 1
2. Punic Wars and Culture Wars 23
3. Classical Christian Education: A Sampling of Some History 41
4. History After Grammar School: Teaching Jr. High 59
5. That Bully Sandie Pendleton 79

HISTORIANS & HISTORY TEACHERS
6. Eusebius—Father of Church History 87
7. Augustine and The City of God 99
8. Another Christopher, Another Christ-bearer 111
9. The Making of a History Teacher 123
10. Goads and Nails: Reformed Influences 139
11. Otto Scott and the Sacred Fools 163
12. Did You Hear the One About the Three Historians? 175

WESTERN CIVILIZATION: CHRISTENDOM
13. Greek to All of Us 187
14. It Takes a Monk to Save a Civilization 199
15. Some Not So Good Ole Days 205
16. The Great Siege: Then and Now 213
17. Light on the Enlightenment 225
18. The Crooked Road from Darwin to Hitler 235
19. The Saved Generation 245

AMERICAN HISTORY—A CALVINIST'S INTERPRETATION
20. The Protestant Reformation—American History, Chapter One 255
21. The Reformation in America 281
22. The Presbyterian War 321
23. 1776 and Washington's Crossing 345
24. A Southern Perspective 351
25. The Greater Depression 373
26. The Legacy of Francis Schaeffer 387

AFTERWORD 399
An Annotated Bibliography 403
Index 439

Dedicated to George Grant and Andrew Sandlin
Scholars, Faithful Pastors, Friends

"He who prophesies speaks edification
and exhortation and comfort to men"
1 Corinthians 14:3

Acknowledgements

"Writing is the best way to talk without being interrupted."
Jules Renard

But I was interrupted—many times—in the writing of this book. Thanks be to God for *most* of those interruptions. The greatest interruptions—not always appreciated at the moment—were those from my wife and children. Along with family, having to pull away from the laptop computer and go to teach my classes for both school and church were further interruptions. The siren lure of books already written pulled me away from this book I was trying to write. The search for a reference often led to a diversion down some path unrelated to the topic at hand. Prayer itself is an interruption—a much needed one.

This book is an answer to many prayers. God has blessed my many years of accumulating, reading, marking, and teaching from shelves and shelves of books. To the many books and authors from which I have gathered ideas, words, and beliefs, I offer this book as a testimony of gratitude. It has grown from a series of unrelated essays, as random as life itself seems at times, into what I hope is a unified whole, which also is true of life itself. At points, it is surely repetitious; perhaps, at points, inconsistent; hopefully, at points, helpful to all who love history and see God's hand directing its course. For most of my life, I have been spared having to work at a job merely to pay the bills. Being a history teacher, my vocation is also my avocation. Hopefully, other teachers can find a few resources or ideas here.

This book is dedicated to Dr. George Grant and Dr. Andrew Sandlin, two true doctors of the church, who are largely responsible for this book coming together. Over the course of several years, both men faithfully posted essays of mine on their web-sites. Both men encouraged me by drawing me out of the wilderness and into a larger fellowship with the saints. Both are models of Christian piety and thought. Both exemplify the best of the Reformed faith and life. Thank you, George, for your unfailing encouragement and for your ministry to both great causes and obscure ones, like helping

Acknowledgements

unknown want-to-be writers. Thank you, Andrew, for pronouncing blessings upon my more quirky ideas and recommending that I get a laptop computer. May God continue to bless both of your ministries to your congregations and to your wider reading and listening audiences.

Randy Booth has always been close at hand when I needed help, encouragement, and friendship. Along with his duties as pastor of Grace Covenant Church in Nacogdoches, Texas and as moderator of the Confederation of Reformed Evangelical Churches, he formatted the chapters of this book and oversaw its production. Second only to Randy's performing a most significant wedding ceremony back in 1991, this book is, in my opinion, the greatest thing ever done by this friend who is doing many great works for God's kingdom. I hope our mutual mentor, Dr. Greg Bahnsen, would approve of this work.

Thanks to Grace Covenant Church in Texarkana, Arkansas and to the session of elders for supporting this work. Thanks also to Sean Mahaffey for all of his personal encouragement from the days when he was a mere student in my classes to now as a fellow pastor. Thanks also to Veritas Academy, the faculty, board, and students for allowing me to teach and serve as headmaster of the school. Thanks also to my Humanities students who have been models of youthful scholarship and potential. Those of you who were either part of the Elite Six of 2005-06 or the Terrifying Ten of 2006-07 are testimonies to the vision and wisdom of our forefathers concerning classical Christian education.

Thanks also to Patch Blakey and Steve Wilkins for their kind, but exaggerated endorsements of this book. Patch, as director of the Association for Classical Christian Schools, labors in a new Reformation taking place in Christian education in America. Pastor Wilkins has not only taught and ministered to his own congregation and many fellow pastors, but also he has influenced many Christian teachers, students, and homeschoolers in his lectures and books.

Thanks to Bojidar Marinov, a translator for the Bulgarian Reformation Society, who encouraged me to write something weekly and who translated and posted the original version of the essay, "Punic Wars and Culture Wars," into the Bulgarian language. I enjoyed the legendary fifteen minutes of fame—in Bulgaria.

Thanks also to Toni Lemley, my sister-in-law and fellow teacher, for doing serious proof-reading. You spared me many mistakes. Thanks to Betty Nix for printing out the early chapters. Thanks to Ryan Brown for collating proofs for the book, and to Ryan, Eli Ramsey and Graham Alexander for our 2006 odyssey to the Christian Worldview Student Conference in Newport

Acknowledgements

News, Virginia. That great conference was exceeded only by the fellowship of three thousand miles and nine days of all too close proximity. For me, at the half-century mark, it was a last youthful fling, and it gave me the inspiration to complete the initial draft of this book.

The many authors I have cited, the many books that have creased the gray matter of my brain, and the many words that have awakened or redirected my ideas are all to be credited for anything worthwhile in this book. Any overlooked acknowledgments, any ideas that are marketed here second-hand, and any mistakes are all the fault of the author.

A special thanks goes to Stephanie, my wife, and my four children, Nicholas, TaraJane, Nathaniel, and Louisa Caroline. The family pays a high price when Daddy writes. Their nearness to where I am working, the sounds of play and laughter, the interruptions of daily family life, and all such are distractions from the computer screen or book at hand, but it is my family which made this book possible. I love you all.

Anytime I reflect upon my education and career, I am reminded of the debt I owe to my father and mother, Joe Mac and Jodie House. Their labors, sacrifices, and love for their children are an abiding inheritance now being enjoyed by their grandchildren. I especially thank them for raising me in church and supporting my desire for a college education.

God rules history. His wisdom, power, and love will advance His kingdom through all the ages. My prayer is that this work will be a means used by God to achieve His purposes.

Ben House
Initially written on December 28, 2006, my fifty-first birthday, and Feast of the Holy Innocents Day;
Revised and completed in the spring of 2008.

Foreword to *House Wars, Punic and Otherwise*
By George Grant

  In his remarkable book entitled *The Moral Sense*, James Q. Wilson makes the point that "the best things in life" invariably "cost us something." We must sacrifice to attain them, to achieve them, to keep them, even to enjoy them.

  That is one of the most important lessons we can learn in life. It is the message that we know we ought to instill in our children: patience, commitment, diligence, constancy, and discipline will ultimately pay off if we are willing to defer gratification long enough for the seeds we have sown to sprout and bear.

  A flippant, shallow, and imprecise approach to anything—be it sports or academics or the trades or business or marriage—is ultimately self-defeating. It is not likely to satisfy any appetite—at least, not for long.

  It was the modern abandonment of this kind of cultural substantiveness, this pattern of lifetime reading that provoked G.K. Chesterton to remark, "The great intellectual tradition that comes down to us from the past was never interrupted or lost through such trifles as the sack of Rome, the triumph of Attila, or all the barbarian invasions of the Dark Ages. It was lost after the introduction of printing, the discovery of America, the coming of the marvels of technology, the establishment of universal education, and all the enlightenment of the modern world. It was there, if anywhere, that there was lost or impatiently snapped the long thin delicate thread that had descended from distant antiquity; the thread of that unusual human hobby: the habit of thinking."

  Happily, Ben House has, in this book as in his life, undertaken the costly, difficult, and arduous process of reconnecting that long, thin, delicate thread for all of us. He has begun reconnecting it by preserving the practical lessons and profound legacies of Christendom without the petty prejudice of humanistic fashions or the parsimonious preference of Enlightenment innovations. He has begun reconnecting it, all the while avoiding the trap of noticing everything that went unnoticed in the past while failing to notice all that the past deemed notable.

Reading these chapters, it is evident that Ben understands that the best sort of history is always a series of lively adventure stories—and thus should be told without the cumbersome intrusion of arcane academic rhetoric or truck-loads of extraneous footnotes. History from that perspective is a romantic moral drama in a world gone impersonally scientific—and thus should be told with a measure of passion, unction, and verve. In Ben's hands, history, books about history, and books about books about history come to life. Thus, these "irrelevant things," as he has dubbed them, actually prove to be among the most relevant of all things.

But, to have undertaken such a work as this, it is readily evident that Ben has had to work hard. By dint of great intellectual ardor, he has disciplined himself to think, concentrate, make connections, and draw conclusions—affording him a richness of insight that otherwise would not have been possible.

Ben ably demonstrates the fact that a healthy appreciation for the gritty work of history not only enables us to recall many of the famous lives, deaths, movements, triumphs, disasters, opportunities, and controversies, but it provides us with tantalizing details of some of the most important lessons and profoundest inspirations that the long legacy of human civilization has to offer us as well. In other words, Ben has undertaken the practice of that old discipline of moral philosophy—and he has done so without apology.

Henry Cabot Lodge once asserted, "Nearly all the historical work worth doing at the present moment in the English language is the work of shoveling off heaps of rubbish inherited from the immediate past." This is precisely the kind of work that Ben House has undertaken here. Lots and lots of shoveling. Together with the great historians of the Christian tradition, he has snapped the spell of smothering modernity with a sane backward glance at the worldview that gave flower to the remarkable liberty, justice, and hope enjoyed by the lands of the West.

There are only a certain few books that actually have the power to ruin a reader. All too uncommon is the volume that can actually reshape your way of thinking, seeing, and living. Ben talks about a few of those rarities within these pages. What he fails to tell us is that this book, his book, must necessarily take its place among them. So work through it—knowing that it very well may in fact, ruin you.

Chapter One
The Importance of Being Irrelevant

Experience slowly taught him that he who takes all history for his province is not the man to write a compendium.
Lord Acton

Indeed, Peyton Williams, the late editor of the Mississippi Quarterly, once remarked as he saw Cleanth Brooks at a distance at an academic conference, "There's one of the great classroom teachers, and finally that's what all this is about." [1]

    This is a self-help book. But, reader, beware. It is highly irrelevant to the everyday world, pressures, and challenges you face at home, in the neighborhood, and at the marketplace. The essays in this book will not give you a working list of seven or ten or one hundred habits of highly effective people. In point of fact, it is written by a most ineffective person. It contains no secrets for climbing the ladder to success or making money. It won't find you a spouse, make you a better spouse, or help you with home repairs. It does not even include remedies for allergies or advice on which mineral supplements to use.

    If you follow the prescriptions of this self-help book, you will likely end up with less money, less time, and lots of around-the-house tasks left undone. For this book looks backward, not forward. It calls for reading and meditation, not action. It is not a bridge to the future, but a pleasant path to the past. This is a book about history. The focus is on reading history, enjoying history, and sharing history, particularly sharing it in a classroom. This book sprang up from other books, and like a spider web, its many strands of thought are connected to books and authors. It is the product of little original thought, but lots of borrowed thoughts. It is not the musings of a scholar, but the

---

[1] Benjamin B. Alexander, "The Man of Letters and the Faithful Heart" in *A Defender of Southern Convservatism: M.E. Bradford and His Achievements*, ed. Clyde N. Wilson (Columbia, MO: University of Missouri Press, 1999), 28. Just the mere mention of those great Southern men of letters, Cleanth Brooks and Mel Bradford, is almost enough to distract me from the purposes of this book.

gatherings of a bookish gadfly, going from place to place, picking an idea here, a quote there, an observation over yonder, and hopefully tying them all together with proper footnoting and acknowledgment of the sources.

Since this book is about history, and since its author is a Christian, it is a book about God. As a believer, I love God because He first loved me (1 John 4:19). As a believer, I know God through His revelation in Scripture. The Bible reveals the Sovereign and Triune God, the Creation and Fall of man, the Redemption of Christ, and our proper response to God, which in the Presbyterian tradition we describe as "glorifying God and enjoying Him forever." Part of that enjoying God is enjoying Him as He is revealed in history, for the Bible is a book of God's work in history and His foundations for understanding history.

God gives gifts to His people. Just today, my older son asked, "Why aren't you a CEO of a big company?" If I were a CEO, I could perhaps write a good book on how to apply the faith in the corporate world and encourage other Christians with the right gifts and callings to join me in the marketplace. Such a calling, and such a book, would be quite beneficial and relevant. Instead, my calling and this book are irrelevant.

I am attracted to the irrelevant. Trends, fads, the latest gadgets, and the newest technologies pass me by. My whole teaching career has been aimed at the irrelevant. For over fifteen years, I taught about irrelevant things in history in a government school. For the past ten years I have been in a classical Christian school environment continuing to teach irrelevant things in history and literature. It all makes sense, for I got a bachelor's degree in irrelevant things, that is, history and literature. When people asked what I was going to do with such a degree, I had no answer other than saying that I was going to teach school. My master's degree had some relevance, for it was a degree in education and a stepping-stone to a pay raise, but I had rather not talk about that. I much preferred the irrelevance of studying British monarchs than the relevance of learning theories of educational psychology.

It isn't just that I taught irrelevant things: I lived what I taught. While some other man might come home at night and remodel the kitchen, I would come home and rethink Pickett's Charge, with the result that I now believe it is better viewed as Pickett and Pettigrew's Charge.[2] Someone else might repair the carburetor or transmission on their car, but I was trying to figure out the impact of the Agrarian poets on Southern literature and how their vision of the past could enrich my own study and teachings. A real man would have

---

[2] See Clyde N. Wilson, *Carolina Cavalier: The Life and Mind of James Johnston Pettigrew* (Athens, GA: The University of Georgia Press, 1990).

gone elk hunting in Colorado, but I chose to hunt through bookstores for biographies of John Calvin.

I have never taught or acquired a marketable skill. Nothing I have taught has ever made anyone rich—certainly not myself. No one has patterned his life or career after me to insure success. And at this stage in life, with the needs of four children and a wife to think about, I should be a bit regretful. Like King Lear, to have grown older and still remained foolish is most tragic. Some sort of worldly wisdom should now compel me to at least warn others of the path that I have followed. I admit I am repentant over my past and wiser than I was thirty years ago. But I only repent that I did not pursue history and literature more. I only regret the books I have not read or did not buy. A wiser life would have been even more irrelevant.

The streams of history and literature that I followed are now leading to rivers that my students and children will be able to enjoy. Christian education, as it is now flourishing in day schools and home school settings, is revolutionizing a new generation. This revolution is better termed a reformation, because the form already exists and has existed in the paideia[3] or worldview of God found in the Bible. Along with the Bible, we have the records, the trials, the successes, and the prayers of two thousand years of Christian living, Christian culture, and Christian institutions, including schools. Our Christian heritage is a seemingly inexhaustible treasure of riches, which we are just beginning to rediscover. This treasure has been deeded to us, and to our children, and to our children's children, forever.

An Odyssey

The world of education—especially in the governmental and public school sectors—has been fad driven for several decades. Our public schools are always just one new program away from achieving Utopia. With no child left behind, with values clarified, with exit exams, with merit pay for teachers, with the next school tax proposal passed by a resounding majority, the public schools keep promising to solve society's problems inside their classrooms and ever-expanding administrative buildings.

Like most Americans, for twelve years I was institutionalized by the state in a public school, and as such, was a victim of such fads as existed in the 1960s. We had something called New Math at that time, which the teachers complained of, but taught anyway. I got New Math without knowing what

---

[3] Douglas Wilson defines 'paideia' as the all-encompassing enculturation of the future citizen. See Douglas Wilson, *The Paideia of God* (Moscow, ID: Canon Press, 1999), pages 9-15.

old math was. Thankfully, I caught the tail-end of phonics. I remember phonics because of the puppy dog on the book we used. Not so thankfully, for the time I was in school, grammar books stopping including exercises on diagramming sentences.

Prayer was taken out of school, and racial integration was brought in. People often seemed more concerned about the latter than the former. The textbooks were vapid, out-dated, and forgettable. A few teachers stood out for being really wise, apt to teach, and patient with the numskull that I was. Thankfully, a few really encouraged reading, and turning book pages was the most athletic trait I had.

In my last year of high school, when my mind was eager to read and learn, I spent two class periods a day taking a course on office education. It was relevant. We learned to use the adding machines with the big handles. I learned to type up to thirty words a minute with mistakes on an IBM Selectric typewriter. I learned to use a mimeograph machine and an offset duplicator (the kind that had the ink that smelled good).

College was challenging intellectually. By this I mean that it was hard to keep up with the assignments. There were good teachers, gifted lecturers, and true scholars amongst the lot. But structures cannot be built without foundations. So never having been taught Latin, never being immersed in the ancient classics, and only skimming the surface of history and literature, college students, like me, arrived in need of basic education. College became the vehicle for acquiring a good high school education. The literature teachers did actually assign literature, and the history teachers lectured on history. The particulars we learned were quite good, but what was lacking was a philosophical unity, a center to hold it all together. Such a center, such a core set of presuppositions is inescapable. Even in such a vacuum where the university becomes a multiversity, worldviews are still to be found in the classroom or elsewhere on campus.

I went to college as a John Locke Christian. This means that I went tabula rasa, that is, with a philosophically and theologically blank slate. I could have become anything. Being socially inept, dull by personality, and shy and introverted, I was spared the decadent college experience so often financed by parents and subsidized by the state. By this, I mean that I never experienced fraternity life, and the only late night drinking binges were black coffee while finishing overdue research papers.

By background politically, I could have made a good moderate Democrat, in the older Jeffersonian tradition.[4] As such, I could have been personally

---

[4] The species basically went into extinction somewhere in the late 1980s. Occasionally there are still sightings; for example, Georgia Senator Zell Miller, a Democrat, gave the keynote

opposed to abortion and an advocate of charter schools in the public sector. I would have also been a good Methodist Sunday School teacher and been quite a decent citizen in suburban America. Maybe had I met a Christopher Dawson-like history teacher or a Joseph Pearce-like literature teacher, I might have taken the road to Rome. I am still attracted to that route, but only for book buying purposes, meaning, I like the Monday through Saturday Catholic books on history, literature, and culture. Had I been influenced by Marxists, I might have become a Communist. But economic theory bored me and Marxian Revolution implied too many risks and sacrifices. If I had become a Marxist, I would hope that I would have been the Eugene Genovese-kind and would have pursued Southern history in the same manner he has.

Instead, I became a Calvinist.[5] The stamp of the Genevan Reformer was pressed upon the blank slate of my soul. Whereas Cornelius Van Til grew up in an environment saturated with Reformed theology, it was grafted on to my life after I entered college. Reformed theology became the center that held for me.[6] Because of my Calvinism, I have always viewed teaching as a mission and myself as a missionary and an educational revolutionary. Calvinism was not an easy teaching to swallow. Better stated, having been Christianized on skim milk, steaks were hard to digest. When Professor Henry Wood explained the Five Points of Calvinism in a lecture on American Colonial religion, I wondered how anyone could believe such a thing.

Some months later, Professor Wood recommended a couple of books to me by Loraine Boettner. I wondered who she was and how she had reformed the doctrine of predestination, which certainly seemed like something that needed reforming. When I started reading, I learned that Loraine Boettner was a man, and he, like me, had been a Methodist. His theology changed when he was reading Charles Hodge's *Systematic Theology* over a holiday break. (My kind of man!) Boettner's book *Studies in Theology* changed me more than his book *The Reformed Doctrine of Predestination*.[7]

---

address at the 2004 Republican National Convention. An excellent, but dated, account of this species is found in *The Natural Superiority of Southern Politicians* by David Leon Chandler (Garden City: Doubleday, 1977).

[5] The terms Calvinist and Reformed are basically synonymous in my usage. Other Calvinists or Reformed Christians can make their own distinctions in their own books.

[6] William Butler Yeats, "The Second Coming." Lines 3-4: "Things fall apart; the center cannot hold; Mere anarchy is loosed upon the world." Southern Agrarian Donald Davidson wrote an essay upon that phrase, called "The Center That Holds" which can be found in *So Good A Cause: A Decade of Southern Partisan*, edited by Oran P. Smith. (Columbia, South Carolina: The Foundation for American Education, 1993).

[7] Boettner's books were published by Presbyterian and Reformed Publishing Company.

Before *Studies in Theology*, I had no or few theological pegs. I read the Bible slightly and devotionally. Some verses I read helped me, and wasn't "Me" what it was all about? Boettner's topics included the inspiration and authority of Scripture, Christian supernaturalism, the Trinity, and the Person of Christ. These doctrines, laden with Scripture references in his book, changed me. I remember a night of reading the book while sitting under a dim light in a camping trailer at the Little Missouri River. It was a life transforming experience. What I had unknowingly recited in the Apostles Creed suddenly became Incarnate Truth.

I determined ahead of time that I would not believe the last chapter of Boettner's book that dealt with the extent of the atonement. I was not going down the road of election and predestination. By the time I got to that section of Boettner's book, I had been so battered down by Scripture that I was gullibly willing to believe anything God's Word said. So, in short order I became a Calvinist theologically. But a Sovereign God is a big God to keep in a small box.

God's sovereignty spilled over into all areas of life. Of course, the changes in theology led to changes in ecclesiology, or the doctrine of the church. So, church changes were inevitable. But more than that, theological changes meant changes in the way that I viewed history, literature, government, philosophy, art, music, family, and all areas of life and thought. Calvinism has been likened to a Copernican Revolution of the soul, and it was such for me.

Reformed theology became the grid that defined my thinking and life in all areas. Like nearly all young Calvinists, I would have benefited from being confined in an insane asylum for a few years.[8] Like all young Calvinists, every verse of Scripture echoed one of the Five Points of Calvinism. Like all young Calvinists, I sought to pound all fellow Christian brethren into full-orbed Calvinism in short order. I was fanatical, unbalanced, zealous, and uncontrolled, and looking back on those days, I can now say that it was a great and glorious time to live through—once.

Reformed theology became the foundation for my life. It awakened me to the marvelous grace of God in salvation. Theologian Benjamin Warfield's explanation of the Calvinists' spiritual experience defined mine:

> The Calvinist is the man who has seen God, and who, having seen God in His glory, is filled on the one hand, with a sense of his own unworthiness to stand in God's sight as a creature, and much more

---

[8] George Grant has repeatedly recommended several years of confinement for new Calvinists to protect both zealot Calvinists and anyone coming in contact with them.

as a sinner, and on the other hand, with adoring wonder that nevertheless this God is a God who receives sinners. He who believes in God without reserve and is determined that God shall be God to him, in all his thinking, feeling, willing—in the entire compass of his life activities, intellectual, moral, spiritual—throughout all his individual, social, religious relations—is, by the force of that strictest of all logic which presides over the outworking of principles into thought and life, by the very necessity of the case, a Calvinist.[9]

This all encompassing theology, this worldview, this total mind-loving vision of God gave definition to my planned teaching career. It furiously rearranged and then vastly expanded my bookshelves. It dominated my reading schedule. Theology became pleasure reading. It reshaped my thinking at every point. Every opinion was referred back to and contoured by some doctrine of Reformed theology. A friend, Pastor Keenan Williams, once said that a Calvinist can see a dead dog in the middle of the road, and from that sight construct a whole theology. I experienced that very thing.

Even as I was only beginning to become familiar with the name Abraham Kuyper, I was beginning to see Kuyper's vision through the spiritual dawn of Sovereign Grace when he said,

> One desire has been the ruling passion of my life. One high motive has acted like a spur upon my mind and soul. And sooner than that I should seek escape from the sacred necessity that is laid upon me, let the breath of life fail me. It is this: That in spite of all worldly opposition, God's holy ordinances shall be established again in the home, in the school and in the State for the good of the people; to carve as it were into the conscience of the nation the ordinances of the Lord, to which Bible and Creation bear witness, until the nation again pays homage to God.[10]

In my zeal and Jehu-like fury, I was often wrong then, but it was the wrongness of Peter slicing off the ear of the guard rather than the wrongness of the atheist philosopher who doubts that ears even really exist. I was always one book away or one chapter away from being an expert on some matter of

---

[9] Benjamin B. Warfield, *Calvin and Augustine* (Phillipsburg, N.J.: The Presbyterian and Reformed Publishing Company, 1980), 491.
[10] Abraham Kuyper, *Lectures on Calvinism*, Tenth Printing (Grand Rapids, MI: Wm. B. Eerdmans Publishing Company, 1978), iii.

theology and life. The learning curve was fantastic; the imbalances occurring on a daily basis were likewise fantastic. I had the hunger of a new convert with fanatical zeal. But for the patience of God, I would have called down fire on any who were slow to learn or reluctant to accept Reformed theology.

Somehow or another in spite of all my sound and fury, the world was not radically changed during those years. I finished college with my degrees in irrelevant subjects and discovered I needed a job. A belief in Christian education had sprung up during the stages of continual paradigm shifts, but there were no Christian schools where I lived. I willingly accepted the opportunity to work in government schools. Of course, I thought I could be an influence there for good. God was good to me there. I actually taught history from a self-consciously Christian viewpoint. I emphasized Protestant Reformers and Puritans, preachers and theologians, and Christian themes. My administrators and the parents graciously supported me or ignored me. So did most of my students. In some more pleasant cases, students became Christians in part because God used the books I gave them or things I said.

In time, God opened the door for me to leave the government school system and become a teacher in a Christian school. One of my first exposures to Christian education was through the ACE program. ACE stood for Accelerated Christian Education, which was faithful at being Christian, but questionable in regard to being accelerated. This was a program, a whole curriculum, which enabled small groups with no trained staffs to quickly start up schools from kindergarten through twelfth grades by using paces or workbooks. A paces program removed the central actor/entertainer/sage, in other words, the teacher, from the classroom, for each student worked individually with help from adults, usually moms, watching for them to raise their little American flags of distress. These schools also removed that most cherished of settings—the classroom itself. Students worked their way independently in little cubicles with their flags and booklets and with a Bible.

I am thankful for ACE schools and for the host of methods and materials that were developed in the late 1960s, 70s, and 80s that enabled parents to begin rethinking Christian education. I am also thankful that I never had to work in such a program. Even today, the Christian school movement is still relatively new. The internal growth in understanding in the movement is amazing. We as Christian educators have not solved all our problems. Still being new and inexperienced, we are only able to graduate students who are better educated in all academic fields, able to read books, and grounded in the Bible. Beyond that, we are still struggling.

I read Dorothy Sayers' article "The Lost Tools of Learning" from the *Journal of Christian Reconstruction* sometime around the early 80s.[11] I thought it was a great article, and I passed it on to my friend Randy Booth, who concurred. I read books and listened to cassette tapes by R. J. Rushdoony on Christian education, and I thought he was both brilliant and right. I read Samuel Blumenfeld's *Is Public Education Necessary?*,[12] agreed with him completely, and quoted from and promoted his book. Still, I remained in the public school system, content to weave in Reformed tidbits amidst the drivel, swill, and mush of the system.

Several people provided the motivation that ultimately changed my battle station. The late Dr. Greg Bahnsen once sat in my living room and argued for my leaving public schools. And no one ever bested Dr. Bahnsen when he used his primary logical tactic—defending the right position. My fellow pastor and friend Randy Booth began talking seriously about starting a school. We had been talking for a dozen years about Christian education, and in our church circles we had tried homeschooling, a teaching co-op, working with other Christian schools—both ACE and other types, and everything except starting our own school. Then Douglas Wilson showed up one evening at our church, by invitation. He preached to a congregation that was already convinced of the desirability of starting a school. He said, "If God tells you to jump through this wall, your task is to get up in the air." If God tells us to do something, we do it and He takes care of those little things, like solid walls. Sometimes I wish God had given us the easier task of jumping through a cinderblock wall. Instead, God put it in our hearts to start a classical Christian school.[13]

The fourth person to convince me of the need for a school was my own firstborn, Nicholas. I might have been content to teach other helpless victims in the public school system, but when Nicholas arrived in 1993, there never was any question but that he would have a Christian education.

I am thankful to be involved in the early stages of the revival of classical Christian education. I am more thankful to already have so many who have blazed the trails for us to follow. In a short time, God has raised up a number of Christian teachers, writers, and thinkers who are developing, or recovering, the philosophy of classical Christian education. And they and others are

---

[11] *The Journal of Christian Reconstruction*, Symposium on Education, edited by Gary North (Volume 4, Number 1, Summer 1977).

[12] Samuel Blumenfeld, *Is Public Education Necessary?* (Old Greenwich: The Devon-Adair Company, 1981).

[13] Douglas Wilson, *Recovering the Lost Tools of Learning: An Approach to Distinctively Christian Education* (Wheaton, Illinois: Crossway Books, 1991).

developing the curriculum for such learning.

To attend the conferences of teachers, administrators, and board members of classical Christian schools, to view the heavy-laden book tables at such conferences, to hear the speakers, to overhear the conversations between sessions are all testimonies to the great work God is doing in our time. This movement is still under the radar screen of America's media and government. Classical Christian teachers are now entering the ranks of the profession who are themselves the products of such education at all levels. The materials and methods are expanding and offering different approaches to reach the goal. There is not and will not be a centralized department somewhere regulating what our children learn in Classical Christian schools. The advocates of ecclesiastical Latin may someday take up arms and pronunciations against the advocates of classical Latin. Teachers of Socratic logic will clash with teachers of symbolic logic. The rivalry will be healthy. *Uniformity* of education is a stranglehold. We know, for many of us have been *uniformly* taught next to nothing.

I offer this collection of essays on history as an aid to teachers in Christian schools. While much of the content leans toward classical Christian schools, I still think any Christian teacher could benefit from it. While the book is heavy laden with Calvinistic sources and references, Christians of all persuasions are encouraged to glean from these essays. Like any author anxiously watching the sale of books, I hope the market reaches more than just a few teachers. I think teachers of history and literature will find much here that will delight them, but teachers of all grade levels and subjects can benefit from this book. Students in both Christian schools and homeschools can enjoy this book. Parents can learn from it, as can pastors and laymen. So can CEOs of large corporations.

In the first several essays, I make the case for classical Christian education. This section includes a series of essays on different aspects of classical Christian education. You don't have to subscribe to the classical models and methodology to benefit from the first part. This book is irrelevant, not practical. If you want to know practically speaking how to start a school and organize a board, there are good books on that subject. If you want to know why you should start a school, or what its philosophy should be, or how different academic disciplines are to be developed, the books are out there that provide such.[14] But not this one.

This book is about teaching, and it is about teaching in the only ways

---

[14] Perhaps the best book on a Christian philosophy of education is Stephen C. Perks, *The Christian Philosophy of Education Explained* (Whitby, England: Avant Books, 1992).

that I know to teach about teaching. I cannot tell you what good teaching is, but I think I know when it happens.[15] Good teaching involves a good subject or lesson. History teachers are incredibly blessed. The stuff of history is fantastic. History teachers really have to work hard to make the lessons boring. The second part of this book focuses on historians and history teachers, and the best historians are teachers, who have influenced me. The third and fourth parts of this book include portions of history that are vital to know. Hopefully, these chapters visit familiar ground, like the American War for Independence, with the emphasis on how a Christian perspective changes, enriches, and revises our outlook on history. Laced throughout this book are references, recommendations, and commendations of books and authors, a small number of the vast cadre who have blessed my understanding.

Historians and authors dominate this book. In fact, they are the ones who wrote it. I just did the job of editing, cutting, and pasting. My best ideas are usually the reflections of what others have already said. History teaching really gets down to two things, stories and outlines. Sometimes, the best thing a history teacher can do is to pass out a really good book and jump out of the way and let the book take center stage. And, as Andrew Nelson Lytle said, "It is not the books you read, but with whom you read them." So you cannot teach better than when you join in the Great Conversation and bring your students into that ongoing grand discussion.

As I emphasized in the beginning, in terms of everyday practical concerns, history is largely irrelevant. There is very little we Christians can do with history, other than use it to change the entire worldview and culture of the future. Read that sentence again. Our history classes are not eulogies and memorial services for the past; rather, they are the commissioning of the future. Our task of changing worldviews and culture must be accompanied by humility and prayer. In preparation for it, we teachers and students of history have a lot of work to do.

The Role and Purpose of History

> The great weapon with which the disciples of Jesus set out to conquer the world was a mere comprehension of eternal principles. It was an historical message, an account of something that had recently happened, it was the message, "He is risen."
> J. Gresham Machen[16]

---

[15] For help on knowing how to teach, read John Milton Gregory, *The Seven Laws of Teaching* (Grand Rapids: Baker Book House, 1993).

[16] *Christianity and Liberalism* (Grand Rapids, MI: William B. Eerdmans Company, 1923), 28-29.

History may very well be the most important subject taught in Christian schools. One might object by saying that the Bible is more important. But consider this: With the Bible, the issue of a textbook for classroom use is pretty much settled. We grant that there are seminaries and courses on the Bible where theologically liberal and heretical books have been used. But with the Bible, you cannot escape the text itself. This is why revival and reformation keeps breaking out. The plowboy with a Bible in hand will eventually, by the Spirit of God, see the truth. Occasionally, so will the seminarian immersed in Hebrew grammars and liberal theology.

Also, it is likely that the Bible will be in some sense correctly taught in the church and home. Correct teaching in this instance would mean a correct foundational understanding. As the Westminster Confession says, "...those things which are necessary to be known, believed, and observed, for salvation, are so clearly propounded and opened in some place of Scripture or other, that not only the learned, but the unlearned, in due use of the ordinary means, may attain unto a sufficient understanding of them."[17]

Unlike the Bible class, choosing a textbook or deciding the content for history class is challenging. There are many books to consider when choosing a history text, and while many may superficially appear to be alike, the interpretations of history found in the textbooks are varied.

Some say that we can just read the actual original documents. The sheer multitude of historical documents is staggering. You can have a 'read the Bible in a year' program, but you cannot have a 'read history in a year' program. Unlike the Bible, neither original sources nor secondary books are infallible either. It is easy enough after seeing a movie based on the Bible to read the corrective texts, but accurate background to historical movies can be difficult to find. Even when the study of history is reduced to a particular country or a particular time period, the amount of material is unfathomable.

Many Christian parents are wary of Evolution being taught in the public school classrooms. Darwinism has dominated the field of science for over a century. It has caused the public schools ongoing angst. School boards feel threatened by parents who assume they have some say so in regard to their children's education. The "Scientific Community" is shocked that myth and superstition still prevail after decades of pounding the Darwinian gospel from the pulpits of science classrooms. The media holds the Christian public in amused contempt, for they looked at Evolution and pronounced it good at the Scopes Trial of the 1920s.

---

[17] Westminster Confession of Faith. Article I "Of the Holy Scripture": Section VII.

The Importance of Being Irrelevant

While the teaching of Evolution[18] has provoked some parents to protest textbooks and some to even pull their children out of the system, it has not enraged parents nearly enough. All too many are willing to accept a compromise and accept an educational demilitarized zone around their personal faith and hearts. If a sticker can be attached to the cover of a textbook or a comment made in the book that Darwinian Evolution is only a theory, then many Christians are content to let their children rest comfortably within the compound of the remaining chapters of the book. A Darwinian worldview can reign supreme as long as the E-word is not used.

Here on this front, the advocates for Intelligent Design are battling against the entrenched scientific community of Darwinists. If only the books will allow that the structure of a cell, the rotation of the planets, and the stripes on a tiger evidence a Designer, an Intelligent Being, then all will be well. As Ann Coulter says in her otherwise quite powerful attack on Darwinism, "Design in the universe may well be explained by something other than God...."[19]

Christianity does not teach Intelligent Design in the universe. It teaches creation by the Triune God.[20] The Bible does not present Creation as the work of an unnamed, undefined source of intelligent existence beyond our pale. Colossians 1:16 and John 1:3 teach that the entire universe was the handiwork of a Man who once did carpentry work in an obscure Roman province in the Middle East. An acknowledgment of some sort of Intelligent Design is not Christian education or an acceptable compromise.

I applaud the scientists and thinkers who are writing scholarly papers and are tilting the tottering paradigms of the Darwinians.[21] They are upsetting lots of school boards and science programs and have introduced chaos into the camps of those who believe in chaos. The opponents of Intelligent Design claim that the movement is a false front for bringing religion into the classroom. I totally disagree: Intelligent Design is the bringing of *another* religion into the classroom. Christianity is at war with unbelief on a wide number of fronts. The labors of guerrilla fighters and partisans fighting inside enemy occupied territory should not be despaired of. Let them continue, but what they are doing is not the true main offensive of the Christian, and it does not provide the true needs of Christian students.

---

[18] Should Evolution be capitalized? I capitalize the names of other religions, like Hinduism and Islam.

[19] Ann Couter, *Godless: The Church of Liberalism* (New York: Crown Forum, 2006), page 245.

[20] Ralph Smith, *Trinity and Reality: An Introduction to the Christian Faith* (Moscow, Idaho: Canon Press, 2004). See chapter 6: Trinity and History: Beginnings.

[21] See William A. Dembski, editor, *Uncommon Dissent: Intellectuals Who Find Darwinism Unconvincing* (Wilmington, Delaware: ISI Books, 2004).

It is amazing that Christians are so often incensed over one of the three essential Biblical themes, but not the other two. Yes, it is just plain wrong and insane when we are taught that we are the descendants of lower life forms and that humans are the result of a frog turning into a prince over a period of billions of years of being kissed by time and random chance mutations. But what about the Fall of Man and Redemption?

Herman Dooyeweerd, a Dutch Christian philosopher pegged the essentials of a Christian view of history when he said,

> Ultimately, the problem of the meaning of history revolves around the question: "Who is man himself and what is his origin and final destination?" Outside of the central biblical revelation of creation, the fall into sin and redemption through Jesus Christ, no real answer is to be found to this question.[22]

For the sake of argument, grant that the science teacher bypasses the "chapter" on evolution.[23] At some point, a bell will ring and the student will leave biology class and go to world history class across the hall. How will the history teacher explain man? Forget for the moment how he got here, just answer and tell me, "What is this rational biped?" The doctrine of Creation and the Doctrine of the Fall are linked. How do we explain man's potential for greatness apart from being in the image of God? How do we explain his wickedness apart from a doctrine of the Fall? History class basically is a combination of theology, philosophy, and anthropology illustrated by examples. But those subjects, especially theology, must provide the foundations to make any sense of history.

The failure to present an adequate historical doctrine of man undermines all the rest of history. As Phillip E. Hughes said, "...it is axiomatic that if we are in error about the origins of things, whether of the universe, or life, or religion, or salvation, we shall be in error about all that follows."[24] An explanation of human evil has to be forthcoming or history ceases to have purpose other than convincing us of despair. The Biblical doctrines of the Creation and the Fall provide an adequate foundation for understanding history. Man has to be at some point of elevation to fall, and the Biblical doctrine

---

[22] Herman Dooyeweerd, *In the Twilight of Western Thought* (Nutley, NJ: The Craig Press, 1990), 111.

[23] Isn't this typical of Christian non-thinking? If the chapter or section that has the word evolution is skipped, then the problem is averted. Christian thinking, if it is such, has to be presuppositional.

[24] Philip Edgecumbe Hughes, *Christianity and the Problem of Origins* (Phillipsburg, N. J.: The Presbyterian and Reformed Publishing Company, 1974), 37.

of man being created in the image of God explains the height from which he fell.[25] It is only within the framework of man as the fallen image-bearer of God that the ambiguity of mankind makes sense. This explains why the culture that produces builders of cathedrals or jet planes can quite readily turn to murderous war-making skills and exhibit a depravity far worse than the violence found in the animal world. Knowing then that man bears both God's image and lives as a fallen subject under Satan's thralldom explains how civilization ascended to produce the art of the Renaissance and descended to the horrors of the Holocaust.

Teachers and parents are usually happily inconsistent. Darwinians accept, by faith, that beings emerging from primordial ooze somehow attain unalienable rights, perhaps granted by governing authorities that are still emerging from that same primordial ooze. We are all actually random atoms and molecules, constantly colliding and bumping by meaningless chance, which accounts for the present stage of order and evolutionary development, but certain actions by particular molecules and atoms are judged immoral and others are judged righteous, at least for the time being by society. We are all products of DNA and/or environment, but some DNA reactions are acceptable by the majority of DNA reactions, while others DNA reactions are politically incorrect.

The only alternative to a Christian view of history is a meaningless chance universe of chaos in which history has no meaning. To quote Dooyeweerd again, "There would be no future hope for mankind and for the whole process of man's cultural development if Jesus Christ had not become the spiritual center and his kingdom the ultimate end of world history."[26] Philosophies undergirding history narrow down to two: Christianity or Despair. So, choose your Frenchman: John Calvin or Jean Paul Sartre.

Ethics cannot exist in a Darwinian universe.[27] Can we hope for an Intelligent Ethicist to be introduced into the classrooms along with the Intelligent Designer? Public schools try everything in an effort to maintain crowd control and to convince parents that they still have the institution in place that grandmother attended in the 1950s. Character words, such as honesty and loyalty, are taught to the students. Self-esteem is lathered over the students to make them virtuous; anger management programs are offered for students still propelled by those Darwinian instincts of the jungle; values clarification, with values being personal and arbitrary, is offered so that students can make

---

[25] Ralph Smith, *Trinity and Reality*, 61-64, 92-96.
[26] Dooyeweerd, 111-112.
[27] Richard Weikhart, *From Darwin to Hitler—Evolutionary Ethics, Eugenics, and Racism in Germany* (New York: Palgrave Macmillan, 2004).

wise choices over their evolutionary destiny. Bars cover the windows and police officers patrol the halls to aid the weaker species in their struggle for survival in the primordial halls and lockers.

Stamp out Original Sin and watch for the results of that liberation. Quite simply, as stated in Romans 1, the result is even more sin. Even unbelieving man, from Voltaire to the present, cannot quite abide in a universe devoid of the effects of believing in God. From Gilgamesh to the present, man has searched for eternal life, for hope, for some salvation to lift us out of the despair and certain death that this world offers.

Along with the doctrine of the Fall, there is the doctrine of Redemption. Yes, as Christians we are quite adamant about God creating the world. But are the incarnation, teachings, death, and resurrection of Jesus Christ negotiable as parts of teaching? We are currently in a culture war that includes debating even over what year we are living in. Is this Anno Domini (In the year of our Lord) 2008 or is this 2008 C. E. (Common Era)? And if this is the Common Era, what was it that happened that became a common assumption for Western Civilization? Was it Caesar's decree that all the world be taxed? Or was it a birth in Bethlehem, providentially brought to fulfillment by that tax?

Speaking of Bethlehem, the war has engulfed Christmas. We now have "Season's Greetings" and "Happy Holidays" and "Winter Break." The issue again is the Incarnation, that Divine interruption in the history and events of life on this planet. If the life of Jesus is simply a matter of a good and entertaining teacher getting a bad rap from the governing authorities, we might as well watch *Dead Poets Society* or read Plato's account of the death of Socrates. Skip the chapter over Evolution in the biology book; it is probably outdated even by the standards of evolutionists. Skip chapter one in the world history textbook that deals with Cro-Magnon man and his hairy, hunch-backed children. Skip right on over to chapter seven, titled "The Roman Empire." What happened of any significance during the reign of Augustus Caesar? He defeated his uncle's assassins and his successor. Fits more with dog-eat-dog Darwinian real-politik than with anything moral and ethical. The Republic became an Empire. So what? Latin speaking DNA molecules pushed non-Latin speaking DNA molecules around a large mass of H^2O, called the Mediterranean Sea. Or was there something else during Augustus Caesar's reign, relating to his tax policies, but more than mere economics?

History cannot be taught correctly without an acknowledgment of the Incarnation of Christ. It would be easier to teach American history by claiming that George Washington was only a farmer and never a general or president than to teach history and claim that Jesus was only a man. Jesus was not merely another religious teacher, meriting equal attention with Buddha and Mohammed. As C. S. Lewis explained so powerfully, the choices are that Jesus was a liar, a lunatic, or Lord.[28]

Malcolm Muggeridge once pondered in writing how "God could become a Man in a particular place and at a particular time; that this having happened, God who was a Man, or, amounting to the same thing, a Man who was God, could be nailed to a cross and left to die, only to rise from the dead, and, after spending a few days with His disciples, then a brief sojourn in hell, disappear into heaven, there to watch over mankind evermore."

He asked the question, "Who in his right mind could believe such a story?" And then he answered his question:

> Well, to begin with, all those who have believed it. That is to say, the greatest artists, mystics, sculptors, saints, builders—for instance, builders of the great medieval cathedrals—over the Christian centuries, not to mention the Christians of all sorts and conditions whose lives, generation after generation, have been irradiated, given a meaning and a direction, through this great drama of the birth, ministry, death and resurrection of Jesus of Nazareth.
> …Who would not rather be wrong with St. Francis of Assisi, St. Augustine of Hippo, all the saints and mystics for two thousand years, not to mention Dante, Michelangelo, Shakespeare, Milton, Pascal, than right with Bernard Shaw, H.G. Wells, Karl Marx, Nietzsche, the Huxleys, Bertrand Russell and the like?"[29]

Peter Kreeft and Ronald Tacelli identify key aspects of the importance of the Christ's Divinity and Incarnation in history. They write:

1. The divinity of Christ is the most distinctive doctrine of all. A Christian is most essentially defined as one who believes this. And no other religion has a doctrine that is even similar. Buddhists do not believe that Buddha was God. Muslims do not believe that Muhammed was God....

2. The essential difference between the orthodox, traditional, biblical, apostolic, historic, creedal Christianity and

---

[28] C. S. Lewis, *Mere Christianity* (New York: The MacMillan Company, 1958), 41.

[29] Malcolm Muggeridge, *Confessions of a Twentieth Century Pilgrim* (San Francisco: Harper & Row Publishers, 1988), 65-66.

revisionist, modernist, liberal Christianity is right here. The essential modernist revision is to see Christ simply as the ideal man, or "the man for others"; as a prophet, rabbi, philosopher, teacher, social worker, psychologist, psychiatrist, reformer, sage or magician—but not God in the flesh.

3. The doctrine works like a skeleton key, unlocking all the other doctrinal doors of Christianity. Christians believe each of their many doctrines not because they have reasoned their own way to them as conclusions from a theological inquiry or as results of some mystical experiences, but on the divine authority of the One who taught them, as recorded in the Bible and transmitted by the church....

4. If Christ is divine, then the incarnation, or "enfleshing" of God, is the most important event in history. It is the hinge of history. It changes everything....

5. There is an unparalleled present existential bite to the doctrine. For if Christ is God, then, since he is omnipotent and present right now, he can transform you and your life right now as nothing and no one else possibly can. He alone can fulfill the psalmist's desperate plea to "create in me a clean heart, O God" (Ps. 51:10). Only God can create....

6. And if Christ is divine, he has a right to our entire lives, including our inner life and our thoughts. If Christ is divine, our absolute obligation is to believe everything he says and obey everything he commands. If Christ is divine, the meaning of freedom becomes conformity to him.[30]

To attempt to structure a history curriculum without this cornerstone leaves history without form or purpose. Is Lordship an issue in the teaching of history? Or is history simply one fact after another? Jesus Christ is the Lord of the Church. Some Christians are content with Christ's Lordship over the church. Most believers would rise up in revolt if Christ's Sunday

---

[30] Peter Kreeft and Ronald Tacelli, *Handbook of Christian Apologetics* (Downers Grove, IL: Inter Varsity Press, 1994), 151-152.

Lordship over the church building, the pews, the stain glass windows, and the choir loft were denied. But a Monday through Saturday Lordship of Christ is something that is kept up close and personal. Christ can be in your heart; He can walk with you in the garden; He can be the object of your quiet time. But the Lordship of Jesus Christ is unwieldy, bulky, and intrusive. Christ's political agenda, emphasized in Psalm 2 and Revelation 19, is quite all encompassing, totally undemocratic, and in fact, tyrannically holy.

Lordship and sovereignty are inescapable in history. Something has to be defining. No culture, no era, no leader can be explained without reference to lordship and sovereignty. Albert Gore, Jr. will be forever irked that in American politics, three electoral votes from North Dakota outweigh the sentiments of several million Californians. It is a question of sovereignty and lordship with the earthly temporal sphere. In some cases in that same sphere, historical circumstances, geography, and economics hold the keys to understanding who rules. Hence German or British history trumps the history of Luxembourg or Monaco. Often, the rulers rule and have sovereignty because they control the swords and guns. As Bismarck said, "Das macht geht vor das Recht," which means that the claims of might go before the claims of right. This is the ad baculum fallacy parading as governmental philosophy. Is there anything wrong with this? Is there some objection to either guns or majority votes determining history?

Some judgment has to be made in history class. If it is democratic procedures, then Hitler gets a nod of improvement. If it is success pragmatically speaking, then fault Hitler but note that Stalin earns his plaudits as a successful ruler.

Most history texts presuppose the primacy of the State over the Church, and in fact, they presuppose the State over all other institutions. Most history texts are products subsidized by the State apparatus. Forms of government, names of rulers, and laws enacted form the bulk of the text. In cases where the Christian Church became a bit too pushy—as was all too often the cases in the Middle Ages—the books lean toward the side of civil government over the Church. The rise of nation-states and absolute monarchs rescued mankind from the Church. In some cases, voting rights are exalted over theological truths. It does not matter that Puritan women were taught the truth about Christ; they could not vote in colonial Massachusetts.

Isn't history just facts, in fact, the same old facts for everybody? Or is history really a philosophy of life and theology deciding which facts are more important, more defining? In the 1500s, men like Luther battled over the content of Biblical teaching, while men like Henry VIII battled over political sovereignty. Which matters most, the sale of relics or the marriage of a king?

In the 1930s, Franklin Roosevelt greatly expanded the political parameters of the American government through his New Deal legislation. During that same era, J. Gresham Machen battled for the soul of American Presbyterianism in his warfare against theological liberalism.[31] Which has the greater impact on history—the WPA or the OPC? In terms of a philosophy of history, something has to have preeminence. History is philosophical and theological and cannot function as a chronological potpourri. Either Luther's labors at Biblical exegesis or Henry's efforts to beget a male heir get top billing. Either the failure of FDR's Court Packing Plan or Machen's failure to save the Presbyterian Church, USA, has had the greater impact on history.

Examples like this can be multiplied without end. So history class is quite important, and how history is taught may be more critical than how the Bible is taught. Without a biblical doctrine of Creation, history has no foundation. Without a biblical doctrine of the Fall, history has no accurate interpretation. Without a doctrine of Redemption, history has no true goal or purpose. Without a final judgment, history has no meaning.

Too many Christians either don't think or think in fragments with random Bible verses and even more random tidbits of ideas picked up from the surrounding culture.[32] They are devotionally monotheists, even Trinitarians, but practically on a day-by-day basis, they are dualists and polytheists. All of life has to be brought under the lens of Scripture. History, in particular, is a key starting point for this reorientation of life and thought. David Naugle said,

> Thus, when believers can understand the all-encompassing significance of the doctrine of creation, when they recognize radical consequences of sin across the whole spectrum of created existence, and when they understand the Lord Jesus Christ in his larger roles as the cosmic creator and redeemer of all things—then perhaps the doctrinal bits and pieces can be fit together into a totality, the narrative connections can be made between the Old and New Testaments, and the danger of dualism can be destroyed once for all.[33]

---

[31] See J. Gresham Machen, *Christianity and Liberalism* (Grand Rapids: Wm. B. Eerdman's Publishing Company, 1923). Among the excellent accounts of Machen's struggle are Ned B. Stonehouse's biography, *J. Gresham Machen: A Biographical Memoir* (Edinburgh: The Banner of Truth Trust, 1987).

[32] See Harry Blamires, *The Christian Mind: How Should a Christian Think?* (Ann Arbor, MI: Servant Publications, 1978).

[33] David Naugle, *Worldview: The History of a Concept* (Grand Rapids: William B. Eerdmans Publishing Company, 2002), 342.

Every subject is then crying out to the Christian to bring it into subjection to the Lordship of Christ. Albert M. Wolters said, "If Christ is the reconciler of all things, and if we have been entrusted with 'the ministry of reconciliation' on his behalf (2 Cor. 5:18), then we have a redemptive task wherever our vocation places us in this world."[34] This book is focusing just upon those of us whose vocation places us in the history classroom. If there were no other subject to consider than history, we would by that measure alone have adequate reason for desiring Christian education. Unbelievers and epistemologically inconsistent Christians may be able to teach historical facts, but they cannot teach a true meaning for history. Only a Christian can do that.

Within that broader framework of Christian teaching, there is lots of room for differences and lots of room for errors. So Christians will differ on the positive or negative effects of Constantine's Edict of Milan, and American Christians will line up shoulder-to-shoulder with their Enfield rifles, figuratively speaking, on opposite sides of the Mason-Dixon line in teaching about the War Between the States. But the greater context will be sound as long as the central Biblical doctrines of Creation, Fall, Redemption, and Sovereignty are taught and God is acknowledged as Lord of History.

The Commission

Christian doctrines impact our understanding and teaching of history at all points. Robert L. Dabney said, "[N]o man but the believer is capable of understanding the philosophy of history." Why is this so? Dabney continues, "He who learns from the Scriptures, and he alone, can possibly understand the meaning of events or interpret them aright."[35] History has a certain unity and coherence because of its Creator. It has a certain direction politically and culturally because of its King. It will come to a certain conclusion and judgment because of its Lord. As Gordon Clark said, "God has not only controlled history so far, but He will bring it to its end and culmination."[36] Before that end comes, those of us who read, write, and teach history have lots of work to do. The enormity of the task before us is exceeded only by the delight of attempting it.

---

[34] Albert M. Wolters, *Creation Regained: Biblical Basics for a Reformational Worldview*, Second Edition (Grand Rapids, MI: William B. Eerdmans Publishing Company, 2005), 74.

[35] Robert L. Dabney, "Uses and Results of Church History" from *Discussions*, Volume II, Evangelical (Harrisonburg, VA: Sprinkle Publications, 1982), 23.

[36] Gordon Clark, *A Christian View of Men and Things* (Grand Rapids, MI: Baker Book House, 1981 reprint), 89.

Chapter Two
Punic Wars and Culture Wars

> We are mistaken when we compare war with "normal life."
> Life has never been normal.
> C. S. Lewis[1]

Americans rarely ponder the Punic Wars. In the midst of a legion of spiritual, political, social, economic, and intellectual problems, we should not lament this negligence of the Punic Wars. Of course, this historical gap in our mental history is but another result of the loss of a wider consciousness of the Greek and Roman languages and literature that was part of the foundation for Western education and which included the major events and historical figures from the Greco-Roman World.[2] For most, there are issues more urgent to be learned and taught than the details of the Punic Wars. But for those of us who are called to the profession of the muse Clio, knowledge of the Punic Wars needs to be an occupational skill. Questions arise, as it always does in teaching history, concerning the relevance of the Punic Wars, and hence all history.

Is history a quest for knowledge in and of itself, an accumulation of odd facts and interesting stories, or does it provide great models for action and paradigms for imitation? History must either echo Macbeth's despairing vision of life as "tale told by an idiot, full of sound and fury, signifying nothing"[3] or it must be like what Paul said of the Old Testament: "Now all these things happened to them as examples, and they were written for our admonition, upon whom the ends of the ages have come" (1 Cor. 10:11). We assign a different weight to the importance of the examples in the Old Testament than to the stories from Ancient History, or specifically, between the wilderness wanderings of the Jews and the Punic Wars. Yet, using the Scriptures as

---

[1] From "Learning in War-Time" found in *The Weight of Glory and Other Addresses* (New York: Touchstone, 1996), 45.
[2] Adrian Goldsworthy, *The Punic Wars* (London: Cassell & Co, 2000), 9.
[3] Shakespeare, *Macbeth*. Act V, Scene V, Lines 26-28.

a model for both history and application of history, we acknowledge Paul's approach of teaching history as moral philosophy as essential to the Christian learning and teaching of history.

Punic Wars

The Punic Wars were a series of three wars fought by the then up-and-coming expansionist Roman state against the mercantilist Carthaginian empire. The name *Punic Wars* came from the Roman word for Phoenician. Winners in history get to name the wars. The Punic Wars, which took place between the years 264 B.C. to 146 B.C., mainly centered on the question of "Whose pond is the Mediterranean Sea?" From our perspective, the inevitable final answer was "Rome." But humanly speaking, the outcome judged by examining the contestants was far from certain. What was inevitable was conflict itself. As historian Carleton J. H. Hayes said, "Each power was strong where the other was weak. Each was subject to ambitions and fears that were easily magnified. Their conflict was inevitable."[4]

Rome was a land power, interested only in whatever lands were adjoining their own property lines. Rome's entry into the power politics of its day came upon its conquest and consolidation of the Italian peninsula. Given time, this would place Roman legions and tax programs over a huge expanse of land stretching from Britain to Egypt. Rome was already expanding eastward and south to the cities founded by Greece, to the west toward Spain, and throughout the islands in the Mediterranean Sea. Adrian Goldworthy comments upon Roman expansion:

> In the late fourth and early third centuries Roman expansion assumed great momentum. The Samnites, Etruscans and Gauls were all defeated, despite some Roman disasters....The cities of Magna Graecia—the "Greater Greece" heavily colonized by Hellenic communities—were subdued....Rome continued to expand, turning defeated enemies into loyal, but clearly subordinate allies. As Rome expanded so did her citizen population which, combined with her allies, gave Rome vast resources of military manpower, far greater than those of Carthage.[5]

---

[4] Carleton J. H. Hayes, *Ancient Civilizations: Prehistory to the Fall of Rome* (New York: Macmillian Publishing Co., Inc., 1983), 358. Hayes is an older historian whose works were written mainly from the 1930s to 1950s. His books are worthy of study and were respectful of Christianity, although not always reliable from a Christian perspective.

[5] Goldworthy, 39.

Carthage, an offshoot of the Phoenician trade empire, was the Ancient World's equivalent of Wal-Mart and Sam's Wholesale Clubs, with a few divisions of the marines joined onto it. If it could be bought, sold, or traded for, the Carthaginians wanted it. If it needed to be defended, Carthage would procure allies and mercenaries for protection. Carthage had its roots in the famed cities of Tyre and Sidon and had as legend the queen Elissa, also known as Dido, who sacrificed herself on a funeral pyre to protect her people.[6] Both empires had republican forms of government, ruled over by aristocratic senators. Rome had more of a tendency to expand rights toward the plebians, and this resulted in the plebians having a greater stake in Rome's military triumphs.[7]

Goldworthy comments upon Carthage's assets:

> In 300 the land controlled by Carthage was significantly greater than the *ager Romanus,* the lands owned by the Roman people, and rivaled the sum of these and the territories of Rome's allies. Its yield was probably significantly greater, for much of the land in Italy had poorer soil….Carthage proved reluctant to extend citizenship and political rights to the peoples within the areas she came to control….Therefore the extension of Punic hegemony over Africa, Spain, Sicily, and Sardinia did not result in a great expansion of the Carthaginian citizen body.[8]

Let the Contest Begin

The first Punic War took place from 264 B.C. to 241 B.C. and started over control of the island of Sicily. Rome was initially able to win interior land battles, but was hindered from victory by the Carthaginian ability to supply coastal cities by sea. Rome embarked upon what would become a typically Roman methodology. The Romans captured a shipwrecked Carthaginian ship, studied it, and began building their own versions. Roman legionnaires learned to handle ships by sitting on benches in the sand and practicing rowing. Imitation was part one of the Roman strategy. Innovation was part two. The Romans installed drawbridges on their ships that enabled them to latch on to enemy ships, allowing them to board them and engage in hand-to-hand conflict.[9] From this, the Romans became a naval power, able to check the Carthaginians at sea.

---

[6] Goldworthy, 26. See also Virgil's *Aeneid* (any edition).
[7] Carl J. Richard, *Twelve Greeks and Romans Who Changed the World* (Lanham, MD: Rowman and Littlefield Publishers, Inc., 2003), 143.
[8] Goldworthy, 29.
[9] Hayes, 359.

For over two decades, the war shifted back and forth; at times, with land battles being waged in North Africa; often with sea battles in the Mediterranean; and repeatedly, with the war shifting back to Sicily. The advantage shifted to the Carthaginians when Hamilcar Barca rose to power and began a guerrilla war against the Romans. His lightening attacks kept the Romans at bay, but guerrilla warfare is generally incapable of effecting a final victory. Hayes quotes Polybius, who along with Livy gave us the earliest accounts of this war: "Polybius compared the contestants to two well-bred gamecocks 'which fight to the last gasp. You may see them often, when too weak to use their wings, yet full of pluck to the end, striking and striking again.'"[10]

A more recent historian used a different metaphor. Carl Richard compared Rome to "a pit bull that would not release its grip on the enemy's leg, no matter how many times it was beaten on the head or offered the milk bone of peace"[11] In this long war of attrition, Rome responded by calling upon its patriots to fund the building of a new fleet each time one was lost. Although Rome ultimately lost seven hundred warships to the Carthaginian loss of five hundred ships, the Roman fleet ultimately bested the Carthaginian navy off the Agates, a group of islands to the west of Sicily.[12] Carthage then sued for peace.

Better remembered than Hamilcar Barca and the first Punic War is Hannibal Barca, son of Hamilcar, and the second Punic War, which was fought between 218 B.C. to 201 B.C. In the intervening years between the first and second wars, Hamilcar Barca fought to put down mutinies within the Carthaginian Empire among its mercenaries, but his greater act was consecrating his son to a lifelong task. The son, Hannibal Barca, was taken to the pagan shrine of Melkarth. In his historical novel about this event, Ross Leckie, has Hannibal tell of this dedication:

> From behind, a eunuch covered me in a mantle of blood red. Two more brought a black dog. One held its head, one its feet above the fire before the stone. My father stepped forward, took a sword and with one stroke cut the dog in two.... 'My this fate befall you, Hannibal, son of Hamilcar, if you break this oath.'[13]

---

[10] Hayes, 360.
[11] Richard, 144.
[12] Richard, 145.
[13] Ross Leckie, *Hannibal: The Novel* (Washington, DC: Regnery Publishing, Inc., 1996), 47. Yes, I quoted a historical novel in a non-fiction historical essay. I am even prone to think of Leo Tolstoy and William Faulkner as historians. So much for my scholarly pretensions.

After a few more rituals, incantations, and bloody sacrifices, Hannibal swore this oath:

> By the eight fires of the Cabiri, by the stars, meteors, and volcanoes, by the Cave of Hadrumetum and the Passage of Ashroket, by slaughter, by all that burns, by desert, by sun, moon and earth...I swear by the serpents of Melkarth, by Eschmoun, by the blackness of Panit I swear this great oath of the seven hates to Rome, undying enmity to Rome, no peace to Rome, no truce with Rome, no mercy unto Rome as long as I shall live or any Roman walk upon the land or sail upon the sea.[14]

The seeds were thus planted for the second Punic War, a war not just for commercial and territorial interests, but one that would determine whether the future would be Roman or Carthaginian. The conflict began in Spain. The Carthaginians had been plundering portions of Spain south of the Ebro River for iron and silver. A young twenty-five year old Carthaginian general then carried his troops north of the Ebro and attacked a Roman ally. Rome demanded the surrender of this young general named Hannibal. Carthage refused and the second war began.[15]

The most commonly remembered image and story of the Punic Wars is Hannibal crossing the Alps with elephants. It really happened; it was an ordeal to move an army of 50,000 infantrymen with 9,000 cavalry and eighty elephants through the passes between snow banks and landslides, across rivers, and over mountain crags.[16] To make matters worse, the locals weren't too hospitable. Hannibal had to fight both natives and nature to cross the Alps. The elephants did not fare too well; along with about half Hannibal's army, a number of elephants perished in the making of that historical drama.

Hannibal is the most fascinating figure out of the Punic Wars. The son of a great general, Hamilcar Barca, and the brother and brother-in-law of other great Carthaginian generals, Hannibal fulfilled from his youth his pledge of undying enmity toward Rome. For fifteen years, he roamed up and down the Italian peninsula turning Roman armies by thousands into spaghetti sauce. For fifteen years, little children had the spaditles scared out of them by the whispered words "Hannibal ad portas"—"Hannibal is at the gates." For fifteen years, he dominated the local gossip and political news as his armies

---

[14] Leckie, 48.
[15] Hayes, 362.
[16] Bevin Alexander, *How Great Generals Win* (New York: W. W. Norton and Company, 1993), 37.

alternately won allies, creamed disloyalists, pillaged wheat fields, and ravaged the land.

G. K. Chesterton gives this vivid description of Hannibal's battles and successes:

> At the worst crisis of the war Rome learned that Italy itself, by a military miracle, was invaded from the north. Hannibal, the Grace of Baal as his name ran in his own tongue, had dragged a ponderous chain of armaments over the starry solitudes of the Alps; and pointed southward to the city which he had pledged by all his dreadful gods to destroy.
>
> Hannibal marched down the road to Rome, and the Romans who rushed to war with him felt as if they were fighting with a magician. Two great armies sank to right and left of him into the swamps of Trebia; more and more were sucked into the horrible whirlpool of Cannae; more and more went forth only to fall in ruin at his touch. The supreme sign of all disasters, which is treason, turned tribe after tribe against the falling cause of Rome, and still the unconquerable enemy rolled nearer and nearer to the city; and following their great leader the swelling cosmopolitan army of Carthage passed like a pageant of the whole world; elephants shaking the earth like marching mountains and the gigantic Gauls with their barbaric panoply and the dark Spaniards girt with gold and the brown Numidians on their unbridled desert horses wheeling and darting like hawks, and whole mobs of deserters and mercenaries and miscellaneous peoples; and the grace of Baal went before them.[17]

Hannibal was one of history's all time great military leaders. Whatever characteristics we associate with Alexander the Great, Napoleon, Genghis Khan, Hernando Cortez, Robert E. Lee, or Douglas MacArthur that made them military geniuses can be found in Hannibal. He was courageous, tactically brilliant, innovative, sneaky, recklessly bold, ruthless, and most often successful. He was admired and studied by Napoleon. Likewise, German military officers and academics studied Hannibal's campaigns in detail.[18] Even to the present day, Hannibal's influence is felt. Goldworthy notes, "As recently as the Gulf War in AD 1991, the UN commander claimed to have

---

[17] G. K. Chesterton, *The Everlasting Man* (San Francisco: Ignatius Press, 1993, reprint.), 146.
[18] Goldworthy, 16.

drawn inspiration for his swift and highly successful operation from Hannibal's campaigns."[19]

With infantry forces inferior to the Romans, he shifted the emphasis in battle to his pike- and sword-armed heavy cavalry and missile-throwing light cavalry.[20] He used mobility, speed, shock and awe, subterfuge, and a host of other battlefield maneuvers to keep the tactical edge of his army sharper than the enemy forces. He typically drew the Roman army onto ground of his own choosing. At the Battle of the Trebia River, he enticed the Romans to cross the river to attack his army. Once engaged in battle, the wet, shivering Romans were then hit on the flanks and rear by cavalry units Hannibal had concealed upstream.[21] On one occasion, he confounded the Roman army blocking his path by moving his own army through a swamp.

Alexander says of this battle:

> [H]e sent his army directly through the flooded swamps for four days and three nights of misery, the men now half drowned in the soft mud, now sinking deeply in the water. Many succumbed to exhaustion and died. Though he rode on the remaining elephant to keep above the water, Hannibal caught an eye infection and lost the sight in one eye.[22]

This eye-sacrificing maneuver put Hannibal between the Roman army and Rome. The Roman army then rushed into an ambush Hannibal had set for them on the shores of Lake Trasimene. Thirty thousand Romans were killed, including their commander, and another ten thousand were scattered at what was the greatest ambush in history.

At the Battle of Cannae, he succeeded in a textbook-perfect double envelopment of the Roman army's flanks. In that one engagement, he slaughtered 40,000 plus Romans. In that battle, Hannibal positioned his less dependable infantry in the center, where they gave way to the advancing Romans. The Carthaginian battle line sagged and Romans poured into the ever-collapsing center. With his African infantry poised and waiting on both flanks, Hannibal was in control of the seemingly chaotic Carthaginian rout.

---

[19] Goldworthy, 16.
[20] Alexander, 41.
[21] R. Ernest Dupoy and Trevor N. Dupoy, *The Encyclopedia of Military History from 3500 B.C. to the Present* (New York: Harper and Row Publishers, 1986), 63.
[22] Alexander, 41.

Alexander says,

> At this moment Hannibal gave the signal and the African foot suddenly wheeled inward from both sides, striking the Romans in flank and enveloping them into a tightly packed mass. Meanwhile, Hannibal's heavy cavalry on the left wing had broken through the weaker Roman cavalry on that side and had swept around the Roman rear to drive away the cavalry on the Roman left flank. Leaving the lighter Numidian (Algerian) cavalry on the right wing to pursue the Roman horsemen, Hannibal's heavy cavalry delivered the final stroke by bursting onto the rear of the Roman legions, already enveloped on three sides and so compressed they were unable to offer effective resistance.[23]

Commenting on this battle, Dupoy and Dupoy said, "The Romans became a herd of panic-stricken individuals, all cohesion and unity lost."[24] Thus ended what has gone down in history as the perfect battle of annihilation. With a force smaller than his enemies, on the homeland of his enemy, with his supply sources far away, Hannibal and his rag-tag mercenary war machine ranged up and down the Italian peninsula, defeating Roman legion after legion, killing consuls and commoners, and always threatening the city of Rome itself.

Whether bribery or threats, diplomacy or intimidation, cavalry raids or set battles, Hannibal was the master of the art of war. Years after the Punic Wars, Scipio Africanus (the only Roman to truly defeat Hannibal on the battlefield) asked Hannibal to name the three greatest military leaders in history. Hannibal gave first place honors to Alexander the Great, second place to Pyrrhus, a king of Epirus, who invaded Italy in 280 B.C., and third place to himself. "And what if you had defeated me?" Scipio asked. "In that case, I would place myself as number one," Hannibal replied.[25]

Yet, despite his greatness on the battlefield, despite his perseverance, despite his unswerving dedication to opposing Rome, Hannibal joins the losers of history. He is a brilliantly attractive loser, but still a loser. There are no second place honors on the battlefield.

With that in mind, we should focus a bit of attention to the winners; that is, we should look at the Roman generals and Roman system that did triumph in that war. Hannibal will not lose his attractiveness as a historical

---

[23] Alexander, 46.
[24] Dupoy and Dupoy, 65-66.
[25] Ernle Bradford, *Hannibal* (New York: McGraw-Hill Company, 1981), 208.

figure, anymore than will other losers like Napoleon, whose tactical victories are only surpassed by his ignominious retreat from Moscow, or Rommel, the Desert Fox of World War II fame who won both battles in North Africa and praise from his enemies.

G. K. Chesterton, in his wonderful book *The Everlasting Man,* makes the point that the defeat of Carthage and the triumph of Rome was a great blessing to the world. The Baal religion of the Carthaginians was, he said, much more pagan and oriented to human sacrifice than were the Roman idolatries. Chesterton noted, "These highly civilized people really met together to invoke the blessing of heaven on their empire by throwing hundreds of their infants into a large furnace."[26] The Carthaginians were Phoenicians, of whom we read in the Bible, and Hannibal's very name meant 'the grace of Baal.' The victory of Rome helped prepare the Ancient World for the advent of Christianity—'when the fullness of time was come.' The alternative, Chesterton notes, "would have been very different if there had been an empire of Carthage instead of an empire of Rome."[27]

Maybe Chesterton is right; he quite often was. His defense of Rome against Carthage is entertaining and thought provoking. But whether the Carthaginian paganism and commercialism (which does not sound all that foreign to us) would have aided or inhibited the later spread of the Gospel is a question of speculation only. God in His wise providence predestined that Carthaginian strip malls and human sacrifices would be buried under Roman salt and sandals and North African sand. Meanwhile, the Gospel would travel through the cultural conduits devised by crafty Greeks and controlled by imperialistic Romans.

How did Rome win? Obviously, they did not have anything like the modern American media broadcasting defeatism and pessimism while Hannibal and his multi-national army terrorized Italy. Rome had its peace-at-any-price party, as did Carthage. But Rome had enough of a long-term commitment, enough of a stable structure, enough of an eschatology of victory (to borrow a phrase from Marcellus Kik[28]), that it sustained over a decade of defeat before it decisively defeated Carthage. Rome survived battles like Cannae, which destroyed not just the flower of their youth, but a large number of political and military leaders. Even after the unprecedented losses at Cannae, Rome was able to quickly mobilize young boys and old men into the ranks of the legionnaires to encourage Roman allies.[29] Even when threatened

---

[26] Chesterton, 145.
[27] Chesterton, 150.
[28] Marcellus Kik, *An Eschatology of Victory* (Phillipsburg: Presbyterian and Reformed Publishing Company, 1978).
[29] Alexander, 48.

with eminent invasion, land prices in and around Rome remained stable and high, indicating a conviction that Rome would prevail. In fact, the very piece of land that Hannibal's army was occupying sold with no reduction in price.[30] Rome survived economic disasters that make the American Great Depression look like a bull market. Rome even survived an inept political system that put two rulers in at a time for a period of one year, giving them divided, often incompetent leadership. Thus Rome survived political incompetence of a magnitude that can only be found in a gathering of Democrat presidential hopefuls every four years in January in Iowa. Rome survived a terrorist attack on their soil for a decade and a half; Rome did not have a 9-11; Rome had a 218 B.C. to 203 B.C.

Rome obviously never seriously considered such alternative courses of action as those made famous by defeatist cultures and civilizations. Bernt Engelmann tells the story of guarding French soldiers who had surrendered to the Germans during the battle for France in 1940: "There lay close to a thousand French soldiers....Most of them were sleeping, in the shade of the bushes and trees. Others had taken off their shirts and were sunning themselves....We swallowed hard when we noticed how many of them were still armed....But all the French soldiers I spoke with on the way were overjoyed that for them the war was over."[31] We have witnessed in the last century those who were ready to cede the battle and surrender—with ample weapons still at hand—to the forces of Nazism, Communism, and now Islamic Terrorism. All too many have preferred sun tans to freedom. But Rome at this stage in its history did not opt for the downward spiral of retreat, surrender, collaboration, and then fawning adoration of their conquerors.

Two men of the Roman army presented different, yet complementary, approaches to the threat that Hannibal posed. These two men were Quintus Fabius Maximus and Publius Cornelius Scipio. Fabius became known as 'the Cunctator' or 'the Delayer.' From Fabius, we get the term "Fabian tactics." Alexander describes this strategy as "a policy of evading decisive confrontation to gain time by using guerilla-like pinprick attacks and harassment to improve morale and preventing potential allies from joining the enemy."[32] Unlike his more bold predecessors and successors, Fabius avoided direct confrontation with Hannibal and thus avoided allowing himself and his army to be "the delicate feasting of dogs, and all birds."[33]

---

[30] Bradford, 148.

[31] Bernt Engelmann, *In Hitler's Germany: Everyday Life in the Third Reich* (New York: Pantheon Books, 1986), 207.

[32] Alexander, 45.

[33] From *The Iliad of Homer*, translated by Richmond Lattimore (Chicago: The University of Chicago Press, 1951), Bk. 1, lines 4-5.

Ernle Bradford said, "The one thing that Fabius had to do, he realized, was avoid defeat."³⁴ Just like the Russians in their later campaigns against the French in 1812 and the Germans in 1941, Fabius practiced a 'scorched earth policy.' Every field, every delicious animal, every warm shelter, and every farm that lay within the reach of Carthage's mercenaries was destroyed. Fabius was dedicated to the long-term, gradual wearing down of Hannibal's army. Just like President Bush's campaign against Iraqi terrorists, Fabius' campaign came under severe criticism. But he avoided his critics, just as he avoided Hannibal.

While Fabius never won the acclaim and honors of the battlefield victor, his methods worked. He made use of resources that Hannibal did not have: Time, supply sources, patience, and long-term vision. The more offensive minded Romans were not happy with Fabius' methods, but Bradford says that Fabius "had done more than any other to teach the Romans the way to wear down and finally defeat" Hannibal.³⁵

In later centuries, Fabian Socialists borrowed Fabius' name and methods to 'successfully' bring about a socialist evolution in Britain.³⁶ The term 'Fabian Tactics' is still used to refer to the use of methods of slowly wearing down the opposition. Wearing down the enemy buys time, but usually by itself, it does not completely defeat the opposing forces. Patience is a virtue both in everyday life and in history, but at some point, confrontation is called for, and that point of confrontation must come when victory is attainable.

The other and more prominently successful Roman general was Scipio, the scion of a famous family of warriors. Unlike Fabius the Cunctator, Scipio was confrontational. Like all great men, Scipio studied his enemy. He had plenty of opportunities. He saved his wounded father on the battlefield during one of Hannibal's early battles in Italy. Later, he fought in and survived the Battle of Cannae. When confronted with defeatism among his fellow officers, Scipio was always quick to remind them of their duty and to inspire them with new confidence.³⁷

Like all great military men, Scipio figured out the vital, but weaker chinks in the armor of his enemy. Scipio's early successes were not against Hannibal himself, but against the Carthaginian army fighting in Spain. He tilted the military fortunes in Spain toward Rome. The loss of Spain to Carthage meant the loss of money and metals. The metals were used to forge weapons and

---

³⁴ Bradford, 95.
³⁵ Bradford, 193.
³⁶ Clarence Carson's book *The World in the Grip of an Idea* (New Rochelle, NY: Arlington House Publishers, 1979) shows how Socialism brought about by evolution—slow change—was often more successfully accomplished than that done by revolution.
³⁷ Richard, 152.

the money was used to pay armies. Carthage, as implied throughout this essay, depended on a hired band of assorted warriors. After turning the war in Spain to Rome's favor, Scipio began to draw away Carthage's key ally, the North African Kingdom of Numidia.

Rather than fielding an army in Italy and adding to the ever-increasing list of deceased warriors for Rome near Rome, Scipio proposed porting his army across the sea to the outlying areas near Carthage. Alexander says, "Scipio saw beyond Hannibal's army. The main deterrent to peace was the will of the enemy to continue the fight."[38] Even Fabius disagreed with Scipio's plan. After the Roman senate gave lukewarm consent, Scipio invaded Africa and began sacking the countryside surrounding Carthage. Through his own battlefield tricks and schemes, now it was Carthaginian armies that were being massacred on their own homeland. Scipio, like Hannibal, hinged his battlefield successes on a skilled and maneuverable cavalry. Now encamped fifteen miles away from Carthage, Scipio began receiving requests for terms of capitulation. Yet, surrender was not Carthage's only option since it still had armies in Italy.[39]

By whatever methods of contact available, Carthage 'e-mailed' Hannibal and said, "Please come home. Now." At this time, Hannibal's raid into Italy was in its fifteenth year, and his near invincible army's heyday had long since passed. Whatever ragtag troops he still had were loaded into ships then taken back with him to Carthage.

Amazingly, Hannibal the Carthaginian was geographically disoriented back in Carthage. He knew Italy better than his home turf. Meanwhile Scipio had used his time in North Africa to build up his army, win allies, and bruise the locals. Before actually confronting Scipio on the battlefield, Hannibal tried to wheedle a peace agreement out of the Roman general. In doing this, Hannibal in effect revealed his vulnerabilities. Scipio used even the negotiations to his advantage by drawing up his allied units to the battlefield while he and Hannibal talked.

So, in 202B.C. at the Battle of Zama, the world changed forever as Scipio defeated the Carthaginians and Hannibal. The tactical elements of Scipio's success consisted in arranging his army in such a way that Hannibal's front line of elephants proved ineffective when Scipio's men blew trumpets to first scare the elephants and then left gaps in their lines for the elephants to pass harmlessly through. After the confused and injured elephants lumbered off the battlefield, Scipio hit Hannibal's flanks with the skilled Numidian cavalry units, which once served under the Carthaginian flags. As lines of Romans

---

[38] Alexander, 58.
[39] Alexander, 58-62.

and Carthaginians converged with the clashing of swords, spears, and shields, the Carthaginians slowly got pushed back. When the Carthaginian army realized that the enemy cavalry had flanked their army, a rout ensued. In the mix and confusion of battle, Carthaginian mercenaries turned upon the newly recruited and untrained Carthaginian civilian soldiers. Roman soldiers, meanwhile, grew weary with hacking the enemy to bits, and for a time struggled more to keep from slipping on the ground littered with hewed limbs, blood, and gore than from facing the enemy itself. In the end, Carthage suffered twenty thousand killed to the Roman loss of fifteen hundred.[40]

Hannibal escaped both death and capture. He lived on to rule Carthage for a time, until later pressures sent him into exile. Scipio, for his accomplishments, was given the title "Africanus," the only Roman given a name of the land he conquered.

As a result of his battlefield successes, Scipio enabled Rome to continue in its quest to dominate the Western world. Rome would repackage and further spread Greek culture. Rome would make its own contributions through language, literature, law, politics, and architecture. Roman Caesars, legions, and provinces would ultimately prove to be vital chess pieces in the advance of God's greater kingdom that was ushered in with the birth of Christ.

The Lessons of History

What, if any, are the 'lessons of history' for us? Personally, I tend to want to find my lessons from Hannibal. He's a historical loser, an underdog, and a brilliant man who is bested by a bureaucratic organization. But for the Christian in today's culture wars, we would be better served by observing history's winners. Christ promised us that the gates of Hell would not prevail against His church. We tend to read it as though it says that we shall not be totally defeated by the enemy who is camped at our gates. We sell off the remnants of Christian culture at reduced prices. We surrender the claims of Christ's Lordship bit by bit to the enemy, holding on to Sunday school and church camp and Christian trinket stores to the end, but willingly conceding art, music, literature, and politics to the dark side. We fight with a bizarre twist to the Fabian model by telling the enemy, "You can only have our children five days a week for the most vital thirteen years of their lives." But such tactics are not Biblical. Jesus' proclamation against the gates of Hell is a call for victory, not a message of defeat or a plea of the underdog or an image of a noble loser.

---

[40] Richard, 156.

The first key for Christians to realize is that we are at war. Jesus and the Apostles used military terminology and analogies to describe the warfare between Christianity and the world. We grant that the martial imagery of Scripture has been and can be misused; we acknowledge that our weapons are not carnal, but mighty in God (2 Cor. 10:4); and we distinguish between the responses of individual Christians to insults and that of Christian magistrates to attacks on the commonwealth. Still Christians need to realize that people outside of Christ will oppose and hate the faith. "Enemy-occupied territory" is how C. S. Lewis describes the world. He adds, "Christianity is the story of how the rightful king has landed, you might say landed in disguise, and is calling us all to take part in a great campaign of sabotage."[41]

Theologian and apologist Cornelius Van Til devoted his career to teaching about this warfare:

> The War between Christ and Satan is a global war. It is carried on, first, *in* the hearts *for* the hearts of men. Through preaching and teaching in the church and in the home, through the witness borne by individual men everywhere, the allegiance of men is turned away from Satan to Christ. But the warfare is also carried on where you might least expect it. It is carried on in the field of reading and writing and arithmetic, in the field of nature study and history….
>
> So far we have been speaking of the victorious struggle of Christ against Satan for the hearts of men. This struggle is global in character. There is not a square inch of ground in heaven or on earth or under the earth in which there is peace between Christ and Satan. And what is all-important for us as we think of the Christian school is that, according to Christ, every man, woman, and child is every day and everywhere involved in the struggle. No one can stand back, refusing to become involved. He is involved from the day of his birth and even before his birth. Jesus said, "He that is not with Me is against Me, and he that gathereth not with Me scattereth abroad." If you say that you are "not involved" you are in fact involved on Satan's side. If you say you are involved in the struggle between Christ and Satan in the area of family and in the church, but not in the school, you are deceiving yourself. In that case you are not really fully involved in the family and the church. You cannot expect to train intelligent, well-informed soldiers of the cross of Christ unless the Christ is held up before them as the Lord of

---

[41] C. S. Lewis, *Mere Christianity* (New York: The Macmillan Company, 1958), 36.

culture as well as Lord of religion. It is the *nature* of the conflict between Christ and Satan to be all-comprehensive.[42]

As Christians, the lessons of history are there for us. We find in history examples, ideas, and insights into how we ought to conduct our faith and life. All such historical findings have to be submitted to the filtering process of Scripture. Christians cannot be Machiavellian in tactics or pragmatists in methods, meaning that we can never allow the ends to justify the means or use methods simply because they work. Still, the wealth of the sinner is laid up for the righteous, so history is there for us to glean.

Christians need to learn from Fabius (and even from the Fabian Socialists). We need to fight long-term battles, avoiding foolish defeats, destroying enemy resources, and using time and patience to our advantage. Why battle for prayer in public schools? A vague prayer to an indefinite supreme being for unclear direction in a setting that does not recognize God is not Christian prayer. Why not pray for Christians to leave public schools? A more Fabian approach would be to build Christian schools and concentrate on changing the next generation and the one after that. Boycotts against movies, companies, and institutions, with occasional exceptions, achieve little or no success and never result in a saved soul. When we are already out of the mainstream, to announce that we are boycotting the mainstream is of no avail. We are like fish boycotting dry land.

Fabian battle tactics are frustrating for impatient people on both sides of the battle. As Christians, we should patiently confront the culture war with such slow methods as prayer, family time, reading books, worshipping, and singing hymns and Psalms. A Christian president, and I rejoice at having a President who acknowledges his faith in Jesus Christ, is not as necessary and effective in winning the culture war as Christian families, churches, and schools that are faithful to their callings.

Wear down the opposition. Preach, pray, evangelize, and build churches. Support Christian education, read Christian books, and live Christian lives. Abortionists and homosexual unions and hedonists and atheists cannot produce either families or culture. Hannibal was never able to effectively recruit long-term allies on the Italian peninsula. The fruits that secular humanism and unbelief offer are very puny and most unappetizing. Don't despair if unbelieving modern-day Hannibal's are camped outside the gate. Hannibal never got inside Rome's city limits, and Christ's church will never succumb to His enemies. The Romans persevered against a long-term enemy. We have

---

[42] Cornelius Van Til, *Essays on Christian Education* (Phillipsburg: Presbyterian and Reformed Publishing, 1969), 26-28.

the advantage over the Romans of having a greater cause, a greater kingdom, and a much greater King. And we have the promise, not of an empire that will dominate the Mediterranean Sea, but of a kingdom that will fill the earth and never be destroyed. (Daniel 2:44)

Aim toward producing godly grandchildren. Have a long-term vision of victory. Be Fabian, be Augustinian, be Medieval, be Reformational, be Puritan, be anything that is Christ-centered, but don't be impatient. Focus on cathedral building and be multi-generational in expectations.

Along with this long-term Fabian approach to changing culture and building Christian institutions, Christians need to learn from Scipio Africanus. Goldworthy says,

> Hannibal in particular was to prove far more skilful in the careful maneuvering before a battle, exploiting the instinctive desire of his Roman opponents to meet him as soon as possible to ensure that the battle was in fact fought in a situation and place of his own choosing. Yet it was a striking feature of the Romans, especially in their military enterprises, that they were willing and able to learn from their opponents and adapt.[43]

Study about and from our enemies. Learn to discern their wrongful and wicked ways from the insights and gifts they have received, but not acknowledged from God. If unbelievers develop better universities, write better novels, create taller skyscrapers, and make more money, learn from them. Anything they do right, they accomplish because they have stolen from God. Take back the technology and artistry. Find the sources of the enemies "metals and money" and win it back. Again, Christian schools are battlefields for confronting the enemy—both short-term and long-term. But Christian schools have to be outposts and forward lines of battle, and not refuges to protect our children from harmful ideas.

Mel Gibson's movie *The Passion of the Christ* did more to draw the enemy out of Italy and back to North Africa than anything else Christians have done in decades.[44] Tolkien and Lewis both had actual war experiences in the trenches during World War I. But their greater military service was as soldiers of the Cross of Christ where they waged war with pens, writing books, in large part writing imaginative literature describing wars and battles among creatures of their own devising. Their books still confront the enemy on his ground. The arts and sciences are beckoning Christians to enlist and fight.

---

[43] Goldworthy, 62.
[44] Gary North, *The War on Mel Gibson* (Powder Springs, Georgia: American Vision, 2004).

Whether it's Hannibal's elephants or Mordor's oliphants, the bloated enemy forces are vulnerable. It may take a few more arrows than usual, but big ugly things die when punctured enough times. Fascism and Marxism, though once quite formidable and frightening, did not last out the twentieth century. Darwinian Evolution, Freudianism, Nietzsche's philosophy, unbelieving Existentialism, Humanism, Feminism, Abortionism, Homosexual Fanaticism, and whatever other deviations are lined up for battle, are all easily outflanked or directly defeated by a vigorous Christian confrontation with faithful doctrine, life, and culture.

Victory is often simply a matter of not having a culture of defeat.

Chapter Three
Classical Christian Education:
A Sampling of Some History

> A wise man devoutly thanks God that the price of knowledge
> is labor, and that when we buy the truth, we must pay the price.
> If you wish to enjoy the prospect at the mountain's
> summit, you must climb its rugged sides.
> —Boston Schoolmasters, 1844

> Ours are the only farmers who can read Homer.
> —Thomas Jefferson

The modern public education system has been weighed in many scales and found wanting. There have been no shortage of critiques and critics of the system. Critiques of the system in the form of books, articles, news stories, speeches, sermons, government reports, and test results have catalogued the numerous failings of state schools. Public schools have received failing grades. Remediation has failed, and whole generations of students have been left behind. Within the public education establishment, teachers, administrators, and students heap on even more criticisms of the system. Whether one considers the arguments of the right or conservative end of the political spectrum, where the call is for a return to "the basics" and prayer, or to the left or liberal wing of the political spectrum, where the call is for more government money, Outcome Based Education, more classrooms, more money for teachers, pluralism, or whatever might be the latest and often perverse trendy innovation, the call is clearly for change.

Government schools are expected to do everything: provide day care, pre-school care, meals, prepare students for college or vocational technical jobs, enable both brighter and slower students to excel at their respective levels, inculcate the "right" values, teach someone's standard of proper sexual behavior, teach students to think critically—but with open minds, enable students to pass standardized tests, raise the self-esteem of students, discipline children—without jeopardizing self-esteem, prevent them from turning to drugs, alcohol, or suicide, teach a wide-ranging curriculum, create racial, sexual, and gender understanding and harmony, win ball games, and do all of these things in a manner that is pleasing to the students so they will not be bored or discouraged. In spite of these messianic expectations,[1] government schools are not sure what they are supposed to be doing. In the midst of a host of bugle commands, they are not sure which way to charge. There is no clear philosophy or direction.

While the two major political parties claim to present different perspectives on issues, they are remarkably close together on the education issue. Granted that Republicans speak more often on parental choice or traditional values with promises to return to the basics in the classrooms, they generally opt for more governmental control over the schools and legislative choices rather than parental choices determining where and how our children are schooled. The No Child Left Behind legislation, proposed by President George W. Bush and supported by many Republicans, has been criticized by the liberal Democrats, but only because the program has supposedly not been adequately funded.

In an age of cultural rootlessness, moral relativism, religious pluralism, social disintegration, and future uncertainty, how can we expect anything other than educational chaos?[2] Unstable times call for a return to theological foundations and historical forms. Many Christians mistakenly think that the cultural and social mores of the 1950s provide the answers. But the families, churches, and schools of the 1950s produced the 1960s. The rediscovery of theological foundations and historical forms must go further back in history.

The theological foundations must be established upon the Scriptures. In education, Christians have too often seen the Bible either as a book to be studied in a separate subject, i.e. Bible class, or as a devotional book. Christian education must teach not only selected Bible verses and stories, but Biblical systematic theology and Biblical Christian worldview thinking. William N. Blake points out:

> There is...no textbook more important in all the curriculum than the Bible. It is not merely a text alongside other texts, but it contains the interpretive principles to determine the content and structure of all texts. It is the Light of all lights. Christian education has

---

[1] Rousas J. Rushdoony, *The Messianic Expectations of American Education* (Philipsburg: Presbyterian and Reformed Publishing Company, 1963).

[2] See Gene Edward Veith, Jr., *Postmodern Times: A Christian Guide to Contemporary Thought and Culture* (Wheaton: Crosssway Books, 1994).

frequently failed to situate the self-attesting Scriptures at the center of the curriculum. The Bible as the voice of God must be the central orienting principle around which all knowledge becomes knowledge and becomes knowable. When this is done the teacher makes God the final reference point in all predication. God becomes knowable; man becomes knowable and so does the world he lives in.[3]

Phonics and traditional math with an armload of classics are all essential elements of an educational reformation, but for that reformation to work, it must be centered on the Bible. The importance of the Bible in education can be seen in an ironically prophetic defense of the use of the Bible in public schools given by Benjamin Rush in 1786. Rush said:

> I do not mean to exclude books of history, poetry, or even fables from our schools. They may and should be read frequently by our young people, but if the Bible is made to give way to them altogether, I foresee that it will be read in a short time only in churches and in a few years will probably be found only in the offices of magistrates and in courts of justice.[4]

From the study of Scripture and theology, Christians must be nurtured into a worldview that applies biblical concepts to every area of life. It is not adequate or faithful to develop a view of Scripture that attends to the soul, but ignores the mind. We are to love God with both soul and mind. The Christian worldview must be comprehensive and its development is a lifelong task that is to be pursued in academic life, in church and family life, and in the workplace. But thankfully, Christians have been building upon these foundations throughout the history of Christianity. The history of the church is a rich success story, replete with examples, instructions, and forms for producing Christian students that are educated in all academic areas, grounded in Biblical knowledge, and discerning of the wider cultural trends. Classical Christian education has revived in our age, but it was not invented in our age. This is a rediscovery, a reformation, a renaissance. It is also a treasure trove, an inheritance, a glorious blessing.

---

[3] William N. Blake, "Van Til's Vision for Education" from *Foundations of Christian Scholarship–Essays in the Van Til Perspective*, edited by Gary North. (Ross House Books,), 108.

[4] Benjamin Rush, "Thoughts Upon the Mode of Education in a Republic," from *American Political Writing during the Founding Era, 1760-1805,* Volume 1, edited by Charles S. Hyneman and Donald S. Lutz (Indianapolis: Liberty Press, 1983), 684. Certainly, Rush would be shocked at the exclusion of the Scriptures from modern courts of justice.

Historian Christopher Dawson has described the beginnings of Classical Christian education:

> From the time of Plato the Hellenic paideia [system of instruction] was a humanism in search of a theology, and the religious traditions of Greek culture were neither deep nor wide enough to prepare the answer.....The new Christian culture was therefore built from the beginning on a double foundation. The old classical education in the liberal arts was maintained without any interruption, and since this education was inseparable from the study of classical authors, the old classical education continued to be studied. But alongside of—and above—all this, there was now a specifically Christian learning which was Biblical and theological and which produced its own prolific literature.[5]

Classical Christian education borrows from and heavily utilizes ideas and concepts taken from the Greeks. So, Homer and Aeschylus, Plato and Aristotle, Herodotus and Thucydides, all beloved pagans, are essential parts of the curriculum. Whereas the Greeks were creators of forms and ideas, Romans imitated and refined more so than created, so Roman thinkers like Virgil, Cicero, and Quintillian built upon the Greek models. And these authors, along with their Latin language, also became foundational in Western education. In *Who Killed Homer?*, authors Victor Davis Hanson and John Heath observe:

> For over two millennia the educated and enlightened in the West had been dragged through 'the Classics' from an early age. The study of Greek and Latin languages and literatures was acknowledged to be the perfect training for nearly every profession, whether one was heading towards business, law, medicine, the voting booth, or a constitutional convention.[6]

But Latin and Greek culture were the inheritance of Christians, and it was always accompanied by and refined by the Christian faith, which of course sprang from Hebrew roots. The Hebrew roots of the Christian culture were

---

[5] Christopher Dawson, *The Crisis of Western Education* (Stuebenville, Ohio: Franciscan University Press, 1989), 8-9.
[6] Victor Davis Hanson and John Heath, *Who Killed Homer? The Demise of Classical Education and the Recovery of Greek Wisdom* (New York: The Free Press, 1998), 5.

not without their own rich educational heritage. As Augustine points out, Christians were to plunder the Egyptians for the gold and goods, but these treasures were to be refiltered and renovated through the Scriptures.[7]

Basic to classical Christian education is the concept of the Trivium. The Trivium breaks the stages and level of learning down to three parts: Grammar, logic, and rhetoric. The Greeks and Romans may have been the ones to use the terminology of the Trivium as the means of teaching and knowing, but the concept was Biblical. Randy Booth says the following about this:

> The development of the trivium model of classical learning is, perhaps, an example of how unbelievers borrow truth from God's world and yet fail to give God the credit....The Scriptures are our *only* rule of faith and life, not the Romans or modern pedagogues....While the Romans did not start or end with the fear of God; nevertheless, they did get part of it right. The 'trivium' has reference to educational method—*how* to educate. The model is comprised of three phases of learning: Grammar, Dialectic, and Rhetoric. These are but new labels for the biblical concepts of Knowledge, Understanding, and Wisdom.[8]

The Christian Church itself did not always get the right balance. Tertullian asked the question, "What does Athens have to do with Jerusalem?" Along with many church fathers, he wrestled with whether Christians should embrace or distance themselves from the classical learning developed by Greek and Roman pagans. From the early church through the Medieval period and after that, from the Reformation to the present, we are still laboring to answer that question. Hanson and Heath point out:

> [T]he challenge facing the early Christian Fathers of the Roman Empire was how to take advantage of a successful pagan system of education without teaching paganism, how to graft the older and more complex Greek idea of a useful body/soul duality onto the Christian notion of eternity, how to apply previously heathenism rituals in the service of a new God.[9]

---

[7] Augustine, *On Christian Teaching* (New York: Oxford University Press, 1997), Book 2.

[8] Robert R. Booth, "The Trivium in Biblical Perspective" (First published in promotional materials published for Veritas Academy in Texarkana, Arkansas, 1996).

[9] Hanson and Heath, 9. All too often the Church Fathers failed at this by assuming that the body/soul duality was something Greek. Neoplatonism and Gnostic thinking all too often

The early Church took up the challenge. Christianity being a religion of the book and being a religion for all kinds of people became, by definition, the religion of education. The early Church set up catechetical schools to instruct both its own covenant communities as well as new converts. Augustine's profession before his conversion was teaching rhetoric. After his conversion, he simply built upon his past labors by theologically retooling his mind and teachings.[10]

In his book, *Christianity and Culture*, T. S. Eliot noted:

> To our Christian heritage we owe many things besides religious faith. Through it we trace the evolution of our arts, through it we have our conception of Roman Law which has done so much to shape the Western World, through it we have our conceptions of private and public morality. And through it we have our common standards of literature, in the literatures of Greece and Rome. The Western World has its unity in this heritage, in Christianity and in the ancient civilizations of Greece, Rome, and Israel, from which, owing to two thousand years of Christianity, we trace our descent.[11]

The Middle Ages, the era from approximately 500 to 1500 A. D., constitutes a whole millennium that witnessed frequent educational revivals and missionary expansion. The course of classical and Christian education in this period is too vast to survey here. Education became one of the prime missions of the monastic orders. They preserved the Roman culture, but established that learning upon Christian foundations. As Christopher Dawson said,

> In the West…the educational institutions of the Roman Empire were swept away by the barbarian invasion or declined or died with the declining culture of the Latin world. It was only by the Church and, particularly, by the monks that the tradition of classical culture and the writings of classical authors, "the Latin classics", were preserved. And already in the sixth century we have an outstanding example in the case of Cassiodorus (496-575) of the way in which

---

hindered even the best of Christians. Consider in regard to marriage and sexuality (but please don't imitate) Augustine and Origen, for example. (By the way, Hanson and Heath miss the point too. Also, they did not capitalize God in the book.)

[10] *On Christian Teaching* is a manual for Bible teachers that incorporates Biblical thinking with ideas from rhetoric and other classical fields of study.

[11] T. S. Eliot, *Christianity and Culture* (San Diego: Harcourt Brace & Company, 1976), 200.

the old tradition of learning found a refuge in the monastery, and the monastic schools and libraries and scriptoria became the chief organs of higher intellectual culture in Western Europe.[12]

Herbert Schlossberg seconds this testimony by saying:

When the cultural life of antiquity collapsed with the Roman Empire, and a centuries-long era of darkness followed, it was a corps of Christian intellectuals who kept the manuscripts, and the skills to use them, from disappearing from the face of the earth.[13]

Both Dawson and Schlossberg envisioned Christians following this pattern of Christian cultural renewal. Schlossberg applies this history to the needs for our age, as the antidote to the idolatries of modernity:

We cannot say how long or how serious the present decline will prove to be, but once again Christians can stand in the gap against barbarism. Just as the biblical doctrine of creation demystified the world and made science possible, so other aspects of the faith are needed to destroy the follies of the modern idolatries.[14]

There is nothing new about barbarian or secular humanist in-roads with resulting idolatry and cultural decline. We simply have been too busy lamenting the evening news instead of reading of the early church and the Medieval era. Once again, note Christopher Dawson's observation about the Medieval period:

At first glance it seems as though the fall of the Empire must have involved the disappearance of the classical tradition, since the Church remained the only link between the barbarian peoples and the civilizations of the ancient world; and the monasteries, which were the chief centers of literary culture, were devoted by their institutions to the ascetic ideals that seem most irreconcilable with the spirit of classical humanism. In fact, however, it was the monasteries that secured the survival of the inheritance of classical cul-

---

[12] Christopher Dawson, *Religion and the Rise of Western Culture: The Classic Study of Medieval Civilization* (New York: Image Books, 1991), 44-45.
[13] Herbert Schlossberg, *Idols for Destruction* (Nashville: Thomas Nelson Publishers, 1983), 253.
[14] Schlossberg, 45.

ture through their adaptation of the old liberal education of the schools of the Later Roman Empire to the needs of the new ecclesiastical culture. The preservation of the old curriculum of the Liberal Arts meant that classical literature remained the basis of Western intellectual training. Virgil and Cicero, Ovid and Seneca, Horace and Quintilian were not mere school books, they became the seeds of a new growth of classical humanism in Western soil. Again and again—in the eighth century as well as in the twelfth and fifteenth centuries—the higher culture of Western Europe was fertilized by renewed contacts with the literary sources of classical culture. At first this influence only reached a small clerical minority, but it steadily increased throughout the later Middle Ages until, by the time of the Renaissance, it became the basis of lay education and inspired the development of vernacular literatures.

In this way the tradition of classical culture, which is also the tradition of humanism, became one of the great formative elements in Western culture. But this did not involve the denial or supercession of the Christian tradition, as has often been suggested by the historians of the Renaissance or the Enlightenment. As the humanist tradition remained alive during the Middle Ages, so the Christian tradition preserved its vitality in the post-Renaissance period, and it is only when both these traditions remain in living and fruitful contact with one another that Western culture attains its highest and most characteristic achievement.[15]

Dip anywhere into the history of the Middle Ages, and you find Classical Christian education. The Carolingian Renaissance, the educational impetus of Alfred the Great, the rise of the universities, and the founding of the schools of the Brethren of the Common Life are all but a few of the examples of education in the Medieval world. The same story can be found by reading the Medieval literary and theological works.[16] Chaucer and Dante are perhaps the most well known examples of the breadth and depth of learning found in the Medieval world. Learning did not begin with the modern age and books did not originate with Gutenberg. Medieval culture was a book culture. In *The Discarded Image,* C. S. Lewis points out,

---

[15] Christopher Dawson, *The Movement of World Revolution* (New York: Sheed and Ward, 1959), 91-92.
[16] See Peter Leithart, *Ascent to Love* (Moscow, Idaho: Canon Press, 2001), "I Have Come to the Garden: The Classics, the Bible, & Love in Medieval Literature," 13-42.

> The Medieval mind had an overwhelmingly bookish or clerkly character....When we speak of the Middle Ages as the ages of authority we are usually thinking of the authority of the Church. But they were the age not only of her authority, but of authorities. If their culture is regarded in response to environment, then the elements in that environment to which it responded most vigorously were manuscripts.[17]

The richness of Medieval schooling only intensified with the Renaissance. From there the Reformation itself was an outgrowth of Medieval and Renaissance education. A key transitional figure here was Gerard Groote (1340-1384), the founder of the Brethren of the Common Life. Christopher J. Lucas said, "The diffusion of schools sponsored by the Brethren of the Common Life did more for a general improvement of education than any other single movement."[18] That great devotional classic *The Imitation of Christ,* rated as the second most read spiritual book after the Bible, was a collection of Groote's thought and the work of one of his students, Thomas á Kempis.[19] Desiderius Erasmus, known for his satirical critique of the Roman Catholic Church and his labors over the Greek New Testament, was a product of a Brethren school.[20] Erasmus was a great scholar and influence over the later Protestant Reformers. Those Reformers, particularly Luther, Melancthon, and Calvin, were also educated in Brethren schools.[21] Lucas said, "From out of the scriptoria of their houses came a profusion of devotional tracts, textbooks, and Bibles. The Brethren staffed church and private municipal schools where they found them, and established models for other schools....That by 1400 opportunities to attend some form of grammar school were common was owed partly to the Brethren's zeal for schooling."[22]

From the Reformation, this educational tradition was part of the cultural heritage brought over to the New World. Education that was classical and Christian dominated Colonial American history.[23] Education that was

---

[17] C. S. Lewis, *The Discarded Image* (New York: Cambridge University Press, 1964), 5.

[18] Christopher J. Lucas, *Our Western Educational Heritage* (New York: Macmillan Publishing Company, Inc., 1972), 247.

[19] Thomas á Kempis, *The Imitation of Christ,* translated by Ronald Knox (San Francisco: Ignatius Press, 2005, reprint from 1959). This spiritual classic is available in numerous editions with different translators.

[20] Lucas, 247.

[21] George Grant and Gregory Wilbur, *The Christian Almanac* (Nashville: Cumberland House, 2000.), 492. Also, this story is brought out powerfully in the numerous versions of Dr. Grant's lecture "The Brethren of the Common Life."

[22] Lucas, 247.

[23] Richard M. Gummere, The American Colonial Mind and the Classical Tradition (Cambridge: Harvard University Press, 1963).

classical and Christian defined the educational experiences of the Founding Fathers.[24] Read any biography, study any part of early American schools and the elements of classical and Christian education are pervasive.

Let the first witness appear. Richard M. Gummere's book *The American Colonial Mind and the Classical Tradition* is a handbook of examples of how pervasive classical education was in Colonial America. Just picking one section—almost at random—will suffice. Gummere writes,

> As to literacy, in certain well-settled regions the proportion of those who could read and write was as high as 90 percent: on the frontier the ratio was much lower. At all events, the ambitious individual could rise on the educational scale. The Moravians provided schoolmasters who could prepare youth for the Latin courses at the seminary in Bethlehem, Pennsylvania....Peleg Folger, ambitious to be Nantucket's schoolmaster, took his classics with him on his whaling voyages, despite the banter of a shipmate who scribbled in one of Peleg's books: "Peleg Folger is a rum soull (sic) for writing Latin." This young relative of Benjamin Franklin attained his objective: he gave up whaling and taught Latin to the young Nantucketers. A rapid glance at the careers of Edmund Pendleton, George Wythe, and Patrick Henry makes it clear that mastery of the classics was not confined to college graduates. Henry, studying at home with his father and clergyman uncle, read Livy and Vergil in the original and continued his "homework" with Grotius, Bacon, Horace, Juvenal, Homer, Ovid, and translations of Demosthenes as a model for oratory.[25]

This same story, filled with an incredible number of examples, is told in Carl J. Richard's *The Founders and the Classics*. The political discussions in the Founding Era assumed knowledge of Latin and Greek political figures, writings, and oratory. Here is how Richard begins his study:

> The eighteenth-century educational system was the institution most responsible for the classical conditioning of the founders. It was mostly in the schools that the founders learned to venerate the classics. The socialization process was so complete, and the classics

---

[24] Carl J. Richard, *The Founders and the Classics: Greece, Rome, and the American Enlightenment* (Cambridge: Harvard University Press, 1996).

[25] Gummere, 62.

themselves so attractive, that even bad teachers, employing the most brutal and unimaginative pedagogical techniques, often instilled a love of the literature in their students. The founders' classical conditioning was so successful that most learned to relish the classics as a form of entertainment and to consider the ancients wise old friends. The founders loved and respected the classics for the same reason that other people love and respect other traditions: because the classical heritage gave them a sense of identity and purpose, binding them with one another and with their ancestors in a common struggle; and because it supplied them with the intellectual tools necessary to face a violent and uncertain world with some degree of confidence.[26]

Richard quotes John Witherspoon, President of the College of New Jersey, who said, "A man is not, even at this time, called or considered a scholar unless he is acquainted in some degree with the ancient languages, particularly Greek and Latin."[27]

The college entrance exams exceeded modern day graduation requirements. Richard notes that "when John Jay entered King's College (now Columbia), he was obliged to give a "rational account of the Greek and Latin grammars, read three orations of Cicero and three books of Virgil's *Aeneid*, and translate the first ten chapters of John into Latin."[28] The entrance exam at Princeton required the ability to write Latin prose and to translate Virgil, Cicero, and the Greek Gospels, with a thorough knowledge of Latin and Greek grammar.[29]

Of course, students grumbled and groaned as they struggled with difficult texts. Richard notes several students' confessions of less than spectacular study habits. He writes, "Another (student) complained that he had managed to read only six books of the *Aeneid* and one oration of Cicero during a break, while yet another confided his embarrassment at having read only seven books of Virgil and having 'looked at Greek grammar, mind, looked at it.'"[30]

In his magnificent biography of John Adams, David McCullough describes Adams correspondence with his son, John Quincy,[31] who wrote describing his reading in history. McCullough summarizes the father's response:

---

[26] Richard, 12.
[27] Richard, 20.
[28] Richard, 19.
[29] Richard, 20.
[30] Richard, 23.
[31] John Quincy Adams' educational background is yet more fodder for classical learning.

History was the true source of "solid instruction," Adams wrote to the boy encouragingly. He must read Thucydides's history of the Peloponnesian War. There was no better preparation, whatever part he was called to play on "the stage of life." It was best read in the original Greek, of course, but he could find a reliable translation among his father's books.[32]

At points the classical emphases overshadowed the Christian elements in the culture and education. Students translated portions of the New Testament, but the emphasis was more on classical languages than on theological understanding. Schools did not often label themselves as Christian institutions, but Christianity did underpin much of the culture. There were critics of classical education and schools that had different goals and curriculums. Often these schools were differentiated from classical schools by being labeled as English schools or writing schools. Students less apt at intellectual learning and parents less able to afford classical education opted for such educational choices. Paul Revere received such an education and went on to pursue a successful career as a silversmith. He then was able to achieve enough success to provide classical education for his sons.[33]

The tradition of classical Christian education predominated the American education scene at least up to the earlier part of the twentieth century. Instructors were quite often ministers whose training was a combination of classical languages and literature and Protestant theology. In other words, they studied the Bible in its original Hebrew and Greek, and they read Homer's *Iliad* in Greek, Tacitus' histories in Latin, as well as studying John Calvin's *Institutes of the Christian Religion.*

Consider yet a few more examples found particularly in the Southern states. Moses Waddell, a Southern Presbyterian preacher and teacher (1770-1840), began studying Latin at age eight, and after six years of school, he had finished courses in Greek, Latin, and mathematics. After his conversion and entrance into the ministry, Waddell established, in a log building, a school with an enrollment of as many as 180 students a year. In his book *Southern Presbyterian Leaders,* Dr. Henry Alexander White made these comments about Waddell's school:

> The food furnished to the students in Waddell's log college was plain, for it was usually nothing more than cornbread and bacon. A

---

[32] David McCullough, *John Adams* (New York: Simon & Schuster, 2001), 170-171.
[33] Esther Forbes, *Paul Revere and the World He Lived In* (Boston: Houghton Mifflin Company, 1942), 27-29.

blast from a ram's horn called them all together from morning and evening prayers. When the weather was mild the students sat or lay beneath the trees to prepare their lessons. The sound of the horn told the class in Homer when to assemble, and all of the members rushed at once to the recitation hall in the main building. Then the horn called up, in regular order, the Cicero, the Horace, and the Virgil classes, as well as those engaged in the study of mathematics and English.[34]

The success of this school obviously did not come from expensive facilities and modern technology or even a good cafeteria. (This shows the fallacy of those who promote higher school taxes to improve education.) Jack Maddex, Jr. said, "Waddell's students mastered the classical curriculum at an exacting pace, interspersing long study periods with recitations."[35] Many of Waddell's students achieved prominence in academic and civil affairs.

The type of student classical Christian education produced in the past astounds modern readers. The difficulty and rigor of education made it a prized commodity. The compulsory and egalitarian education system of today has debased the value of the commodity. While academic degrees are expected in many professional fields today, they are rarely seen as evidence of academic or intellectual ability. By contrast, education in the past was equated with book knowledge, and that knowledge was acquired only by hard work. Young Moses Hoge was noted for fastening a book to his plow as he worked the fields. He would plow a furrow, stop and read a page, and then ponder the contents as he plowed the next furrow.[36] David Caldwell, as a student, would sit near an open window and study into the late hours of the night. Then he would fold his arms on the table, lay his head down, and sleep until morning.[37]

James Henley Thornwell, who was given to studying fourteen hours a day, commented on his own need to improve his speaking and writing skills:

> Language was my great difficulty in early life. I had no natural command of words. I undertook to remedy the defect by committing to memory large portions of the New Testament, the Psalms, and much of the Prophets, also whole dramas of Shakespeare, and a

---

[34] Henry Alexander White, *Southern Presbyterian Leaders* (New York: Neale Publishing Company, 1911), 59-60.
[35] Jack P. Maddex, Jr., "Waddell, Moses," *Encyclopedia of Religion in the South,* edited by Samuel S. Hill (Macon: Mercer University Press, 1984), 819.
[36] White, 193.
[37] White, 196.

great part of Milton's *Paradise Lost*; so that you might start me at any line in any drama or book, and I would go through to the end.[38]

As a young teacher, Thornwell continued his study habits:

> I have commenced regularly with Xenophon's works, and intend to read them carefully. I shall then take up Thucydides, Herodotus, and Demosthenes. After mastering these I shall pass on to the philosophers and poets. In Latin I am going regularly through Cicero's writings. I read them by double translations; that is, I first translate them into English and then retranslate them into Latin. In German I am perusing Goethe's works. My life, you can plainly see, is not a life of idleness.[39]

After Thornwell committed his life to Christ, he entered the ministry and became one of the greatest Presbyterian ministers and theologians ever produced in America.

Professor Clyde Wilson has described the curriculum and its purposes in the University of North Carolina in the middle of the 1800s. He said:

> The college curriculum consisted chiefly of Latin, Greek, and pure mathematics, with smaller amounts of modern languages, chemistry, geology, physics, botany, zoology, metaphysics, logic, rhetoric, political economy, and constitutional and international law. More than half of a student's time in four years was spent in languages ancient and modern; three-fifths in the languages and pure mathematics together. The intent of these studies was to develop the powers of reason, analysis, and perspective, and by familiarity with the classical republics to inspire an understanding and love of American institutions. The curriculum also reflected a highly verbal and personalized society in which fixed status and institutional rigidity had not robbed words of their power to persuade and move.[40]

This ability to use reason, analysis, and perspective comes from reading. Neil Postman said, "From Erasmus in the sixteenth century to Elizabeth Eisenstein in the twentieth, almost every scholar who has grappled with the

---

[38] White, 309-310.
[39] White, 309-310.
[40] Clyde N. Wilson, *Carolina Cavalier: The Life and Times of James Johnson Pettigrew* (Athens: The University of Georgia Press, 1990), 15.

question of what reading does to one's habits of mind has concluded that the process encourages rationality; the sequential, propositional character of the written word fosters what Walter Ong calls the 'analytical management of knowledge.'"[41]

Since so many students in classical schools were training for the ministry, the intellectual ability was cultivated in order for future ministers to understand and implement the Scriptures. Susan Alder has stated that education in Colonial America was Christian not only in teaching the doctrines of the Christian faith, but in defining all reality by precepts and principles laid out in the Bible. She references historian Clinton Rossiter who said, "The colonial mind was thoroughly Christian in its approach to education, philosophy, and social theory...."[42]

Even the nature of the questioning of classical education and the debates such education engendered reveal an educated climate far different from ours today. Classicist Basil L. Gildersleeve was once asked to write a defense of classical education. He refused and in a letter commented upon the topic:

> If there is any subject that has been discussed to death, and that I have helped discuss to death since 1854, it is the place of the ancient classics in education; and I cannot get up enough interest in the matter to undertake the commission which you offer me. For the wider question, the discussion of which the ancient classics form only a part, I have neither the equipment nor the courage. The truly deplorable tendency of today is to break with the past altogether. There is to be no such thing as literary tradition, nothing but a succession of new births; and those who come after us will need elaborate commentaries in order to understand the text of the men of my time, which is rapidly becoming a remote past.
>
> With many thanks for considering me a possibility in what Matthew Arnold calls 'these bad times.'[43]

From the time the subject of classical education was "discussed to death" until our own time, education has suffered at the hands of many pedagogical

---

[41] Neil Postman, *Amusing Ourselves to Death: Public Discourse in the Age of Show Business* (New York: Penguin Books, 1985), 15.

[42] Susan Alder, "Education in America," in *Public Education and Indoctrination* (Irvington-on-Hudson: Foundation for Economic Education, 1993). Alder quoted Clinton Rossiter from *Seedtime of the Republic: The Origin of the American Tradition of Political Liberty* (New York: Harcourt Brace, 1953), 119.

[43] Basil L. Gildersleeve, *The Letters of Basil Lanneau Gildersleeve,* edited by Ward W. Briggs, Jr., 300.

physicians. The break with the past—that "deplorable tendency"—has become the mode for modern education. The cost of having jettison classical learning and the cost of abandoning the Bible at the core of the curriculum have been devastating. The result has been that we have produced generations of students—and we ourselves are such products—who do not know how much they do not know.[44]

None of this is to imply that colonial or early American or late nineteenth century education was perfect. None of this is to imply that teaching Greek and Latin will save the soul. The study of history cannot be like Coronado's quest for a city of gold—ever seeking for something on earth that was perfect. There was no golden age of Christian education, but there have been dark ages of Christian education. We study these past examples, we do history by anecdote and story, in order to find glimmers of light in our times of darkness.

C. S. Lewis makes this case in his essay "On the Reading of Old Books" when he says:

> Every age has its own outlook. It is specially good at seeing certain truths and specially liable to make certain mistakes. We all, therefore, need the books that will correct the characteristic mistakes of our own period. And that means old books....Not, of course, that there is any magic about the past. People were no cleverer then than they are now; they made as many mistakes as we. But not the same mistakes. They will not flatter us in the errors we are already committing; and their own errors, being now open and palpable, will not endanger us. Two heads are better than one, not because either is infallible, but because they are unlikely to go wrong in the same direction.[45]

The old books will help immensely in educating a newer generation and re-educating ourselves. Of course, by themselves, neither Homer or Augustine, nor Shakespeare or Flannery O'Connor will correct us without the Bible as the foundation for Christian education. Classically trained pagans are no more desirable than illiterate pagans. The Bible must be a subject in the educational curriculum, but more: The Bible must form the presuppositions for the truth of all subjects and the framework for all curriculum goals.[46]

---

[44] Credit George Grant with this phrasing of our situation.

[45] C.S. Lewis, "On Reading Old Books" as found in *God in the Dock* (Grand Rapids: William B. Eerdmans Publishing, 1978), 202.

[46] See Roy Clouser, *The Myth of Religious Neutrality* (Notre Dame, Indiana: University of Notre Dame Press, 2005).

This essay, this look at some history, is heavy laden with stories and examples from the past. An endless number of other examples could be given of classical Christian education as it existed in America from our colonial beginnings to the early decades of the twentieth century, and such much more could be added by looking at examples from Europe. Very obviously, the academic standards of the past centuries were high, the worldview was Christian, and the results were amazing. But what is the message for us?

Some would object to this discussion and point out that not all Americans received the level of education described above and that not all American students were James Henley Thornwell or Patrick Henry in inclination and ability. This is true; likewise, not all basketball players today are future NBA draft picks, but that should not cause us to lower the basketball goals to five feet high. The example of educated men of the 1700s and 1800s is daunting.

How can we teach in such a way as to achieve this when so many of us teachers today do not have the classical Christian training of the past? The answer is that we cannot achieve the same results—in one generation. We must be future oriented, and we must begin with what we have.

Tracy Lee Simmons is just one of a growing number of writers who is calling for a restoration of classical education. His book builds upon the metaphor of the mythical Mount Parnassus as the image of the task before us. He says,

> Climbing Parnassus once helped to form the unformed mind. The arduous ascent fostered intellectual and aesthetic culture within those who had endured the strain. It helped to bring mental and even emotional order out of chaos. And a classical training still provides the surest footing for the educated mind and a high perch from which to view other periods and nations. The foundations of the modern world are viewed more competently from this height. Poetry, drama, democracy, idealism, scientific curiosity, and so much else furnishing our minds are better grasped, and better judged. We drift without classics, floating on our own deracinated, exiguous islands. And we become fodder for demagogues. We need not a revolution, but a restoration.[47]

---

[47] Tracy Lee Simmons, *Climbing Parnassus: A New Apologia for Greek and Latin* (Wilmington, DE: ISI Books, 2002), 20.

There is much that Simmons, as well as Hanson and Heath and others, call for that may not be achievable for us as teachers or for our schools at the present. For example, Simmons does not think reading the classics in translation is true classical education. But we cannot pick up where the classical academies of the 1800s left off. We have to start where we are in this time and culture.

We have the Bible, so we can teach theology. We have books—centuries' accumulation of books at affordable prices. While we may begin with language restrictions, since few are trained in Latin and Greek today, we can, following John Adams' advice, master the great works of literature, history, and theology either written or translated into English.

Another objection might be: Why this type of education? Why not something more relevant, more modern, more accommodating to a non-literate, non-theological age? Classical Christian education is not designed to fit the student for *our times*. It is designed to transform the student to *God's times* (Romans 12:2). It is designed to produce a student with the mental discipline and ability to read an in-depth book (even one with more than one hundred pages), write discerning, thoughtful essays on the book, present lectures or debates on the contents of the book, and evaluate its contents in light of the Christian worldview. "Paces," multiple choice questions, computer games, and entertaining films cannot accomplish these results. Classical Christian education is "word-oriented." It can and has produced workmen who can rightly divide the Word of God and who do not need to be ashamed to confront and unmask the idols of our age.

Let's climb to the summit.

Chapter Four
History After Grammar School: Teaching Junior High

> My object will be, if possible, to form Christian men, for Christian boys I can scarcely hope to make.
> —Dr. Thomas Arnold, 1828,
> on being appointed headmaster of Rugby[1]

In Paul's great one-line testimony of his salvation, he said, "This is a faithful saying and worthy of all acceptance, that Jesus Christ came into the world to save sinners." (I Timothy 1:15) In the broader covenantal picture of Christ's work in time and history, we can expand this faithful and worthy saying to say that since Jesus Christ came into the world to save sinners, Jesus Christ came into the world to save history.[2]

Christ's subsequent salvations in history do not compare with or duplicate the once-for-all-time great sacrificial offering of Himself on the cross. Rather, the ongoing saving work of Christ flows from the salvation accomplished at Calvary. "For He must reign till He has put all His enemies under His feet" (1 Corinthians 15:25). All Christians acknowledge the personal salvation of ourselves and others. But we should also recognize the great works of salvation that Christ has brought about in the great events of history.

Providentially, God has saved history many times. Sometimes, as in the Noahic Flood, it is by direct intervention. In that case it was the intervention of judgment upon a wicked world mixed with grace upon Noah and his family.[3] In some cases, as in the story of Joseph in the Old Testament, God

---

[1] From *The Oxford Dictionary of Quotations*, Third Edition (Oxford: Oxford University Press, 1980), 16.

[2] To view history covenantally, see Ralph Smith's *Trinity and Reality* (Moscow, Idaho: Canon Press, 2004), chapters 6 and 7 and Norman Shepherd's *The Call of Grace: How Covenant Illuminates Salvation and Evangelism* (Phillipsburg: P & R Publishing, 2000), chapters 1-4.

[3] The theme of blessing and judgment coinciding is prevalent in Biblical and historical studies.

uses a righteous man to accomplish His purposes of saving many people both in time and eternity. In His sovereign freedom and power, God can and does also use the wicked to accomplish His purposes (Acts 4:27-30).

Because of the salvation brought by Christ, Christians have been used of God to save history many times. Western Civilization–Christian Civilization–Christendom–has been saved many times by Christians. All too rarely has our history been cast in terms of being salvation experiences. Secular historians have generally failed completely to see the role of the Christian faith in preserving our civilization.

Let us consider a few examples:

In 410, Alaric led the Visigoths into Italy, and after several sieges and negotiations, the Visigoths sacked Rome. The Roman world was shocked. The pagans controlled the spin on this news story: Rome fell because it had forgotten its old gods and had abandoned them for the Christian God. Here was a disaster of great magnitude. And what is always worse than a disaster is its accepted interpretation. One Christian stood up against that interpretation. He began to write the answer; it took over a dozen years to complete the answer, but in 426, Augustine, bishop of Hippo and Christian theologian, presented the first systematic case for Christian history in his magisterial *City of God*. This study presented all of history as the story of two cities, the city of man and the city of God. It provided the intellectual and theological blueprint for a thousand years of Christian civilization, now called the Middle Ages.

In 527, an unlikely man and woman succeeded to the throne of the Byzantine Empire, or the eastern Roman Empire: Justinian I and the Empress Theodora. This empire provided the boundaries of the eastern fringes of Christendom. Together this man and woman ruled for a time in what would be a 1000-year Christian empire, imperfect, flawed, yet Christian.

Justinian is best remembered for the *Corpus Juris Civilis*, a codification of the laws of the empire. Theodora, a woman with a miserable background, but a remarkable Christian testimony to God's saving grace, was responsible for seeing that the laws protected women. She made certain that Biblical principles guided Justinian's laws so that other women would not be abused as she had been.

The Byzantine Empire faced many dangers and threats from all sides. Harold Lamb, in his book *Constantinople: Birth of an Empire,* used a portion of a letter written by a Confederate soldier to describe the rulers of the Christian Byzantine Empire: "Men who saw night coming down about them could somehow act as if they stood on the edge of dawn."[4]

In the early fifth century, an Englishman, a fugitive slave, a young man with a burden from God, returned to the land of the ones who had enslaved him. He returned to bring them the Gospel of Jesus Christ. Thus St. Patrick of Ireland began the Christianization of the Emerald Island and created the Celtic Christian faith that not only evangelized Ireland, but enabled his successors to seize the small island of Iona, between England and Ireland, and from there they re-Christianized England and Scotland, and from there faithful Irish monks sent missionaries throughout Europe. These missionaries copied the great manuscripts, thus saving the intellectual heritage of Christendom, and they evangelized the people, thus saving the flock for whom Christ had died.

In 1565, a band of Christian nobles, who alternately served as warriors or nurses, whatever the need called for, fought against odds of something like ten to one, and defeated the Islamic Ottoman Turks invading army that set out to capture the small island of Malta in the Mediterranean. From that small island, the Ottomans would have moved on to Sicily, then Italy, then into the heartland of Christian Europe. Thus at Malta and later at Lepanto, the Islamic Turks were stopped from invading Europe.

Earlier in that same century, in 1521, theology professor and preacher Martin Luther stood at the Diet of Worms in the presence of the Holy Roman Emperor, Charles V, and political and ecclesiastical representatives from all over Europe, defended Scripture and conscience against tradition and church authority and thus saved Christendom in its Protestant and Catholic forms from institutional and heretical threats from within.

On Christmas night in 1776, Anglican vestryman and Virginia agricultural genius, George Washington put into action what his fellow

---

[4] Harold Lamb, *Constantinople: Birth of an Empire* (New York: Alfred A. Knopf, 1959), 2.

Virginian Thomas Jefferson had put into writing that same year—1776. On Christmas night, Washington launched an audacious and bold attack across the Delaware River right into the camp of the highly trained and skilled German mercenaries, the Hessians, encamped at Trenton, New Jersey. The victory netted the Continental army a large number of prisoners. In overall effect, it saved the Patriot cause. It would be five long years between that triumph and the next greatest one of Washington. In 1781, a coalition of soldiers consisting of New England Congregationists, Middle Colony Presbyterians, and Southern frontiersman, mainly of Presbyterian/Scots-Irish stock, along with our French allies would all join together for a great battle in Yorktown, Virginia. There they captured a British army under Lord Cornwallis, whose underlings had raided the Southern colonies, destroying churches and communities mercilessly. This victory would put an end to effective British military opposition to the Patriot War for Independence.

In the 1860s, waves of revival would sweep through the Confederate armies, and to a lesser extent through the Union armies, and thousands of men would be converted, thus providing the spiritual resources that would be necessary to enable the South to survive defeat and Reconstruction with a strong Bible base still intact. Compare the spiritual culture of the postwar South to that of postwar Britain, France, Germany, or Russia after World War I. The spiritual heritage of the revival in the Confederate army still survives in the South today.

In 1941, Franklin Roosevelt, an Episcopalian whose favorite chapter of the Bible was First Corinthians 13, and British Prime Minister Winston Churchill, who described himself, not as a pillar, but more like a flying buttress of the Church of England, met together on warships off the coast of Newfoundland. There they discussed Allied war aims and post-war expectations. Churchill had long understood the nature of the war against Nazism: It was a war of good against evil, of Christian civilization against the forces of darkness. What is significant about that meeting is not the particular objectives—several of which we would disagree—what was significant was the gathering on Sunday morning when the officers and political leaders gathered around Pres. Roosevelt and Prime Minister Churchill to worship. There together they sang "Onward

Christian Soldiers" and acknowledged in prayer and worship the true God.

In the late 1980s, an aging actor and former governor stepped to center stage to perform his greatest role: Winning the Cold War. President Ronald Reagan, of a Disciples of Christ upbringing, a man with a continual reliance upon God and a belief in a special mission from God, stood before the Berlin Wall, and to the consternation of his aides and to the disgust of his many liberal enemies, he demanded—he didn't ask: He issued a demand to the pragmatic Soviet premier and media idol of the Left, Mikhail Gorbachev, "Mr. Gorbachev, tear down this wall." Within a period of a few years, much to the surprise of Reagan's enemies, but not to Reagan himself, that very wall came tumbling down.

Christian history teachers have such a wealth of resources. Next to the Bible, history is our greatest resource as teachers in Christian schools and as the cultural preservers of Christendom. We have at our disposal such an embarrassment of riches. Whether it is teaching American history or World History, whether the focus in on the Ancient, Medieval, or Modern world, the reading and studying of history is one of the most pleasurable experiences in life. The personal pleasure of the study of history is exceeded only by joy of sharing history with others in the classroom.

And yet with all this abundance of material, with the wealth of stories, with the beauty of the glimpses of God's purposes being fulfilled, we have to admit those experiences where God's glorious story as revealed in the events of history is lost on the poor students under our charge.

Sometimes we as teachers are to blame. Our sheaf of notes with names, dates, and details is quite exhilarating—to us. Our discoveries and insights are life-transforming experiences—to us. Beware the lazy spring afternoon when your twenty-seven point outline on tariff issues competes with classroom weariness or youthful hormones or calls of nature. Yes, we teachers sometimes fail to adequately deliver the historical goods.

Sometimes the students are to blame. Their intellectual immaturity, their lack of historical curiosity, their contentment with ignorant mediocrity makes us earn those big bucks we get paid. Sometimes the students are lectured-out from other classes by the time they arrive in our classroom. Sometimes they are stubbornly rebellious. Sometimes they are just not apt to receive the fine delicacies offered up in our lecture banquets. And then sometimes our students are suffering from a particular malady that we characterize by a grouping terminology: They are junior high students.

Some teachers are called to teach elementary students and are imbued with a love for small children. Elementary children bubble with eagerness to hear stories, to read aloud, to make cardboard castles and construction paper crowns. Some of us are called to teach high schoolers. Being in the rhetoric stage of learning, high schoolers can take notes at an increasingly fast clip, read increasingly fatter books, and see the connections between ancient warriors and modern shopping malls.

But somebody has to teach junior high students. Somebody has to take on the task of instructing students during the logic or dialectic stage. Dorothy Sayers calls it the Pert Stage. Of it she says that the students' 'nuisance value is very high.'[5]

The Junior High Years: Proof of a Fallen World

Some time back I had the occasion to lecture at the annual conference for the Association for Classical Christian Schools. In most cases at such conferences, those who teach the teachers do so because they are smarter, or more experienced, or better than those who listen. I felt more like I had been called to the front and singled out as an example of how bad I was and how slow I was to learn.

Just mark this down: No matter how much experience you have teaching, no matter how great a success you are in the classroom, no matter how prepared you are academically and personally to control a learning environment, there is out there somewhere a group of junior high students who can take you to the mat. Keep score when it happens and make sure that the final score is in your favor, but never forget that it will happen.

It happened to me with a junior high class during the school year preceding my ACCS talk. In my upcoming lecture, I had wanted to give an anecdote-to-anecdote recitation of success stories. These stories would have included an example of the students beginning a daunting book with fear and dread and ending with them loving the book. It would include the story of the poor struggling student who, under my tutelage, discovered that he could learn. It would have included the story of the child who started out hating history who now wanted to be a history teacher, just like me. Instead, I merely survived that year, and most of the students moved to other towns that summer or transferred to other schools. I survived the year of teaching junior

---

[5] As found in Appendix A of Douglas Wilson, *Recovering the Lost Tools of Learning* (Wheaton, Illinois: Crossway Books, 1991), 154 ff.

high as a sadder, but hopefully wiser man. Thankfully, the next year's class was much better, but I had no opportunity to speak about them.

Why are junior high students so hard to teach? Consider the following: First, they are too old to color a rabbit, too young to love *The Iliad*. This does not mean that they cannot still color rabbits; they just usually don't want to. The excitable hands-on type of activities that characterized the elementary years are beneath them. But since the depths of rhetorical and poetic learning have not opened up, the aching beauty of *The Iliad* often escapes them. They are people caught in a series of betweens: Between elementary and high school. Between grammar and rhetoric. Between childhood and adulthood. Between the cute characteristics of young children and the maturity found in older teenage students.

The social, physical, and spiritual awkwardness of the early teenage years give hints about the situation. The human body is more challenging to them than is the curriculum. Their immaturity is exasperating. Their senses of humor are crass. Vulgarity, grossness, obnoxiousness, rudeness and the like are the fruits of the age. Any statement can, with a junior high student, be turned into sexual humor. Unfortunately, their humor is usually not even remotely funny.

Added to all that is the overwhelming influence of the adolescent society in which we live. Our culture as a whole is locked into a permanently junior high adolescent mentality. Why is there so much sexual humor on television? We are in a junior high culture. Why is so much of modern advertising so me-centered? We are a junior high culture. Why does our culture question everything antagonistically? ("Who says girls are different from boys?") We have an adolescent culture. Why is our culture so crass, so crude, so rebellious, so individualistic, and so immature? We live in an adolescent culture.

There is no piece of literature so grand, no selection of theology so awesome, no musical composition so moving, no poem so profound, and no lecture so well crafted as to not be able to bore a junior high student.

Don't feel bad if you bore the adolescent. Shakespeare, Bach, and Calvin bore them as well.

What's Happening Inside There?

What is going on in the minds of our junior high students? Sometimes we think nothing is going on. Sometimes we discover that more is going on than we really want to know. The human mind is a non-stop information and sensation processing machine that simultaneously is accessing information empirically, recalling information historically, creating information imaginatively, and is randomly connecting all sorts of facts, words, sensations, thoughts, memories, and current happenings.

William Faulkner used the stream-of-consciousness technique to show the workings of Benjamin Compson, a retarded man, in his novel *The Sound and the Fury*. Once the reader figures out the jumps from time to time in Benjy's memory, the word associations, and the ways that Benjy processes these things, the novel begins to make sense.

Far more difficult than this variation of "a tale told by an idiot"[6] are the mental processes of junior high students. Here are some of the features that dominate their approach to the classroom:

First of all, junior high students have school figured out. It is a perpetually long sentence that has already occupied two-thirds of their lives. When we tell them that before long they will be graduating from high school, they think we are crazy. As adults, we remember the time when the days from Christmas to Christmas seemed to last forever. As time goes on, a year goes by quickly. For the adult, five years and even ten years go by with breathtaking speed. I find myself surprised at the middle-aged man that stares back at me in the mirror.

But the junior high student has a perspective on time that is different. In his mind and memory, school has been there since almost the beginnings of time itself. The urgency that drives teachers—"You need to know this so you can get a job someday"—is offset by the interminable lengths of time spent in the classroom gulags.

Second, much of the excitement of learning has ceased. Most of what can be known is already known by the average junior high student. "We already know that." "We learned that last year." "We already read that." Again teachers, and especially those of us whose post-college education has been devoted to realizing how incredibly ignorant we are, are painfully aware of how much we don't know. In fact, for me there are two areas where I feel really terribly deficient in my own knowledge: The first is in those areas, like Latin, science, and logic, where I have little or no education. The second is in those areas like American Colonial history, history of the War Between the States, Southern literature, and Twentieth Century political history where I have read widely and deeply.

As a teacher, I may be turning somersaults over a realization that Poland had the fourth largest air force on the allied side in World War II,[7] but the

---

[6] After you get to know Jason Compson in Faulkner's novel, you realize that Benjy is not the real idiot in the family.

[7] Lynne Olson and Stanley Clous, *A Question of Honor: The Kosciuszko Squadron—Forgotten Heroes of World War II* (New York: Alfred A. Knopf, 2003).

worldly wise and experienced eighth grader is able to file that fact under irrelevant historical mush and yawn.

Third, junior high students have figured out how to short-cut classwork in order to get the lesson done quickly. Whole essays can be completed in one paragraph. Paragraphs can be completed in one sentence. Such details as capitalization, punctuation, spelling, and grammar are not applicable. Thought questions are answered tritely. Discussion questions are answered with brevity. The whole goal of schoolwork is shutting the book and getting back to talking to a neighbor. Quality of work, original thought, and intellectual growth do not appear on their radar screens. Occasionally, the junior high student will venture to explore more deeply if he finds the answer a springboard for junior high wit or insults against a fellow student.

Dorothy Sayers points out that at this stage the student is making connections between facts. Beware of thinking that you as the teacher can present the facts, draw the lines of connection between them, and see the faces light up with excitement. Junior high students are far more committed to making their teachers earn their pay than that. All too often, they still think facts are things to learn, to recite, and to give back to the teacher.

Uses and Limitations of the Trivium

Dorothy Sayers was a bit unbalanced in her life; her story is unseemly and dark at certain points; she was not the model for Christian womanhood we want our daughters to follow. All that being said, she was a trophy of God's grace, and she was brilliant. Her essay "The Lost Tools of Learning"[8] has still only just begun to make an impact in this day when many schools, teachers, and homeschooling families have used her essay as a roadmap.

But her essay is simply that—an essay. Many of the topics she raised call for more examination. Miss Sayers stood at a crossroads in history and pointed backward at a time when everyone was racing forwards. She called for a return to the Trivium as the methodology of teaching. I have a Master's Degree in education and most of what I studied and read to attain the thirty-six hours of graduate credit for that degree is stubble compared to Sayers's "The Lost Tools of Learning."

Still, we suffer limitations. Many of us are limited because we are the products of an education that was neither classical, nor Christian. It took a while for the education establishment to weed out all of the old school marms

---

[8] Found in many sources including Wilson's *Recovering the Lost Tools of Learning* as Appendix A, 145-164.

and the Mr. Chips-types who held on to the older and better ways of educating students. When I was taking education courses, I was taught, for example, several "nevers": Never have students memorize poetry. Never use rote learning (which we learned by rote). Never correct grammar or spelling. Never impose values. Underlying it all was a philosophy that assumed that great books should never be assigned to graduate students.

Many of us find ourselves trying to teach students and simultaneously trying to both learn for ourselves and learn how students should be taught. In such a pedagogical desert, the Trivium is a veritable oasis. But several precautions need to be noted, especially for junior high classes.

The junior high years are the hardest years in which to implement a classical methodology. Here is what I have noticed in myself and others: It is all too easy for junior high classes to evolve into upper elementary. Some students have insufficient historical grammar. They may arrive without a background from either a classical Christian school or a school with academically rigorous standards. Sometimes junior high children seem to be the victims of severe cases of amnesia. There is grammar level material that needs to be taught or re-taught. Sure, they may have learned the thirteen colonies, the fifty states and capitals, the countries of Europe, the seven continents, the four oceans, and the emperors of the Ming Dynasty, but now all that is forgotten. Lists of facts need not be the driving force of the curriculum at the logic level, but they may have to be reviewed or relearned or learned for the first time.

The junior high teacher will find that memory work assignments, specifically, learning lists, is quite successful. It puts grades in the gradebook; the learning is measurable; and the children get lots of correct answers. The high school teacher finds the same results possible on the same types of assignments. But this is not the classical Christian methodology or goal. Junior high students need to be mentally connecting ideas, mentally grappling with the legality or illegality of the Boston Tea Party, mentally seeing similarities and differences between the Holocaust, Apartheid, and Jim Crow Laws. Such learning is harder to measure, test, and grade.

On the other extreme is the classical workcamp mentality. The problem above is the result of teacher frustration over the students' poor backgrounds. The problem here is zeal with the high ideals of the new convert. We as teachers entering into classical Christian education grasp that in many cases we did not get the education we should have. We recognize that our own educational experiences were dumbed-down, so we take to the streets, or more likely, the classroom with the fervor of the revolutionary. I think to myself: "I got a Master's degree without having once opened Herodotus and

Thucydides, but my eighth graders must read them in a week." In college you have lectures and research papers, so let's get started in junior high with the same level of work. After years of wandering in the academic wilderness, I've discovered the promised land, so I force march my kids through the classics. Load them down and require them to love it. Ad fontes—to the sources—tolle lege—take up and read—and let's recapture one hundred and fifty lost years of educational excellence in one fell swoop before the Thanksgiving break.

How is a balance achieved? What does a classical Christian education look like at the junior high level? How is it implemented when the students are not where they ought to be at all points?

If the "nuisance value" of junior high students is very high, how are they to be taught?

Outlines

Along with incredible teaching skills, which translates into energy, intellectual aptitude, ability to lecture in interesting ways, and lots of patience, the junior high teacher must be the master of stories. Biographies of famous people, biographies of obscure people, stories of saints, tales of scoundrels, anecdotes, jokes, puns, mysteries, adventures, romance, and above all WAR must make up the content of history at the logic level. Stories really should be a big part of the content at the grammar and rhetoric levels, too.

For the sake of covering the material, history teaching consists of two parts—stories and outlines. Stories will be the focus further down, so let's consider outlines. Outlines, as I am using the term, are any tools that line up and list the events or that take a time period or an event and presents it in a simplified format. Lists of leaders, names of battles, key terms, chronologies, charts, and maps all fit under the broad category of outlines. Chronologies are most useful in presenting lectures for history. History is, as Stephen Mansfield notes, more than dates and dead people, but chronologies are dates and dead people.[9]

Consider George Washington, John Adams, Thomas Jefferson, and James Madison, the first four Presidents. The names fit into a chronology of events in American history. We could supply the dates of their Presidencies or of their lives. In some way, we need to use charts, lists, chronologies, and even pictures to present an outline showing these four presidents. We need the list

---

[9] Stephen Mansfield, *More Than Dates and Dead People* (Nashville: Cumberland House Books, 2000).

of facts about these men, but more is needed to teach history. Most of those people who are remembered as bad history teachers were not history teachers at all. Often, they taught outlines, lists of facts, and chronologies. Chronologies dominate traditional history textbooks.

Chronologies are not bad. We need good textbooks that put events in chronological order, that list the causes of events by dates, that record the terms of office of leaders. We also need those useful resources for teachers and students that chronologically recite the facts of history. If the names Peloponnesian Wars, Napoleonic Wars, and World War II don't cause certain chronological bells to ring, you are not able to understand history. If you cannot remember that Roosevelt's vice presidents were John Nance Garner, Henry Wallace, and Harry Truman—in that order—then chronologies are useful.

It is most helpful to learn and memorize dates. In 1492 Columbus sailed the ocean blue. Without that peg, it is hard to then even roughly place Cortez, John Smith, and Daniel Boone in history. You can never learn too many historical facts and dates, and students need to memorize dates, but our goal is not fulfilled by making little encyclopedias out of our students. We want them to know how to think and how to research facts, not simply to remember and recite.

Within the skeletal framework of chronological outlines of history, stories are needed to flesh out the fullness of history.

J. R.R. Tolkien as Historian

J. R. R. Tolkien was a philologist and a literary scholar and not a historian. Although *The Lord of the Rings* began appearing during World War II, the trilogy was not, he emphasized strongly, an allegory of World War II.[10] The shire was not England and Mordor was not the Third Reich. Tolkien's creative writings were fiction, more exactly, fantasy. But Tolkien also said that Middle Earth and *The Lord of the Rings* felt like history.[11] More than that, Tolkien presented a vision of history that history teachers can benefit from incorporating into their teaching style. At least five elements of Tolkien's vision can be formatted for use by teachers.

---

[10] J. R. R. Tolkien, *Fellowship of the Rings* (Boston: Houghton Mifflin Company, 1982), Foreward, 6-7.

[11] Stratford Caldecott, "Over the Chasm of Fire: Christian Heroism in The Silmarillion and The Lord of the Rings" from Tolkien: *A Celebration*, edited by Joseph Pearce (San Francisco: Ignatius Press, 1999), 18.

First, history must be cast in terms of a story. From our earliest years, we respond to stories. Dr. Louise Cowan has repeatedly emphasized that literature appears in four major forms or genres and that these four types of literature are modes of knowledge. They are epic, tragedy, comedy, and lyric. Each encompasses stories. Even lyrics, or what we would usually think of as both poetry and songs, express stories. The sound of language and the rhythms of language are sources of delight for both infants and adults, but along with the sense and sound, there is the story.

Daniel Taylor said,

> Stories link past, present and future in a way that tells us where we have been (even before we were born), where we are, and where we could be going....Our stories teach us that there is a place for us, that we fit. They suggest to us that our lives can have a plot. Stories turn mere chronology, one thing after another, into the purposeful action of plot, and thereby into meaning....Stories are the best single way humans have for accounting for our experience.[12]

Take his quote and insert the word "*history*" for "*story*," and it reinforces my point. The most plain and obvious etymological fact about the word history is that it has the word "story" as its root. Herodotus first used the word *historia,* which can also be translated as *inquiry*. The word *inquiry* seems more to call for a gathering of facts, an assembling of pertinent details, an archiving of key documents. But even the driest of historical facts are the kernels of stories. Herodotus' *Histories* is more a collection of stories than a documentary of historical facts. To simply state the number of battlefield casualties at Gettysburg is to reveal the number of stories at that battle that end in death.

Douglas Wilson has said, "Children need to hear stories. The reason is they must learn to interpret stories, and they must do this so that they come to understand the story of their own life. The gospel story is, of course, the center of this process."[13] In the flow of history, children begin finding stories that contain the patterns, the archetypes of the issues of life they face. What does the day-by-day experience of a twelve year old have to do with Napoleon's retreat from Moscow? Well, for one thing, he might readily associate the

---

[12] Daniel Taylor, *The Healing Power of Stories: Creating Yourself Through the Stories of Your Life*—as quoted in Brian Godawa, *Hollywood Worldviews* (Downers Grove, Illinois: Intervarsity Press, 2002), 33.

[13] Douglas Wilson, *My Life for Yours* (Moscow, Idaho: Canon Press, 2004), 110.

experiences of his enduring history class with the experiences of the retreat of the Grande Armee across the barren steppes of Russia. Will he make other connections? Connections like the dangers of pride, the necessity for perseverance (perhaps better illustrated by the Russian side in that conflict), or the fact that life is not a just one big happy party, but is—at moments— more like a retreat in the midst of a Russian winter?

Along with the facts for the upcoming test, the map assignment, the worksheet, and the terms and people listed at the end of the chapter, students need to get a feel for, or sense of, the story. Lectures will need to be structured around narratives, biographies, and anecdotes. The best supplementary readings will be stories. Even fictional accounts of history, such as Michael Shaara's *Killer Angels,* are quite useful. Another example of great historical fiction is Esther Forbes's book *Johnny Tremain,* which portrays events in Boston leading to the American War for Independence. The stories woven into the course lectures and readings need not tell the whole story of history, but only illustrate certain aspects, such as courage or leadership or providential turning points.

Second, the story must be cast in terms of good and evil. In the universities today, historians steer clear, so they say, of making moral judgments. For moral judgments, they tell you to go to the religion and philosophy departments. (Don't expect to find the correct judgments there either.) But there was a time when history was viewed as a branch of philosophy, specifically moral philosophy. Quite often historians of the past were overly nationalistic, moralistic, and biased. Because of this, they wrote with a flair and passion for their chosen cause. Sometimes the writing was too flowery, sometimes too adulatory. Then historians began focusing on objectivity. Analysis replaced conviction. Why can we not have both—an analysis of historical events with moral judgments?

Tolkien's story was cast in terms of good and evil. Bradley Birzer said, "It is in the goodness of the heroes who are fighting for Middle-earth that one understands the evil that good opposes."[14] The kingdoms of Mordor and Sauraman were the forces of evil. Orcs were not simply misunderstood; they were not just doing their duty like the horsemen of Rohan; rather, Orcs were fighting for an evil cause. Tolkien was wise enough and Christian enough in his story to reveal the faults of good men, the limitations of dwarfs and hobbits, and the ambiguities of mankind. Gollum, an evil character, plays a major role in the defeat of the evil forces, just as Stalin helped to defeat

---

[14] Bradley J. Birzer, *J.R.R. Tolkien's Sanctifying Myth* (Wilmington: ISI Books, 2002), 92.

Hitler. Good and evil as concepts disappeared from American culture until September 11, 2001. Then the word "evil" returned to our vocabulary.[15] Moral relativism cannot work in the world or the classroom without resulting in a philosophy of meaninglessness.

The teacher has to be careful when casting the story of history in terms of these moral absolutes. In some cases, it is quite clear. Nero was wicked and Paul was righteous. In other cases, the right and wrong sides are questionable. Are we better off because of the band of brave Spartans who defended the pass at Thermopylae, or could Western Civilization have been better served by the removal of the wicked and perverse Greek civilization?[16] The American experience has been taught in such nationalistic and adulatory ways that are not sound from a Christian worldview, but being hyper-critical of the country can be dangerous too. I cannot look at Grover Cleveland's Presidential victory in 1892 when he recaptured the White House from Benjamin Harrison and say that good triumphed over evil or visa versa. (After all, both were Presbyterians.) In many instances in history, I believe good men truly differed in their beliefs. I have great respect for both the Federalists who wrote and promoted the Constitution and the Anti-Federalists who opposed it.

So, don't force an absolute moral judgment on every event. Don't follow the party line found in the secular public school textbooks and university classes. Don't create straw men, or to broaden the fallacy, straw history: for example, "At the Battle of the Wilderness in 1864, the drunkard, Butcher Grant led the Unitarians against the American Christians in Lee's Army of Northern Virginia."[17] But when the occasion is appropriate, and the historical documents bear up the case, and the lessons of history stand in need of dramatic presentation, present the story in terms of good and evil.

I think Winston Churchill was far from a perfect man or perfect leader. He exercised poor judgments on many occasions and made moral and political blunders. Still, he was a good man of moral vision, political savvy, and Christian rhetoric who stood steadfastly against Hitler who was evil. Puritans were guilty of failings and inconsistencies, but their opposition to Queen Elizabeth in matters ecclesiastical and later the Stuart kings in matters political cast them as good against evil. Otto Scott documented the careers of a few scoundrels he termed sacred fools, specifically Robespierre, King James I,

---

[15] David Wells, *Above All Earthly Powers: Christ in a Postmodern World* (Grand Rapids: Eerdmans, 2005), 3.

[16] See Thomas Cahill, *Sailing the Wine-Dark Sea: Why the Greeks Matter* (New York: Nan A. Talese, 2003) Cahill highly honors the Greeks although he readily documents their perversities.

[17] Yes, I have been tempted to teach the War Between the States this way, but have resisted the more extreme characterizations.

and John Brown. These men were evil and served evil purposes. Cromwell was a great Christian leader; not everything he did was great and neither was it consistent with his Christian faith. And just as the Bible openly portrays the sins of great men, like King David, we must in our histories portray the failures and shortcomings of our heroes, as well as successes.

Third, history, as a study of the past, has to be relevant to current times. This is a challenge for the junior high students because they have such a limited capacity and experience with both historical and contemporary relevancy. Relevance was what the Hobbits did not understand in the early parts of the *Lord of the Rings* series. The dark gathering clouds over Middle-earth all seem to concern distant kingdoms and events from ages past when Elves and Men battled against the forces of evil. But Frodo and Sam's education comes as they realize more and more how distant events will ultimately destroy the shire.

Just as preaching has to include practical exhortations, so teaching has to include exhortations of practical relevance. Luther's stand at Worms is relevant to my Christian walk; the attack on Pearl Harbor is relevant to America's role in the world today; and Washington's decision to retire after two terms as President is relevant to the preservation of my freedom. Often when I am teaching on some seemingly distant event in history, I will tell my students to remember that event at Wednesday night prayer meeting. Remember, I tell them, to give thanks that Cortes defeated the Aztecs and ended the horrible human sacrifices.[18]

Children need to realize that their lives and circumstances are the product of historical forces. Ancient history was not the era before the invention of VHS's and DVD's; the Middle Ages were not when the teachers were young. Time and history define our lives and culture here and now. To God one day is as a thousand years and a thousand years is as one day, but to a junior high student, a long historical era is the length of time he is sitting in your classroom on a Tuesday afternoon. It is their mental, historical timelines that need developing. Thankfully, there will always be some students who will like history and who will lap it up like pudding. But all students—even those without a predisposition for history—need to develop a sense of historical relevance. They need to go out of the Shire and see the battles facing Middle Earth.

Fourth, history has to be taught in terms of the survival of civilization being at stake. This point builds upon the previous ones. To close out a

---

[18] Gary DeMar and Fred Young, *A New World in View* (Powder Springs, Georgia: American Vision, 1996) See chapters 11-13, 105-132.

lecture by saying, "And so, the tariff was lifted and commerce continued as it had before," will likely cure insomnia, but it cannot energize the soul of a junior high student, or me either. "So What? Who cares? What difference does it make?" These are three of the greatest questions you can ask and three you better answer before the kid at the back of the room asks those questions.

History is best written or taught by focusing on hinges or turning points. Thomas Cahill's series of histories are developed around this very theme.[19] History consists of salvations and destructions. History always has flow to it and is never stagnant. Our country is at this point either rising or falling, as are all other nations. General Washington's surrendering of his sword to the president of the Continental Congress was a turning point in history. Franklin Roosevelt's attempt to pack the Supreme Court was another turning point. There is a ripple effect to every event in history.[20] Amidst the vast expanses of factual datum, historical crossroads are what teachers need to discern and teach.

The Lord of the Rings is not just about friendship, or an adventure journey through troubled lands, or jewelry. The survival of civilization was at stake in Middle Earth, just as it was in the world where Tolkien was penning this work. While we can accept Tolkien's insistence that the books are not allegorical to World War II, they are in a greater sense allegorical to all of history.[21] As Russell Kirk point out:

> Some critics may identify the evil power in Tolkien's *Lord of the Rings* with Nazi or Communist dominations; yet Tolkien himself did not intend to be bound by yesterday's or today's ideological encounters. His three volumes are a picture of the perpetual struggle between good and evil; his concern is the corrupting intoxication of power.[22]

For that reason, the story of Middle Earth resonates in our time when we are seeing this global war on terror, and it will continue to resonate on earth among men until swords are hammered into plowshares. It is a shame

---

[19] This series began with *How the Irish Saved Civilization*.
[20] Victor Davis Hanson, *Ripples of Battle* (New York: Doubleday, 2003).
[21] Tolkien emphasizes in the forward to *The Fellowship of the Rings* that World War II was not the inspiration of the book. World War I had a greater impact on the book. See *Tolkien and the Great War* by John Garth (Boston: Houghton Mifflin, 2003).
[22] Russell Kirk, *Enemies of the Permanent Things* (Peru, Ill.: Sherwood Sugden, 1988) 13, as quoted in Birzer, 92.

that George Orwell's two classics *Animal Farm* and *1984* are less noticed today because the Soviet Union disintegrated. Both of his books had clear parallels to events in the Communist world, but the greater messages of his books transcend Communism. The false egalitarian promises with real elitist results exemplified by Orwell's pigs and the ever-encroaching nature of governmental overreach were not evils confined simply to Stalin and his successors.

Fifth, Tolkien understood that history always has a theological and spiritual dimension. Something is always central to the interpretation of history. For Marxists, it is economics and class differences. For nationalists, it is the nation marching in Hegelian fashion as God on earth. For the Christian, history has to be ultimately grounded in a theological and spiritual perspective. Tolkien rewrote his trilogy in an earlier draft to better incorporate his Catholic worldview. The theological issues are presented in *Lord of the Rings* in ways that do not moralize, allegorize, or weigh down the central story. Unbelievers read and enjoy Tolkien and miss the connections. Believers more quickly catch the symbols, often with a little help from the great number of good studies on Tolkien by Christian authors. Here C. S. Lewis's *Chronicles of Narnia* were more direct, the symbols more obvious, and the issues more clearly stated. This is not to criticize either author, but to point out the obvious. Every war is in some sense a clashing of two rival philosophies of life. Every philosophy is based on some religious presuppositions. Every war and every event in history is in some sense Man acting in accordance with what God has ordered or in rebellion against it. Most often it is the latter.

We as teachers may not always be able to completely or correctly give a theological analysis of historical events. I can better see the theological underpinnings of the Reformation than I can of the War of the Roses. Sometimes, all I can know is that men are sinners, but God's purposes will be established. As much as is possible, we as teachers need to know more about the theological climate of periods of history. It is vital to see that the religious presuppositions of many of the people who joined the Patriot army and opposed King George were different from those who stormed the Bastille and opposed King Louis XVI.[23]

The Easy Part

So, how do you teach junior high history? First, find the best textbook that you can. Consider the textbook to be both a dispensable and an indispensable tool. A textbook will no more teach junior high students than a

---

[23] Compare Kevin Phillips's *Cousins' Wars* with James H. Billington's *Fire in the Minds of Men*.

recipe book will feed your family, but both are useful. In the history classroom, it is lifeless to teach history by relying totally on a textbook; however, history class can end up being formless without a textbook. A good textbook should provide chronology, outlines, definitions, maps, and additional details. Perhaps it will also be supplemented by tests and worksheets that reinforce key concepts and free up teacher time for lecture preparation.

The biggest problem with most textbooks is the lack of narrative; that is, the lack of a good story. This happens because textbooks try to squeeze everything in. A good textbook will likely be strong on narrative—meaning war and gore—and less than complete, meaning lots of things are left out.

Supplemental books will give life where the textbooks lack it. History classes need some primary source materials. Many collections of good original source materials are available. George Grant's book *The Patriots Handbook* is an outstanding source in American history.[24] Books like *Yankee Doodle Boy*, an actual account of serving in the War for Independence, by Joseph Plumb Martin, or *Company Aytch* by Sam Watkins, who served in the Confederate army, are two wonderful, first person accounts of men who were actually "there."

Movies and films can be used to increase the interest level, but lots of cautions need to be used. Documentaries suffer from being uninteresting, and movies frequently are inaccurate or contain material inappropriate for the classroom. Still, a good movie can create love for history, and a good documentary can enhance love for history. Never allow a long documentary with talking heads and still photos to become the death march through an historical era. Never use a movie without previewing it and without researching the actual history.

The movie *Gettysburg* and the book it was based on, *The Killer Angels* by Michael Shaara, are both outstanding dramatizations of actual history. Both are interpretive approaches to history; both can enhance a student's interest in history. Using movies should be used as the occasion to teach a bit about critical viewing of movies as art, about the differences between historical facts and dramatized entertainment, and about having a feel for history. Movies are, after all, art, entertainment, interpretation, worldview, and by the artistic nature of the case, for better or worse, distortion. Here Brian Godawa's book, *Hollywood Worldviews: Watching Films with Wisdom and Discernment,* is indispensable for the teacher.[25]

---

[24] George Grant, *The Patriot's Handbook*, (Nashville: Cumberland Book House, 1996, 2004).

[25] Brian Godawa, *Hollywood Worldviews: Watching Films with Wisdom and Discernment* (Downers Grove, IL: Inter Varsity Press, 2002).

Lectures present another great challenge to the teacher. A good teacher has to be able to read two things: He or she has to be able to read some useful books before the lecture and then read the audience during the lecture. If the lecture releases enthusiasm, but does not convey enthusiasm, it is doomed. Sometimes, a lecture is doomed for other reasons. On a Friday afternoon in the spring, a lecture on tariffs is fatal. We sometimes hear (or hope to hear) comments about history teachers like this: "He really made history interesting." But it is not true. History is already interesting, far more interesting than any teacher. The teacher who supposedly "made" history interesting was a good lecturer. And if you cannot be good, develop a good brief outline, and find some good stories.

Somebody has to teach history to junior high students. It will be the best workout you ever experience.

Chapter Five
That Bully Sandie Pendleton

> I believe him to have been, in spite of his youth,
> the most brilliant staff officer in the Army of Northern Virginia
> and the most popular with officers and men.
> Brave, courteous, resolute, quick,
> and of high intelligence he was a model.
> —Henry Kyd Douglas[1]

> Ask Sandie Pendleton. If he does not know, no one does.
> —General Stonewall Jackson[2]

Have you ever had the experience of being afraid to walk down a certain street because a bully there intimidated you? Or maybe you avoided some parts of the school playground so as not to run into big kids who would pick on you. I have long since outgrown those fears and experiences, but I am still intimidated.

It is not a street or a part of the playground that intimidates me, but it is the past; it is history that intimidates me. I dread the 19th century, the 18th century, the 17th century, and so on. Like a gang, like bullies, all too many figures from those centuries threaten me and belittle me.

In short, each time a new school year approaches, I confess that Sandie Pendleton intimidates me. Sandie Pendleton—his full name was Alexander Swift Pendleton—is in all respects a very minor historical figure. I was reminded of him a few years back when I watched the movie *Gods and Generals*. Without digressing too far into a movie review, *Gods and Generals* was an outstanding portrayal of the faith and courage of the men who fought in the War Between the States. Men on both sides wrestled deeply with the issues of the war and then fought bravely for the cause they chose. Surprisingly, this movie very favorably portrayed the Southern cause and the strong religious commit-

---

[1] *I Rode With Stonewall* (Chapel Hill, NC: The University of North Carolina Press, 1984) Seventeenth Printing, 313.
[2] James I. Robertson, Jr., *Stonewall Jackson: The Man, The Soldier, The Legend* (New York: Macmillan Publishing USA, 1997), 670.

ments of so many Southern soldiers. Richard Weaver's contention that the Old South was the last bastion of Christendom was reinforced by the movie. The kind of men that Southern Christian civilization produced was highlighted in the movie's depiction of the life and death of General Thomas J. "Stonewall" Jackson. As a husband, as a soldier, as a Christian, Jackson epitomized Christian manhood. [3]

On Jackson's staff was a young man named Sandie Pendleton. In the movie, like in real life, he played a subordinate and little noticed role. Pendleton's father, William Nelson Pendleton, was an ordained Episcopal minister with a military background. Armed with sword and Bible and prayer book, he served in the Confederate army. He held the title of Chief of Artillery in Lee's Army of Northern Virginia, and he, like fellow minister Robert L. Dabney, preached to the troops on all occasions. Pendleton was sometimes mistaken for Robert E. Lee in looks, but sad to say, not in military ability. His daughter Susan Pendleton Lee wrote a laudatory biography of her father,[4] but apart from the judgments of a devoted daughter, few have found reason to praise Pendleton's military skills. I refrain from further hinting at a criticism of one who served in the Army of Northern Virginia.

General Pendleton's son, Sandie, joined the Confederate army in 1861 at age 21. Perhaps due to his college education and perhaps aided by his family connections, he obtained a position as an ordinance officer in the famed Stonewall Brigade of the Army of the Shenandoah. Soon he was promoted to chief of staff under General Jackson, who like the Pendleton family, had lived in Lexington, Virginia before the war. He had a brilliant, but short career as a staff officer. In 1864, just a few days before his 24th birthday, Sandie Pendleton died from wounds received at the Battle of Fisher's Hill. A few months after his death, his young wife gave birth to a son who was given his father's name, but died the next year.

As fascinating as his military career was, Pendleton's intimidating challenge to me precedes his short, tragic, but brilliant service as a staff officer. In 1853, Rev. William Nelson Pendleton accepted a call to serve as rector of Grace Episcopal Church in Lexington, Virginia. Like any family moving to a

---

[3] Among the many good biographies of Stonewall Jackson, a good one to start with is J. Steven Wilkins's *All Things for God: The Steadfast Fidelity of Stonewall Jackson* (Nashville: Cumberland House Books, 2004). A good second read is Robert L. Dabney's *Life and Campaigns of Lt. Gen. T. J. "Stonewall" Jackson* (Harrisonburg, VA: Sprinkle Publications, 1976). The books noted above by Robertson and Douglas are excellent secondary and primary accounts of Jackson's life and military genius.

[4] Susan Pendleton Lee, *Memoirs of William Nelson Pendleton,* (Harrisonburg, Virginia: Sprinkle Publications, 1991). Originally published in 1893.

new town, one of the first tasks was to enroll his children in school. Rev. Pendleton took Sandie to Washington College (now called Washington and Lee University) where he was enrolled as a freshman. This was not simply a matter of bringing along a copy of his school records, an ACT score, and writing a check, as in our day. Most of his education had consisted of being home-schooled by his father, with some time spent in a private school for boys. (Sandie was the only boy in a house full of sisters, so his parents wanted him to have opportunity to develop manly qualities.[5]) So before he could matriculate, that is, be enrolled, as a freshman, he was given a "rigorous examination in Greek, Latin, and mathematics" by a group of professors.[6]

One of the examining professors asked Rev. Pendleton why he sent this "delicate looking child to face us alone." The father replied, "I knew that he was well prepared, and my son must learn to depend upon himself and not on me. I wish him to be a good scholar, but still more a strong, self-reliant man."[7]

As I said, I am intimidated, I am bullied, I am afraid of this "delicate looking" college freshman in Lexington, Virginia from the year 1853. Sandie Pendleton was age thirteen when he entered Washington College.

If this thirteen-year-old stepped out of the past and walked into my office to face me alone, I could not give him a rigorous examination in Latin, Greek, and mathematics. I say that not as a college freshman, or as a thirteen year old, but I say that as one whose years are multiples of thirteen, as one who has a college undergraduate degree, a Master's degree in education[8], many hours beyond a Master's degree, over two decades of teaching experience, and a personal library of several thousand volumes. I am, in our modern dark age, a well-educated man, or at least I have been told that.

I could not teach this kid anything, except maybe 20th century history—in English. He could not be enrolled—matriculated—in my school, even though we pride ourselves as a classical Christian school on our high academic standards. I would have to give him an application to teach at my school rather than attend here as a student. In my classroom, this teenager could challenge me in almost any area and make mincemeat of my state teaching certificate.

---

[5] W.G. Bean, *Stonewall's Man: Sandie Pendleton*, (Wilmington: Broadfoot Publishing Company, 1987), 7.
[6] Bean, 7-8.
[7] Bean, 8.
[8] I know what education is and I know what degrees are, but I don't know what a degree in education means.

In time, this bully Sandie Pendleton only got worse. While at Washington College, Sandie was invited to join the Graham Literary Society. Honorary members of this society included his father, Rev. Pendleton, and Major Thomas J. Jackson (later known as Stonewall). The guys in the society gathered for formal debates on such topics as the following: "Is free discussion the best way of propagating truth among the masses?" and "Is more honor due to the soldiers than the statesmen of the Revolution?" Sandie participated in the debates and served as librarian for the group.[9]

In the typical college curriculum of his time, Sandie studied ancient and modern languages, mathematics, philosophy, chemistry, elocution, and composition. He became an assistant mathematics instructor at the college during his junior year, and upon the death of the Latin instructor, Sandie began teaching Latin at the college during his senior year. He graduated at the top of his class just prior to his seventeenth birthday.

After this, Sandie began working on a Master of Arts degree from the University of Virginia. The requirements for this degree called for the study of Latin, Greek, Modern Languages, Mathematics, Natural Philosophy, Chemistry, and Moral Philosophy. Before graduating, the student had to prove "an accurate and comprehensive acquaintance with his entire course of study, by an examination in the presence of the Faculty, on all the foregoing subjects, at the close of his academical career; and lastly he must prepare and submit to the Faculty an essay, exhibiting a due degree of literary ability; and this he may be requested to read on the Public Day [commencement]."[10]

One thing that the University of Virginia did not offer was sports. Sandie lobbied for sports to be added to the program. I have had the experience of coaching basketball for younger students and the experience of working with lots of athletic students, so I am familiar with the way athletes usually describe sports. Sandie wrote the following in an article calling for sports:

> When the pulse beats high and the life blood bounds like a courser, it kindles the feelings irrepressibly. The exuberance of animal life even exhibits itself in gladness. It makes the grasp of the hand more cordial; there is a kinder smile to greet the acquaintance; and the joy of the heart, awakened by sympathy with the body, bursts forth in the merry laugh or song; the whole man is happier, and therefore better….All the finer feelings are developed by acquain-

---

[9] Bean, 9.
[10] Quoted in Bean, 18, from Catalog of 1859-60, University of Virginia Catalogues, 1850-1860.

tance with Nature. The works of the Creator have…a wonderful ameliorating and elevating effect. They give strength, no otherwise obtained, to sincerity, cordiality, generating the high-souled honor—those emotions that raise man most nearly to God; and they impart vigor to his whole being.[11]

In his two years at the University of Virginia, Sandie only had time to take and pass examinations in four of the seven required areas. Events leading to the War Between the States pulled him and a whole generation of students out of the classrooms and onto the battlefields. The academic training and Christian nurture proved effective at making Sandie Pendleton a quick study in military matters and staff leadership. His attainments are attested to by the quote at the beginning of this from a fellow staff officer, Henry Kyd Douglas. Douglas himself was a bit intimidating. During the war, he notes that he read the New Testament and most of the Old Testament, portions of Tennyson, Browning, Shakespeare, Thackeray, Dickens, Horace, Victor Hugo's *Les Miserables,* a two volume biography of Napoleon, and quite a few military manuals. This bookish tendency seemed to have resulted from his childhood, for Douglas noted, "In those days Virginia boys read *The Federalist* and all the debates of the framers of our government and the Constitution."[12] It was a veritable age of bullies.

I would not be so bothered if Sandie Pendleton were the lone, or at least rare, case of genius. I can even accept Pendleton and Douglas and a few others and not be overly awed. We all read of those rare and gifted people who can calculate incredible square roots in their heads or who can memorize whole passages with one reading, but Sandie Pendleton was no genius. He was smart; he was gifted; but he was not unusual for his time.

Turn any corner in the past centuries, step into any classroom, glance at any textbook or writing assignment, check out any list of assigned readings, and the same patterns appear. Ministers, teachers, politicians, doctors, lawyers, military officers, and many a common laborer and farmer had educational experiences that make our modern degree factories look like kindergarten.

Even though thirteen-year-old Sandie Pendleton intimidates me, I keep stepping back into those centuries, knowing I am going to be humiliated again. For many of us who are teachers and pastors today, one of our main callings is to call attention to how far we have fallen and make a few steps on the

---

[11] Bean, 24.
[12] Douglas, 5, and scattered references throughout the book.

journey back. My hope is for children, grandchildren, and great grandchildren who can regain what Sandie Pendleton once had.

I pray that in regard to the future I will be intimidated by bullies again.

1

HISTORIANS & HISTORY TEACHERS

Chapter Six
Eusebius—Father of Church History

And here, fathers and brethren, you will all assent that I have bestowed upon my science the most magnificent encomium which is possible, when I have said that the history of the church is one of the studies and enjoyments of heaven.
Robert L. Dabney[1]

Following is always easier than leading. Building upon foundations is always easier than building the foundations themselves. Foundations are vital for the rest of the structure. The Church itself is built upon the foundation of the apostles and prophets with Jesus Christ Himself being the chief cornerstone. Pioneers and founders face great difficulties. When we build on foundations already established, we may think we have troubles, but at least we have patterns or forms to follow. Imitating is easier than creating. Traveling a road is easier than blazing a trail. In spite of the difficulties, various saints are called by God to venture into areas where none have ventured before.

In the first several hundred years of the Church, God raised up an amazing lot of men. We know them as the Church Fathers. By the faithful testimonies of their lives, their generally voluminous writings, and sometimes by their martyrdom, we remember these men as pillars of the Faith. Their sermons and theological treatises are daunting. When all joined together in volume upon volume, the collected writings of the Church Fathers are intellectually daunting and breathtaking. Added to the extensiveness of their writings is the Fathers' depth and erudition: These men were very familiar with the Scriptures—in the original languages, with Greek philosophy, and with the intellectual cross currents of their age.

Offsetting all these strengths is the uneven orthodoxy, let us even suggest heresy, found in almost every Church Father at some point or the other.

---

[1] Robert L. Dabney, "Uses and Results of Church History," 25, as found in *Discussions: Evangelical*, Vol. 2 (Harrisonburg, VA, Sprinkle Publications, 1982).

As much as we admire these men, we could not approve ordination of these men for our churches in our time. We see glaring errors in their systematic theology, huge gaps in their Biblical theology, odd exegesis in their hermeneutics, imprecision in their soteriology, Greek syncretism in their apologetics, and so on. We can out think these founders and do theology better than they did, but not because of anything in ourselves. We stand where we are because of the foundations for Biblical theology that they built for us. We see their errors because they taught us how to spot error. We think because they wrote. The church lives today because they were willing to die if necessary.

Building upon Scriptural foundations, they were pioneers. The Church of the Apostles quickly became the Church of the Gentiles. The Greco-Roman world presented new challenges and obstacles to Christianity at all points. In this confrontation, in this bringing of truth of Jerusalem to bear upon thought of Athens and the power of Rome, the Church Fathers blazed many new trails and built many new foundations for the next two millennia of the Christian Faith.

Historian Philip Schaff speaks of these Church Fathers in this way:

> This third period is uncommonly rich in great teachers of the church, who happily united theological ability and practical piety, and who, by their development of the most important dogmas in conflict with mighty errors, earned the gratitude of posterity. They monopolized all the learning and eloquence of the declining Roman empire, and made it subservient to the cause of Christianity for the benefit of future generations. They are justly called fathers of the church; they belong to Christendom without distinction of denominations....[2]

One such Church Father who was a pioneer for the Faith was Eusbius of Caesarea. Eusebius, whose dates are c. 260 to c. 340, wrote, taught, and preached extensively. He wrote on Biblical doctrines; he wrote defenses of Christianity against the critics and heretics of his day; he wrote Bible dictionaries and study guides; and he wrote letters, sermons, and orations; however, he is primarily remembered today for his historical writings. These included stories of martyrs, church leaders, and an account of the life of the Emperor Constantine.[3] His best remembered work was *Ekklesiatices Historias*, which

---

[2] Philip Schaff, *History of the Christian Church*, Volume III (Grand Rapids: Wm. B. Eerdmans Publishing Co., 1977 reprint), 872.

[3] Paul Maier, "Introduction" from *Eusebius—The Church History: A New Translation and Commentary*, (Grand Rapids: Kregel Publications, 1999), 13-14. I recommend Maier's translation of Eusebius.

we usually call either *Ecclesiastical History* or *Church History*. His labors to compile the records and collate the details of the first several centuries of church history earned him the title "The Father of Church History." His ecclesiastical classic covered the time from the Apostles up through the age of Constantine. The first three centuries in which Christianity was born and began spreading is a marvelous story of the success of the church. Quite often, the successes were as Herbert Schlossberg describes in *Idols for Destruction* "a string of God's triumphs disguised as disasters."[4]

Paul Maeir gives this testimony of Eusebius:

Had his *Church History* never been written, our knowledge of the first three centuries of Christendom would have been pockmarked by missing figures, facts, documents, and data of major importance. With his vast erudition, the Bishop of Caesarea sifted through mountains of material to gather valuable information for subsequent ages that might explore it more deeply than he did.[5]

Philip Schaff gives this testimony:

The theological and literary value of Eusebius lies in the province of learning. He was an unwearied reader and collector, and probably surpassed all the other church fathers, hardly excepting Origen and Jerome, in compass of knowledge and acquaintance with Grecian literature both heathen and Christian.[6]

Schaff continues,

He is temperate, upon the whole, impartial, and truthloving—rare virtues in an age of intense excitement and polemical zeal like that in which he lived. The fact that he was the first to work this important field of theological study, and for many centuries remained a model in it, justly entitles him to his honorable distinction of Father of Church History.[7]

---

[4] Herbert Schlossberg, *Idols for Destruction* (Nashville: Thomas Nelson Publishers, 1983), 304.
[5] Maier, 17.
[6] Schaff, 876.
[7] Schaff, 876.

But not all of Schaff's comments are as favorable. He continues:

> Yet he is neither a critical student nor an elegant writer of history, but only a diligent and learned collector. His *Ecclesiastical History*…gives a colorless, defective, fragmentary, yet interesting picture of the heroic youth of the church, and owes its incalculable value, not to the historic art of the author, but almost entirely to his copius and mostly literal extracts from foreign, and in some cases now extinct, sources.[8]

"Colorless, defective, and fragmentary"—not exactly the best review for a book. But Schaff is correct, and there are certainly lots of church histories available today that are more thorough, accurate, and certainly more up to date than Eusebius, including Schaff.

Church Histories

Justo Gonzales said, "Every renewal of the church, every great age in its history, has been grounded on a renewed reading of history."[9] The renewal of God's people is the task and prayer of Christian teachers and pastors. Along with a devotion to the Bible, basic learning skills, logical thinking, composition skills, and manners and morals, Christian teachers must read, teach, and know history. Along with theology and counseling, preaching sermons and leading in worship, pastors and elders must read, teach, and know church history. Eusebius saw this need in his day. Between the deaths of the Apostles and the new found freedom granted by Constantine, much had happened to the church that had to be remembered.

Let us consider just a few of the more recent historians and histories we need to add to our collection of books, along with Eusebius.

Philip Schaff (1819-1893) was well equipped to judge Eusebius. Schaff was a German theologian and historian who came to America in the 19th century. He compiled a history of some eight volumes in the late 19th century, titled *A History of the Christian Church*. He also compiled a collection of creeds and confessions in a three volume work called *The Creeds of Christendom*. His inaugural address for the theological seminary of the Reformed Church of Mercerberg was titled *The Principle of Protestantism*. In it, Schaff described

---

[8] Schaff, 877.
[9] Justo Gonzales, *The Story of Christianity*, (Peabody, Massachusetts: Prince Press, 1999), XVIII of the preface.

Church history as the merger of Protestantism and Roman Catholicism with it all being part of God's divine purposes. The Reformation, according to Schaff, was "the greatest act of the Catholic Church itself, the full ripe fruit of all its better tendencies...."[10] All of these works of Schaff remain in print.[11] Schaff was an evangelical believer and a first rate scholar, whose work included the latest and greatest scholarship of his time. He described this combined faith and knowledge by saying, "A theologian without faith is like a sky without a star, a heart without a pulse, light without warmth, a sword without edge, a body without soul."[12] His history begins with the New Testament and covers events both by chronology and topics all the way up through the Protestant Reformation, so it covers more time and covers it more accurately than Eusebius' history. Schaff's research and writing earned him the title "Father of American Church History." In the academic iron sharpening iron process, even the valuable works of Schaff can be supplemented with better scholarship and more insight.

Two older Christian historians who came on the scene after Philip Schaff were Williston Walker (1860-1922) and Kenneth Scott Latourette (1884-1968). Walker was a professor of church history at Yale. His most noted book is *A History of the Christian Church* (1918), and he also wrote biographical works, including a study of John Calvin.[13] Latourette also taught at Yale. He produced several multivolume histories of the church. His titles include *A History of the Christian Church* (most recently reprinted in two volumes), *History of the Expansion of Christianity*, and *Christianity in a Revolutionary Age* (reprinted in five volumes).[14] Just the mere mention of Latourette beckons us to quote him on his overall view of history. He writes concerning the Christian historian's vision:

> He perceives as he looks back across the years that, measured by the criteria of area covered, inner vigor, and the effect on mankind as a whole, Christianity, beginning in a very unpromising fashion,

---

[10] Philip Schaff, *The Principle of Protestantism* (Eugene, Oregon: Wipf and Stock Publishers, 1845, 2004), 224.

[11] Robert Schnucker, "Philip Schaff," from *Dictionary of the Christian Church*, edited by J. D. Douglas (Zondervan), 881-882.

[12] Quoted in Philip Schaff: *Christian Scholar and Ecumenical Prophet*, by George Schriver. (Macon, Georgia: Mercer University Press, 1987), 13.

[13] Williston Walker's *History of the Christian Church* has undergone subsequent revisions and reprintings. It was published by Charles Scribner's Sons in New York.

[14] *A History of Christianity* (2 volumes) has been reprinted by Prince Press, Peabody, MA, and *Christianity in a Revolutionary Age* has been reprinted by Zondervan.

has gone forward by a series of pulsations of advance, retreat, and advance. Each advance has carried the Christian tide farther than its predecessor, and each major recession has been shorter and less marked that the one before it.[15]

The works of both these men are scholarly, well researched, and based on the best documentation of their times. Yet their works reveal some of the theological deviancies of their age as well; so I suggest that you collect and read Walker's and Latourette's histories, but read with discernment.

The multi-authored Penguin History of the Church is well worth collecting, especially any volumes written by Owen or Henry Chadwick. Reference works like Zondervan's *New International Dictionary of the Christian Church* and *Eerdmans' Handbook to the History of Christianity* are helpful for both referencing and reading.[16] R. B. Kuiper's *The Church in History* is a standard Christian school text that is great for younger students and useful for all ages.[17] Books like *100 Most Important Events in Christian History* by Curtis, Lang, and Peterson, aptly introduces key names and events.[18] The history of Christianity is told with stories and biographies in Richard Hannula's *Trial and Triumph: Stories from Church History*. This account lends itself to reading aloud to your class or family. Paul Johnson's *History of Christianity* displays the usual Paul Johnson traits of literary delightfulness, unconventional insights, and a general defense of traditional faith and culture, with bits and pieces of liberal Catholic theology and interpretive quirkiness thrown in. Jaroslav Pelikan's five volume *The Christian Tradition: A History of the Development of Doctrine*[19] is a modern treatment by a scholar respected by people from all angles and particularly well-liked by my friend and scholar Andrew Sandlin.

Two histories that I consult most frequently are Bruce Shelley's *Church History in Plain Language*[20] and Justo Gonzales' *The Story of Christianity*. Shelley's book is notable for the short chapters, well-written narrative format, and usefulness for reading aloud. He aptly takes stories from history and weaves

---

[15] Kenneth Scott Latourette, *The Twentieth Century Outside Europe*, Volume V of *Christianity in a Revolutionary Age* (Grand Rapids: Zondervan Publishing House, 1969), 534.

[16] *New International Dictionary of the Christian Church,* edited by J.D. Douglas (Grand Rapids: Zondervan, 1978) and Eerdmans *Handbook to the History of Christianity*, edited by Tim Dowley (Grand Rapids: William B. Eerdmans Publishing, 1978).

[17] R. B. Kuiper, *The Church in History* (Grand Rapids: William B. Eerdmans Publishing Company).

[18] Curtis, A. Kenneth, J. Stephen Lang, and Randy Peterson, *The 100 Most Important Events in Christian History* (Grand Rapids, MI: Fleming H. Revell, 1991).

[19] Published by the University of Chicago Press.

[20] Bruce Shelley, *Church History in Plain Language* (Dallas: Word Publishing, 1995).

them into the more difficult theological issues in history. Gonzales' study is in a more scholarly format, but is still quite readable. I am using Gonzales as a textbook for my Medieval and Modern World Humanities courses. A work in progress that is most promising is N.R. Needham's *2000 Years of Christ's Power,* which is noteworthy for its emphasis on the main theologians and ideas found in the early and Medieval church. So far, there are three volumes in this set: The first volume is *The Age of the Early Church Fathers* and second is *The Middle Ages,* with a third volume covering the Reformation.[21] Needham includes good selections of the actual writings of the church fathers that illustrate his main points and gives the Medieval Church a far more extensive and favorable coverage than many Protestants are used to seeing.

Along with a consideration of the books listed above, don't neglect the more narrow church histories, meaning, those with more definite denominational biases. My basic principle is to buy every book that has either the word Reformation, Calvinism, Puritans, Reformed, or   in the title. Every Christian history teacher needs some studies written by Catholics, Orthodox, Calvinists, Methodists, Baptists, and others. Trying to study church history while maintaining sectarian "my church's view of history is THE correct view" is like trying to swim without getting wet. Church history humbles us. It humbles us to see the faults of our heroes and to see how God has used all sorts of people, churches, and events to advance His kingdom. And mere mention of people, entices me to want to venture off into biographies, but I can only say, to your study of church history and for your devotional growth, add biographies.

An exhaustive bibliography of books on church history would be beyond the comprehension of even so rapacious a book collector as I am. Studies just on the early church, that is, on the same time period that Eusebius covered, still entail the listing of thousands of books. In the many black holes of historical and theological ignorance that characterize my frustrated life, knowledge of the early church is one of the greatest of my own deficiencies. Just a few years back I would have thought that the word "Patristics" referred to an exercise program. While I now know the term refers to the early church fathers, yet I am still laboring to learn just who these church fathers were. My reading on the church history has often entailed skimming the first fifteen centuries and then getting serious when Luther and Calvin appear. Portions of the latter Medieval period were read in light of how they paved the way for the much needed Protestant Reformation. The story of the church after the Book of Acts and in the centuries shortly following has sorely been neglected.

In this age of relatively cheap reprints, works of the church fathers are

---

[21] N. R. Needham, *2000 Years of Christ's Power* (London: Grace Publications Trust).

available. I recently obtained the thirty-eight volume Church Fathers set. I can have lots of wisdom near me, even if I have far too little in me. This multi-volume set looks good on my shelf and my momentary perusals of the contents continually testify to the intellectual attainments and successful defense of the faith during the first several centuries.

Surrounded by so great a cloud of recent scholarship and books hot off the presses, along with the reprints, why read Eusebius? After all, he operated with limited resources; he made many mistakes; some of the sources he used were flawed; and his style and organization beg for severe editing.

Back to Eusebius

Something is to be said for going to the sources. Modern scholars have studied Origen, one of the great church fathers, in detail, and modern scholars have examined the life and conversion of the Emperor Constantine. Eusebius, however, personally studied theology under Origen. He was also personally acquainted with Constantine. Many Christians find reading accounts of the martyrs of the early church inspiring. Eusebius escapted the fate of martyrs, but he knew fellow Christians who were martyred in the early church. This lends a freshness and power to this original work, even in translation. We look at Eusebius' account from a perspective where we know of the ultimate triumph of the early church over its enemies. We ourselves are evidence nearly seventeen hundred years after Eusebius that the faith survived those early challenges and continues to grow. Yet for Eusebius, that assurance of victory in his history is based on faith and not on evidence. The witness who from the trenches sees the triumph amidst the smoke and haze of battle can be quite compelling, even when the perspective from the trenches is not the most accurate.

Eusebius' account of the early church sheds light on many theological issues. Among these are his discussion of the church's recognition of the canon of New Testament Scriptures, the power of the testimony of the martyrs, and the favorable change that Constantine ushered in with the Edict of Milan in 312.

The Canon

The canon of Scripture has been the center of battle in the past several centuries just as it was in the early centuries. The parameters of the battle have changed, but part of contending for the faith entails contending for the centrality of Scripture. In recent times, particularly since the rise of the Higher Critical movement in the 19th century, Scripture was put in the dock and judged by theologians and scholars, the ones who should have been the Scriptures' defenders. In contrast to faithful churchmen who submitted to the authority of Scripture and pronounced the judgment of Scripture on the world, the higher critics pronounced judgments on the Word of God to the world. Their beginning presupposition was that whatever else a portion of the Bible might be—literary work, historical document, or sectarian tract—*what it is was not* was an infallible revelation from God. Accepting that on faith, they then proceeded to analyze (or psycho-analyze) authors, determine the dates of composition, and accept or reject the theological content with frenzied abandon. The Bible was demythologized, humanized, deconstructed, psychoanalyzed, feminized, and subjected to every variety of modern apostate thought available.

The struggle in the early church was different. Some, perhaps many, of the early Church Fathers differed over whether particular books should be included, like John's Revelation, or whether certain others should be excluded, like Clement's Letters. But they did not reject the belief that a revelation from God did exist. Dan Brown has gotten rich off his doubly fictional screed casting doubt on the development of Scripture and Christology in his best selling novel *The Da Vinci Code*. Pseudo-gospels, Gnostic gospels, and spurious writings are nothing new, nor, from a Biblical perspective, surprising. Neither are heretical writings new or surprising. Eusebius commented on the heretics:

> Writings published by heretics under the names of apostles, such as the Gospels of Peter, Thomas, Matthias, and others, or the Acts of Andrew, John, and other apostles have never been cited by any in the succession of church writers. The type of phraseology used contrasts with apostolic style, and the opinions and thrusts of their contents are so dissonant from true orthodoxy that they show themselves to be forgeries of heretics. Accordingly, they ought not be reckoned even among the spurious books but discarded as impious and absurd.[22]

Eusebius was quite judicious and careful in his judgments of books, even when subsequent history has shown him in error. He recognized the four Gospels, Acts, Paul's Letters, and I John and I Peter. He was not sure about James, Jude, II Peter, and II and III John. He noted that some works,

---

[22] Maier, Paul, *Eusebius—The Church History: A New Translation and Commentary.*,(Grand Rapids: Kregel Publications, 1999), 115.

such as the Shepherd of Hermas, were instructive and often cited, but still regarded such as spurious.

Questions about the canon of Scripture arose early in church history. Eusebius' writings appeared less than a century before the issue was settled. The church was challenged—and sometimes attacked—over the issue of canonicity. We can rejoice in the scholarly dimensions of the Church Fathers and the way they confronted the issue. We can rejoice even in the good effect of the heresies they combated: Paul Maier points out, "[S]uch heretical challenges…forced Christian thinkers to agree on an authoritative canon of Scripture and a unifying tradition of its interpretation and compelled them to teach and express church doctrines with greater precision and a deepened theology."[23] The early church was much more Berean and careful in discerning the will of God concerning the canon than the Bible's critics today. And it must be made clear that they were recognizing what constituted the Word of God rather than questioning whether there even was a revelation from God.

This struggle for the canon of Scripture necessarily entailed a separation between orthodox thought and heresy. The church then strove to find the truth. R. J. Rushdoony, in his excellent study of the early church, *The Foundations of Social Order*, points out a key difference between the early church and the modern church: "First, the early councils had as their primary purpose the defense and establishment of truth, not unity. Unity had to be established on the foundation of truth, not truth as a product of unity."[24] Spurious books and heretical doctrines were an ever-threatening danger to the future of the church. Providentially, God preserved the truth. One of the key ways He did so was by bringing the early church to a recognition of what constituted the New Testament.

Testimony of the Martyrs

American Christianity is, above all else, comfortable. We are comfortable in our padded pews in air-conditioned sanctuaries behind our stained glass windows. Most of us are middle class; we enjoy easy access to the great American lifestyle; and our Christian faith is relatively easily acquired and easily lived out. For these reasons, we need large doses of tales of martyrs and missionaries. Since we are hindered from Sunday worship by staying up too late on Saturday night, we need to read of those hindered from worship by chains and tortures.

---

[23] Maier, *Eusebius*, 166.

[24] R. J. Rushdoony, *Foundations of Social Order* (Phillipsburg, NJ: Presbyterian and Reformed Publishing Company, 1972), 19.

Eusebius recounts the sufferings of Christians in Gaul and other parts of the Roman Empire. Some of the stories of martyrdom, like that of Polycarp, are quite famous, while others are less so. At the heart of this persecution was the Roman state, which was humanistic, polytheistic, and fickle. The Roman Caesars were more than tyrants or, in some cases, perverted monsters. They claimed to be gods. Ethelbert Stauffer's classic study, *Christ and the Caesars,* notes these tendencies:

> Suetonius tells us that the imperial missives dictated by Domitian himself began with the words 'The Lord our God commands'. Martial quotes a proclamation of Domitian which begins in almost the same words, 'Edict of the Lord our God.' A wooden tablet has survived with the beginning of an imperial order in the official style of Oriental despots: "The words of the emperor, son of the God Vespasian, Domitian the worshipful."[25]

Long before Domitian, Augustus had been proclaimed as deity. Stauffer points out that the Roman state, in effect, was claiming: "Salvation is to be found in none other save Augustus, and there is no other name given to men in which they can be saved."[26] Christians died not for simply following Christ, but for refusing also to bow the knee to Caesar. We live in a time that exalts tolerance, compromise, and polytheism, so here again, we need Eusebius to enrich our thanksgiving for freedom and increase our diligent contending for the Faith.

Eusebius does not spare the reader the gory details of the tortures inflicted on martyrs. His theology enabled him to describe martyrdom in these ways: "Faustus, who nobly confessed the faith…was fulfilled in martyrdom by beheading…." And "…three prominent confessors of Christ at Caesarea in Palestine were also crowned with martyrdom by becoming food for wild beasts."[27] This is central to a Christian view of history. Death for Christ is not an end, but a fulfillment. History always moves toward the final judgment and the glorification of God's people.

---

[25] Ethelbert Stauffer, *Christ and the Caesars*, translated by K and R. Gregor Smith (Philadelphia: Westminster Press, 1955), 158.

[26] Stauffer, 88.

[27] Maier, *Eusebius*, 261.

Constantine's Legacy

After ten waves of persecution over the course of three centuries, Constantine's issuing of the Edict of Milan signaled a change in the treatment the church received. Christians have differing views on both Constantine as a professing Christian and on his policy toward Christianity. Some view him as the model of a Christian emperor and accept his testimony as indicating true faith. Some think his edict opened the doors of the church to worldly people and ideas. A textbook for Christian schools states, "The church of the saints and martyrs had conquered the Roman Empire, but now the Roman Empire conquered the church and institutionalized Christianity."[28]

Eusebius is a key source for the more favorable views toward Constantine. In fact, the latter part of his history is a panegyric—or essay giving praise—to Constantine. Since Eusebius served as a court historian and close associate with the Emperor, he would naturally be writing in praise of his boss. His close association with Constantine neither proves nor disproves the overall effects of Constantine's faith and rule. But it is critical to see how a believer who saw the effects of persecution first hand reacts when the emperor becomes a professing believer.

C. S. Lewis makes the case that reading old books makes us aware of ideas and perspectives that we are blinded to in our own age. When we talk about what modern Christians need or what the church today needs, we can provide endless answers and directions. Eusebius will not provide us a model to direct our next presbytery meeting or church planting effort, but he will give us much insight and encouragement. We will see how the church has grown, but also how it has, in some ways, regressed. Eusebius blazed a trail by committing the story of the church to writing. Once a trail is blazed, it goes both ways. Anytime we seek to move ahead, we need to consider looking back as well.

---

[28] George T. Thompson and Elizabeth Laurel Hicks, *World History and Cultures in Christian Perspective* (Pensacola: A Beka Book, 1985), 122.

Chapter Seven
Augustine and *The City of God*

Like Eusebius, Augustine translated apologetics into history.
Jaroslav Pelikan[1]

Charles Dickens begins his *Tale of Two Cities* with the now famous words, "It was the best of times; it was the worst of times; it was the age of wisdom; it was the age of foolishness." Centuries before that novel, Augustine wrote a tale of two cities that grew out of the worst of times and that gave an age of foolishness, an age of wisdom.

The year 410 A.D. and the time following saw two terrible events occur. And these events occurred during a stage of the decline of the Roman Empire where bad news was common. For several centuries, the factors that would ultimately topple the empire were competing for future historical notice. Political instability was rampant; the violent death of an emperor was no longer newsworthy. During one forty-nine year time period, there were twenty-six different emperors, of whom, only one died of natural causes. Economic problems abounded. Roman currency was debased to the point that silver coins consisted of less than two percent silver. The currency was so bad that the Roman government would not accept it as tax revenues.[2]

Barbarian invasions had destabilized the frontiers and yet had furnished the only new blood in the empire willing to man the armies. Thomas Cahill has written on the transformation of the Roman army:

> With the moral decay of republican resolve, the army became more and more a reserve of non-Romans, half-Romanized barbarian mercenaries and servants sent in the stead of freemen who couldn't

---

[1] *The Emergence of the Catholic Tradition*, Volume 1 from *The Christian Tradition: A History of the Development of Doctrine* (Chicago, IL: The University of Chicago Press, 1975), 41.

[2] Carl Richard, *Twelve Greeks and Romans* (New York: Rowman and Littlefield Publishers Inc., 2003), 236.

be bothered. In the last days of the empire, men commonly mutilated themselves to escape service, though such a crime was—in theory—punishable by torture and death. Military levies, sent to the great estates, met such resistance that influential landowners were allowed to send money, instead of men to the army.[3]

In the first century, Paul had written of human depravity most graphically in the opening portion of his Epistle to the Romans. Confirming evidence of such depravity was to be found in the pre-conversion lives of the recipients of that letter. And apart from the Christian community, such behaviors still abounded. The salt and light effects of Christianity were only incrementally able to push back the tide of paganism, ignorance, and immorality.

Edward Gibbon, the author of *The Decline and Fall of the Roman Empire,* said,

> The Roman government appeared every day less formidable to its enemies, more odious to its subjects. The taxes were multiplied with the public distress; economy was neglected in proportion as it became necessary; and the injustice of the rich shifted the unequal burden from themselves to the people…they [the people] adjured and abhorred the name of Roman citizens, which had formerly excited the ambition of mankind.[4]

Able emperors, such as Diocletian and Constantine, had found innovative ways to divide and rule the increasingly unmanageable Roman world. Yet, as William Butler Yeats would write of a later era, the center could not hold. Officially Christian, but practically multicultural and pluralistic, Rome tottered and stumbled every step of the way to dissolution.

As if there were not enough internal problems, the presence of barbarians on the frontier brought in new dimensions to the decline. Sometime after 395, Alaric, a barbarian chieftain and leader of the Visigoths, occupied Illyricum and plundered Greece. Rome responded with great enthusiasm: They sent troops who also plundered Greece and then recognized Alaric's rule over Illyricum.[5]

Alaric and company represented the external forces for cultural breakdown that plagued the empire. The Visigoths had broken through the eastern

---
[3] Thomas Cahill, *How The Irish Saved Civilization* (New York: Nan A. Talese, 1995), 39.
[4] From Edward Gibbon, *Decline and Fall of the Roman Empire,* as quoted in Richard, 236.
[5] Richard, 240.

frontier over a century before. Romans originally found them a nuisance as invaders, but then decided they were useful as purchasers of Roman commodities. When tensions developed in the Visigoth-held regions, Rome responded with its characteristic solution to political problems—it sent in its feared legions. At the battle of Adrianople in 378, under the Emperor Valens, this Roman army boldly marched in and gave bystanders a picture of a military shellacking. Only this time, it was the Romans who were shellacked.

In 410 Alaric led his horde to the Italian peninsula down to the very gates of Rome. What Hannibal had failed to do after fifteen years of trying, Alaric accomplished quite handily. After he besieged the city and the population began to starve, Roman city officials met with Alaric. They threatened him, in effect, with the promise that their big brother could beat him up; specifically, they warned him that a million Romans were armed and ready to defend the city. Alaric yawned and answered, "The thicker the hay, the more easily it is mowed."[6] Then they asked him what it would take to buy him a one-way ticket away from Rome. Alaric presented a list of demands that included immense amounts of gold, silver, silk cloth, and almost every other moveable kind of property. The city officials asked, "But what will we have left?" Alaric answered, "Your lives."

The city officials refused Alaric's demands and so he and his Visigoth army enjoyed three days of good old-fashioned barbarian pillaging, plundering, and raping. All the things the city fathers had refused him, he now took, with interest. Buildings were destroyed, people were killed, and chaos reigned. (Amazingly, the Visigoths did respect church buildings and those hiding there for the Visigoths were, like the empire itself, nominally Christian.)

Will Durant describes the sack of Rome:

> A slave opened the gates; the Goths poured in, and for the first time in 800 years the great city was taken by an enemy (410). For three days Rome was subjected to a discriminate pillage that left the churches of St. Peter and St. Paul untouched, and spared the refugees who sought sanctuary in them. But the Huns and slaves in the army of 40,000 men could not be controlled. Hundreds of rich men were slaughtered, their women raped and killed; it was found almost impossible to bury all the corpses that littered the streets....Gold and silver were seized wherever found; works of art were melted down for the precious metals they contained; and many masterpieces of sculptor and pottery were joyously destroyed....[7]

---

[6] Will Durant, *The Age of Faith*, from *The Story of Civilization*, Volume IV (New York: Simon and Schuster, 1950), 36.
[7] Durant, 36.

Augustine and *The City of God*

The sack of Rome in 410 was earth-shaking news. Rome had not been sacked or invaded in 800 years. Despite the fact that the political and economic center of the empire had long since been relocated, Rome was still centrally and symbolically the heart of the empire. People of all walks of life were shaken by the events. We can identify in part because of the shock we felt on September 11, 2001.

The theologian Jerome expressed the shock felt by many in a letter when he said,

> Rome had been besieged and its citizens forced to buy their lives with gold. Then thus despoiled they had been besieged again so as to lose not their substance only but their lives. My voice sticks in my throat; and, as I dictate, sobs choke my utterance. The City which had taken the whole world was itself taken.[8]

Jerome commented again on this event in his preface to a commentary on Ezekiel, referring to it as the time "when the Roman Empire was decapitated, and …the whole world perished in one city." He went on to say, "'Who would believe that Rome, built up by conquest of the whole world, had collapsed, that the mother of nations had become also their tomb…?'"[9]

The Spin

As devastating as was the news of the sack of Rome, there was something even worse. As people asked why and how this happened, a certain interpretation arose concerning the attack on Rome. It was what we now call the analysis or spin on the event. And as is common today, the spin on the story was worse than the story itself.

In our own time, our country has conquered and occupied two enemy regimes across the world from us—Afghanistan and Iraq—in record time and with a record low casualty count. Whether or not we should have done that is another matter, but the fact is that the conquest and occupation has been quite astounding—unless you follow the spin and the interpretation given so often in the major media.

Likewise, in 1968 during the Tet Offensive in the Vietnam War, the ground fighting changed from being a guerrilla-type war based on raiding parties, and

---

[8] *Jerome: Letters and Select Works*, translated by W. H. Fremantle, Volume 6 from *Nicene and Post-Nicene Fathers*, edited by Philip Schaff and Henry Wace (Peabody, MA: Hendrickson Publishers, 4th Printing, 2004), 257.

[9] *Jerome: Letters and Select Works*, 500.

it became a full fledged war with the North Vietnamese army openly engaged against the American and South Vietnamese forces, and the result was an overwhelming American victory in the fields. But that was followed by an interpretation or spin that destroyed the American cause.[10]

The liberal media have often proved to be better theological thinkers than Christians, for they have recognized the truthfulness of Cornelius Van Til's oft-repeated saying that there are no brute facts: All facts are interpreted facts.

What was this interpretation of the sack of Rome that was so devastating? After the events of 410, pagans attributed the sack of Rome to its failure to adhere to its historic gods and myths. Although the empire had been tolerant of Christianity for almost a century and Christianity had been the official religion for a little over 30 years, paganism remained a strong force. "Why did this happen?" everyone asked. "Simple," answered the pagans, "Rome abandoned her former gods and goddesses who had protected her. It is the fault of the Christian God and the Christian people." According to Etienne Gilson, there were two problems that pagans had with Christians. The first had to do with Christian renunciation of the world, which influenced Christian citizens to turn away from state service. As Durant noted, "Pagan civilization was founded upon the state, Christian civilization upon religion."[11] The second complaint of the pagans, according to Gilson, was retribution of the gods. He says, "When the Christian religion first began to spread, the pagans proclaimed that their betrayed gods would visit terrible punishments upon the Empire."[12]

From our perspective, the Roman idolaters look pretty silly. But all defunct idolatries look silly. To imagine that Jupiter and Juno were miffed at being snubbed may not give us an apologetic challenge, but we have to repent of our own fear of the idols of our age before we can truly understand. The empire was in the midst of its own culture war. There were not red states and blue states; there were no referendums on gay marriage; but there were cultural battles being waged all around the Mediterranean Sea.

George Grant comments on the culture war of that time:

---

[10] Victor Davis Hanson, *Carnage and Culture* (New York: Doubleday, 2001), 389-439.

[11] Durant, *Caesar and Christ* from *The Story of Civilization*, Volume III (New York: Simon and Schuster, 1944), 647.

[12] Etienne Gilson, Foreword to Saint Augustine's *The City of God: An Abridged Version*, edited by Vernon J Bourke (New York: Image Books, 1958), 16.

Though a decree of toleration was passed in 313, such high-minded pluralism is an impossible equilibrium to maintain—as the whole of human history proves beyond any shadow of a doubt. Because opposing religions manifest opposing cultures, a multicultural society is merely a euphemism for a society in the midst of transition—a society in the midst of a Culture War.[13]

Christians were stunned by the charges of the pagans. Family gatherings were tense where pagan mothers-in-law berated Christian sons-in-laws for abandoning the old ways. Nominal and weak believers woke up on Sunday mornings and questioned whether to go to the house church down the street or the temple of Diana across town. "See, I told you so" became the rebuke of pagans to Christian converts. The gates of hell may not have been on the offensive, but they seemed strong and secure.

By 413, a North African Christian political leader, Marcellinus, recognized that something had to be done. Christian refugees were arriving on the shores of North Africa daily. This was a genuine Christian retreat. The church militant was becoming the church defeatist. All that was needed to ice the pietistic retreatist cake was some clever team writing the *Left Behind in Rome* series.

Marcellinus appealed to the Bishop of Hippo in North Africa to refute the charges of heresy. That bishop, Aurelius Augustinius or as we know him, St. Augustine, got up from his sickbed, went to his study, and began dashing off a tract to answer the pagans. Bits and pieces of his work appeared over the next several years.

Thirteen years later, the completed massive tome hit the shelves of the local Scrolls-a-Millions. Titled *De Civitate Dei* or *The City of God,* this book laid the vital foundations for subsequent centuries of Christian scholarship, philosophy, apologetics, and theology. It established clearly a Christian view of history, and like all historical paradigms, it provided a vision for future Christian civilization.

More than any other book of its time or since, *The City of God* signaled the end of the ancient world and the beginning of that new frontier era now known as the Medieval period. More than any other book, it made clear that the central meaning of history was to be found in the kingdom of God and not the kingdom of man, no matter whether that man was in Rome or Paris or London or Washington. More than any other book, this book defined the difference in the only two ways that life exists here in this world: Life is either

---

[13] George Grant, "In the Midst of a Culture War: Augustine's City of God" (www.kingsmeadow.com/stirling_archive.html).

in covenant with the true and the living Triune God or it is in rebellion against that same God. More than any other book, this book showed the utter bankruptcy of the pagan worldview, which offered no happiness or blessings to people either in this world or the world to come. More than any other book, this book, showed the blessings of being the covenant people of God.

The book has had a tremendous influence on a host of writers and thinkers. George Grant comments on this influence:

> According to Martin Luther, this one book "set the very course of Western Civilization." According to John Knox, it is the very essence of "incisive Christian thought applied to the circumstances of this poor fallen world." When Peter Lombard compiled his *Sentences,* providing the Medieval world with its basic handbook of theology, he acknowledged his "supreme debt" to the "masterful work" of Augustine in *The City of God*. When Gratian compiled the principle handbook of canon law, he too recognized the "vital import" of the "seminal foundations" laid in Augustine's *City*. Cassiodorus and Boethius both relied heavily on Augustine's worldview paradigm as exposited in *City,* as well as his tripartite arx axiom methodology in establishing the Western pattern of covenantal and classical education. Anselm, Aquinas, Petrarch, Pascal, Bellarmine, and Kirkegaard all counted *The City of God* as the first and primarily intellectual influence.[14]

Augustine devoted the first ten books or portions of *The City of God* to a devastating and informed critique of pagan mythology and philosophy. Combing through the histories, the beliefs, and the fruits of paganism, Augustine traced the corruptions to their very sources. He studied and quoted extensively from the best historian on paganism, a man named Varro. He also went to the philosopher he considered the best of the lot, Plato. Like a young seminarian right out of a Van Tilian apologetic class, he turned his intellectual flamethrowers to the contradictions and incoherencies of the world of pagan thought.

Christians before and after Augustine have grappled with the question, "What has Athens to do with Jerusalem?" However one answers that question, some, like Paul in his day and Augustine in his time, have to march right into the middle of Athens, right past the idols, and declare the idol-toppling truth. In his powerful critique of the enemy's worldview, Augustine not only

---

[14] Grant, "In the Midst of a Culture War.".

taught readers in his day to rest assured in the bankruptcy of Christianity's opponents, he also taught future generations how to battle its own demons.

G. K. Chesterton's confidence in shrugging off Darwinism and other heresies echoes Augustine. C. S. Lewis' certainty of the vindication of "God in the Dock" reminds us of Augustine. Machen's *Christianity and Liberalism* is a twentieth century application of Augustine's methods. The critiques of modern philosophies and theologies found in the works of Rushdoony, Schaeffer, Van Til, and Schlossberg are updated versions of Augustine. Christopher Dawson simply applied Augustine's historiography to European history. Gregg Singer applied Augustine's precepts to American history. The works of Phillip Johnson and Nancy Pearcey, as well as the older works of Henry Morris, in answer to the Darwinian scientific worldview follow the model of Augustine.

After shredding the pagans for ten books, Augustine turned his attention to constructing a Christian view of God, the world, man, history, and reality. Well trained in rhetoric and philosophy, Augustine did not establish his worldview on the fruits of his classically developed reason. Instead, Augustine takes the reader step-by-step through the Bible. As Gordon Clark pointed out,

> Augustine got his ideas from Scripture, as must be the case for everyone whose view is truly Christian. Though deeply influenced by Plotinus and Platonism on some points, his fundamental principles of history come from the Bible alone. He accepted the Old and New Testaments as the written word of God, as a divine revelation, and his historiography has this revelational basis.[15]

In the Bible is found the precepts, the examples, and the mandates for a Christian culture. In those pivotal doctrines of creation, the fall, and redemptive history, the patterns for building an earthly city with eternal foundations are found. Like the great theologians who would follow in his footsteps, Augustine did theology by mining the text of Scripture. Gregg Singer said this about Augustine's overall theological accomplishments:

> The Augustinian theology not only made possible a Christian philosophy but also pointed out the way toward the formulation of a systematic arrangement of the world according to biblical presuppositions. More particularly, in his *De Civitate* (begun shortly after

---

[15] Gordon Clark, *Historiography: Secular and Religious* (Nutley, NJ: The Craig Press, 1971), 246.

the fall of Rome to the Visigoths in 410) Augustine provided the church with a biblical philosophy of history which served as the basis for most historiography in the West until the advent of humanism in the fourteenth century and the coming of the Reformers in the sixteenth century. Although his successors in the Middle Ages were never able to reach the heights which Augustine reached in his great classic, it is nevertheless true that they consciously followed the pattern of interpretation which he laid down and kept it alive until it could be refined and deepened by the Reformers of Geneva and Scotland.[16]

Of course, Augustine stumbled over the intellectual currents and philosophical influences of his time. Since his world was swimming in a sea of Greek and Roman humanism, he could not help but get wet. While his theology could not transcend Greek philosophy or Latin culture, he still managed to lift the Christian world of thought to a higher level. His mistakes and flaws are clearly visible. Augustine's theology is tainted at points by the retreatist and ascetic aspects of much of the early church. Hence, Augustine is not the man to go to for directions for intimacy in marriage. Sometimes, he made poor applications or weird interpretations of Scripture. But mistakes and missteps in theology are readily correctable if Scripture is the foundation for theology. Scripture provides a self-renewing, self-correcting epistemology. So even when Augustine was wrong, he was right, for he kept pointing to the Bible as the source of truth.

The fall of the Roman Empire is now the stuff of history and, occasionally, movies. The Roman religions and myths are long since reduced to trivial pursuit questions. The Visigoth threat to Europe is long gone. North Africa has long since ceased to be a center of Christian thinking. The crisis of 410 is forgotten, but Augustine's *City of God* lives on. It is more relevant to our own culture wars than are the latest best sellers. As Cornelius Van Til said, "I can hardly think of a more relevant book than *The City of God*."[17] It is both a model for us and instruction to us. Andrew Nelson Lytle said, "Augustine's time was all too like our own: a world in rebellion against the truth had fractured into opposing forces with only the Gospel offering any hope of reconciliation or restoration."[18] A child saying, "Tolle lege" or "Take it and read it" prompted Augustine's conversion. We can do no better than follow that advice with *The City of God*.

---

[16] C. Gregg Singer, *Christian Approaches: To Philosophy; To History* (Craig Press, 1978), 28.
[17] As quoted by George Grant.
[18] As quoted by George Grant.

Reading *The City of God*

The City of God is a large book with many references to people and ideas that are foreign to most readers. Augustine is repetitive and wordy; he strays away from the point and sometimes strays away from the point he originally strayed away from too. He branches off into theology, philosophy, mythology, rhetoric, and what were then current events and Mediterranean gossip. Encased in the twenty-two books of *The City of God* are brilliant statements, uplifting theological meditations, and philosophical bombshells. The reader has to work through the greater mass of material to mine the nuggets of gold and silver. Allen Tate said, "Reading most classics requires a sturdy constitution and a carefully wrought plan; not so *The City of God*. It is so well organized that it is read with ease by even the most novice of theological readers." And those who have read both Augustine and Allen Tate might confirm that Augustine is far easier than Tate.

The abridged version of *The City of God,* a translation by several scholars, edited by Vernon J. Bourke, is a great way to tackle the book.[19] This edition reduces a work of over 1000 pages to a mere 550 page pamphlet. Some passages Bourke judged to be obscure and less essential to the overall text are cut out and summarized, but enough remains for the reader to still get a thorough taste of Augustine's work. This edition also contains a forward by Etienne Gilson, a brilliant twentieth century Catholic scholar, which is helpful and thought provoking.

Perhaps as a warm-up for reading *The City of God,* the reader might begin with Augustine's *Confessions,* which is a devotional classic. It is part autobiography; part prayer of praise to God. It testifies of the faithful devotion of that great saint of God, Monica, Augustine's mother. Gilson says that Augustine viewed *Confessions* as a companion to *The City of God*. "[T]he evolution of world history is a no less striking 'confession' of the love and power of God than the sight of His creation, and the awareness of the wonders wrought by grace in the soul of His servant Augustine."[20] In this work, Augustine wades through the philosophical attractions of the pagan world, especially the philosophy of the Manicheans, and the varied ways in which he tried to escape the pressing claims of God's truth. Augustine's account of his own conversion is a classic story.

---

[19] Published by Image Books, a division of Doubleday.
[20] Gilson, 33.

Thomas Cahill testifies to the power of Augustine's *Confessions:*

> Augustine is the first human being to say 'I'—and to mean what we mean today. His *Confessions* are, therefore, the first genuine autobiography in human history. The implications of this are staggering and, even today, difficult to encompass. A good start is made, of course, by reading the *Confessions* themselves and falling under their spell.[21]

Another shorter work that is valuable of itself and helpful to get the reader used to Augustine is *On Christian Teaching*. This book is a manual for Bible teachers. In it, Augustine deals with the issue of the canon of Scripture, the use of secular learning in theology, and the benefits of rhetoric and grammar. Above all, he emphasizes the absolute necessity of the Bible teacher living the Word before and along with his teaching it to others.

There are, of course, many other works of Augustine and books about him and *The City of God*. Christopher Dawson said that Augustine was "to a far greater degree than any emperor or general or barbarian war-lord, a maker of history and a builder of the bridge which was to lead him from the old world to the new."[22] Simply pick it up and start reading. Give yourself plenty of time and be patient and prayerful. But above all, read Augustine.

---

[21] Cahill, *How the Irish Saved Civilization*, 39-40.
[22] As quoted on the opening page of Bourke's edition of *City of God*.

Chapter Eight
Another Christopher, Another Christ-bearer

History is philosophy from examples.
—Dionysius of Halicarnassus

The doctrine of the Incarnation which is the central doctrine of the Christian faith is also the center of history.
—Christopher Dawson[1]

For years the story of Columbus's discovery of the New World was a part of the history catechism of American children's schooling: "In 1492, Columbus sailed the ocean blue." The event was celebrated in stories and poems and later, movies. Columbus was hailed for his perseverance, leadership, and resourcefulness. He was in title and in truth "Admiral of the Ocean Sea."

Then everything changed. New perspectives on history began focusing on his personal flaws and discrediting his discoveries. There were explorers before Columbus; the lands Columbus discovered were already inhabited by civilizations; many atrocities took place as a result of such conquests. With the historical revisionism, the language changed. The New World was not discovered, it was brutally conquered. Columbus's voyage was the opening wave of a conquest, not the beginning of a new world. Civilizations were not advanced by Columbus, but were destroyed by the Columbian invasion. October 12, the traditional date for celebrating Columbus's arrival, became a time of mourning and protests.

Then everything changed again. The year 1992 marked the five hundred year anniversary of Columbus's voyage, and battle lines were drawn. Due to a renewed Christian interest in history, the interpretations of Columbus began taking his faith into account. His name—Christopher—meant Christ-bearer. In his voyage, he did not set out to prove the world was round, but

---

[1] "The Christian View of History" from *Dynamics of World History* (Wilmington, DE: ISI Books, 2002), 313.

he primarily sought to bring fulfillment to certain prophecies in Isaiah concerning the worldwide spread of the Gospel.

So what was Columbus? Was he a brave admiral and explorer, advancing man's knowledge of the world against the prejudices of his day? Was he a ruthless exploiter of native American cultures? Or was he a Christian, albeit flawed at many points, who was motivated by Christian interests? Was it gold, God, or glory that drove him westward with that fleet of three ships?

Too often, we have all learned history in ways that presupposed nationalism, economics, social forces, or individual psychology as the prime motivating factors in human action. Too often Christianity has been pushed into the background: Of course, Columbus was a Christian, note the historians, for he lived in an age when all Europeans were Christians. Too often the role and impact of the Christian faith has been interpreted in negative terms: Columbus sometimes used Christianity as a justification for his less than Christian actions, and he had no qualms about brutality toward the native races. Columbus was a complex figure: He was more than just a Christian by cultural upbringing. He was a man of Christian conviction and piety, and he was a sinner.

A Christian study of history, which calls for a Christian reinterpretation of history, will not mean whitewashing the sins of individuals, eras, or cultures. But it will recognize the salt and light impact of Christianity on culture and life.

Christians are rediscovering history. Along with a recovery of historical knowledge, we need to rediscover Christian historians. One who deserves such honor is Christopher Dawson.

The Other Christopher

Without distracting in the least from the well-deserved honor and holiday of Christopher Columbus' arrival (or discovery or rediscovery) of the New World, another man also should be honored on October 12. Another Christopher, Dawson in this case, a discoverer of history, was born on that date in 1889 in Wales. Like the big man of 1492, this Christopher had a mission of being a Christ-bearer.

Christopher Dawson's mission field was the study of history. His contemporaries included such men as G.K. Chesterton, T.S. Eliot, and C.S. Lewis. They were more than just contemporaries in a time-spatial sense; they were the intellectual and spiritual peers of Dawson. Together with a host of other writers and thinkers such as Dorothy Sayers, J.R.R. Tolkien, and Hilaire Belloc, they were a part of the "m" of I Corinthians 1:26a ("...not *many* wise...are called"—as opposed to 'not *any*...).

In the post-Christian culture of 20th century Britain, as the sun was setting on the empire, as Matthew Arnold's sea of faith echoed "its melancholy, long, withdrawing roar," the sun continued to blaze brightly on that Kingdom that is greater than even Albion at its height. Of this greater kingdom, this kingdom not bound by seas and mountains, the prophet Daniel said it would never be destroyed, but would increase until it covered the earth (Daniel 2).

Put simply, God converted and commissioned a host of novelists, poets, and intellectuals from among the peoples of Britain. Some produced great novels, poems, and literary essays. Some, and here we think of Chesterton and Lewis, wrote brilliant apologies (that is, defenses) of the Christian faith. Some, and here we think of Martyn Lloyd-Jones, rediscovered Puritan writings, Calvinistic theology, and expository preaching from the Bible. At least one, Winston Churchill, defended Christendom against Teutonic tyranny, the menace of the Nazi juggernaut, and the scourge of the Bolshevik threat, and then chronicled the account in an historical epic. And one, Christopher Dawson, restructured a Christian interpretation of the history of Europe and the world.

The twentieth century was in one sense a time of maturity for the field of history. Universities claimed the field, usurping what had once been the domain of true scholars, that is, men of leisure who read and reflected and wrote. In another sense, the twentieth century was a time of historiographical, adolescent foolishness. Some historians flirted with Hegelian theories of history and saw the State as god marching upon the earth. Before World War I, they were bounding with optimism over the brave new world of the future. After 1918, some despaired of life or history having any meaning or purpose.

Some historians courted Marxian theory with its economic determinism and its eschatological vision of a utopian society. It finally took more than one account of the gulags and holocausts to break them of their romantic love affair with Marx, Lenin, and Mao. Alas, some never abandoned their love or their tenured posts. Into the late 1980s and 1990s, they still gushed over the brilliant Mikhail Gorbachev and scorned the reactionary Alexander Solzhenitsyn and the foolish Cold Warrior Ronald Reagan. Those not quite Marxist courted the equally ugly twin sister of Communism—Socialism.[2] There have been Marxist historians whose honest presuppositions and historical scholarship have added greatly to our understanding of history, and here one thinks of British historian Christopher Hill, whose books on the Puritan Revolution are useful, and American historian Eugene Genovese, whose studies of Southern history are boldly brilliant.

---

[2] An analogy originally given by Dr. Greg Bahnsen.

The brutal edges of political history cut too sharply for some historians. Hence, they looked at social institutions; they bemoaned the plight of women and the dispossessed classes; they ignored the great men of history in search of the underlying social causes; they exalted environment over rhetoric, chance over destiny, and academic trivia pursuit (which produces dissertations and tenure) over the grand sweeps of history.

History as a field of study precariously teeters between extremes. The teaching and writing of history can easily become ideology. History is then used to support and buffer particular viewpoints. Historians become the moral watchdogs of society. Historical activists, like judicial activists, can handily marshal facts and direct studies to prove whatever they set out to prove. Hence, the oppression of women, the plight of the lower classes, or either the failures or successes of centralized government can all be shown from history, depending upon the historians' presuppositions, whims, patrons, and ideological hatchets. Opposite the ideologues are the more objective historians. The study of history leads to ever increasing archival collections. The accumulation of facts yields no certainty, only more studies.

Historical studies can become as arcane as any branch of philosophy. They can be inconclusive since either there are too few sources or too many. History can become so complex that both man and story are lost in the historical processes. History then becomes an academic field where historians write for historians.

Just as art can lose beauty and literature lose power, so history can lose direction. The Nine Muses don't live on Parnassus independently. All intellectual and creative work is built upon some presuppositions about the meaning of life. Even pagan presuppositions can promote coherence for a time. In the twentieth century, as art became disjointed and ugly and literature became Nihilistic and full of despair, history as a subject faced the same pressures.

Then God raised up Christopher Dawson. This was nothing new for God. He had done the same in the fifth century when Augustine's blockbuster *The City of God* hit the shelves of the Scrolls-a-Million franchise and stayed on the bestseller list for a millennium. God's enemies always seem to know that it is not the facts of the event, but the interpretation of the event that matters most. Barbarians sacked Rome: It was the Christians' fault, so they said. Then spake Augustine. God has continually revived His work and His kingdom. Sometimes He has raised up a Catholic Aquinas or Dante; sometimes a Protestant Luther or Calvin; sometimes a Calvinistic Whitefield and the Arminian Wesley brothers. Sometimes God's special instruments have been theologians, preachers, and missionaries, sometimes poets, sometimes statesmen, sometimes musicians, and sometimes, even historians.

This brings us back to Christopher Dawson. Dawson was quite an unexciting man. He was quite ordinary looking and suffered from poor health. He was never an athlete, warrior, or political figure. He was a studious young man, who was physically frail, and who suffered from chronic insomnia and bouts of depression. What he lacked in physical and social attributes was offset by intellectual strength and obstinacy.[3]

Dawson was raised in the Anglican Church, was homeschooled at points by private tutors, and attended an Anglican school at age sixteen. The Christian nurture of his home was offset by the spiritual lifelessness of his formal schooling.

Dawson wrote of the loss of the faith in the school and culture of his time:

> The haze of vagueness and uncertainty which hung around the more fundamental articles of Christian dogma…[and how] the one standard of authority in the Protestant religious world, namely the Bible, was being swept away by the tide of the new Biblical criticism.[4]

Spiritual struggles led Dawson to a period of agnosticism. In time, due to the influences of friends and books, including the Bible, Dawson became a Roman Catholic. When he was nineteen and had not yet decided on his theological convictions, Dawson went to Rome where he received his calling from God on Easter Sunday in 1909.

His daughter Christina tells what then happened:

> Looking back on that Easter day in 1909 Christopher remembered that he went to visit this church and sat on the steps of the Capitol in the same place where Gibbon had been inspired to write *The Decline and Fall* and it was there that he first conceived the idea of writing a history of culture. An entry in his journal later that year refers to "a vow made at Easter in the Ara Coeli" and stated that he had since "had great light on the way it may be carried out. However unfit I may be…I believe it is God's will I should attempt it."[5]

---

[3] Christina Scott, *A Historian and His World: A Life of Christopher Dawson* (New Brunswick: Transaction Publishers, 1992), 42.

[4] As quoted in Scott, 37. Protestantism without a commitment to Scripture is hopeless.

[5] Scott, 49.

Since Gibbon had blamed Christianity for the fall of Rome and had embraced the skepticism of Voltaire,[6] it is ironically humorous that God called Dawson at the same location to repair the damage Gibbon had done. Dawson committed his life and intellectual career to writing about history and culture from a Christian perspective. His life was then devoted to study. He read books, he gave lectures, and he wrote essays. Books evolved out of the essays and lectures.

Once when T. S. Eliot was lecturing in the United States, he was asked what writer was the most powerful intellectual influence in England. Eliot answered, "Christopher Dawson."[7] Not everyone recognized or noticed Dawson. The academic community, as is all too often the case, largely ignored this diminutive man with his beard and thick glasses. He wasn't in line with the trends of the political 'isms' and academic printing presses of his day. Still Dawson plugged away, winning a plaudit here or there, and reaching a small number of scholars on both sides of the Atlantic. In his latter years, Dawson was invited to the United States where he taught at Harvard University for a time, chairing a professorship in Catholic historical studies. Returning to England, he died in 1970. In time, many of his books and essays fell to the wayside and were forgotten.

But God is gracious to us in matters relating to the printed word. Those obscure books tucked away in college libraries and used bookstores continued to fall into the right hands here and there. The cultural renaissance and reformation of our time has resulted in the rediscovery of Christian scholarship. Books and essays by Dawson began to be reprinted. His daughter wrote a worthy biography of him, and scholars began revisiting his writings and building upon his insights. For a time back in the 1980s, I received a newsletter devoted to the thinking of Christopher Dawson. I did not quite understand his importance then, but I did recognize that here was a scholar worthy of note.

Not all of his books are yet reprinted. Some are still treasure finds in used book markets and library sales, but there have been reprints of some great Dawson works and on-going scholarly studies of his historiography.

One of the best places to begin studying Christopher Dawson is in his biography, *A Historian and His World: A Life of Christopher Dawson,* written by his daughter Christina Scott. Dawson's Victorian childhood is told by both his daughter and himself in a memoir he penned. The book gives the background of Dawson's lectures and essays, and it describes the influences he had upon others. For example, C. S. Lewis sent Dawson a letter after reading

---

[6] Thomas Cahill, *How the Irish Saved Civilization,* 14.
[7] Scott, 210.

Religion and Culture in which he said, "I embarked on it at once and indeed by greedily reading it at lunch and splashing it with gravy have already deprived the copy of some of its freshness." Lewis went on to brag about the book, and then added, "But I mustn't go on regurgitating plums from your own cake."[8] Besides such delightful anecdotes, the biography shows how Dawson remained faithful to his calling as a Christian historian.

An excellent collection of his essays is found in *Christianity and European Culture: Selections from the Work of Christopher Dawson,* edited by Gerald Russello.[9] This book includes the whole of another Dawson book titled *The Historic Reality of Christian Culture: A Way to the Renewal of Human Life.*[10] The essays in the Russello collection include different angles on the topics of Christian culture, Christianity and history, and the impact of secularism. Another work focusing on how a Christian philosophy of history looks and works is *The Dynamics of World History*[11]*,* which outlines Dawson's Christian approach to history. This book begins with ten essays on the sociological foundations of history. This is followed by another ten essays on different broad aspects of history. The second half of the book deals with how Christianity provides meaning with history, and the last part examines key historians, ranging from St. Augustine to Karl Marx to Arnold Toynbee.

Religion and the Rise of Western Culture and *The Making of Europe* are both useful surveys of the impact of Christianity upon European cultural history. Both of these books survey movements and events in European history from the end of the Roman Empire up through the latter Middle Ages and the Renaissance. More on the Medieval period is found in *Medieval Essays,* which has played a key role in the whole field of Medieval studies.[12] This book is a topical study and also includes chapters on Medieval literature, including discussions of Dante's *Divine Comedy* and Langdon's *Piers Plowman.*

The Dividing of Christendom surveys events from the Renaissance and Reformation through the Enlightenment and the French Revolution.[13] Certainly, my historical sympathies are much closer to Luther and Calvin than was Dawson's. But even though he might not always have judged history "cor-

---

[8] Scott, 158-159.

[9] Gerald J. Russello, editor, *Christianity and European Culture: Selections from the Work of Christopher Dawson* (Washington, D.C.: The Catholic University of America Press, 1998).

[10] Christopher Dawson, *The Historic Reality of Christian Culture: A Way to the Renewal of Human Life,* (New York: Harper and Brothers, 1960).

[11] Christopher Dawson, *Dynamics of World History,* edited by John J. Mulloy (Wilmington, Delaware: ISI Books, 2002).

[12] Christopher Dawson, *Medieval Essays,* (Washington, D.C.: The Catholic University of America Press, 1954).

[13] Christopher Dawson, *The Dividing of Christendom* (New York: Sheed and Ward, 1965).

rectly," Dawson always judged it judiciously and insightfully. His insights into the further theological, political, and philosophical developments after Europe's spiritual unity was fractured are most worthy of consideration. The French Revolution and other revolutionary upheavals are given more coverage in *The Gods of Revolution*[14] and *The Movement of World Revolution*[15] Dawson's works overlap at many points. He generally focused on the larger movements and did not particularly look at biographies and source materials. His focus was on culture in its broader dimensions and not on the lesser details of history.

The Crisis of Western Education first appeared in 1961. It was an appeal to Catholics, making the case for the necessity for Christian education which has never been more strongly stated. Notice just this one quote: "But for the Christian the past can never be dead, as it often seems to the secularist, since we believe the past and the present are united in the one Body of the Church and that the Christians of the past are still present as witnesses and helpers in the life of the Church today."[16]

Key Themes

Dawson's many works can be reduced down to several key themes or ideas, the main one being this: The key determining factor in a culture is religion—not politics, not economics, not geography, but religion. All those other things matter, but religion is central. Gerald Russello comments on this theme as it appears in Dawson's early works: "These early works reveal the central core of Dawson's thought, which he would express in various forms throughout his writings: religious cult is at the heart of every culture, and the society that disregards its spiritual foundations will collapse, no matter the level of its material well-being."[17] Whether Dawson was looking at the Ancient, Medieval, or Modern Worlds; whether his attention was directed to the east or the west; whether his focus was on political changes, religious revolutions, or literature, his main interpretive principle was religion.

A second key idea in Dawson's thinking follows: The true religion is Christianity. Hence, Dawson's study of European history titled *The Making of Europe* is essentially a study of the Christian faith in Europe. The main

---

[14] Christopher Dawson, *The Gods of Revolution* (New York: New York University Press, 1972).

[15] Christopher Dawson, *The Movement of World Revolution* (New York: Sheed and Ward, 1959).

[16] Christopher Dawson, *The Crisis of Western Education* (Steubenville, Ohio: Franciscan University Press, 1989).

[17] Gerald Russello, "Introduction." Page xii.

interpretive principle of education is religious, or more specifically, Christian education. Christian presuppositions formed the basis for the development of law, education, government, literature, and other aspects of life in Europe. The most apparent divisions of history into epochs or time periods are to be determined by theological, not political, institutions and revolutions. In fact, Dawson's essay "The Six Ages of the Church" is a useful outline for looking at history.[18] Any hope for civilization is to be found not in technology or evolution or some subjective experience, but in a revival of the Christian faith. Describing Christianity, Dawson said, "For Christianity is essentially the religion of the Incarnation, of the divine intervention in history at a particular time and in a particular social context and of the extension and incorporation of this new spiritual creation in the life of humanity through the mediation of an historical institutional society."[19]

Open almost any book by Dawson, at almost any point, and Dawson will be reiterating these themes. He is not a narrative historian like Winston Churchill or Paul Johnson. His stories will not keep you up late at night, turning pages, gulping coffee, and awaiting the final charges of the cavalry. Dawson was not a storyteller like Herodotus. He analyzed history: he explained the causes, the moving forces, and the underlying currents of history. He gives the interpretive framework for the great stories.

At least one more quote must be given: "It is hardly too much to say that it is Christian culture that has created Western man and the Western way of life." "It is hardly too much to say" and yet with the exception of one faithful Christian history teacher and a scattering of books I came across here and there, I never heard it said by most of my professors or came across it in the history books I read. Christianity—or Christian culture or better yet, Christendom—was ignored, minimized, ridiculed, distorted, or attacked. Christianity was responsible for the Crusades, the Inquisition, the burning of witches, the suppression of drama, and the oppression of women—so we have all been told. Young Christians should never head off to the university without the major premises of Dawson's thinking in their minds and hearts.

Yes, there is a third key theme to Dawson. Religion is the key and Christianity is the religion, and the branch of Christianity that Dawson converted to and loved and defended was the Roman Catholic Church. Like Chesterton and Tolkien in Britain, like Flannery O'Connor and Walker Percy in America, Dawson was Roman Catholic—through and through. So what is the lonely Calvinist (of Richard Tawney's myth) to do?

---

[18] "The Six Ages of the Church" is found in Russello and in *The Historical Reality of Christian Culture*.

[19] Russello, "Christian Culture as a Culture of Hope" 49.

Simple, recognize that you are not ordaining Dawson (or Chesterton or Tolkien or even Lewis, for that matter) as your pastor, but rather are gleaning from him in those areas where we believe he was most correct. In the Apostles' Creed we affirm belief in the "communion of saints" and for now, that communion is enhanced by us using what other saints have garnered for the glory of God. With thanksgiving, borrow heavily from Dawson for understanding history Christianly, and thank God for raising him up. Practically speaking, Protestants may best read many a fine Dawson paragraph by substituting the word "Christian" for "Catholic." Christians have got to get beyond a narrow sectarianism that cannot reach beyond our Sunday services toward those who battle the same enemies.

Dawson himself, though zealously Roman Catholic, bemoaned the effects of the breakup of Christian Europe and blamed both sides. He said, "It is difficult to exaggerate the harm that was inflicted on Christian culture by the century of religious strife that followed the Reformation."[20] The ultimate harm was the secularization of European culture. As is always the case when Christians are divided, the enemy triumphs. Dawson notes, "The convinced secularists were an infinitesimal minority of the European population, but they had no need to be strong since the Christians did their work for them."[21]

A fourth theme in Dawson's historiography is hope. His hope is not that of the early twentieth century progressives. Dawson says that the church wins "not by majorities but by martyrs and the cross is her victory."[22] In his lectures and essays, he did not simply point out the high peaks of the past, but rather urged that Christians again venture into mountain climbing. In his *Medieval Essays,* he issued this thoughtful exhortation, "If the semi-barbarous society of feudal Europe could create such a remarkable cultural unity under the influence of Christian ideas, what might the modern world achieve with its vast resources of knowledge and power which are now running to waste or being perverted into instruments of social destruction."[23]

Having lived through the worst half of the twentieth century—an era destructive of human life and largely dismissive of the Christian faith—Dawson maintained this hope. He said in 1960,

> We today are living in a world that is far less stable than that of the early Roman Empire. There is no doubt that the world is on the move again as never before and that the pace is faster and more

---

[20] Dawson, *The Dividing of Christendom,* 9-10.
[21] Dawson, *The Dividing of Christendom,* 10.
[22] Dawson, *Dynamics of World History,* 299.
[23] *Medieval Essays,* 14.

furious than anything that man has ever known. But there is nothing in this situation which should cause Christians to despair. On the contrary it is the kind of situation for which their faith has always prepared them and which provides the opportunity for the fulfillment of their mission.[24]

Tolkien saw the destruction of his world from the trenches of World War I. He envisioned Middle Earth and told the story of its redemption. Dawson saw the same cultural 'No Man's Land' from his book-lined study. He saw that cultural redemption would result as an outgrowth of the Christian faith. Calvinist scholar Henry Van Til would aptly state this by saying, "Culture is religion externalized." Christians have to think beyond merely evangelizing the lost and planting churches—and those are both worthy efforts. A Christian culture must be created. It has been done before—not perfectly—but still done well. Christian culture will be advanced when Christians prepare for the future by reaching into the past for wisdom. Christian historians like Christopher Dawson have led the way.

---

[24] As quoted in Scott, 211.

Chapter Nine
The Making of a History Teacher

There is not a square inch in the whole domain of human existence
over which Christ, who is Sovereign over all, does not cry: Mine!
—Abraham Kuyper[1]

Only one historian ever won a Nobel Prize for Literature. The year was 1953 and the historian was Winston Churchill. He won the prize largely due to his massive six volume series titled *The Second World War*, which came out beginning in 1948 up through 1953. Also contributing to his being honored was his other numerous histories and his brilliant oratory. What made Churchill's histories of both World Wars so compelling was his dual roles as the storyteller and participant. Often Churchill himself was the story. Samuel Eliot Morison, himself an outstanding historian, noted this about Churchill as an historian:

> There is no question but that Churchill is a great historian. He has verve, style, honesty, imagination, and, above all, superb craftsmanship. How did he learn this craft? The young men and women today who are training to be historians wish to know. Well, my answer is background, innate capacity, experience, and a vigorous course of self-teaching: that was essential, but no one would have worked without the others.[2]

But Morison continued with the main ingredient he found that made Churchill a great historian. It was that he "absorbed history through the skin" and he had a prodigious memory.[3] Churchill, although he hated it and

---

[1] As quoted in *Abraham Kuyper: A Centennial Reader*, ed. by James D. Bratt (Grand Rapids, MI: William B. Eerdmans Publishing Company, 1998), 488.
[2] Samuel Eliot Morison, "Winston Churchill: Nobel Prize Winner" from *Sailor Historian—The Best of Samuel Eliot Morison,* edited by Emily Morison Beck (Boston: Houghton Mifflin, 1977), 377-378.
[3] Morison, 378.

did poorly at it, received a classical education. Surpassing his formal education was his home life and personal history. He was the distant descendant of the Duke of Marlborough, a great English military commander, and the son of a prominent Victorian politician. "History was in the air during his youth," Morison said.[4]

So here was a man whose life was rich in personal history, both his own and that of his ancestors. This same man was blessed with a good memory, providential opportunities of being in key places at critical moments in time, and outstanding writing and literary skills. And he lived a long time, and drank heavily, and was witty. It is no wonder that my shelf of Churchill biographies is so large, including William Manchester's uncompleted two volumes, the shorter biographies of John Keegan and John Lukacs, and particular volumes focusing upon Churchill's oratory and leadership, . It is amazing to consider how many books Churchill wrote. It is personally vexing for me to consider how many books by and about Churchill I do not have.

With Churchill in mind, in this case, not Churchill the politician or war leader or soldier or journalist, but Churchill the historian in mind, I embark on my own autobiography as a history teacher. Churchill, either as a soldier, journalist, or political leader, or all three, was in an uprising in British-controlled India in 1897, the Sudan Uprising, which included the Battle of Omdurman, in 1898, and the Boer War in South Africa in 1899, where he was captured by the Boers and then escaped. From there, he gained fame as Lord of the Admiralty in World War I, which led to the failed Gallipoli Campaign. After that, Churchill resigned the Admiralty and served in the British army in France. In regard to World War II, he spent the decade before the war warning Britain and the world of the dangers of Naziism, and he served as Prime Minister of the United Kingdom during most of the war.

In contrast to Churchill, my military record consists of a two time membership in the Military Book Club and a short stint as a Civil War re-enactor in the Third Arkansas Brigade. My political career consists of losing an election for class vice president during my senior year in high school. My ambitions in life have always been quite below those of Churchill. My lifelong dream always consists of my standing in front of a group of eager listeners, in particular, young people, lecturing on historical events and people like Churchill. My fantasy world consists of endless bookshelves, a spacious well decorated history classroom, and once again, a group of young people sitting there fascinated by my lecture, laughing at my humor, and marveling at history itself. And I must thank God that the dream and the fantasy world—at least to the extent of having students listen to me—have been recurring realities.

---

[4] Morison, 378.

The Tools

Let me distinguish between the way a history teacher should conceive of history and the way a child should learn it. Although it occurs in a section on eschatology, or last things, Cornelius Van Til made a statement that is vital and foundational to a Christian history teacher's approach to knowledge. Van Til said, "It becomes especially plain here that in the Christian conception of things interpretation precedes facts."[5] Van Til is correct in that this is the way it must happen in the teacher's worldview, but it is not the way it is to be taught and revealed to students. A teacher's understanding of the processes of learning and his or her students' way of receiving of that process are different.

The Christian history teacher should have the following assortment of academic and mental tools in his or her intellectual toolbox and have them in this order:

First, the teacher should have a thorough familiarity with the Bible. This means a reading knowledge of it with a personal and covenantal conviction of its truth. This type of familiarity is best cultivated in a life of hearing and reading the Bible, of being nurtured with Sunday school lessons and sermons from the Bible, and memorizing verses and meditating on key passages of Scripture. Those who grow up without the nurturing effects of the Bible have to do a crash course to catch up.

Much could be said at this point about study tools, study methods, and specific courses of approach to reading the Bible. Much could be said about translations, the study of the original languages, and hermeneutical principles. There are many good books outlining and directing believers in their Bible reading and study. Many of those books are directed toward men preparing for or already engaged in pastoral ministry. Others are directed toward laymen. Almost everything a pastor or pastor-candidate needs to do to familiarize himself with the Bible also needs to be done by the person teaching in a Christian school. Time and other tasks limit us, but all hindrances aside, the Christian history teacher has to be a student of and a devoted reader of the Bible.

Second, building upon the knowledge of the Bible is the need for developing a knowledge of theology. Theology often refers to the formal study of religion, and we usually compartmentalize this as the requirement for pastors and theologians. But just as history is for more than just history teachers, even more so, theology is for more than just theologians. Christian theology

---

[5] Cornelius Van Til, *The Defense of the Faith*, Third Edition, (Phillipsburg, NJ: Presbyterian and Reformed Publishing Company, 1967), 20.

grows largely out of the historic creeds and confessions of the church. Theology, as I am using the term, involves making connections between the many statements in the Bible concerning God, man, and the world. It is the study of doctrines; it is the approach of looking at Bible subjects, such as the Trinity, the atonement, eschatology, family, and personal holiness, and then examining the verses and passages relating to those topics.

Presbyterians use the Westminster Standards for doctrinal and theological statements. These standards include the Westminster Confession of Faith and the Larger and Shorter Catechisms. Believers of all sorts would do well to study the Shorter Catechism, even if you hesitate on accepting certain particular answers. The Heidelberg Catechism is also a wonderful resource. Such studies provide tremendous grounding in theology; however, to delve into creating a reading list on theology would sidetrack us from this essay.

After Bible and theological knowledge, the Christian teacher's worldview begins to come together. We all already have a worldview, but even though we are Christians, we do not always have the condition of our souls in harmony with the thoughts of our minds.

A Christian worldview grows out of seeing the many connecting strands from God's Word to God's World. Cornelius Van Til explores this expansive use of the Bible when he notes,

> The Bible is thought of as authoritative on everything of which it speaks. And it *speaks of everything*. We do not mean that it speaks of football games, of atoms, etc., directly, but we do mean that it speaks of everything either directly or indirectly. It tells us not only of the Christ and his work but it also tells us who God is and whence the universe has come. It gives us a philosophy of history as well as history. Moreover, the information on these subjects is woven into an inextricable whole. It is only if you reject the Bible as the Word of God that you can separate its so-called religious and moral instruction from what it says, e.g., about the physical universe.[6]

Albert M. Wolters seconds Van Til's emphasis on the range of the Bible's application, but he notes that not all Christians are willing to unshackle the broader implications of Scripture. Instead, they want the Bible to be little more than a liturgy for Sunday morning worship and a guide to private devotions. He writes,

---

[6] Van Til, 8.

To be sure, we must be taught by Scripture on such matters as baptism, prayer, election, and the church, but Scripture speaks centrally to *everything* in our life and world, including technology and economics and science. The scope of biblical teaching includes such ordinary "secular" matters as labor, social groups, and education. Unless such matters are approached in terms of a worldview based squarely on such central scriptural categories as creation, sin, and redemption, our assessment of these supposedly nonreligious dimensions of our lives will likely be dominated instead by one of the competing worldviews of the secularized West…In a certain sense the pleas being made here for a biblical worldview is simply an appeal to the believer to take the Bible and its teaching seriously for the totality of our civilization right now and not to relegate it to some optional area called "religion."[7]

An early classic on theology and worldview, titled "Paul's Epistle to the Romans," after having explained our salvation through Christ in detail, then exhorts us to "be transformed in the renewing of our minds" (Romans 12:2). James Orr stated the necessity of a worldview quite well when he said,

He who with his whole heart believes in Jesus as the Son of God is committed to much else besides. He is committed to a view of God, to a view of man, to a view of sin, to a view of Redemption, to a view of human destiny, found only in Christianity. This forms a "Weltangschauung," or "Christian view of the world," which stands in marked contrast with theories wrought out from a purely philosophical or scientific standpoint.[8]

Central to a Christian worldview is understanding God, and then understanding ourselves as created by God, and then by knowing who God is and who we are, we can begin to map out what our purpose is. John Calvin's *Institutes of the Christian Religion* begins with this grand epistemological issue of this self knowledge and knowledge of God. Calvin says, "Nearly all the wisdom we possess, that is to say, true and sound wisdom, consists of two parts: the knowledge of God and of ourselves."[9] Central to this knowledge of God

---

[7] Albert M. Wolters, *Creation Regained: Biblical Basics for a Reformational Worldview*, Second Edition, (Grand Rapids, MI: William B. Eerdmans Publishing Company, 2005) 8-9.

[8] James Orr, *The Christian View of God and the World* (Grand Rapids: Kregel Publications, 1989).

[9] John Calvin, *Institutes of the Christian Religion*, edited by John T. McNeill (Philadelphia: The Westminster Press, 1960), 35

is God's Triune nature. Ralph Smith says, "Obviously, an adequate statement of the Christian worldview must find its center in the Trinity, for the Christian God Himself is the heart of the Christian's understanding of the world." Smith's study of the Trinity, *Trinity and Reality: An Introduction to the Christian Faith,* explores in depth how Christians are to understand themselves, Creation, history, the Bible, the family, and the entire created order through the Triune God of Scripture.[10] The Christian worldview, especially as taught in many good books, branches out to include Christian views of government, art, music, literature, economics, and all areas of life and thought.[11]

The Christian history teacher then needs to be a Bible scholar, a theologian, and a worldview thinker. J. Gresham Machen wisely pointed out, "The student of the New Testament should be primarily a historian. The center and core of all the Bible is history."[12] We can reverse this and say that the history teacher should be primarily a Bible student, for the center and core of all meaning in history is found in the Bible. Like a pastor, the Christian history teacher has to know how to 'rightly divide the Word' and how to apply it. Like a theologian, the Christian history teacher has to have a doctrine of the immanence and transcendence of God, a view of God's covenantal workings in history, a theology of the predestination of God and the free agency of men, a working model of creation, fall, redemption in all of life, and a view of man that incorporates his being created in God's image, but fallen into sin. Also, being a history teacher entails having a Biblical and theological knowledge of how God deals with nations and civilizations.

Bible and theology seem academically foundational to me even from a secular viewpoint or a Christian schizophrenic viewpoint (that being defined as the prevalent view of many Christians where Jesus is Lord of the heart, but everything else is either neutral or Devil-owned and operated). I realized this some years ago while taking a graduate level class on Colonial American history and listening to fellow students discuss religion in Colonial America.

---

[10] Ralph Smith, *Trinity and Reality: An Introduction to the Christian Faith* (Moscow, Idaho: Canon Press, 2004). Every single page!

[11] These books are all must reading: Nancy Pearcey, *Total Truth: Liberating Christianity from its Cultural Captivity* (Wheaton: Crossway Books, 2004; James Sire, *The Universe Next Door: A Basic World View Catalog* (Downers Grove, IL: Intervarsity Press, 1997); Abraham Kuyper, *Lectures on Calvinism.* Dr. Roy Clouser's essay "Is There a Christian View of Everything?" is a difficult, but beneficial read. For some worldview studies on the deeper end of the pool, consider Clouser's *The Myth of Religious Neutrality,* (Notre Dame, IN: University of Notre Dame Press, 2005) and David K. Naugle, *Worldview: The History of a Concept* (Grand Rapids: William B. Eerdmans Publishing Company, 2002).

[12] J. Gresham Machen, *Selected Shorter Writings,* edited by D. G. Hart (Phillipsburg: P & R Publishing, 2004), 97.

How can you possibly understand the Puritans of New England and Virginia without some grasp of the Westminster Standards, particularly the Confession and Catechisms? Likewise, how can you understand Medieval history without understanding the theology of Augustine, Aquinas, and Dante? If I were ever to teach a college level history course in a secular institution, I would repeatedly tell all students of history and literature that to understand their academic fields, they absolutely needed to read the Bible, early Church creeds, portions of Augustine and other Church Fathers, portions of key Medieval Christian thinkers, selections from *On the Imitation of Christ,* at least some writings of Luther and Calvin, the Book of Common Prayer in the oldest of editions, the Westminster Standards, *Pilgrim's Progress,* at least one Dostoevsky novel, and a few modern Christian thinkers, such as C.S. Lewis and Flannery O'Connor. And, I bet I could not stop with that list.

After the foundations of Bible and theology are established, and the structural walls of a Christian worldview are standing, then the teacher is ready to start plugging in history. From there, broad surveys of history, biographies of famous people, key documents in history, and more specialized books on particular eras or topics can start flooding into the mind and onto the bookshelves of the history teacher. If you have missed this point, let me be clear: History teachers have to be nearly unrestrained book buyers and readers. At the point of convergence of Bible, theology, worldview, and historical writings, the teacher should be in need of Ritalin, for how can you stay focused and calm when you are immersed in the Scriptures, in theology, and in history? You will find yourself in a perpetual frenzy, saying, "I want to read this and that and this other and that other, and I want to reread these five books, and I want to take a course on this subject, and I want to begin learning all of this other history and theology, too."

The last tool in the intellectual toolbox is teaching skills. There, Augustine's *On Christian Teaching* has some useful insights for all teachers. John Milton Gregory's *The Seven Laws of Teaching* is a classic on structuring and conveying knowledge to students. Above all, the new teacher needs two things: Personal experience in the classroom and the opportunity to sit under older master teachers.

Putting all this in order, we can list it as follows: Bible, theology, worldview, historical chronology, and pedagogical skills. But how did we receive history on the other end of the spectrum; in other words, how does the child learn history? And for that matter, how does the child learn Bible, theology, literature, art, music, and so on? We realize that we don't begin teaching our babies the eight parts of speech and the distinctive characteristics of English, and yet they learn our language. How then do we approach history?

History begins and is built upon stories. Children have an incredible ability to grasp worlds and times and creations beyond their own little worlds and experiences. They intuitively grasp the One and the Many; for example, they may have a stuffed animal that is a cat; they may watch cartoons with Sylvester the cat; they may have story books with pictures of cats, and they may have a real cat. They identify all these many Aristotlean Particulars of cats with the one Platonic Idea of a cat. Likewise, they have an incredible ability to visualize and enjoy stories. Stories are so real to them that often they are scared to go to bed at night after hearing a story with a big, bad wolf in it. History has to be taught to children as stories. Views of history, such as evolutionary and Marxist views or the Christian view, and determining factors in history, like economics and ideology, cannot be the starting blocks. Neither can dates and dead people. Stephen Mansfield has written a delightful and fun book titled *More Than Dates and Dead People,* designed to hook students into reading history. Both junior high and high school students (and adults) are shown how history is to be read and loved by Christians, and then how stories bring out Christian truths.[13]

Since history is stories, then textbooks are weak conveyors of history. A history textbook approach to history is like telling the story of the three little pigs by examining the eating habits of carnivorous beasts, the real and imaginative habitats of swine, and then the structure of different edifices, particularly straw, wood, and bricks. Textbooks are useful, even invaluable for the teacher. But they are the recipe books, not the meals that are to be served.

Another problem occurs when the history teacher absolutizes the Trivium. By this, I mean that the teacher looks at the methodology of classical education—the grammar, logic, and rhetoric of the Trivium—and teaches history as dates and dead people. Yes, children can and should memorize lots of lists and facts. Chronologies are great; outlines and timelines are tremendous; maps and charts are thrilling; but if these are the components of history class and the stories are lost in the lists of facts, the students will not develop a love for history. The grammar of history is skeletal. We all have skeletons inside us (creepy thought), but they do not define who we are. We are flesh and blood, or better yet, soul and spirit with flesh and blood. Even at the grammar level, even when learning the facts on the history cards, history must be taught as stories.[14]

---

[13] Stephen Mansfield, *More Than Dates and Dead People* (Nashville: Cumberland Book House, 2000). All my junior high students read this book in 7th grade and again in 8th grade.

[14] I am indebted to Evan Wilson for this. I heard him lecture on this topic at the Society for Classical Learning Conference in Dallas, Texas in June, 2003. Mr. Wilson wrote an essay on this topic, titled "Heroism 101," which appeared in "The Classical Teacher," (Winter 2004, Volume 4, Number 1), 16-17.

The goal of teaching history is always the same—romance. The teacher is to romance the subject—history in this case. The student is to grow to love the subject, and that love of history then extends to the God of history.

My Early Journey

In my early years of schooling, I endured, rather than loved, the subject of history. My worst memory is of having to write facts from a filmstrip series we watched in seventh grade over Texas history. Texas has an incredibly fascinating history, from the Spanish explorers through the Alamo and up to the Presidency of George W. Bush. Back in the late sixties, a group of conspirators against the love of history, worked incredibly hard to produce filmstrips that made Texas history boring. Then they found a willing pawn, a teacher who leaned against the wall the whole time in class, overseeing the filmstrip. Added to this was a textbook, which was served as the main course. When we were not taking notes on the filmstrips, we were reading the textbook aloud, one paragraph per person, and then answering questions at the end of the chapter. I associated history with the words, "Read the next chapter and answer the questions at the end."

In some of the more advanced technology of the late sixties, a recording of a sonorous voice reading the script accompanied the filmstrips and a bell dinged signaling the operator to advance the filmstrip. Our filmstrips were not that advanced; someone in class read the script aloud. I never got to be the kid who turned the knob on the projector or who read the script. I only took notes. I did not hate history; I certainly did not hate Texas history. I was a Texan; I thought every boy in Texas played the Alamo, meaning, we played like we were Davy Crocket and Jim Bowie, and we were busy killing countless numbers of Santa Anna's hapless troops. School was endured. It made little sense, but generally, you could get paroled in time for good behavior.

Everything changed in ninth grade. First, I realized that within a century I would be out of school. And I had a good history teacher. Her name was Bonnie Reed. She was probably the most disorganized person to have ever lived. Quite often when she came into class, one of the girls would discreetly go up to her and zip up the back of her dress. She did three brilliant things in class: First, she assigned a book to be read for every six weeks grading period. From there, I started reading history books, particularly biographies. Three of my favorites from that year were Desmond Young's *Rommel—The Desert Fox*, Ernie Pyle's *Brave Men* (a reporter's account of soldiers in World War II that even included a man who lived in my home town of DeKalb, Texas), and a book titled *I was the Nuremberg Jailor*.

The second brilliant thing Mrs. Reed did was to begin World History with World War I. This could have created severe psychological problems if I had gone through life believing that Kaiser Wilhelm lived long before Julius Caesar, but the psychological problems never occurred. (Or if they have, historical chronology was not the cause.) We started World War I in September and by the Christmas break, we were barely through with World War II. We never got into many parts of the textbook. I missed out on defining terms, identifying names, learning many dates, and answering questions at the end of the chapters. But I fell in love with history. I committed my life to being a history teacher. Mrs. Reed taught World War I as stories. Even greater were her stories of World War II. She showed many documentary films of that war, not film strips. We did not take notes; we watched and enjoyed the films.

World War II—back in 1970—was still quite close and personal to my parents' and Mrs. Reed's generation. Her husband, who for a time was my bus driver, had been a prisoner of war in Nazi Germany. Stories were told of him sometimes hitting his wife in the night because of nightmares. In class, she never mentioned his experiences or struggles after the war, even though the films and lectures made many references to brutalities of that war. She talked of heroes, like Churchill, Patton, and Eisenhower, and villains, like Hitler and Mussolini. She talked without lecture notes, outlines, or any structure. From that one year in class, I have continued to read about World War II to this day, and I have never recovered from that class.

The third brilliant thing Mrs. Reed did was to rebuke my ignorance, something I needed then and still need daily. In the second semester, after we got back to the beginnings of history, we had to do an in-depth book report on someone in the Ancient World. I reluctantly picked Alexander the Great for my topic, but I told Mrs. Reed that I was not interested in reading about him because I did not like ancient history. She said, "You don't like what you don't know." That brilliant statement stayed with me. There is much in the arts and sciences that I think I don't like, and even lots of history I don't fancy. I am convinced, thanks to Mrs. Reed, that the main reason for my dislike is that I don't know enough about those areas.

My tenth grade American history teacher was Janie Matteson. She had a reputation as being an incredibly hard teacher. She had a law degree, and the year I was in her class, she was, in Biblical language, great with child. Mrs. Matteson had a totally different style from Mrs. Reed. Mrs. Reed gave me the love for history; Mrs. Matteson gave me the discipline for history. Mrs. Matteson gave rigorous assignments, detailed lectures, and incredibly difficult tests. I made a B the first six weeks on my report card, and decided I would never make a B in history again. Hard as I tried, I never got a discussion question completely right on one of her tests. She forced me to mine the textbook page by page. I learned the recipes. I learned them so well that when I started to college, I took a college placement test in American history, called a CLEP test, and 'clepped' out of both semesters of history.

God was good to me. I never had the proverbial football coach for a history teacher. The football coaches who taught history were around, slinking up and down the halls, scorning all the non-athletes. I saw them in in-action, slumped at a desk reading the sports pages while the students ate the textbooks, but I never had one for a teacher. The only other related course I had was a one-semester government course. Here again I had a good teacher, Mr. Gerald Pinkham, the principal. He was the most intimidating man I ever met. Years later after I grew up, I realized Mr. Pinkham was still the most intimidating man I had ever met. He lectured on government in detail, made us read and report on political issues, and gave the most comprehensive essay tests in the universe. (You could opt out of the essay test and use your books and notes, but the highest you could make on that was 50, but I never considered that option.)

So I left high school with some good background and preparation for a life of teaching history. All I have to do, I thought at the time, was endure four years of college, for I was already prepared for teaching history.

Those of us in private Christian and especially classical Christian education are very critical of government schooling. The main reason we are so critical is because government schooling is so abysmally inept, so intellectually embarrassing, so socially debilitating, and so theologically corrupt; besides that, it is okay. But we have to recognize that government schools have always included both salt and light Christian influences and common grace blessings of God. I received both. Rural and small town American schools, at least back in the 1960s and 1970s, were still dominated by churchgoing people. My parents, and their parents before them, worked hard to send their children to school. Only in time, have we been able, by standing on the shoulders of our parents, to see the need for Christian education, and in particular, classical Christian education.

The primary faults of my high school history experiences are as follows: First, history was taught without a theological base. Second, it was only taught for two years. We had World History and then American History. Third, it was taught apart from a study of literature and original sources. Fourth, it was still too much tied to textbooks. The deficiencies of public school history were offset by my having some good teachers who overcame these deficiencies and by my developing habits of personal reading.

College and Reformation

According to my scores on the College Level Examination Program Test, I did not have to take American History in college. According to some obscure bureaucratic decision—determined by God in part for my sanctification—students still had to take one semester of American history at Texarkana Community College. I was arrogantly incensed, but I submitted to the yoke. A middle-aged lady from my hometown, Mrs. June Shaver, began coaching me on what teachers to take at Texarkana Community College. She had gone back to college to major in history herself. She told me to take a particular professor, who had the reputation for being the hardest and most intractable teacher at the college. I told Mrs. Shaver that my schedule would not allow for me to take his class. And, according to all the talk around the student center, no one made A's in his class.

Here was another one of those rebukes I so often achieve in life: Mrs. Shaver said, "Mr. Wood is the only teacher who teaches the Five Points of Calvinism, and you need to know that for American Literature. And, I never made anything but A's in his class." Humbly, I revised my schedule.

I had no idea what the Five Points of Calvinism were. I thought it maybe had something to do with the Maryland colony, but I looked up Maryland and realized it was Lord Calvert I was thinking of.

I arrived in Professor Henry Wood's class rich in knowledge of history. A week later, I was destitute of all historical understanding and in dire intellectual poverty. Professor Wood is a tall man with a deep bass voice and commanding, stern Old Testament demeanor. He began by asking a rhetorical question, "Is there a law of history?" All of Professor Wood's questions were rhetorical; mere students were to learn, not answer. He then began lecturing on the views of history. This was 1974 and the Cold War was still raging, so the first view of history to be considered was the Marxist view. He described the German philosopher Hegel's dialectic view of thesis, antithesis, and synthesis and how this was incorporated by Marx and Engels into an economic paradigm that then was the prime interpretive factor of history. Wood acknowledged that economics was, indeed, a key factor to understanding history, then foreshadowing what Ronald Reagan accurately predicted, he cast Marxism into the dustbin of history. The year 1974 was at the high point of political liberalism, so Mr. Wood turned next to the Progressive View of History. This philosophy was built upon the liberal ideology and evolutionary views found throughout academia. Wood described how science and social and political planning fit in this view. He described how it affected our views of human nature and society. He looked over what he had described, pronounced it "Nonsense" and moved on.

Then came what he called the philosophy of pessimism and despair. Various shades of Nihilist and Existential modern thought from Nietzsche to Oswald Spengler to Sartre were woven into a position that was most despairing and hopeless for man and history. Professor Wood described this view so vividly that I wondered if that was going to be the view taken in this course: Life is meaningless; history is meaningless; in fact, everything is meaningless; death is the end, so you may as well kill yourself!

"If I had to choose between the Progressive, Marxist, or philosophy of despair," Professor Wood said (and I was personally opting for the Progressive view at that point), "I would choose the philosophy of despair and pessimism." I slumped in my seat, then he continued: "But there is one more view to consider: The Christian view of history."

From there, Professor Wood lectured on Augustine's *City of God* and the development of a Christian worldview, or Weltanschauung, as he called it. This philosophy centered around four key points: God created history, God controls history, God entered history, and God will end history. Much of what Professor Wood said seems to have come from Gordon Clark's book *A Christian View of Man and Things,* particularly the second section, "The Philosophy of History."[15] At the time, sitting in that classroom, I thought it was coming from stones written by the finger of God through Moses, God's mouthpiece.

All of my knowledge of history, particularly World War II, was still there, but it now looked like household items left outside and in need of a home. I began my freshman year of college not knowing what a Weltanschauung or worldview was, but now I was desperately in search of one. Of course, I already had a worldview. As Francis Schaeffer points out, "Most people catch their presuppositions from their family and surrounding society the way a child catches measles."[16]

The lectures continued and I continued to reel in amazement. Soon I learned about the Five Points of Calvinism, the Reformation, the Puritans, the Separatists, and the other groups that settled in the Colonies. Mr. Wood assigned a book *John Calvin: His Roots and Fruits* by C. Gregg Singer. I wrote some profound comments in my book: "Calvinistic exhortations 'dealt in limitless fire and brimstone, and thinned the predestined elect down to a company so small as to be hardly worth the saving,'" according to Mark Twain.[17]

I summarized the book on the inside cover, saying, "Important influence on American History until 1860." And then in my most brilliant mo-

---

[15] Gordon Clark, A *Christian View of Men and Things: An Introduction to Philosophy*, (Grand Rapids: Baker Book House, 1952).

[16] Francis Schaeffer, *How Should We Then Live?* (Old Tappan, NJ: Fleming H. Revell Company, 1976), 20.

[17] From *The Adventures of Tom Sawyer*, by Mark Twain. So, a knowledge of Calvinism did help in understanding American Literature.

ment, I commented on a quote from Irenaeus about predestination by saying, "Why doesn't book quote Word of God instead of Word of Men? JBH." I initialed it so as to get credit from future scholars for my insight.

I read the book twice. Underlined countless portions. Did not like it. And I made 87 on the open book essay test given on the book. I made lower than the girl who sat behind me who told me that she didn't read the book. I just did not get it.

But in spite of my low test grade and complete puzzlement over Calvinism, I loved Mr. Wood's class and his lecture style. His lectures were structured around numbered sequences—four views of history, five points of Calvinism, four Intolerable Acts, and so on. Our textbook was Thomas Bailey's *Pageant of American History*. Mr. Wood liked Bailey's wit, but not his position. Mr. Wood interspersed his lists and explanations with humorous asides, references to books, quips and quotes, and historical anecdotes. He not only had an overwhelming knowledge of history, but it all seemed to connected to the central Calvinistic worldview.

This historical paradigm also included a radically different interpretation of the War Between the States than I had ever heard. I was a Southerner and I loved the South, Robert E. Lee, and my heritage, but I never imagined that it could be defended. Mr. Wood defended the South, displayed a Confederate battle flag in his office, and muttered imprecations against perfidious Yankees. His conservatism, Calvinism, and Confederate sympathies were tied in with his basic Christian commitments.

At the end of the semester, Mr. Wood recommended two books. The books were *This Independent Republic* by R. J. Rushdoony and *A Theological Interpretation of American History* by C. Gregg Singer.[18] The books were assigned to be read and tested over by any student wanting to bring up a low grade. At this point, I had an A average, but I bought the books anyway. Professor Wood, after all, had said, "You need to read both these books if you are a history major."

Over the Christmas holidays, I read Singer's *Theological Interpretation*, underlined countless parts of it, and understood little. Late in the spring semester, I read Rushdoony's *Independent Republic*, underlined a lot of it and understood very little. Two things were happening: I was frustrated by how my educational level had slipped in one year. The more I was reading, the less I was understanding. I did not know how to read a book of ideas and interpretations, in other words, books that presupposed knowledge of intellectual currents and historical events. But, I was beginning to crack the code on how

---

[18] Both published by Craig Press at that time.

Mr. Wood devised all his lectures. Bits and pieces of profound wisdom that were the everyday fare of his class had not originated with him: He had gathered all this knowledge from books, and quite often books written by Calvinists, some of whom had really odd and foreign sounding names.

One day while visiting in Mr. Wood's office and talking about the War Between the States, he gave me a book order form from Presbyterian and Reformed Publishing Company (also known as Craig Press). He recommended a book called *Studies in Theology* by Loraine Boettner. I had no interest in the book, for I was a history major and not a theology student, but I ordered it, and I read it.

But before I read Boettner's *Studies in Theology,* I read a little book called *Tortured for Christ* by Richard Wurmbrand.[19] Wurmbrand had been persecuted by Nazis, rescued by Communists, who then persecuted him even more. The story is one of those incredible testimonies of faith under fire and persecution that have appeared frequently through the centuries since the time of Eusebius. Wurmbrand's perseverance and zeal were daunting. Having reread the book in recent years, I am still moved by the amazing witness and ministry of Richard Wurmbrand, which still continues now even though he has gone on to glory. His book began giving me an understanding of the all-encompassing claims of Christ on my life and of the all-encompassing nature of Christianity. Before that, church was something I attended out of habit and personal preference, and God was something personally believed on in my heart, and the Bible was personally read to find comfort.

When I read Boettner's *Studies in Theology,* my life changed again. It was one of those conversions—not from unbelief to faith—but from faith to faith. I remember sitting in a camping trailer at Camp Albert Pike, under a dim light, reading Boettner late into the night. For the first time, the person and work of Christ, the Triune nature of God, and the authority of Scripture all began filling out what I had learned in seed form in the Apostles' Creed. I balked when I got to the last section of Boettner's book that dealt with the extent of the atonement, or Calvinism.

Always one to finish books, I read on, comfortable with the assurance of being able to just say "No" to God's soteriological sovereignty. Like Singer, Boettner quoted men. Being a book on theology, he quoted Scripture as well, lots of it. When he did not quote verses, he cited them. I had already gotten used to looking up all of Boettner's many verse citations. For the first time in my life, I was actually studying the Bible.

After I finished the last page of *Studies in Theology,* I began Boettner's more formidable *Reformed Doctrine of Predestination.* The Five Points of

---

[19] Richard Wurmbrand, *Tortured for Christ* (Hayfield Publishers, 1967).

Calvinism, which Professor Wood covered in one lecture, were detailed in rather lengthy chapters documented by yet more quotes of men—whose names I began to recognize—and a multitude of Bible verses. After the Five Points, Boettner dealt with objections to the doctrines of grace, which finished off the last remnants of my Methodist Arminian background. Boettner began branching off into other areas of this doctrine. Like Mr. Wood, he seemed to see everything connected by theological doctrine.

One of the last sections of Boettner's book dealt with Calvinism in history. This short history of Calvinist men and ideas is woefully superficial. It is poorly documented, filled with unsubstantiated claims, and almost boastfully triumphal in its tying so much of history to famous Calvinists. All that being said, it is still one of the best essays around about Calvinism. It is still quoted widely in books about history.

Henry Wood revealed to me how little I understood about history. I learned that I knew next to nothing about God and the Bible. I knew facts and anecdotes that all existed randomly in my mind. A Christian worldview was needed to build upon.

From Wurmbrand, I learned what Christianity costs. From Boettner, I learned how to study theology and do so in the light of a sovereign God. When I began reading Rushdoony and Singer again with this worldview in place, they made sense. I now had a foundation for understanding history.

Chapter Ten
Goads and Nails: Reformed Influences

> The words of the wise are like goads, and the words of scholars
> are like well-driven nails, given by one Shepherd.
> And further, my son, be admonished by these.
> Of making many books there is no end,
> and much study is wearisome to the flesh.
> —Ecclesiastes 12:11-12

We are changed by the books we read and the people we meet. Who we are and what we become is largely influenced by those occasions and circumstances where—by assignment of a teacher or by choice—we are engaged in reading a book that forever changes the way we view the world as a whole or at least our own little world. In other cases, we are forever changed by those people whose lives providentially cross our own paths. Sometimes we know these influential people as teachers, sometimes as friends, and sometimes as both. In some very blessed occasions, we know both the book and the author.

Biographies reveal that the most original thinkers were men who learned from others. Mankind is inescapably connected by covenantal bonds of community both spiritually and intellectually. Mankind is inescapably connected historically as well. Paul did not exhort Timothy to find some truth that could be found within himself, but rather he reminds him that he followed Paul's own life and doctrine (2 Timothy 3:10). Earlier when Paul gave instructions to Timothy for training teachers, he presented the Christian model of teaching: "And the things that you have heard from me among many witnesses, commit these to faithful men who will be able to teach others also" (2 Timothy 2:2). Learning within the Christian faith, like all learning, consists in standing on the shoulders of those who came before us.

The Christian teacher has to be taught before he can teach. And the Christian teacher has to recognize an ongoing process of being taught. Especially in a field like history, the teacher has to be a person of many books and much reading. I generally think a person has to read ten books on a particular subject before he can intelligently follow a conversation among the experts. I don't mean ten books on history in a broad sense; what I mean is that you need to read ten books on the American War for Independence, or the Protestant Reformation, or the Crusades before you can follow the conversation on those particular topics. By the time you have read fifty to a hundred books on a particular area, you can begin to really understand the subject. These numbers are arbitrary, but this truth is certain: Never assume that having read a book on a subject makes you an expert in that area. After reading one book you know something, or a lot of somethings. After ten books, you begin to realize how much you don't know. After a hundred books, you might know what it is you don't know.

Along our way, certain writers will influence our thinking more profoundly than others. Maybe it happens because of *when* we read them and maybe it happens because of other external factors. Some books and writers entertain and influence us for the time when we are engaged in reading them. Some influence us for a season. Others influence us for a lifetime. The more foundational books and authors may be reread frequently, but for some books, the original reading has a life-long influence.

In the previous essay, I told about my early experiences in reading the books of R. J. Rushdoony and C. Gregg Singer. Because of the theological changes God brought into my life and thinking, the works of Rushdoony and Singer became foundational for my subsequent study of history. A number of other writers added to the influence of these two. I read books and articles by such Calvinistic thinkers as Gary North, Francis Nigel Lee, Marcellus Kik, J. Gresham Machen, Gordon Clark, Francis Schaeffer, Herbert Schlossberg, Gary DeMar, James Jordan, David Chilton, George Grant, and Greg Bahnsen. While most of these men were not historians and only a few of their books were histories, they still built upon the theological foundations I now had with in-depth Biblical and historical reasoning. Along with Christian thinkers, I did read lots of historical works by academic and popular historians.

I also read lots of political commentators and literary figures. Alexander Solzhenitsyn was a pivotal influence on me, as were other prophetic voices from the Gulags. Biographies, histories, political studies, economic works, and even many novels helped me along the way to better understand the subject of history. Many books piled on the facts, some books broadened my interpretations, and quite a few books supplied anecdotes. But the more important books were those that brought unity to my worldview. It has been those thinkers that drew the lines from history, government, literature, economics, and art back to the Bible that have been most formative.

Goads and Nails: Reformed Influences

These Christian scholars have been goads to me. Like an ox lumbering along the road, I am prone to go ever more slowly and to stop and munch on the grass. Then I read a book, and I am consumed with the desire to know more. Key portions are reread or mulled over. The bibliography is combed over. I keep asking, "How did this writer learn these things?" and "How can I teach this book to others." My mental flanks keep feeling the sharp pricks of these goads, and the effect of one book or topic leads to numerous other ones.

Likewise, the words of scholars are like well-driven nails. Nails bring the random sizes and shapes of boards together to form a structure, a building. Christian scholars emphasize the concept of a Christian worldview. A unity or coherence of thought grows out of this kind of reading. Some authors have focused on the bigger picture of this worldview thinking, while others have focused on particular areas, like government, education, or art. It is like the building of a house. Some of the workmen build the bigger structure, such as the foundations and framing out of the rooms. Other workmen do the detail work, like cabinets. They bring thousands of wooded particulars together into a universal dwelling place.

R. J. Rushdoony (1916-2001)

Rousas John Rushdoony's life history is an amazing story in itself. His parents fled from their Armenian homeland during World War I. At that time, the rulers of Turkey were engaged in efforts to destroy the Armenian Christian population of Turkey. It was the first, and perhaps most neglected, of the twentieth century genocides.[1] Rushdoony's parents barely escaped the murderous Turks, but they made it to the Russian frontier and from there, to New York City where Rousas John was born in 1916.[2] That in itself echoes the terrible nature of their flight: Who ever flees to Russia for asylum and rescue?

Thousands of Armenians fled their homeland and came to the United States. The situation of the Rushdoony's was somewhat unusual in that they were Presbyterians. Armenia has a long history as a Christian kingdom and the Armenian Orthodox Church has been the main source of Armenian Christianity. Protestant missionaries went to Armenia in the nineteenth century, and among the converts to Protestantism was Rushdoony's father.

---

[1] Donald E. Miller and Lorna Touryan Miller, *Survivors: An Oral History of the Armenian Genocide* (Berkeley: University of California Press, 1993).

[2] Mark Rousas Rushdoony, "A Biographical Sketch of My Father" from *A Comprehensive Faith: An International Festschrift For Rousas John Rushdoony*, edited by Andrew Sandlin (San Jose: Friends of Chalcedon, 1996), 21-29.

Rushdoony grew up in a moderately Calvinistic Presbyterian household. The Calvinism, while inescapably present, was diluted, and Biblical orthodoxy was shaky at a few points. But God blesses His covenant people. Our inconsistent, weak, and faltering faith still contains mustard-seed potential. And so, a young Rushdoony came to see the sovereignty of God while reading the Book of Job.

Rushdoony embarked upon a life of ministry and study. His desire for reading and his ability to comprehend vast numbers of books—and remember them—was astounding. Early in life he began a habit of reading a book a day—every day—for the whole of his life. In addition to that, he read articles, magazines, and journals; he researched and referenced books, and he wrote essays, book reviews, sermons, letters, and many books. God was gracious to Rushdoony and the church. Rushdoony would have made a superb academic scholar. By focusing on some particular field, perhaps theology or philosophy, he could have been one of the reigning experts in that area. He would have chaired an important professorship, and his name would have reigned supreme in footnotes of academic journals and the bibliographies of scholarly monographs.

Instead of being an academic scholar, Rushdoony became a lifelong pastor and missionary. Rushdoony bemoaned as a great tragedy the "retreat of scholarship from the pulpit to the school."[3] He pastored churches throughout his career, and during the 1940s, he did mission work at the Duck Valley Indian Reservation in Owyhee, Nevada. But his main pastoral and mission work was outside of the normal bounds we think of when we picture pastors and missionaries. Rushdoony was a pastor to the mind of the Christian church, and he was a missionary to the world of Christian thought.

While his writings often displayed a deep familiarity with the parameters of scholarly debate on theological and other topics, they went even further. Rushdoony was a theologian of both Special Revelation and Natural Revelation. No field of human thought or endeavor seems to have escaped his notice. Hence, he read about science, philosophy, economics, literature, politics, art, music, architecture, sociology, psychology, biography, and above all, history and theology. He was able to synthesize literally thousands of disparate ideas, examples, and insights from the writings of Christians of all persuasions as well as secular writers. From that wide reading, his Christian presuppositions, derived in large part from his reading of Cornelius Van Til, served as a grid or worked like a fish net and caught concepts workable within Christian thinking. He faithfully sought to make every thought captive within the

---

[3] R. J. Rushdoony, *Intellectual Schizophrenia* (Phillipsburg, New Jersey: Presbyterian and Reformed Publishing Co., 1980), Preface, xii.

all-encompassing claims of Christ's Kingdom for the edification of Christ's people. The ideas contained in the following passage from Rushdoony could be replicated from dozens of his books and essays. He writes,

> We need to recognize that nothing is more short-sighted and tragic than the limitations of Christianity to ecclesiastical objectives when its responsibility is in terms of the whole of life, and Jesus Christ is presented as mediator of a cosmic as well as personal redemption. Man is called to exercise his image mandate in knowledge, righteousness, holiness and dominion, subduing the earth agriculturally, scientifically, culturally, artistically, in every possible way asserting the crown rights of King Jesus in every realm of life, claiming the kingdoms of this world as the Kingdoms of our Lord and his Christ.[4]

So many intellectual and Christian streams fed into the river of Rushdoony's thinking that it is an oversimplification to limit it to a few thinkers. Still it is fair to say that along with the full impact of both Old and New Testaments on his heart and mind, Rushdoony's main ideas were largely constructed upon the presuppositional apologetics of Cornelius Van Til,[5] the worldview thinking of Abraham Kuyper,[6] and the postmillennial eschatology of the older Princeton Theological Seminary.

Rushdoony blazed intellectual trails through an astounding number of scholarly disciplines. He began his writing career with a book titled *By What Standard*, which was a defense of the apologetic methods of Cornelius Van Til. But being a true student, he did not simply echo or explain Van Til, he built upon the premises of Van Til's thought. Primarily, Rushdoony applied Van Til's view of factuality and neutrality to all areas of life. If no facts are merely brute facts, but instead are interpreted facts, specifically God-interpreted facts, then this truth applies not just in Biblical exegesis or church work, but it applies to all areas of life and thought. If it is impossible for man in his philosophy, epistemology, and ethics to be neutral, then this too applies to all areas of life. Hence, scientists, historians, philosophers, and plumbers all enter the workplace—be it laboratory, classroom, or cabinet under the kitchen sink—either in covenant obedience to God or in rebellion against

---

[4] Rushdoony, *Intellectual Schizophrenia*, 100.

[5] Cornelius Van Til, *The Defense of the Faith* (Phillipsburg: Presbyterian and Reformed Publishing Co., originally published in 1955).

[6] Abraham Kuyper, *Lectures on Calvinism* (Grand Rapids: Wm. B. Eerdmans, 1978, tenth printing).

him. But even the covenant rebels experience God's common grace; hence, the unbelieving scientist can discover a faster headache remedy, the secular historian can recognize historical truths, the atheistic philosopher can accurately portray the limits of man's choices, and the plumber who goes fishing on Sunday mornings can fix a leaky faucet.

Rushdoony's wide-ranging Christian worldview interests led him to writing books on philosophical problems, political issues, science, and education. His study of the historical problem of the One and the Many, titled *The One and the Many*[7], took this arcane topic and approached it Biblically. In other words, the answer was not to be found in the unity or oneness of all things as proposed by the ancient Greek philosopher Musaeus or in the diversity and randomness of Heraclitus' philosophy. The ancient Greeks succeeded only in laying out the parameters of the problem. The two biggest guns in Greek philosophy parted ways over this issue. It is aptly illustrated in Raphael's painting, "The School of Athens," which shows Plato pointing one finger up, signifying the One Unity or Ideal, and Aristotle pointing his fingers downward, signifying the world of Many Particulars. In the Triune God, both One and Three, this philosophical problem—with its many everyday practical effects—finds it solution.

In his book *The Politics of Guilt and Pity*, Rushdoony commented on the political scene emerging out of the 1960s.[8] This was at the height of the political Liberalism. Democrat President Lyndon Johnson's trouncing of conservative Republican candidate Barry Goldwater portended a demise of the last elements of conservative politics, states' rights, and personal freedom. Goldwater's conservatism, like so much of the conservative movement as a whole, was as much based on secular humanism as was Johnson's big government liberalism. Standing alongside the depressed state of conservatism was the failed state of liberalism. Johnson's presidency was doomed by two wars he waged: The war in Vietnam and the war on poverty. The older establishmentarian liberalism spawned a more radical new liberalism that found itself in the riots on college campuses and in the major urban centers.

Rushdoony did not make the particular hot button issues of his day, like campus rioting on the left or anti-communism on the right, his main focus. Like Robert L. Dabney, Rushdoony looked past the evening news and examined the core issues from a biblical perspective.[9] At the heart of the Liberal

---

[7] R. J. Rushdoony, *The One and the Many: Studies in the Philosophy of Ultimacy and Order* (Fairfax, Virginia: Thoburn Press, 1978).

[8] R. J. Rushdoony, *Politics of Guilt and Pity* (Vallecito: Ross House Books, 1995, originally published by Presbyterian and Reformed Publishing in 1970).

answer to every question at home and abroad was not whether or not injustices had been done to minorities (they had) or whether government aid could cure social poverty (it couldn't). It was resentment and envy that fueled American politics. The American political system implied and enforced the ideas that those who are the "Have's" should feel guilty for those who are "Have Not's" and the "Have Not's" should feel a right to those things denied them. And by governmental expropriations, the "Have Not's" were "entitled" to receive what they lacked. These motivations still underlie much of the political agenda of American politics.

It was this basic impulse toward guilt and pity that gave impetus to all varieties of socialism. Marxism was predicated on this completely. Socialism was only a milder view of the same. American liberalism—stemming from the same roots—offered the same solutions. By going to the most basic premises, Rushdoony wrote a political study that applies as much to the present as it did at the time of its writing. One of the great insights of Rushdoony, repeated many times in his books and lectures, was his emphasis on the different realms of government. We commonly use the word *government* as a synonym for state and federal agencies and offices. But, as Rushdoony pointed out, this was merely civil government, and as such, was just one of several levels of government.[10]

True government is, first of all, the government of God. As always, in true Calvinistic fashion, Rushdoony connected all the lines back to God. Church, family, workplace, and community were all levels of government. This emphasis echoed the sphere sovereignty discussions of such Dutch thinkers as Abraham Kuyper and Herman Dooyeweerd, both of whom influenced Rushdoony.[11] A very critical area of government was the school, and it was here that Rushdoony blazed yet another significant trail. In fact, many Christian schools and homeschooling families today may not be aware of who Rushdoony was, but without him, Christian private and homeschools would likely not enjoy the freedoms and successes they have today.

Rushdoony's initial works on education were two rather weighty books. They were not aimed at showing how people could start Christian schools, develop curriculum, and manage tuition. Those books would have to come later, just like window curtains in a house being built. Rushdoony worked on

---

[9] Mark Rousas Rushdoony, "My Recollection of Chalcedon's First Forty Years" from, *Faith for All of Life*, September/October 2005, 4-5.

[10] Rushdoony, *Politics of Guilt and Pity*, pages 331-343.

[11] Rushdoony wrote introductions to Dooyeweerd's books *In the Twilight of Western Thought* and *The Christian Idea of the State*. See Ben House "Rushdoony and Dooyeweerd" in *Faith for All of Life* (Jan/Feb 2008) 19-22.

the foundations. His book *Intellectual Schizophrenia* showed the Van Tillian necessity of Christian thinking necessary for Christian education. To some degree, it focused on the bulldozing needed before even the foundations could be laid; in this case, the tax-supported, allegedly neutral government school system had to be—and still needs to be—pushed out of the way of Christian thinking before Christian curriculum decisions can be finalized. After that, the focus could turn to other matters. Rushdoony never cared for supposed Christian schools that were actual secular schools with prayer, chapel, and Bible class. Granted that would be better than secular schooling without those things; still it is not Christian education.

Because he understood that Christian salvation is found only in the saving, atoning work of Christ on the Cross, Rushdoony cast out any and all humanistic religious answers to man's problem. This was a basic Rushdoony insight: Every subject, every academic discipline, every philosophy, and every idea is at the heart religious. All thought that attempts to stand on its own legs apart from the God of the Bible is proposing its own autonomous answer to the question "What must I do to be saved?" A national religion and a state church are unavoidable. In the American experience, the public school system became the state church. Horace Mann was Moses and John Dewey was King David. They established public schooling as the means of saving man from himself and from what they saw as the constraints of Christianity. Hence, Rushdoony's magnum opus on education was titled *The Messianic Character of American Education.*[12] Bit by bit, he exposed the humanistic and messianic expectations and aims of American educators. Some of his targets were Christian educators whose theology fatally truncated faith and learning; some were classicists who found the basic answers to life's questions in the Greeks and the Romans.

Gary North described Rushdoony's *Messianic Character of American Education* as "a highly condensed, thoroughly documented, and theologically astute critique of the educational philosophies of over two dozen of the major founders and philosophers of American progressive education, from Horace Mann to John Dewey. Nothing like it had ever been published before, and nothing equal to it has been published since."[13]

The high point of Rushdoony's writing career came in 1973 with the publication of his massive book *The Institutes of Biblical Law*. Next to the *Roe V. Wade* decision of that same year, it was one of the most important theological developments and challenges of that time. Rushdoony took what

---

[12] R. J. Rushdoony, *The Messianic Character of American Education: Studies in the History of the Philosophy of Education*, (Vallecito: Ross House Books, 1995, originally published in 1963).
[13] Gary North, "R. J. Rushdoony, R. I. P." from *Chalcedon Report* (April 2001), 20.

everyone gave lip service to—the Ten Commandments—and he proposed something quite radical: Christians should live by and promote the Bible in its entirety in all areas of life. And when Rushdoony said Bible, he did not mean just the New Testament, or the Sermon on the Mount, or the red-letter words of Christ. This work was a groundbreaking study of Old Testament Law in its particular details. Each commandment was treated in what could have been a separate book, and each commandment was applied exhaustively to personal Christian living and church life, and more. The civil government, society at large, and all social institutions were called into account and made responsible for implementing God's Law-Word.

Being a book by Rushdoony, *The Institutes,* with its title echoing Calvin's classic, was filled with a voluminous range of insights and footnotes from theologians and writers of all stripes. The book-a-day every-day reading schedule had garnered an incredible range of quips, quotes, anecdotes, insanities, and insights that Rushdoony was able to marshal when needed. Like most of Rushdoony's work, this tome reached a core audience of thinkers, pastors, and teachers. Much of Rushdoony's subsequent work, including two companion volumes titled *The Institutes of Biblical Law, Volume 2* and *Volume 3* and *Salvation and Godly Rule,* were expansions and commentaries upon the basic ideas of the first volume of the *Institutes.*

Had the books mentioned above been all that Rushdoony wrote, he would still be a major Reformed thinker in the Twentieth Century. His application of Christianity in the fields of apologetics, philosophy, education, and law were all path-breaking, paradigm-shifting, and Scriptural. But Rushdoony's writings expanded into even more areas. In the 1960s, when political Liberalism was in its heyday and the conservative alternative was an unworkable coalition of John Birch anti-Communists, Southern segregationalists, and establishment Republicans wanting to slow down the New Deal,[14] Rushdoony began Chalcedon Foundation, which began providing Christian blueprints and vision for all areas of life. For many years, this center for Christian studies did not have buildings, but was an outgrowth of Rushdoony's ideas and readings and that of other scholars attracted to that same vision. Just as Gutenberg's printing press had once become the vehicle for spreading Martin Luther's Ninety-Five Theses, so now the mimeograph machine began cranking out essays by Rushdoony on a variety of topics—theology, politics, education, and culture—to spur on a reformation in thinking.

---

[14] Rick Perlstein, *Before the Storm: Barry Goldwater and the Unmaking of the American Concensus* (New York: Hill and Wang, 2001).

The work of Chalcedon, and of Rushdoony in particular, became like a long extended footnote to Abraham Kuyper's 1898 Stone Foundation Lectures delivered at Princeton University and later titled *Lectures on Calvinism*. In those lectures, Kuyper outlined Calvinism, first, as a life-system, or what we more often call a Worldview or World and Life View. Calvinism, then, was not merely Five Points or an explanation of how God saves sinners; instead, it was a life-embracing system of thought. God's sovereignty extended beyond the walls of the church and the soul of the believer. Every square inch of the universe belongs to God, Kuyper asserted. From there, Kuyper examined the Calvinistic worldview in the areas of religion, politics, science, art, and the future. Rushdoony built upon these areas, not always in exact agreement with Kuyper, but expanding beyond him. His goal was initially to found a Christian university, and to some extent, Rushdoony's university campus reached throughout the world.

Being outside the secular academic circles and even viewed suspiciously by the Christian college and seminary circles, Rushdoony was ignored often, scorned occasionally, and kept at a distance frequently. Still, the range and depth of his books and essays managed to intrude his thought into Reformed and evangelical circles. John Frame noted in one of the few reviews given to *The Institutes of Biblical Law* that Reformed thinkers could not safely or wisely ignore Rushdoony's thinking.[15]

Rushdoony gained prominence in time as a theologian and writer. His role in the movement called Christian Reconstruction, in the foundation called Chalcedon, and in the theological emphases of the application of God's Law, of postmillennialism, and of Cornelius Van Til's apologetic method are all highlighted by both his friends and enemies. Along with being a key influence in Christian private and homeschool movement, the Creation Science movement, the political Christian Right, and Christian Reconstruction, Rushdoony was a very gifted historian and history teacher. He taught the importance of history and the delights of history. His philosophy of history echoed his Calvinistic and Kuyperian worldview. His analysis of history was most centrally focused on theology.

Rushdoony's role as a historian is not always as prominent as it needs to be. Perhaps it was the more controversial areas, particularly the debates over Biblical law and postmillennialism—and Rushdoony's connection of the two—that have caused his historical writings to be less noticed. Still, it was in the field of history that his insights first caught my attention and formed my thinking in the field of history.

---

[15] John Frame, *Westminster Theological Journal*, 38:2 (Winter, 1976), 195-217.

Rushdoony the Historian

As Christian history teachers, we are always looking for the perfect textbook. That is, we want the textbook that includes Christian historical figures, Christian influences, and Christian interpretations, all done with high scholarly standards and exciting narratives and lots of original source materials. One such history textbook does exist, the product of a fantastic team of writers and glorious Editor, but its coverage of history does not quite reach 70 A.D. That same text tells us "The works of the Lord are great, studied by all who have pleasure in them" (Psalm 111:2). We are commissioned to bring every thought captive to Christ (2 Corinthians 10:5). One of the Christian tasks, then, is to reconstruct the works of God and man in history.

Jesus preached to the multitudes, but He gave special focus upon teaching the Apostles. Likewise, Ezra, having studied the Law of God diligently (Ezra 7:10), taught the Law to a gathering of all the children of Israel (Nehemiah 7:73b), but then conducted a seminar for the leaders, priests, and Levites (Nehemiah 8:13). Building a movement involves reaching the masses, but more so, it involves educating the core group who will provide the leadership. Rushdoony's key works were geared toward reaching and teaching the core leaders.

Andrew Sandlin noted,

> Despite, or rather, because, of his commitment to the binding authority of God's Word, Rushdoony was an unflagging advocate of liberty: political, religious, and ecclesiastical. Two of his books from the 60s, *The Nature of the American System* and *This Independent Republic* showed that the United States' heritage of freedom is anchored squarely in the Bible and the Christian Faith.[16]

It was in large part from those two books that I began to see the impact of Christianity on American history.

In *This Independent Republic,* Rushdoony presented thirteen essays, previously given as lectures, on issues relating to the American colonial experience and early history as a nation. His goal was to give a Christian view of American history that would counter views overly influenced by Marxian or Enlightenment thought. Concerning the rich, and neglected, roots of American history, Rushdoony said,

---

[16] Andrew Sandlin, "R. J. Rushdoony: Champion of Faith and Liberty" in *Chalcedon Report* (April 2001), 11.

Not only is it the oldest of Western countries in consecutive and unbroken inheritance in civil government, having been free of revolutions and internal chaos, but its origins are Christian and Augustinian, deeply rooted in Reformation, medieval, and patristic thought. It is held, moreover, that the United States, from its origins in the Colonial period on through the Constitution, represented a Protestant feudal restoration.[17]

Rushdoony established several patterns in this book that would characterize his greater approach to history and learning. First, he demonstrated a wide familiarity with scholars of American history, both current and older. Simply reading the abundant footnotes of his book, as well as list of suggested readings he included in an appendix, gives a virtual who's who among American historians. Rushdoony gleaned insights and quotes from his readings, but he also interacted with the scholars, often strongly disagreeing with their conclusions.[18] Rushdoony believed that in the common grace of God, men are able to discover great truths; hence, the wealth of the sinner-historians was laid up for the righteous.

Second, the all-encompassing, wide breadth of reading and study is a requirement for the Christian history teacher. To just read Rushdoony would be to misunderstand the mission of Rushdoony. But this wide sweep of the net has to have a framework, or keeping with the analogy, a network. Rushdoony said, "The writing of history then, because man is neither autonomous, objective, or ultimately creative, is always in terms of a framework, a philosophical and ultimately religious framework in the mind of the historian."[19] It was Rushdoony's Christian worldview that provided the framework. A belief in the Sovereignty of God, the infallibility of Scripture, the particulars of Reformed theology, and the presuppositional apologetics of Cornelius Van Til all made up the key parts of Rushdoony's approach to history. In fact, his second collection of essays, *The Nature of the American System,* is dedicated to Van Til, who Rushdoony calls a philosopher and teacher to the generations. His preface is an application of Van Til's thought to the field of history. There is no neutrality in any area of life, and history especially demonstrates man's recognition of God or rebellion against Him.

In the Book of Daniel we are told that God gave Daniel and his companions knowledge, skill in all literature, and wisdom (Daniel 1:17). Comparing

---

[17] Rushdoony, *This Independent Republic*, Introduction, page vii.
[18] See Rushdoony, *This Independent Republic*, page 145, for example, where he strongly disagrees with Crane Brinton.
[19] Rushdoony, *The Nature of the American System*, A Preface on the Writing of History, page vi.

this to Rushdoony's method of doing history, the knowledge is the Biblical foundations. The skill in all literature comes from the many trips to the library to read what the thinkers and scholars have written. This is the research, the collateral reading, the compilation of books, essays, lecture notes, and examination of original documents. All these facts and interpretations are then sifted through the knowledge portion, or the net. Wisdom is the separation of useful facts and ideas from those that are not needed or are wrong. History teaching never has the goal of producing encyclopedias, but wisdom and insights.

Christians need not shy away from historians who hold different or even anti-Christian perspectives. Historians like Will Durant, Barbara Tuchman, and Perry Miller can yield useful insights for Christian thinkers. Many historians conceal their own religious and philosophical views carefully, but still do history quite well. Whether gleaning from the innumerable books coming off the presses or from sitting in the university classrooms, Christian history teachers need the knowledge of historians outside of their own personal sectarian and political views.

A third characteristic of Rushdoony was his highlighting of particular books, people, and ideas that had been ignored or neglected. Hence, in *This Independent Republic,* we learn of the influence of John Witherspoon, the Calvinist theologian who was a signer of the Declaration of Independence. Witherspoon is still regarded as the forgotten Founding Father.[20] Rushdoony also brought out the influence of the Calvinistic tract *Vindiciæ Contra Tyrannos,* which he contends, based on John Adams' observation, was more influential in the American War for Independence than the works of Thomas Paine. In *The Nature of the American System,* he devotes a whole chapter to a neglected American political thinker, Fisher Ames, and another chapter to an underrated political figure, President Andrew Johnson.[21]

Fourth, Rushdoony boldly ventured forth with strong convictions and interpretations that went against the scholarship and political climate of his day. His writings were quite conservative, without being tied to the conservative movement and figures, with whom he was more than willing to disagree on many issues. Not only did he strongly posit Christianity as the key factor in early American history and thought, he wrote against centralization, egalitarianism, internationalism, and democracy. Never did he present a view simply to be contrary; rather, his arguments were buttressed with quotes of theologians and historians and supported from his theological base and readings. In

---

[20] Jeffrey H. Morrison, *John Witherspoon and the Founding of the American Republic* (Notre Dame, IN: University of Notre Dame Press, 2005), 1-18.

[21] Rushdoony, *The Nature of the American System*, Chapters 2 and 3.

the midst of the Civil Rights Movement, Rushdoony revealed the racial prejudice of Lincoln and the Abolitionists. Such interpretations, along with his support for state governments, but even more for county and local spheres,[22] led to Rushdoony's favorable views of the Southern cause in the War Between the States. Such a position has almost always been unacceptable in both academic and popular circles. But Rushdoony was not captive to neo-Confederate thought any more than he was captive to the political correctness of his day, the conservative movement of the 1960s, or the Yankee hegemony over historical interpretations of the War Between the States. In fact, Rushdoony's dislike of John C. Calhoun's Unitarian leanings led him to frequently describe the war as the Unitarian War.

Fifth, and notice here how I am inescapably imitating Rushdoony, Rushdoony frequently presented his ideas in numerical lists. He explained *Vindiciae Contra Tyrannos* in terms of four key teachings that gave legality to the American Revolution. The limited powers of government, as opposed to centralized sovereignty, are described with three points.[23] Three points are given for the renewal of localism.[24] Seven points are used to clarify the controversial concept of equality.[25] The relationship of Christianity to government is defined in four points.[26] In a brilliant comparison and contrast of the American and French Revolutions, Rushdoony outlined fourteen points that illustrated the philosophy of the Enlightenment, the French Revolution, and all their political and social results.[27] This method reveals that at heart Rushdoony was never primarily the academic scholar garnering research, but instead, he was the teacher giving lecture notes to his students.

Boiling the Enlightenment down to fourteen points, and similarly reducing key issues in history to a few outlines, carries a certain stigma and danger. The stigma is that of being labeled as simplistic. The Christian has to recognize that we have to be simplistic because we are finite. We and our students are not only finite, but ignorant. The whole range of books that have covered the Enlightenment and the French Revolution are beyond my reach, and certainly beyond my students's reach. As a teacher, I must simplify, outline, and make accessible to my own mind and that of my students great and sweeping events of history. Rushdoony made himself vulnerable to the pro-

---

[22] Rushdoony, *This Independent Republic*, Chapter 2 "Federalism and Feudalism."
[23] *This Independent Republic*, 33-40.
[24] *This Independent Republic*, 55.
[25] *This Independent Republic*, 66-67.
[26] *This Independent Republic*, 113.
[27] *This Independent Republic*, 134-155, Chapter 10 "The French Revolution and the American Conservative Counter-Revolution."

fessional historians by his sweeping generalizations, but he was looking at his students, not as his academic reputation. Still, there is a danger in such lists. Without the student, and teacher, reading beyond the list or outline, history is not properly studied. History is incredibly complex and the sources inexhaustible. The list, the lecture points, and the outline can only be the beginnings.

This Independent Republic and *The Nature of the American System* constitute Rushdoony's main work on American history. In the 1970s, he taught a history class at Fairfax Christian School in Fairfax, Virginia. His lectures from that class were recorded. Along with the lectures, he assigned two readings. One was Ernest Lee Tuveson's *Redeemer Nation: The Idea of America's Millennial Role*[28] and the other was Alexis de Tocqueville's *Democracy in America*. Tuveson's book was the type of study Rushdoony often gleaned from with profit. It was the work of a secular historian who examined certain religious themes in America's history. Rushdoony lifted the postmillennial insights from Tuveson's research and combined them with his own study of postmillennial influences on Columbus, the Puritans, and the Founding Fathers. From de Tocqueville, he lifted portions dealing with localism, voluntary agencies, and Christianity as the focus of his lectures. While Rushdoony's writings were generally analytical, heavily documented, and scholarly, his lectures were filled with stories, biographical sketches, and humor. In short, he was the consummate Christian history teacher: Stories and outlines, wit and wisdom, all built upon sound Biblical foundations.

In addition to his studies and lectures on American history, Rushdoony did a ten part lecture series on world history that was recorded. Once again, he demonstrated his ability to marshal great portions of historical research together in a presentable format. Once again, he showed how biography, anecdotes, contemporary application, and humor are all ingredients for teaching history. This lecture series was supplemented by a whole book of notes, published in a spiral bound format and titled *World History Notes.*[29] Both the lectures and the notes are good sources of history and guides to books and topics for study. In *The Foundations of Social Order: Studies in the Creeds and Councils of the Early Church,* Rushdoony examines how the creeds and church councils helped protect the church from the dangers of Greek thought and other heresies. While this book presents neither a history of the early church nor of the West, it once again posits a key emphasis in Rushdoony's thought—the importance of understanding the religious presuppositions of a culture.

---

[28] Ernest Lee Tuveson, *Redeemer Nation: The Idea of America's Millennial Role* (Chicago: University of Chicago Press, 1968).

[29] R. J. Rushdoony, *World History Notes* (Vallecito: Ross House Books, 1945).

He states, "Every social order rests on a creed, on a concept of life and law, and represents a religion in action."[30]

This emphasis on understanding not just history, but the foundations of life and thought undergirding history, was the emphasis in his book *The Biblical Philosophy of History*. This book brought into one central focus what Rushdoony spread throughout all his writings. Again, it was an emphasis on the nature of God as Triune and Sovereign, on Christ as both God and Man, on the Scriptures as infallible and authoritative, and on man's religious nature either as covenant keeper or covenant breaker in both his actions and thought. Repeatedly, Rushdoony appealed to the Sovereignty of God, the truth of Scripture, and the Incarnation of Christ to examine currents of thought among historians, philosophers, and thinkers. Rushdoony said, "Jesus Christ is the exegesis, the declaration, the revelation of God. In Him the exegesis of God and of all God's purposes, including the meaning of history is manifested. Because Christ is the truth, the exegesis of God, the primacy of history is with Him and in Him, and the truth of history."[31]

Rushdoony never penned a best seller or pastored a mega-church or started a university. He did lots of preaching and teaching the Bible, and lots of teaching about history and other subjects from a Christian viewpoint. He encouraged and endorsed lots of Christian thinkers and works. Lots of Christians who don't know his name or never read his books have been influenced by his ideas. If you are a history teacher, read Rushdoony, and then pass on his insights to your students. Also, include Rushdoony himself in your history teaching. Andrew Sandlin said that Rushdoony was the man most responsible for the revival of Christian political action in the 1970s.[32] Right after Ronald Reagan was inaugurated in 1981, *Newsweek* identified Rushdoony's Chalcedon Foundation as the think tank of the Religious Right.[33] His life and labors, and particularly his books, certainly changed the world we now live in.

Charles Gregg Singer (1910-1999)

Gregg Singer was a contemporary with Rushdoony and a fellow combatant in many battles for the cause of Christ in the fields of history and philosophy. Both were Calvinist and Presbyterian scholars. Both were fellow

---

[30] Rushdoony, *The Foundations of Social Order: Studies in the Creeds and Councils of the Early Church* (Thoburn Press: Fairfax, Virginia, 1978).

[31] R. J. Rushdoony, *The Biblical Philosophy of History* (Nutley, N. J.: Presbyterian and Reformed Publishing Co, 1974).

[32] Sandlin, *Chalcedon Report*, 11.

[33] North, *Chalcedon Report*, 19.

contributors of essays to scholarly Christian works.[34] Both were students of Cornelius Van Til, who in turn wrote books applying Van Til's thought to theology and philosophy.[35] While the range of topics and amount of writing that Rushdoony did was incredibly extensive, Singer confined most of his writing to history and philosophy. While Rushdoony was primarily seeking to undergird historical scholarship with Christian presuppositions, Singer was primarily analyzing historical ideas that departed from Christian presuppositions. While Rushdoony, although personally of Presbyterian convictions, labored for the broader Christian community, Singer devoted much of his teaching to Presbyterian interests.

Singer's primary work was *A Theological Interpretation of American History*, which was first published in 1964.[36] This work was far from being a Christian history of America. Instead, it was a supplemental reader, an interpretive sidebar to the general histories of the United States. To borrow from Richard Weaver's title *Ideas Have Consequences*, Singer's book contains a study of intellectual currents in our history and the bad fruit generally spawned from such currents.

Like Rushdoony and Van Til, Singer pointed to the fundamental flaw in otherwise scholarly historians and histories. Commenting on such historians as Merle Curti, Perry Miller, Henry Commager, Charles Beard, and others, Singer notes that they have rightfully "laid hold on some aspect of historical truth."[37] But he goes on to point out:

> As valuable as these studies are, they lose a great deal of their effectiveness as guides to our understanding of history because, all too frequently, they are not presented in the light of the predominant theological and metaphysical issues of the day. Too seldom have these historians given theology its proper place as a determining factor in intellectual life.[38]

---

[34] See *The Philosophy of Gordon H. Clark*, edited by Ronald H. Nash (Philadelphia: The Presbyterian and Reformed Publishing Company, 1968). Rushdoony wrote on Clark's view of education and Singer on his views of the state. Also, see *The Foundations of Christian Scholarship: Essays in the Van Til Perspective*, edited by Gary North. (Vallecito: Ross House Books, 1979).

[35] Rushdoony, *By What Standard* (Tyler, TX: Thoburn Press, 1985), and Singer, *From Rationalism to Irrationalism* (Phillipsburg: The Presbyterian and Reformed Publishing Company, 1979).

[36] Never interpret events from the news headlines. Barry Goldwater's conservative run for the presidency was buried in a landslide in 1964. That same year, Ronald Reagan made his political debut with a speech given on Goldwater's behalf. That same year, key books by Singer and Rushdoony were published.

[37] Singer, *Theological Interpretation*, 3.

[38] Singer, 5.

He goes on to address the great issue in Christian scholarship and the study of history. Intellectual life and faith were divided. There were two stories of reality—the lower story which constitutes this world, and thereby, encompasses scholarship, and a higher story, which is personal and spiritual.[39] Concerning scholars who might actually be Christians—in their own hearts and on Sunday mornings—Singer says, "Whatever may be their personal convictions toward the biblical message of redemption, they refuse its claims of authority in the world of scholarship."[40] In contrast with this subdued faith, Singer asserts that only "in the light of the Christian revelation can American history be brought into a proper perspective."[41]

Singer began his survey of history with the Puritans. He brought out important aspects of the Puritan influence, in particular the Puritan elements in Virginia. In some ways, the Puritan foundations are presented as the standard from which subsequent historical eras would be evaluated. In a surprising contrast to the many optimistic and progressive approaches to history, Singer presents a view of an America that never recovered from its loss of Puritan theology. As he states concerning the decline of Puritanism, "Its dethronement from a position of supremacy has cast its shadow over every succeeding epoch and generation; its effects are seen not only in the life of churches but in American political, social and economic development as well."[42]

At a time when the historians and popular opinions regarded the Puritan era as a time of spiritual oppression and political shackles, to suddenly cast this as the measuring rod for subsequent generations was quite bold. Singer was advancing beyond Perry Miller's scholarship, which said "Respect and study the Puritans." Singer was saying, "Bring back the Puritans." All too often when Christian teachers lift up a person or figure out of history for special attention, our critics go crazy. If we honor Augustine, we must be endorsing the suppression of the Donatists; if we praise Calvin, we must approve the execution of Servetus; if we admire Robert E. Lee, we must want to re-institute slavery. But Christian history is not premised on a reactionary view of time. Recognizing that a steak dinner I ate yesterday at noon is better than a bologna sandwich today is not a call for turning back the clock or repeating mistakes I made yesterday. Biblically speaking, it is wisdom. The

---

[39] This dichotomy has been addressed by many Christian writers, including Schaeffer in *How Should We Then Live*, Nancy Pearcey in *Total Truth*, and recently by David Wells in *Above All Earthly Powers: Christ in a Post-Modern World* (Grand Rapids: William B. Eerdmans Publishing Company, 2005)..

[40] Singer, 6

[41] Singer, 6.

[42] Singer, 21.

Bible praises Abraham, Moses, and David, without endorsing their faults.

So Singer was right in his general approach to history. Details about Puritan failings have their place, but those eras and epochs of history that have a more consistent Christian worldview call for honor and study. Such times and histories include the Byzantine Empire, the Christian Medieval period, and the Puritan eras in England and America. In fact, Singer called upon Christians to "concentrate their efforts in order to write their histories for the glory of God" in such fields as church history itself, the Renaissance and Reformation, the Enlightenment and French Revolution, and the Puritan era.[43]

The prevailing theology that replaced Puritanism, according to Singer, was Deism.[44] Singer goes against Rushdoony and lots of other Christian interpreters of American history, for he proposes that Deism as a political philosophy produced the American Revolution. The American War for Independence would not have occurred, according to Singer, without the decline of Puritanism and the rise of this more democratic theology that denied the Fall of Man, the saving work of Christ, and the Scriptures.

In those naïve days when I first discovered Calvinists, I assumed they were all in lock step agreement on everything. Here early on, I began finding key differences between Singer and Rushdoony. God often tells me, "So you thought it would all be easy?" The Christian study of history is not always easy; Christian interpretations and conclusions are not always exact. Christian studies of history that portray all our Founding Fathers as pious churchmen, the Constitution as a theological appendix to Scripture, and early American life as one big long Sunday school class are as guilty of misrepresentation as those who suppress religious elements of the history.

Singer's study of Deism highlights some of the tensions of the Founding Era. Worldviews then, as now, were in conflict. Ideas and concepts were battled over by the Christians and by the Deists. The language of liberty was appealed to by both Calvinists and Free Thinkers. Gary Amos wrote a whole book on the Christian elements in the Declaration of Independence to answer Singer's contention that the Declaration was a secular and deistic document.[45] Iron sharpens iron, but it does so only by the two being clashed together.

Singer's study of "Transcendentalism and the Rise of Modern Democ-

---

[43] Singer, "The Problem of Historical Interpretation," from *Foundations of Christian Scholarship*, ed. by Gary North (Vallecito, CA: Ross House Books, 1979), 72.

[44] Singer, *Theological Interpretation*, Chapter 2, "Deism in Colonial Life."

[45] Gary Amos, *Defending the Declaration* (Brentwood, TN: Wolgemuth & Hyatt, Publishers, Inc., 1990), 22.

racy" has long been one of my favorite parts of his book. Like Rushdoony, Singer spoke favorably of the South and its role in the War Between the States. In this chapter, Singer strongly defended the South and gave a completely different justification for secession and the war than was usually found. There were three currents that Singer highlighted in this story.

The first was the theological and political aberrations of the New England Transcendentalists. Usually this crowd, in particular Ralph Waldo Emerson and Henry David Thoreau, has been honored as literary and cultural icons of American thought. The more weird and anti-Christian elements of the Transcendentalists have been ignored in light of Emerson and Thoreau's sentiments about nature and individuality. The Abolitionists, who sprang from much of the same cultural milieu, were not merely trying to find solutions to the problem of Negro slavery. There were groups, both in the north and the south, who were vexed over slavery. Generally, such groups were advocating colonization of slaves back in Africa. The Abolitionists, according to Singer, were much more revolutionary and violent in their approach to the slave problem.

The second emphasis Singer makes is that of the Southern response in the 1830s. In contrast with the theological deviations found in New England and other parts of the North, there was a reaction to Unitarianism in the South along with a revival of Calvinistic orthodoxy. Singer says, "After 1830 there was a growing philosophical and theological cleavage between the North and the South. While the North was becoming increasingly subject to radical influences, the South was becoming increasingly conservative in its outlook."[46] Other historians have concurred about this Southern turn toward Calvinistic orthodoxy. Francis B. Simpkins wrote, "After 1830 the Southern mind was captured…by a group of orthodox Presbyterian theologians."[47] At one point in time, students at William and Mary College had been fans of the French Revolution, but in 1836, the president of the college, Thomas R. Dew addressed them as follows:

> The Atheist has long since been overthrown by the light of nature, and the Deist by that of revelation. The Infidel and the Christian have fought the battle, and the latter has won the victory.[48]

Singer's third point builds upon this Southern orthodoxy. He states that Southern theologians prophetically saw the dangers of Abolitionism as an

---
[46] Singer, 83.
[47] Simkins, as quoted in John Boles, *The Great Revival*, 189.
[48] Dew, as quoted in Boles, 190.

ideology and of radical democracy. It was the theological aspects of the war and of the Southern cause that were foremost in the mind of key Southern thinkers, and in this case, thinkers who were primarily Presbyterian ministers. Singer says,

> [A]fter 1840 these same leaders of Old School thought took a very strong stand against Abolitionism as a movement, not because it was opposed to slavery per se, but because of the philosophy and theology it represented, and because they clearly saw that if this radicalism were to gain the supremacy in the national government, then there must certainly come in its wake a radical political and social program which would threaten the established order and constitutional government for the nation as a whole. J. H. Thornwell, Robert Dabney, B. B. Palmer, and William Plumer were all of one mind in their own theological convictions, and in their discernment of the threat which the abolitionist movement held for the American people.[49]

The boldness of Singer's thesis provokes controversy to this day. He picks the "wrong" people for heroes and villains. Defending the Confederacy, and doing so on a self-consciously Christian basis, is hotly contested even within Christian circles. But wherever an individual Christian finally lands on the issue of the causes and conduct of the American War Between the States, the Christian history teacher has to carefully read and evaluate both sides of issues.

Singer's defense of the South has been bolstered in recent years by the wide reprinting of the works of Southern Presbyterians, such as Thornwell, Dabney, Palmer, and Plumer.[50] Also, the historian Eugene Genovese, whose political leanings are avowedly Marxist, has defended the principles of Southern Christian thinkers in his numerous studies. The works of M. E. Bradford and Richard Weaver are also useful in this study. A major study that presents the War Between the States from Christian perspective, with a strong Southern flavor, is John J. Dwyer's *War Between the States: America's Uncivil War*.[51] Within the broader Christian school movement, the War Between the States, and the South in particular, is beginning to be studied and evaluated in a far

---

[49] Singer, 84.
[50] Most of these reprints have been done by Sprinkle Publications, which is the work of a Baptist Calvinist, Lloyd Sprinkle. Sprinkle Publications, Harrisonburg, Virginia.
[51] John J. Dwyer, with George Grant, J. Steven Wilkins, Douglas Wilson, and Tom Spencer, *The War Between the States: America's Uncivil War* (Denton, Texas: Bluebonnet Press, 2005).

more balanced and discerning way than has ever been done before. Here, as in many areas of historiography, Singer helped pave the way.

The second half of Singer's *Theological Interpretation* dealt with Social Darwinism, the Social Gospel, and Theological Liberalism. An updated version of the book carried the discussion up through the 1980s. His Christian worldview, his interpretation of movements, and his emphasis on understanding the intellectual currents over the historical events all impacted my own understanding and teaching of history. Whether one accepts Singer's disagreement with the American Revolution and his agreement with the Southern Confederacy or whether one disagrees with the particulars is not the only point of his book.

No doubt Singer, like all teachers, wanted to persuade his students to agree with him. But his greater emphasis was always on the Christian history students thinking Christianly. In his essay where he applies Cornelius Van Til's insights to history, Singer says,

> No historian is neutral. No historian can passively allow the cold facts to speak through him. At every point in his historical investigations the scholar betrays his own frame of reference in choosing the area of history in which he does his research and in the facts he will ultimately use out of the mass of data he has collected and in the meaning he assigns to those facts. Such neutrality is impossible because man is a thinking being, and as a thinking being he is under compulsion to find meaning and purpose in all that he does.[52]

Reiterating this point even more strongly, Singer declared that every "historian is either a covenant breaker and therefore at enmity with God or through the new birth he is a new creation in Christ Jesus, possessing the mind of Christ as he engages in historical research."[53]

Singer's short book *John Calvin: His Roots and Fruits* is a great introduction to the ideas and influence of the Genevan Reformer. His booklet *Christian Approaches to Philosophy, to History* is a stirring call to Christians to approach both those disciplines with zeal. A more detailed book, *From Rationalism to Irrationality*, is a type of companion volume to his *Theological Interpretation of American History*. In this case, he surveys world history from the Greeks to the twentieth century with a particular focus on philosophical developments. The book is a heavy weight version of what Schaeffer set out to cover in *How*

---

[52] Singer, "The Problem of Historical Interpretation," 69-70.
[53] Singer, 70.

Should We Then Live. Unlike Schaeffer and very much like Rushdoony, Singer directly credits and dedicates the book to Van Til, whose "basic epistemology and apologetical principles…offer the key to the proper solution of this tremendously important question."[54] That "tremendously important question" is implied in Singer's subtitled of this work: *The Decline of the Western Mind From the Renaissance to the Present*. Despite the pessimistic sound of it all, Singer concluded with a call for Christians to reconstruct society along biblical principles, no matter how difficult the task.[55]

Singer's main contribution was as a teacher. He was training a generation of Christians how to think and read. He demonstrated that scholarship can be both academically rigorous and biblical in its presuppositions. James Jordan has commented on the type of Christian worldview books that Singer, Rushdoony, and others wrote in the 1960s and 1970s. Jordan says,

> These books were written by serious Bible-believing Calvinists who were engaged with the Reformation but also with the whole history of Christian thought. They were written by men who sought to think presuppositionally, and who did not mind saying so, even if they differed with each other a bit over how to do so. They were men who took seriously the depravity of the mind, and were not fooled by the majority opinions in society, academy, and church.[56]

Now that it is over thirty years since I first read, then reread and began to understand, history from a Christian viewpoint and from Reformed presuppositions, I am not sure exactly at what points I still would agree with Singer and Rushdoony. I still read portions of their works in awe of their insights and boldness, but I know that time and other readings have widened (and hopefully improved) my perspectives. The philosopher Nietzsche got things right on occasion, and one of those occasions was when he observed that a pupil repays his teacher poorly if he remains nothing other than a pupil.[57] What I got from Singer and Rushdoony, and what a student always gets from great teachers, was the foundations on which to begin my own studies.

---

[54] Singer, *From Rationalism to Irrationality*, (Phillipsburg, NJ: Presbyterian and Reformed Publishing Co., 1979), Dedication, iii.

[55] Singer, 442.

[56] James Jordan, "The Closing of the Calvinistic Mind."

[57] Reference found in Kimball, "The Forgotten Founder" http://www.opinionjournal.com, July 3, 2006.

I got to meet Dr. Rushdoony on several occasions. The most memorable was on July 6, 1991. My fiancé, Stephanie, and I delayed our wedding date for one week so we and others could go hear Rushdoony speak at Rowlett, Texas. Besides the occasions I met him, Dr. Rushdoony sent me handwritten notes on occasion and his Easy Chair tapes brought him and his readings into my life on almost a daily basis. I have bought many books merely on the basis of a Rushdoony recommendation.

I never met Gregg Singer. Along with reading his works, I enjoyed hearing him lecture from tapes, even though he was constantly clearing his throat. His lectures were most interesting, as were his digressions, which is often the mark of a good teacher. A frequent digression of Dr. Singer was his personal story of his involvement in the investigation of the Pearl Harbor bombing. He was to be a speaker at a conference in Monroe, Louisiana in the mid-1990s, but was unable to come because of his wife's health. Not too many years later, he died, and so I missed the opportunity to meet this man who helped me so much.

Only God knows how many of us who preach, teach, and write about Christian thinking have been blessed and changed by Rushdoony and Singer.

Chapter Eleven
Otto Scott and the Sacred Fools

> God is no buttercup.
> —Otto Scott

When a story of his own death reached the still living Mark Twain, he quipped that the rumor was exaggerated. Looking at my collection of books by Otto Scott and remembering his writings and lectures made me think the same of him when I received news of his death in May, 2006. Besides the living voice of Otto Scott in his books and writings, there is also the joyful acknowledgment of his earthly passing being just that: a passing from this world to be with the Lord.

Otto Scott was a master historian. While his fame as a historian was limited to smaller circles and his accomplishments not as widely acclaimed as we might wish, those of us who were privileged to have read his books and met him have esteemed him quite highly. He lived and wrote outside of the academy, outside of university circles, outside the notice of the professional historians.

Perhaps this obscurity was due in part because he wrote quite a few favorable business and corporate histories. Americans have had a strange relationship with the business world. On the one hand, we assume a degree of corruption and greed in big business, but, on the other hand, we happily enjoy consuming what the business market produces. We love success stories, but tend to be more enamored by sports figures and entertainers than businessmen. The crooked and shady businessman is a stock character in our movies and fiction. So, much of what Otto Scott wrote would not have appealed, on the surface, to most readers. I personally don't relish curling up with a history of Purina Dog Chow for an evening's reading.

When I first heard of Otto Scott's biography of oilman J. B. Saunders, titled *The Professional,* I had no interest in the story. Then I heard R. J. Rushdoony recommend it as being one of the best histories of the twentieth century, along with Paul Johnson's *Modern Times*.[1] Saunders, as I learned from reading the book, was a marvelously adaptive and brilliant man who prospered before, during, and after the Great Depression. His life and success in the oil business ran parallel with government programs that tended to stifle the entrepreneurial spirit. It was the success of American innovation as opposed to governmental regulation. It was a biography in the Horatio Alger tradition, which is a vital part of the American story.

Otto Scott wrote history from the vantage point of a journalist looking for a good human interest story. He once said that a publisher criticized him for being too readable to be taken seriously by scholars and yet too scholarly for average readers. He wrote for people in the middle category, who are neither scholars nor merely escape readers. Scott understood this class of people; in fact, he coined the term "silent majority" that defined those people of traditional values, Christian heritage, and conservative principles. He wrote from a conservative perspective, but without being captive to a conservative agenda. His choices for topics were diverse and unorthodox. He seemed oblivious toward trends, impervious toward fads, obstinate toward political acceptability. He made irascibility a desired and lovable trait. His years at sea as a sailor gave him a certain saltiness in his style of writing and demeanor. His time of trekking across the United States during the 1930s gave him a Steinbeck-like feel for humanity, with a dose of disdain toward pretension. Otto Scott was both urbane and cultured, yet street-wise and knowledgeable in the ways of men.

What must have been his downfall for the world of acceptable historians and histories was his irascible tendency to make heroes of villains and villains of heroes. Hence, his praise of business was viewed with suspicion. That his checks came from oil companies and not from universities must have sealed his fate among the professorial elite. Exercising the office of historical prelacy, Scott canonized those he deemed worthy, and then more significantly pronounced his anti-canonizations on those he deemed as sacred fools. Scott was a Christian, a convert in his middle age years; his earlier perspective was cultural Christianity, honed by an upbringing that included living in New York and Caracas, Venezuela, sundry jobs and travels during the Great Depression, and a stint in the Merchant Marine during World War II. He read widely and thought deeply. Such a life of scholarly contemplation led him one evening to begin reading one major classic he had hitherto neglected—

---

[1] Otto Scott, *The Professional: A Biography of JB Saunders* (New York: Atheneum, 1976). Paul Johnson, *Modern Times: From the Twenties to the Eighties* (New York: Harper & Row Publishers, 1983). An expanded version of *Modern Times* carried that history up through the nineties.

the Bible. He read it, was converted, and in time, picked up on a lead in a book review of a work titled *The Myth of Overpopulation* by R. J. Rushdoony.[2] After reading that book, Scott ordered every book Rushdoony wrote.

In time, Rushdoony and Scott met, became intellectual and spiritual friends, and frequent sparring partners in the exchange of ideas. Rushdoony was one of the few Christian leaders who had recognized the theological implications of Scott's books, which he reviewed for *Christianity Today*. Scott's thinking and writing, while never parroting Rushdoony, grew with his understanding of theology and of history from a Calvinistic perspective.

From the 1980s on, his more mature perspective as a writer and historian was self-consciously Christian. As a Christian historian, he could have chosen some safe Christian topics, such as biographies of Christian ministers and missionaries, and he would have been politely ignored by the academy. Instead, having lived a life that went against the grain, he chose more controversial topics; therefore, he was rudely ignored.

Yes, it was the anti-canonizations that defined Scott's most enduring histories. He wrote biographies of King James I of England, Robespierre of France, and abolitionist John Brown. As good historians always do, he used biographies as lenses to view broader historical periods. So, Scott chronicled the Stuart era of British history, the French Revolution, and the ante-bellum tensions of America. He pronounced a stern judgment of his three subjects: They were fools; no, even worse, they were sacred fools. The trilogy of sacred fools was to have been a quartet. The candidates for that fourth position would be legion, but Scott's choice was President Woodrow Wilson. Time and circumstances have spared Wilson from Scott's wrathful pen, although others have exposed him.

Just as saints—at least in the more Roman Catholic sense—have miracles that occur in their names; just as saints influence not just their own age but the ages to follow; just as saints attract willing—and often gullible followers; just as saints inspire others to take up the holy cause for which they spent their lives; just as saints change the world, so sacred fools forever change the world. That religious fervor of the saint is also found in the sacred fool. Just as a saint's commitments rest upon a theological underpinning, so do those of the sacred fool. With that keen theological understanding as a starting point, Scott singled out his three choice candidates and gave them their just historical rewards.

---

[2] R. J. Rushdoony, *The Myth of Overpopulation* (Fairfax, VA: Thoburn Press, 1975). A brilliant short study.

While many historians separate the secular from the sacred with zeal, Otto Scott saw that all men act and function according to a set of presuppositions that are at heart religious and theological. My saint is someone else's sinner, and vice versa. Dante put Mohammed in Hell. Muslim poets—if they have any—would rather put Dante there. Being polite, being politically correct, being non-judgmental were the things that never were part of Otto Scott's historiography. And for that, too, we are thankful.

The French Revolution Revisited

Scott's biography of Robespierre was originally subtitled *The Voice of Virtue*.[3] You can almost hear Scott's chuckle and see his slight smile when reading that ironic subtitle. Robespierre's political career consisted largely of denouncing his enemies as the enemies of the people. Under Robespierre and a host of fellow worthies, the guillotine grew fat under a steady diet of public enemies. Trials were fast and "justice" was swift. The crimes were simply defined: Anyone with ties to the old order was guilty; anyone hindering the revolution was guilty; anyone who was accused was guilty. As Scott observed, "the revolution's rules had grown so numerous that virtually every citizen was now technically guilty of property crimes against the state."[4] What did it matter if some who were truly innocent or noble or good were killed? It was a new age, a new world that was being created on the rubble and corpses of the old.

Robespierre died at the same guillotine at which he had hastily and randomly condemned others. His downfall began when he decreed a state religion that recognized a Supreme Being.[5] But the Revolution lived on. It came in time to be embodied by Napoleon and his Grande Armee. Scott said, "France was fractured, and not only France. Across the face of European culture, injured first by men carried away by their own cleverness into attacking, undermining, and crippling all their own sacred images and their own forebears, the fissures of the French Revolution continued to widen."[6] The Revolution cropped up again and again throughout the old monarchies of Europe. Marx, Engles, Lenin, Stalin, Mao Zedong, and Pol Pot were the children of Robespierre. The Islamic world may hate the European culture, but the Islamic terrorists certainly have imbibed the spirit of Robespierre.

---

[3] Otto Scott, *Robespierre: The Voice of Virtue* (New York: Mason and Lipscomb Publishers, 1974). A later reprinting by a different publisher had the subtitle *The Fool as Revolutionary*.

[4] Scott, *Robespierre*, 221.

[5] Scott, *Robespierre*, 225.

[6] Scott, *Robespierre*, 233.

All too often, the French Revolution has been portrayed as being only a slightly different species of what America experienced in 1776. We celebrate the 4th of July; the French celebrate Bastille Day. We have the Declaration of Independence; the French have the Declaration of the Rights of Man. Clearly, our revolution freed us from the shackles of monarchy, and subtly, it is hinted that it freed us from religious constraints. The French experience thus becomes the lens through which we interpret our own experience. The incongruity of the analogy of the events in the United States and France has been duly noted through the years. From Edmund Burke's *Reflections on the Revolution in France* (1790) to Friedrich Gentz's *The French and American Revolutions Compared* (1800), which John Quincy Adams translated, to Christopher Dawson's *The Gods of Revolution* (1972) to Simon Schama's *Citizens: A Chronicle of the French Revolution* (1989), there have been historians who have recognized the evils of the French Revolution and who, in some cases, clearly demarcated the differences between the American and French experiences.[7] Charles Dickens chronicled the ugliness of that revolution in his novel *A Tale of Two Cities*. The evils that took place in France, as noted by historians and novelists, were not confined to the streets of Paris.

Theologian Alister McGrath comments on the far reaching aspects of the
. He writes,

> What the French Revolution began, the Russian Revolution continued. Soviet political and military expansion after the Second World War led to the imposition of a new order upon much of Eastern Europe and became the inspiration of Communist parties throughout Europe.[8]

Yet there was more to the French Revolution than simply spawning the future Communist regimes. McGrath credits the French Revolution with being the first case where the possibility of an atheist state was accepted, and from this beginning, an age of unbelief began. McGrath notes,

> [T]he real significance of the French Revolution…lies not so much in what it accomplished in the realm of France, but on the impact it created in the minds and above all the imaginations of many alienated individuals throughout Europe. Seeds were planted, mental horizons were extended, and hopes for change ignited.[9]

---

[7] Burke, *The Best of Burke: Selected Writings and Speeches of Edmund Burke* (Washington: Regnery Publishing, Inc., 1963); Gentz (Houston, TX: St. Thomas Press, 1975, reprint); Dawson (New York: New York University Press, 1972); Schama (New York: Alfred A. Knopf, Inc., 1989).

[8] Alister McGrath, *The Twilight of Atheism* (New York: Doubleday, 2004), 2.

[9] McGrath, 46-47.

To add even more references to the case, James H. Billington's *Fire in the Minds of Men: Origins of the Revolutionary Faith* and Michael Burleigh's *Earthly Powers: The Clash of Religion and Politics in Europe from the French Revolution to the Great War* both note the dangers and evils that stemmed from the Revolution both before and after it occurred.[10] Hence, Otto Scott was right on target in singling out the French Revolution and Robespierre as vital for understanding the evils of the centuries that followed.

Scott linked many of the evils of the modern world with the French Revolution. In an essay titled "Hatred of History," he wrote of the effect of the Enlightenment and the French Revolution:

> The cumulative effect was to sow the seeds of hatred toward history that fueled the revolutionary argument that society had to be completely remade, and that all existing institutions from the church to the monarchy to all tradition had to be brought down, and the world remade along new lines.[11]

Scott's indictment of Robespierre was an indictment of the whole French Revolution, of the Enlightenment unbelief that preceded it, and the atheistic revolutionary philosophy that succeeded it. Too much of our political framework, too many of our autonomous attitudes, too much of our modern thinking is still rooted in that era. For a time and in a very Orwellian sense, wickedness was called virtue. After the word virtue was used up, like other children of the Revolution, including Robespierre, it was devoured.

A Blasphemous King

James I was a different sort of sacred fool. He unwittingly left us one great and positive legacy—the Authorized Version of the Bible.[12] Like so much that he did, like so much he sought to do, the good was the overruling providence of God and not James's intention. Otto Scott dealt with the life of James in *James I: The Fool as King* and also in *The Great Christian Revolution*. James's foolishness was that of the squandered life and wasted heritage. It was the foolishness of seeing the house built on rock, but choosing the house built on sand. It was the foolishness of preferring tyranny to wise counsel,

---

[10] Billington, (New Brunswick, NJ: Transaction Publishers, 2003); Burleigh (New York: Harper Collins Publishers, 2005).

[11] Scott, "Hatred of History" in *Compass*: "Charting a Course to Knowledge" (Volume 6, Issue 68, April 1, 1996). *Compass* was a newsletter that Scott wrote and published for many years.

[12] Scott referred to King James' name on the Bible translation as a blasphemous joke.

perversion to grace, and pettiness to nobility. He clung to the doctrine of the divine right of kings, but he caused men to ponder a divine imperative to remove wicked kings.

James was nursed in the strict Calvinism of the Scottish theologian George Buchanan's tutorials. His education contained the seed germs of what became the rudiments of the Westminster Standards a generation later. His schooling was harsh at times, but not radically different from the cane and birch pedagogy of most scholars of his age. Intellectually James had the ability to both learn and write. Politically, however, he was a fool, and spiritually and sexually, he was a pervert. As Scott noted in what might be the most succinct summary of James's life: "There had never been anything wrong with James's intelligence; it was his character that was deficient."[13]

His mother, Mary Stuart, known as Mary, Queen of Scots, had failed as a leader due to her own personal wickedness, overreaching ambition, and political Catholicism. After being forced to abdicate, she fled to England where her distant cousin, Queen Elizabeth I, ruled. In 1587, Elizabeth, after enduring threats to her throne, was compelled to sign Mary's death warrant. Then in 1603, Queen Elizabeth I died without a direct heir to succeed her. Mary's son, James, inherited what his mother had once schemed for herself.

Elizabeth, with all her failings and conniving, had proven to be an apt, even brilliant ruler. The kingdom she left her cousin was strong. Surging with energy within that kingdom and ready to fight foes both within and without that kingdom were the Puritans. Being the headstrong and stouthearted Calvinists they were, they were ready with Bible in hand to reform both church and state.

The Calvinism brimming forth in England was matched by that to the north. Scotland had become one big Reformed Calvinistic Presbytery. Puritans in England, while differing on details, constituted a rugged Calvinistic coalition within the political and religious landscape. Across the channel, Calvinists in the Netherlands, struggling for their own political identity, were valiantly contending for the faith. Calvinists in some of the German states stood steadfast on Reformed theology. Catholic Spain, which dominated Europe's political landscape, was forever vulnerable due to its overreaching empire and had already suffered setbacks in their 1588 attempt to subdue England with the Grand Armada. France had its own internal problems with a Calvinistic element arising in its merchant classes. The spiritual gains of Luther, Calvin, Bucer, and Knox from an earlier century were all in place. The New World was, though largely controlled by Catholic Spain, continuing

---

[13] Scott, *James I: The Fool as King* (Vallecito: Ross House Books, 1986 reprint).

to be explored and beginning to be settled by Protestants.

A brilliant man, holding sway over two kingdoms, with a Christian and Calvinistic upbringing, could have united the Protestant cause and changed the world for the better. James I could have been that man, but instead, he wasted and squandered the greatest opportunity any Protestant Christian king ever had to usher in an age of political Reformation. His memorable phrases are testimonies to his utter stupidity. Of the Puritans, he said that he would "harry them out of the land." Of the desire of many to establish more Biblical norms for church and state by removing the political bishops from power, he retorted, "No bishops, no king." His inability to work with Parliament, his penchant for ruling tyrannically, and his hatred of Reformed theology all contributed to a miserable reign for him. Under his son's rule, matters in England became worse and resulted in the English Civil War and ultimately Charles I's execution. His grandsons—Charles II and James II—were likewise inept.

This being James I's record, Otto Scott gave him the much-earned mantle of the "Fool as King." All too many leaders have seemingly coveted those same honors, perhaps with a modified title, such as "Fool as President" or "Fool as Supreme Court Justice." In God's graciousness, more than one leader has had the opportunity to rule in good, wise, and godly ways, but have traded such chances for the world's mess of potage. One cannot help but remember the charm, political savvy, oratorical skills, and electoral successes of former President Bill Clinton. As a Southern Democrat with an evangelical Christian background, he had the opportunity to rule with righteousness and wisdom, but he opted for King James's pattern of personal immorality and political conniving for personal aggrandizement. Lacking a Puritan controlled Senate, Clinton survived his miserable second term.

Scott retold part of King James's story in *The Great Christian Revolution*. This account appeared first as a collection of essays by various writers, in which Scott's piece occupied over 230 pages of a book of some 327 pages.[14] Scott's extended essay later appeared as a separate volume. This work is an account of Europe during the Reformation of the 1500s and the political upheavals that followed in the 1600s. Luther, Calvin, the Huguenots, Henry VIII, Elizabeth, James I, Cromwell, and others are all covered in this history. It is one of the best surveys of the religious and political aspects of the Reformation ever written. And it is a powerful testimony to Scott's growth in understanding and commitment to the theology of the Reformation. It pro-

---

[14] Otto Scott, R. J. Rushdoony, et. al., *The Great Christian Revolution* (Vallecito: Ross House Books, 1991).

vides a background to the Calvinistic settling of North America and the later influences of Reformed theology on the American experience. Scott credits the Christianity of the Reformers and their heirs with providing the foundation for the liberties we have come to enjoy. It was, according to Scott, the most significant revolution in our history.[15]

John Brown's Legacy

Otto Scott's third subject for his Sacred Fools series was John Brown and by extension, his supporters, known as the Secret Six. John Brown's foolishness nearly destroyed our nation. Like Robespierre, like James I, John Brown did not act alone. The North had no monopoly on foolishness in the years leading up to the War Between the States, for Southern fire-eaters were continually lunging at the chance to destroy the union; however, New England spawned more than its share of utopian insanities during its literary golden age. Deism, Unitarianism, Transcendentalism, secession, utopian socialism, the free love movement, and the public school movement all either sprang from New England roots or was easily grafted into the culture. The more radical positions on the abolition of slavery were also found there.

In short, Brown focused on the problem that was dividing the nation—slavery. Wiser men had struggled and agonized over it in the legislative halls, in the pulpits, and in the press. Without the working class provided by Negro slaves, Southern agriculture would not have developed. Without Southern raw materials cultivated by slaves, Northern industry would have been hindered. All Americans profited from the system. Jefferson compared slavery to the dilemma of holding a wolf by the ears. Time, patience, economic and industrial development, and Christian sanctification could have solved the problem in history. South American countries ended slavery without a war. William Wilberforce and other English Christians worked patiently to end the slave trade in the British Empire. Only America resorted to the ad baculum fallacy, the appeal to force and violence, to deal with slavery.

But John Brown, fool that he was, had no patience with society, with the political process, or with slow cultural change and progressive sanctification. Like those who always think a more perfect world can be dynamited into existence, he opted for a quick answer: Terrorism. Long before either of the bombings of the World Trade Center, our nation was subjected to a political agenda that was promoted by violence. Brown cut his teeth on violence literally by cutting throats, and that included cutting the throats of frontier settlers who had no slaves. Yes, America had a true civil war. It occurred in

---

[15] Scott, *The Great Christian Revolution*, 309.

Kansas in the 1850's before the 1861-1865 conflict. The guilt of "Bloody Kansas" falls on both Northern and Southern hands.

Brown was not content with simply seeing Kansas come into the union as a free state. As Churchill once said of Lenin: His goal was to save the world; his method was to blow it up. Brown and sons instigated a takeover of a weapons arsenal in Harpers' Ferry, Virginia. It was to spawn a slave rebellion throughout the South. Virginians, led by Robert E. Lee, in a typically Southern way took out the terrorists and rescued the hostages. Significantly, the first and perhaps only black American affected by Brown's activities was a free Negro who was shot by Brown's men.

Had Brown succeeded in securing arms and putting them into the hands of supposedly willing slaves, he would probably have caused the destruction of the entire black population in the United States. As bad as the War Between the States was, with huge armies clashing and grinding each other up for four years, Brown's terrorism would likely have caused a real civil war with guerrilla bands fighting for decades. Northern Ireland and Lebanon would be viewed as mild and gentle by comparison.

Brown was just a crazy tanner turned sacred fool. He mouthed religious, even messianic, rhetoric. The state of Virginia disposed of him quite effectively via the gallows. But Ralph Waldo Emerson, a true nut case who aspired to be a transparent eyeball, compared those same gallows to the cross. Emerson was aligned with other factions in New England who were also abolitionists. This coalition consisted of upright, well-schooled, culturally groomed people who might never personally knife a slave owner. Yet they financed and promoted terrorism. Scott says of the Secret Six,

> The members of the cabal were persons of high standing in the community. All were in comfortable circumstances. Some were famous, and others were wealthy. All of them were dissatisfied with the normal process of government, and all were obsessed with the desire to make their opinions—and not the decisions of the elected leaders of the people—the determining factors in the life of the nation.[16]

Brown was their lackey and the martyr for their convictions, and after his death, their saint. The Constitutional avenues for dealing with slavery were of no interest to them. The Bible that motivated their Puritan ancestors

---

[16] Scott, *The Secret Six: John Brown and the Abolitionist Movement* (New York: Times Books, 1979), 3-4.

was not their creed. They were gentlemen revolutionaries; they were refined, cultured paymasters to terrorism.

Otto Scott's bestowing the title of sacred fool on John Brown was yet another evidence of his historical unorthodoxy. Why, you simply cannot blame Brown or the next thing you know, you find yourself defending the Southern Confederacy. Yes, Scott did exactly that. Even though Scott was not a Southerner by birth or ideology, he took his stand beside Jefferson Davis, rather than Abraham Lincoln. Otto Scott was not afraid to defend a cause he believed was right.

I wish Scott had completed his book on Woodrow Wilson. I wish he had added a fifth, a sixth, and on up to a hundred biographies on the foolish men who have warped the ages. He left us lots of homework to complete. Perhaps we need to spotlight some more sacred fools. But what is more important, we may now be able to navigate past the losers and find the greater lights of history.

Scott's life and historiography following his mid-life conversion to Christianity are a testimony to the intellectual as well as spiritual growth resulting from grace. Salvation refined and sanctified his overall view of the world. The theology of the Reformation and of his friend, Dr. Rushdoony, deepened and positively changed his outlook. In spite of his abilities to spot the sacred fools of history, he still could focus on God's greater purposes being accomplished in history. Scott's friend, Jack Phelps of Anchorage, Alaska, comments on this aspect of Scott:

> Otto Scott taught us how to think about history as Christians and the importance of doing so. He believed that history is not a long string of events, interconnected somehow, but random. It is, rather, the unfolding of the purposes of God, directed by his determined hand toward a final goal.[17]

Along with his excellent books, Scott wrote numerous essays in the *Chalcedon Report* and in his own newsletter, titled *Compass*. Christians interested in history would be greatly blessed if these essays were gathered together and published in book form. Otto Scott was too good a historian and thinker to be forgotten. Through his books and testimony, he still lives.

---

[17] Jack Phelps, "Otto Scott—May 26, 1918-May 5, 2006" from the *Chalcedon Report,* June, 2006, 2.

Chapter Twelve
Did You Hear the One About the Three Historians?

> It is in Christianity that our arts have developed; it is in Christianity that the laws of Europe have—until recently—been rooted. It is against a background of Christianity that all our thought has significance.
> —T. S. Eliot[1]

A Lutheran, a Roman Catholic, and a Baptist walked into a college classroom right in the middle of a professor's class on Western Civilization. "You are interrupting my lecture," the professor said. "You are right about **that**," the three men replied.

I admit that the story above lacks real effect as a joke. The beginning is promising, but the punch line is not quite funny for a joke. The actual story should put a big grin on the mouth of Christians.

I speak in reference to three books: *Under the Influence: How Christianity Transformed the World* (now titled *How Christianity Changed the World*) by Lutheran pastor Alvin J. Schmidt, *How the Catholic Church Built Western Civilization* by Roman Catholic Professor Thomas E. Woods, Jr., and *The Victory of Reason: How Christianity Led to Freedom, Capitalism, and Western Success* by Baylor Baptist University Professor Rodney Stark.[2] These three books demonstrate the transforming effect of Jesus Christ and His Church in time and history. These works are like complementing movements in a grand symphony. These three books provide an antidote to the secularized version of history. These three books boldly challenge the anti-Christian bias so often found in the world both inside and outside the academy.

Before we examine the books, we need to examine the issue of history itself. As Orwell said, "Those who control the present control the past. Those

---

[1] T. S. Eliot, *Christianity and Culture: The Idea of a Christian Society and Notes Toward a Definition of Culture* (New York: Harcourt Brace & Company, 1976), 200.

[2] Alvin J. Schmidt, *Under the Influence: How Christianity Transformed Civilization* (Grand Rapids: Zondervan, 2001); Thomas E. Woods, Jr., *How the Catholic Church Built Western Civilization* (Washington, D.C.: Regnery Publishing Company, 2005); Rodney Stark, *The Victory of Reason: How Christianity Led to Freedom, Capitalism, and Western Success* (New York: Random House, 2005).

who control the past control the future." History is anecdotal philosophy. A history lecture is as agenda-driven as a political caucus. Just as ideas have consequences, history lessons have consequences.

Sometimes we speak of something called "the lessons of history," and we talk of needing to learn these lessons. "Those who ignore the lessons of history are bound to repeat them," we are told. What the exact lessons are is not so clear. Does the Alamo teach the lesson of: 1. The necessity of the few sacrificing for the many? Or 2. The inevitability of American Manifest Destiny? Or 3. "Don't mess with Texas"? History does not teach plain, simple, moralistic lessons. It is not the same as *Aesop's Fables*. History teaches perspectives, angles, and inquiries into truth. What history finally teaches us will always be based upon some prior presuppositional commitments.

Herodotus called his founding historical document *Historia,* which we would translate as *Inquiry.* History is always questioning what exactly happened and what caused it to happen. History looks for roots, for common causes, and for cause-effect relationships. History—not just in general, but in specific examinations—can reveal whatever the student is presuppositionally looking for. As Cornelius Van Til said, "It becomes especially plain here that in the Christian conception of things interpretation precedes facts." [3] Andrew Hoffecker applies this to history: "Historians bring to their study of human events a conception that history is either meaningful or meaningless. They disagree over whether transcendent powers influence the course of events and over whether human actions or natural and social actions are the more significant in shaping human destiny."[4]

The First Front and Second Front

History is the second vital front in the Christian culture war. The first front is the battle for the Bible. Without the Scriptures, we have no revelation from God, no marching orders, no army to march, and really, no reason to fight. The truth and authority of God's Word is the foundational presupposition of Christian thought.[5] When the Christian Church battled over the Bible within its ranks in the late nineteenth and early twentieth centuries, the world was able to march unhindered into all areas of territory once claimed and occupied by Christians. When Darwinian Naturalism marched to the gates

---

[3] Cornelius Van Til, *The Defense of the Faith (*Phillipsburg*:* Presbyterian and Reformed Publishing Company, 1967), 20.

[4] W. Andrew Hoffecker, "Preface: Perspective and Method in Building a World View" from *Building a Christian World View,* edited by W. Andrew Hoffecker and Gary Scott Smith (Phillipsburg: Presbyterian and Reformed Publishing Company, 1986) xi.

[5] See everything by Cornelius Van Til and by everyone who follows his thought.

of Christendom from the outside, Higher Critical theology opened the gates to the enemy from the inside. Without the Bible, our churches are nothing more than community family centers. Without the Bible, we Christians have no agenda. For this reason, conservatism and libertarianism, while offering wonderful critiques of the enemies surrounding us, can never work as philosophies or as worldviews to counter the opposition. They can never truly advocate throwing the rascals out; they only call for a new set of rascals.

In a sense, the Bible in a school setting more closely resembles an academic skill than a subject. Our compartmentalization of life leads us to segregate disciplines. A Bible confined to a course called "Survey of the Bible" looks like a lion confined in a cage with the description "King of the Jungle." But just as the knowledge of the alphabet pervades and dominates all other academic disciplines, so the Bible should be the philosophical or intellectual alphabet to all learning. On one occasion, a Jewish lady called our Christian school and asked if her son could attend, but skip the first part of the day or the 'religion part'. Our elementary administrator explained that the Bible and Christianity were not a fifteen-minute segment in the mornings. Anytime the Bible is caged, it ceases to be what is really is and its effect is nullified. So the first front of the culture war is always the battle for the Bible.

History is the second front for three reasons. First, the Bible from beginning to end presents a philosophy of history. Second, the Bible itself contains history. Third, the Bible itself impacted history. To say, "I love the Bible, but I don't like history" is to speak in a contradiction. The biblical philosophy of history is rooted in Augustine's *City of God,* which was written in response to an apologetic challenge from pagans. Gregg Singer says of Augustine's work and times:

> It was at this moment when classical culture had reached the depths of disintegration and the grandeur and glory of Rome were things of the past, that Augustine brought historiological insights into the service of the church. This made possible a philosophy of history which looked to the Bible for its frame of reference.[6]

I am really puzzled when I recall that I acquired a history degree without ever taking a class that defined what history was. Both warnings and encouragements were given in regard to what a history degree could and could not do for you. My professors seemed to have a personal enjoyment of the subject; perhaps, they were merely relieved to be employed at a university

---

[6] C. Gregg Singer, *Christian Approaches to Philosophy, to History* (Craig Press: 1978), 27.

instead of having to do tedious and grimy factory work or having more lucrative, but stressful work in a law office. They encouraged the study of history, but a philosophy of history was never given. Schools of historical thought were never explained. A history of historians was never offered. Interpretations of history were unavoidable, but an explanation of interpretive approaches never showed up.

It would be far easier to make sense of history if universities followed Van Til's approach and allowed interpretation to precede facts. Perhaps the prevalence of humanistic worldviews completely blinded the historians to their own interpretations. Whether from blindness to other views, willful suppression of the truth, or indifference, a Christian philosophy of history is rarely taught about or taught from in the classroom.

Within the Bible and its historical philosophy are detailed histories of the ancient world, the Hebrew nation, surrounding kingdoms and civilizations, social customs, Roman occupation methods, and the interactions between Jewish, Greek, and Roman cultures. Whole books of the Old and New Testaments are histories. In fact, Moses, rather than Herodotus, is actually the father of history, for as Paul Johnson said, the Jews "were the first to create consequential, substantial, and interpretive history." He goes on to say, "[T]he Jews were above all historians, and the Bible is essentially a historical work from start to finish. The Jews developed the power to write terse and dramatic historical narrative half a millennium before the Greeks, and because they constantly added to their historical records they developed a deep sense of historical perspective which the Greeks never attained."[7]

The historical events contained in the Bible makes it both an invaluable original source, particularly for ancient world studies, and a measuring rod for other original sources. One should not claim knowledge of the ancient world without a well-thumbed copy of the Bible, Herodotus' *Histories,* and Livy's *History of Early Rome.* But while the Bible is a supplementary collection of documents in one sense, it is the corrective to and interpreter of source materials in a greater sense.

The third key area of importance for the Bible is its own influence on history. The three histories we mentioned at the beginning all focus on this question. Their titles and subtitles answer the question. Christianity did, as Dr. Schmidt shows, transform civilization. Christianity did, as Dr. Stark shows, lead to freedom, capitalism, and Western success. And the Catholic Church did, as Dr. Woods shows, both in the broader and narrower uses of that word Catholic, build Western Civilization.

---

[7] Paul Johnson, *A History of the Jews* (New York: Harper & Row Publishers, 1987), 91-92.

Just as some historians ignore or avoid presenting the historic Biblical philosophy of history, and just as they ignore or misuse the Bible for source materials, so they ignore, avoid, and misinterpret the impact of the Bible on Western Civilization.

Western Civilization

Western Civilization's roots can rightly be found in the varied streams of the Greek, Roman, and Hebrew cultures. Ancient history contains numerous details of the currents and cross currents, the blending and separating, and the development of these cultures both in their interactions and their separate achievements. From the Incarnation of Jesus Christ to His death and resurrection, these three separate cultures are brought together. That miserable pawn Pontus Pilate had no idea how profoundly he was serving Western civilization in his actions. John 19:19-20 tells us, "Now Pilate wrote a title and put it on the cross. And the writing was, JESUS OF NAZARETH THE KING OF THE JEWS. Then many of the Jews read this title, for the place where Jesus was crucified was near the city; and it was written in Hebrew, and Greek, and Latin." This King of the Jews was being revealed to the three major cultures of Western Civilization as the true unifying ruler whose kingdom would have no end.

If this was the proclamation of the creation of Western Civilization as a unity, Acts 16:9-10 was the inauguration of this civilization: "And a vision appeared to Paul in the night. A man from Macedonia stood and pleaded with him, saying, 'Come over to Macedonia and help us.' Now after he had seen the vision, immediately we sought to go to Macedonia, concluding that the Lord had called us for to preach the gospel to them."

As historian Christopher Dawson said, "When St. Paul, in obedience to the warning of a dream, set sail from Troy in A.D. 49 and came to Philippi in Macedonia he did more to change the course of history than the great battle that had decided the fate of the Roman Empire on the same spot nearly a century earlier, for he brought to Europe the seed of a new life which was ultimately destined to create a new world."[8]

From this point on through the next thousand plus years, Western Civilization became the primary domain of Christianity. Western Civilization became Christendom. The story is progressive and developmental; the story is uneven; the story is both thrilling and uplifting to the mind and the soul at points, and depressing to both mind and soul at other points. The story of

---

[8] Christopher Dawson, *Religion and the Rise of Western Culture* (New York: The Image Books, 1991), 27.

Western Civilization parallels the stories of both individual Christians and churches, in that it demonstrates grace and sin, sanctification and backsliding, growth and failure. Still, Christianity has been salt and light to this civilization. It has defined the norms of morality and justice. It has regulated the affairs of kings and rulers. It has provided the foundations for social, political, and economic institutions.

Schmidt, Stark, and Woods are not the first historians to chronicle the influences and celebrate the successes of Christianity in history. In fact, each of their books contains good bibliographies and endnotes citing both secular and religious histories. None of the three books is a complete history of European Christendom or a history of the Christian Church. All three books are topical in their presentations.

From the Lutheran, Baptist, and Catholic

Alvin Schmidt says, "On the basis of the historical evidence, I am fully persuaded that had Jesus Christ never walked the dusty paths of ancient Palestine, suffered, died, and risen from the dead, and never assembled around him a small group of disciples who spread out into the pagan world, the West would not have attained its high level of civilization, giving it the many human benefits it enjoys today."[9]

Schmidt's book, *Under the Influence,* then presents the historical evidence. He quotes from original sources, from scholars and observers, and from both friends and enemies of the faith. Many current issues, such as abortion, marriage, sexual morality, and freedom, are discussed from a historical Christian perspective. He divides the subject of Christian influence into such topics as transformation of individual lives, sanctity of human life, sexual morality, women, charity, health care, education, labor, economics, science, art, music, and literature. Each topic, according to Schmidt, is worthy of a book length study by itself. Each topic is then developed with references showing the Christian impact in each of these areas. Many of the quotes Schmidt uses can be found in numerous books and articles, but they are all easily found here, well documented, and supplemented with charts and illustrations.

Rodney Stark's principal assertion parallels that of Dr. Schmidt. Stark says,

> Christianity created Western Civilization. Had the followers of Jesus remained an obscure Jewish sect, most of you would not have learned to read and the rest of you would be reading from hand-copied scrolls. Without a theology committed to reason, progress,

---
[9] Schmidt, page 14.

and moral equality, today the entire world would be about where non-European societies were in, say, 1800: A world with many astrologers and alchemists but no scientists. A world of despots, lacking universities, banks, factories, eyeglasses, chimneys, and pianos. A world where most infants do not live to the age of five and many women die in childbirth—a world truly living in "dark ages.[10]

Stark's book, *The Victory of Reason,* as the title implies, stresses that because Christians embraced reason and logic as gifts from God, Christianity was oriented to the future and to progress rather than being enslaved to the past. This future orientation included economic development during the Medieval period, a time often underrated by both Protestant and non-Christian historians for its economic growth. Stark outflanks Marxist historiography by showing that economics is not the key to history; rather, it is built upon religious foundations. Then with those foundations in place, economic activity develops its course of action. It is significant that Stark reclaims the word *reason* for the Christian faith. He says, "While the other world religions emphasized mystery and intuition, Christianity alone embraced reason and logic as the primary guide to religious truth."[11] The Enlightenment stole the concept of reason from Christianity and portrayed Christianity as the antithesis of reason and logic. In the best of cases, and it was far from being the best, Christians assumed that they could be people of faith in the cathedral and prayer closet, but would have to exchange those garments for reason and logic at the workplace or study. This work sets aside that dichotomy and reminds us that all the treasures of wisdom and knowledge are found in Christ (Colossians 2:3).

Another useful insight in this work is Stark's re-evaluation of the significance of the Fall of Rome. Quite often, Roman civilization is measured as the height from which Europe fell during the "Dark Ages." Stark disagrees. He says, "[T]he fall of Rome was not a tragic setback; had the empire prevailed, there would be nothing to call Western Civilization. If Rome still ruled, Europe would be mired in a brutal command economy, there would have been little innovation of any kind, and the rest of the world probably would be much as Europeans found it in the fifteen and sixteenth centuries."[12]

Echoing both Schmidt and Stark is Thomas Woods. He says,

---

[10] Stark, 233.
[11] Stark, "Introduction," x.
[12] Stark, 75.

The Catholic Church did not merely contribute to Western Civilization—the Church built that civilization. The Church borrowed from the ancient world, to be sure, but she typically did so in a way that transformed the classical tradition for the better. There was hardly a human enterprise of the Early Middle Ages to which the monasteries did not contribute. The Scientific Revolution took root in a Western Europe whose theological and philosophical foundations, Catholic at their very core, proved fertile soil for the development of scientific enterprise.[13]

Thomas Woods's book, *How the Catholic Church Built Western Civilization*, calls for a bit of patience for the Reformed and evangelical Christian reader. His trumpeting of the Roman Catholic Church is much like listening to proud grandparents brag about grandchildren. Calvinists and evangelicals need to do two things while reading this book, and we do need to read this book: First, we need to recognize that the church was not raptured for a thousand years during the Middle Ages. The Medieval Catholic Church was Luther and Calvin's church. They loved it. They loved the church so much that they and countless others labored to bring reform to it. Catholics during the Middle Ages, like Protestants now, had their shining moments and dark stages. Dr. Woods wrote this book so that his daughters would know the heritage of their faith. So this leads to the second reason for we Reformed types to read this book: We can grow through understanding the impact of Medieval Christian thinkers on law, politics, and science, and we can get busy seeing to it that our children know about the contributions made since the Reformation by Reformed Christians.

Woods' book is especially strong on the Christian impact on the foundations of science and moral law. He also covers art, architecture, and education. In fact, he plants the Catholic banner over a whole range of territories. He says, "All of these areas: economic thought, international law, science, university life, charity, religious ideas, art, morality—these are the very foundations of a civilization, and in the West, every single one of them emerged from the heart of the Catholic Church."[14] A key point he emphasizes and then develops near the end is that the accomplishments within Christian circles was not the result of a coincidence; meaning, certain scientists discovered key truths and coincidentally, they were Catholics. It was the historic Christian Church's view of God that made all these things possible: These doctrines

---

[13] Woods, 219-220.
[14] Woods, 221.

that differentiated Christianity from other religions were Monotheism, God's absolute sovereignty, God's transcendence, and God's goodness.[15]

Laughing in the Trenches

Learning history brings humility. It brings humility to our intellect and memory as we realize how much we do not and cannot know. It humbles our sectarian pride as we see how God has worked through men, churches, and time. Our theological heroes have their faults; and those of other traditions have their strengths. The advance of God's Kingdom has not been confined to our guys, our churches, and our times.

We should never forget that we are in a culture war. Those who acknowledge the Incarnation of Christ, who worship Him as the Son of God, who believe His blood was shed for sinners, and who rejoice in His resurrection are all part of the same army. From our trenches, we must rejoice in any and every advance of those who fight alongside us in the cause. We must learn to recognize allies and co-belligerents and differentiate them from our true enemies.

So, did you hear the one about the three historians? A Lutheran, a Roman Catholic, and a Baptist walked into a college classroom right in the middle of a professor's class on Western Civilization. "You are interrupting my lecture," the professor said….

I still cannot think of a good punch line to finish this joke, but for some reason, I cannot stop laughing.

---

[15] Woods, 218

WESTERN CIVILIZATION: CHRISTENDOM

Chapter Thirteen
Greek to All of Us

> Fair Greece! Sad relic of departed worth!
> Immortal, though no more; though fallen, great!
> —Lord Byron

> Do not trust the horse, Trojans. Whatever it is, I fear the
> Greeks even when they bring gifts.
> —Virgil

> The genius of Christianity is a reversal of the genius of the Greeks.
> —Cornelius Van Til[1]

Edith Hamilton was the very image of the prim and proper headmistress of a girls' school in the late Victorian Era. She was exactly that. Her dates were 1868—1963; her school was the Bryn Mawr School of Baltimore; the high point of her life was being made an honorary citizen of Athens, Greece, in 1957. Miss Hamilton taught literature. I bet she called it 'lit—tra—chure.' Her specialty was the Greeks. After her retirement from teaching at age 63, she began to write.

She left a literary legacy in books on Greek and Roman mythology and history. Her book *Mythology* remains a classic in its field. Miss Hamilton combed through the ancient sources—Homer, Hesiod, the playwrights, and the Roman poet Ovid (whose style and treatment of mythology she despised). She then retold the stories of the pesky Greek pantheon of gods and goddesses with both style and restraint. The shorter myths and legends are also told, along with accounts of the fall of families, like the House of Atreus, and the story of Oedipus. She summarizes the three great ancient epics—*The Iliad, The Odyssey,* and *The Aeneid*—by combining these accounts into the greater story of the Trojan War. She even includes a section on Norse mythology.

---

[1] Cornelius Van Til, *A Survey of Christian Epistemology* (Phillipsburg, NJ: Presbyterian and Reformed Publishing Company, no date), 24.

Edith Hamilton's mythology is safe, sanitized, and brimming with the love of a teacher who was a real and female version of Mr. Chips. *Mythology* is a great read, a useful reference, and an enjoyable textbook for classroom use. My copy has been read several times.

Miss Hamilton's other books, particularly *The Greek Way* and *The Roman Way*, merit attention as well. *The Greek Way* is a useful survey of Greek thinkers. The opening paragraph captures the flavor of her appreciation of the Greeks and style of praising them:

> Athens had entered upon her brief and magnificent flowering of genius which so molded the world of mind and of spirit that our mind and spirit to-day are different. We think and feel differently because of what a little Greek town did during a century or two, twenty-four hundred years ago. What was then produced of art and of thought has never been surpassed and very rarely equaled, and the stamp of it is upon all the art and all the thought of the Western world.[2]

Bruce Thornton comments on Miss Hamilton's style, saying, "Hamilton, can, to be sure, sound at times a bit too earnest for our jaded taste. After all, she was born in 1867, so her prose and her enthusiasm are decidedly late Victorian."[3] More modern writers may have advanced beyond Miss Hamilton's flowery prose, but they still credit the Greeks with creating Western Civilization.[4]

The Greeks themselves and their larger historical context, the Greco-Roman world, draws us all in. The Greek language is second only to Latin as a source for roots of our English language. All literature—novels, poetry, and drama—is structured around the forms set by the Greeks. The epic cosmos of Homer (to use Louise Cowan's term)[5] contains the modes of knowledge or the essential archetypes of reality that structure our lives. Modern movies often simply retell the epic tales. The novel *Cold Mountain* by Charles Fraser is a retelling of *The Odyssey* set in Civil War Virginia.. The Coen Brothers' movie *O Brother, Where Art Thou?* is a humorous telling of the same story in the Great Depression Era South. The book *Killer Angels* by Michael

---

[2] Edith Hamilton, *The Greek Way* (New York: Discus Books, 1973), 11.

[3] Bruce Thornton, *Greek Ways: How the Greeks Created Western Civilization* (San Francisco: Encounter Books, 2000), 3.

[4] Hence titles like those of Thornton's and Cahill's books.

[5] Louise Cowan, "Introduction," in *The Epic Cosmos,* edited by Larry Allums (Dallas: The Dallas Institute Publications, 1992).

Shaara and the movie version *Gettysburg* retells the story of *The Iliad* in a Civil War setting.

The American political order is structured around terminology from both Greek and Roman models. In the early eras of American history when education meant classical education, political figures tossed about classical names and references with the same ease with which they now toss about platitudes.[6] All philosophy, according to Alfred North Whitehead, is a footnote to Plato. Aristotle, Plato's most famous student and most polar philosophical opponent, created or catalogued whole disciplines of thought and is still regarded as a major original thinker in philosophy, political science, biological science, rhetoric, and the field of literary theory. Cicero called Herodotus 'the father of history', and his successor, Thucydides, is hailed by many as the better and more accurate historian.

Runners still complete in marathons. The world's best athletes meet every four years at the Olympic games. Greek columns adorn major buildings of both church and state. College fraternities and sororities pick their names from Greek letters (that being the closest thing to a classical education available at many higher learning institutes). Gymnasiums and academies still testify to the enduring nature of the Greek language and culture. According to many scholars, Western Civilization itself was heroically defended and saved at a mountain pass called Thermopylae by 300 Greek Spartans, along with their allies. Movies such as *Troy*, featuring Brad Pitt as Achilles, *Alexander*, and the older movie classic *Three Hundred Spartans* and the more recent version of that same battle at Thermopylae, titled *300*, still testify to our interest in Greek history and legend, even when the movies create more myths, distortions, and misunderstandings than history. In an age of cultural illiteracy, more than a few still know of the Trojan Horse and the warning to 'beware of Greeks bearing gifts.'

The Christian faith itself—Biblically and historically—is interwoven with Greek strands. The Book of Daniel prophesied the military blitzkrieg of Alexander the Great and the subsequent breakup of his short-lived conquests. Greeks approached the Apostle Philip in John 12, saying, "Sir, we wish to see Jesus." The early church suffered a near split when Hellenic (or culturally Greek) Jewish widows fought Hebrew Jewish widows over distribution of food in Acts 6. The most successful missionary team ever turned west and headed into Macedonia and Greece after the Apostle Paul had a dream of a Macedonian asking for help. Many of the letters of the New Testament were written to churches in Greek cities, or written from Greek cities, or to

---

[6] Carl Richard, *The Founders and the Classics: Greece, Rome, and the American Enlightenment*. (Cambridge: Harvard University Press, 1996).

missionaries, Greek Jews like Titus and Timothy, serving in Greek cities. And to top it all off, the New Testament itself was written in Koine Greek, the true lingua franca of the Latin ruled Roman Empire. The early Church Fathers both borrowed from and fought against Greek concepts.

The pervasiveness of things Greek calls attention to a book by Thomas Cahill, titled *Sailing the Wine-Dark Sea: Why the Greeks Matter.* Cahill's reputation itself draws attention to the book. An earlier work of Cahill's, *How the Irish Saved Civilization,* is outstanding. There he devised a way of looking at history by studying key "hinges of history," which he describes as "narratives of grace, the recountings of those blessed and inexplicable moments when someone did something for someone else, saved a life, bestowed a gift, gave something beyond what was required by circumstance."[7] The 'hinge of history' swings at those "essential moments when everything was at stake, when the mighty stream that became Western history was in ultimate danger…" then some transformation saves civilization.[8] Cahill's overall approach to history is quite insightful. In his book on the Irish, he tells how courageous, dogged Irish monks, like the non-Irish St. Patrick and St. Columba evangelized the obscure Irish world steeped in paganism and on the fringes of a disintegrating Roman civilization. From the miniscule island of Iona, located between Ireland and Scotland, monks launched missions that saved souls by evangelism and saved civilization itself by the faithful copying of manuscripts. That work is a brilliant piece of Christian history; it is one of the best around.

Sad to say, *Sailing the Wine-Dark Sea* does not live up to the standard of *How the Irish Saved Civilization.* Cahill's writing is always thought provoking; his topics are academic without being obscure, and his style is readable and enjoyable. Cahill believes that history has applications, that it has meaning and purpose. The book is well structured in terms of the topics covered; it contains a useful glossary and timeline; he quotes from original sources, often making his own translations; his bibliography is delightful; and his interpretations are quite often most helpful.

So where does the book fail? It fails in terms of the darker side of the subject itself, the Greeks, and it fails in terms of Cahill's method of portraying that darker side. Everything said in this essay above praising the Greeks stands; most of what Edith Hamilton says of the Greeks stands; and Cahill's overall thesis that the Greeks matter stands. But the Greek world was perverse.

---

[7] Thomas Cahill, *Sailing the Wine Dark Sea: Why the Greeks Matter* (New York: Nan A. Talese, 2003). From "The Hinges of History" found at the beginning of each of the books in the series.

[8] Cahill, op. cit.

Greek to All of Us

Beautiful at points, brilliant often, far reaching intellectually, astounding—all that and more, but perverse and perverted. The world of idolatry, homosexual debauchery, and wickedness described by Paul in Romans 1, verses 18 and following, was not given in a "Ripley's Believe It or Not" fashion. Paul wrote that letter in the Greek city of Corinth to the Church in Rome. From either location—Corinth or Rome—that perverted world existed, not just confined in the bad part of town, but in all parts of town. The congregation in Corinth consisted in part of people whose lives before conversion were embroiled in all manner of wickedness (1 Cor. 6:9-11).

Cahill does his readers a favor to bring up this side of Greek culture. He spares no effort to soften the total nastiness of the Greeks in his descriptions and illustrations. His post-modernism fills in the details that Edith Hamilton's Victorianism never mentioned. Bruce Thornton also notices what Edith Hamilton politely overlooked. He says, "Hamilton appears to slight what Nietzsche convinced our century was really most fascinating about the Greeks: the dark, wild, Dionysian forces seething beneath their sunlit, marmoreal repose. Finally, Hamilton says little about the topics our therapeutic culture enjoys brooding over, such as slavery, homosexuality, and the status of women."[9]

Cahill spares no sensibilities in resorting to the crudest and most vulgar language to describe the Greeks. The book reads like a hybrid of a scholarly history and a pornographic tract. While reading the book, I kept questioning the subtitle and asking, "Do these perverted Greeks matter?" We might re-examine the question of the importance of the Greek contribution to Western Civilization. Was there any real advantage to the Greeks halting the Persian advance at Thermopylae? From the glimpses we see of the Persians in such Old Testament books as Ezra and Esther, could not they have been more worthy founders of the West? Instead of framing the issue in terms of our debt to the Greeks, perhaps we should see it more in Biblical and Augustinian terms: The wealth of the sinner is laid up for the righteous and we are to plunder the Egyptians—and Greeks.[10]

My advice: Read books, like Cahill's, and read the Greeks themselves, wash your soul out after each reading, take note of the brilliant insights, and take heed to the accurate depictions of Greek depravity. Teachers, and especially teachers in classical Christian schools, need to research both sides of the Greek world. There are no truly noble pagans. Even Christian cultures include many ugly and depraved elements of those who profess a higher

---

[9] Thornton, 3.
[10] Proverbs 13:22 and Augustine's *On Christian Teaching*, Book II.

standard. God's common grace poured out many gifts on the Greeks. God used the Greek culture as a springboard for the Gospel.

Even God-hating, truth suppressing, sin-laden men can produce wonderful and beautiful things. We can, like Paul in Act 17, walk through Athens and note their idolatry. We can, as Paul recommended in another context, in speaking to Greeks living in Philippi, meditate on whatever things the Greeks created that were true, noble, just, pure, and lovely (Philippians 4:8-9). We can wax eloquent over Greek glory of old as the poet Byron did when he wrote,

> The isles of Greece, the isles of Greece!
> Where burning Sappho loved and sung,
> Where grew the arts of war and peace,
> Where Delos rose, and Phoebus sprung!
> Eternal summer gilds them yet,
> But all, except their sun, is set.[11]

We can kick around the ruins of Greek civilization and retain the good, just as God Himself did in using the rich Greek language for the New Testament. Cahill recommends, in his bibliography, that the reader should immerse himself in both Greek and Hebrew writings to understand the two worlds, the two cultures.

Homer

The works of Homer, Herodotus, Aristotle, Aeschylus and others are useful tools for comparison and contrast with the study of Scripture. Greek epics are great fun to read and are common bonds with educated people from the past. Greek drama is intense, warped at many points, but still revelatory of man's capacity for both wickedness and good. The influence of the Greek philosophers is not disputed, even by those who dispute their premises and conclusions.

And then there is Homer, almost in a class by himself, and those two foundational works of literature and history, *The Iliad* and *The Odyssey*. In regard to what we have often termed the "Greek Bible," I grow closer to Homer each time I read him. I often nourish a hope that Homer stumbled across the works of Moses and believed them and subsequently went to Heaven. Homer created two epics that have defined the course of literature for the Western World. Whether Homer was a real, live blind man who

---

[11] Lord Byron, "Don Juan," Stanza 86.

composed the two great poems, as legend suggests, or whether the works were compiled by multiple unknown authors, the result is the same.[12] Both *The Iliad* and *The Odyssey* have inspired and influenced many subsequent literary and poetic works and are unsurpassed as literature.[13]

The Iliad first appears to be a rather long and overly violent war story. Homer seems to have contemplated every possible entry and exit wound location in the human anatomy. If it could be pierced, punctured, crushed, or lopped off, Homer saw to it that it was. Where is the line between ancient world slasher-fiction and Yeats' "terrible beauty"?[14] Homer understood the brutal nature of war, and the voices of poets, historians, and soldiers who have echoed his understanding show that though the weapons change, the results are still the same.[15] Woven into his combinations of animal-of-prey similes and gory descriptions are brief biographical glimpses of the soldiers. These soldiers killed in war are not just casualty figures, but are men who had hopes and families back home. The violence is unrelenting, but not unnecessary.

Each battle, each violent episode, serves as a buildup to the point in the story where Achilleus returns to action and kills Hektor. Homer crafts a series of *aristeia,* man-to-man duels, that keep raising the level of men's valor and military skill. Achilleus' plight is that of mortality. His greatness in battle is linked to his certain death in battle. He is god-like; he is even 'half-god'; he should have been the greater son of Zeus.[16] Achilleus is a failed Christ. He brings us face to face with our own mortality. While we may lack his physical prowess, we feel the loss of something in this world that keeps us from attaining what we potentially could. The Christian sees that sin—Adam's and our own—has cursed our existence in spite of our being in God's image. But pagan Homer in his double blindness yet stumbled upon this same problem.

The key image or symbol of *The Iliad* is Achilleus' shield. Just as Christians associate the image of the cross with Christ dying for the world, so the

---

[12] Mark Twain commented that the works of Homer were not written by Homer but by another poet with the same name. I found this in Douglas Wilson's *The Case for Classical Education.*

[13] Upon reading Shelby Foote's magisterial history of the American War Between the States, titled *The Civil War,* his close friend, Walker Percy told him, "You have written the American Iliad."

[14] In the poem, "Easter 1916," Yeats uses the refrain "And a terrible beauty was born." *The Collected Poetry of W.B. Yeats* (New York: Scribners Paperbackback Poetry, 1989), 180-183.

[15] While reading Max Hasting's book *Armegeddon: The Battle for Germany 1944-45* a few years back, I was struck by how he used Homer's mini-biographical devices throughout his account.

[16] See "The Sacrifice of Achilles" in *Why Literature Matters* by Glenn Arbery (Wilmington, Deleware: ISI Books, 2001).

Greek could associate the shield of Achilleus with the world he is dying for. With the many details of life in the community, the shield revealed the patterns and contours of the life that Achilleus could not enjoy, but that would be saved by his sacrifice. The community, mankind, vividly etched into the shield by Hophaestus' skill, would be protected by the great warrior Achilleus. In part, his return to battle, after having stormed out of the ranks in Book 1, is a recognition of Achilleus' choice to fight and die for others rather than live for himself.

The last portion of the *Iliad* is surprising. Warlike Achilleus has not only killed Hektor, but has treated his corpse to a host of indignities. Yet when King Priam comes to Achilleus and pleads for his son's body, Achilleus shows mercy and pity. Indeed, the fate of rich Troy and poor Priam are the same as that of Achilleus. The first-time reader expects the story to go on. He anticipates the death of Achilleus from the wound in his heel and the capture of Troy by the Trojan horse. But Homer in a grand bit of restraint only foreshadows Achilleus' death and funeral by ending the work with the funeral of Hektor.

Homer's second epic, *The Odyssey*, builds upon several themes that constitute the core of many great stories—journeys and the revealing of the true king. Along with *The Odyssey*, works ranging from the Books of Exodus through Deuteronomy in the Bible to *Pilgrim's Progress* to *The Adventures of Huckleberry Finn* contain well-crafted stories about journeys. Books ranging from 1 Samuel in the Bible to Tolkien's *Lord of the Rings* build suspense and plot around the revealing of the rightful king. Because of the sense of life being a journey, because of the metaphorical image of this world being a journey, the main motif of the book resonates with modern readers.

Surprisingly, in the first four books of *The Odyssey*, the focus is not on Odysseus. There is some introduction to his plight, now ten years after the Trojan War ended, but the story turns to the terrible conditions back in Ithaka, his homeland. The key character in the early books is Telemachus, Odysseus' son. Telemachus, who would have been past twenty years old, must grow up and become the true son of his father. These first four books deal with Telemachus' growth into manhood and the role of the mentor, the teacher, in this case, the goddess Athena. She awakens Telemachus to his need to take control of matters in the banquet hall and then to leave in search, not of his father, but of his father's story. Telemachus goes and visits both the ever-aged and ever loquacious Nestor and King Menelaus and Helen. His model for behavior is Orestes, the son of Agamemnon who avenged his father's death.

In Book 5, the story shifts over to the journey of Odysseus. Again, the technique of Homer is amazing. Most of Odysseus's story is told not by the narrator, but by Odysseus. The amazing events we associate with Odysseus—the Trojan Horse, the Cyclops, and the Sirens—are relayed by the hero to his listeners. Homer is reminding us that we all have a story, and that story is our lives. Hence, *The Odyssey* is not just a story, but many stories within a story.

The key interpretive image or symbol of *The Odyssey* is the shroud Penelope is weaving. It is a fabric, a fabrication or a created thing, woven together and rewoven again; likewise, our stories are woven things, things made and fashioned out of our images and memories. Telemachus had to leave home to create his own story and to learn his father's story. Images of weaving are used throughout the book. Penelope is the most powerful character in the story, for it is she who is weaving her husband back home.[17]

More of Penelope's role can be seen by the comparisons of her with all of the other women Odysseus meets. Whether it is Queen Helen, Circe, or Nausica, no woman in the *Odyssey* can match the attraction of Penelope to Odysseus. Helen in all of her beauty, Circe with the power of everlasting life, and Nausica in the freshness of her youth all fall short of the attraction of Penelope.[18] Odysseus' trek home and his reclaiming of his rightful position entails much bloodshed, but order only comes with the sacrifice of blood.

Herodotus of Halicarnassus

The Histories by Herodotus is one of those great monumental works that I once started, put aside, and then read fully after starting the Ancient World Humanities program at my school. The history Herodotus preserved can be found in better organized, shorter, more accurate accounts. But Herodotus tells you how to teach history: Tell stories, mix the incredible with the chronological; insert humor and fantasy; give your sources; raise doubts; bounce along the details; ascribe the results of history to God's purposes and man's sins (hubris or pride); and teach the greater themes, such as the victory of freedom over tyranny.

The experts who point skinny fingers of factual indignation at Herodotus' errors would do well to ponder his success. History without stories and without passion is impossible. Again, as Augustine encourages us, borrow well

---

[17] I am indebted to Dr. Dennis Slattery for this material about the weaving motif. I heard this from him in a lecture and seminar on *The Odyssey* given at the Dallas Institute for the Humanities in Dallas, Texas, in June 2001.

[18] I am indebted to a colleague, Kent Travis, currently a teacher at Brookhill Academy in Tyler, Texas, for this insight.

from the wisdom of the pagan ancients. This book contains many truths worth borrowing and plundering.

Herodotus' *Histories* is an indispensable help in understanding the world and culture found in the Bible. Sacrifices, oaths, cultural habits, the inescapability of religion, and much more that is central to the Bible are also found in Herodotus. It has been described as a work that exists somewhere between the worlds of the Homeric epics and the Bible.

The central message of this work of the Father of History is the conflict between the East and the West. Herodotus devotes the last several books to a detailed study of the Greco-Persian Wars. One can profit from reading using just this portion of Herodotus, but there is so much more to Herodotus that one is really compelled to purchase and read the whole work.

Modern Light on Ancient Athens

While I still consider myself an elementary student when it comes to understanding the Ancient World, I can recommend the following books as secondary sources:

A Student's Guide to the Classics and *Greek Ways: How the Greeks Created Western Civilization* by Bruce Thornton.[19] *A Student's Guide* is a part of a useful series of short introductory books by different authors for high school or college students. The series is published by Intercollegiate Studies Institute. This particular book surveys the key authors and titles in literature, history, and philosophy in the Greco-Roman world. This is a great starter for both Greek and Roman literature. Thornton's book *Greek Ways* is similar to Cahill's book. It covers Greek thought, government, and literary achievements. Thornton's account is honest enough to include some shocking material, but is more restrained than Cahill's book. Thornton says,

> What was unique about the Greeks, however, was their 'spirit,' the ideals they introduced into the world, their 'sheer originality and brilliance,' as Bernard Knox put it. That those ideals could be contradicted by the Greeks' behavior reflects only the banal truth that humans rarely live up to their own aspirations; it does not mean that the ideals themselves are faulty, or that the Greeks should not be appreciated for articulating them.[20]

---

[19] Published by ISI Books.
[20] Thornton, 4.

Heroes in the City of Man by Peter J. Leithart is *the* book on ancient literature from a solidly Christian perspective. Subtitled *A Christian Guide to Select Ancient Literature,* this book is a study guide—with questions for classroom use—on Hesiod, Homer, the Greek dramatists, and Virgil. This is a book to keep close at hand when reading the ancient Greeks. As useful as the outlines and commentaries on the stories found in this book are, Leithart's introduction is *indispensable* when thinking through the Christian justification for reading pagan Greeks. Titled "The Devil Has No Stories," it is a brilliant defense of the world of the Greeks and Romans. Leithart says,

> Hesiod and Homer, Aeschylus and Aristophanes, as much as Moses and Samuel, are 'for Christ.' We must exercise great care and pray for wisdom in our study of this literature. We must never embrace enemies as friends or treat 'Greek wisdom' as sound and true. Yet, it is fully within the rights of Christians, to whom, in Christ, belong 'all things' (1 Cor. 3:21-23), to plunder these stories and make what use of them we can. Because some treasures of Athens, purged with fire, may, like the gold of Egypt, finally adorn Jerusalem.[21]

Complementing Leithart's book is *Omnibus I: Biblical and Classical Civilizations,* edited by Douglas Wilson and Ty Fisher. This book is the first in a series of textbooks designed to help teachers and students in Classical Christian schools to benefit from great works of theology, literature, and history. Different authors, all Christian, have contributed essays to this work, along with study guides and supplementary materials. Homer, Herodotus, and others are covered in this work, along with particular books of the Bible.[22]

Victor Davis Hanson is not only one of the best military historians today, but he has a particular expertise in Greek military history and is an advocate for studying the classics of Greek antiquity. His military histories, *Carnage and Culture, The Ripples of Battle, The Soul of Battle,* and *The Wars of the Ancient Greeks* are all excellent studies that contain insights into the contributions of Greeks to the Western way of war. He believes that our modern age could learn lots from the Greeks on how and why we should fight the war on terrorism. He has also written *A War Like No Other,* which covers the Peloponnesian War. *Who Killed Homer?,* which Hanson co-authored with John

---

[21] Peter Leithart, *Heroes in the City of Man.* (Moscow, Canon Press, 1999), 38.

[22] Douglas Wilson and Ty Fisher, *Omnibus I: Biblical and Classical Civilizations* (Lancaster, PA: Veritas Press, 2004). Subsequent books in this series cover the Medieval and Modern periods of history.

Heath, provides a rousing defense of classical education and a call for recovering the wisdom of the Greeks. This book contains useful commentaries on Greek literature, along with a castigation of modern education's abandonment of classical learning. Hanson has a Renaissance Era-like exuberance over the classics, but he lacks a Reformational sense of biblical limitations to the Greek worldview. Read him with caution, but read him.

Russell Kirk's *Roots of the American Order,* Richard Gummere's *The American Colonial Mind and the Classical Tradition* and Carl J. Richard's *The Founders and the Classics* all bring out the influence of Greek civilization on America's founding.

With the revival of classical education, books extolling the benefits of learning the ancient languages and cultures are increasing. I recommend Tracy Lee Simmons' *Climbing Parnassus: An Apologia for Greek and Latin,* which like *Who Killed Homer?,* extols the benefits of Classical studies, even calling for such in the original languages. Both books also bemoan the decline of our educational and social ideals because of the loss of Greek and Ancient wisdom.

Greek philosophy is filtered through Christian lenses in select chapters of Gordon Clark's *From Thales to Dewey,* R. C. Sproul's *The Consequences of Ideas,* and W. Andrew Hoffecker's *Building a Christian Worldview.*

The closest the Greeks came to truth was their altar inscribed "To the Unknown God." The God who made the world and everything in it has been proclaimed to us. As His children, we can know what the Greeks did not know. The Greek ruins belong to us as Christians. We are free to borrow them, rebuild from them, use them as models, scorn them as depraved, or whatever else is useful for the building of the Kingdom that will never end.

Chapter Fourteen
It Takes a Monk to Save a Civilization

> "But while in the Mediterranean the monks were retreating from the dying culture of the ancient world, in the North monasticism was becoming the creator of a new Christian culture and a school of the Christian life for the new peoples of the West."
> —Christopher Dawson[1]

Art historian and critic Kenneth Clark wrote, "It is hard to believe that for quite a long time—almost a hundred years—western Christianity survived by clinging to places like Skellig Michael, a pinnacle of rock eighteen miles from the Irish coast, rising seven hundred feet out of the sea."[2] This rocky island located off the southwestern coast of Ireland was one of the outposts of early Irish Christians who in the fifth and sixth centuries rescued European civilization.

This took place in a time when the old order and power of the Roman Empire had completely disintegrated and when illiterate, pagan, barbaric hordes, who were devoid of understanding the Greco-Roman heritage, were rearranging Europe. While Greece lay in ruins and Rome was being pillaged and plundered, the best of their accomplishments were preserved only in books.

But books too are perishable. Thomas Cahill notes, "A world in chaos is not a world in which books are copied and libraries maintained. It is not a world where learned men have the leisure to become more learned."[3] Great libraries, like that of ancient Alexandria, were vulnerable to destruction, and with the destruction of books, the knowledge, thought, and poetry of whole cultures were subject to extinction.

---

[1] Dawson, *Religion and the Rise of Western Culture,* 49.
[2] Kenneth Clark, *Civilization* (London: The Folio Society, 1999), 17. Quote originally found in Cahill.
[3] Thomas Cahill, *How the Irish Saved Civilization* (New York: Nan A. Talese, 1995), 35.

Yet instead of this fate, books were copied, libraries maintained, and learning preserved and increased. For a time, about all that stood between the preservation of European civilization or its descent into a true dark age was a hardy band of Irish monks who were dedicated to copying books and evangelizing people. Usually we think of the Irish as the victims of colonization and oppression. In their later history, English policy toward the Irish ranged from trying to absorb them to trying to obliterate them. Just as the Emerald Isle is on the edge of Europe, so the Irish have been on the edge of the progress and forward tug of history—most of the time.

Although there was never a time when Irish armies occupied Europe or Irish leaders dominated the councils of power, there was a time when Ireland did save civilization. We recognize the name of Patrick, but most know little about his successors, like Columcille and Columbanus, who spread the Christian message beyond Ireland to Britain and then to continental Europe. Thomas Cahill's book, *How the Irish Saved Civilization,* is a delightful account of this history.

Two things were done primarily by the Irish during the fifth and sixth centuries. First, they carefully copied and preserved the books that fell into their hands. Latin literature would have been lost without the Irish; furthermore, as Cahill points out, "[T]here would have perished in the west not only literacy but all the habits of mind that encourage thought."[4] Second, the Irish monks established monasteries all over Europe that were devoted to preaching, teaching, and ministering to the local populations. Cahill said, "While Rome and its ancient empire faded from memory and a new, illiterate Europe rose on its ruins, a vibrant, literary culture was blooming in secret along its Celtic fringes. It needed only one step more to close the circle, which would reconnect Europe to its own past by way of scribal Ireland."[5] That one step was taken when the Irish colonized Europe through establishing monasteries. From Ireland, they went to Scotland and the rest of Europe. Cahill says,

> Monks began to set off in every direction, bent on glorious and heroic exile for the sake of Christ....Some went north....Others went northwest, like Brendan the Navigator, visiting Iceland, Greenland, and North America....Some set out in boats without oars, putting their destinations in the hands of God. Many of the exiles found their way to continental Europe, where they were more than a match for the barbarians they met. They, whom the Romans had never conquered....fearlessly brought the ancient civilization back to its ancient home.[6]

---

[4] Cahill, 193-194
[5] Cahill, 183.
[6] Cahill, 187-188.

Imitating the Irish

Cultivating a book culture and doing mission work: These two characteristics of the Irish monks point out the way for Christians to take dominion over the future.

I recently had a conversation with a friend who teaches history at a junior college. He was bemoaning the fact that his college students could not locate key American cities on maps of the United States. I smiled and said, "Well, my tenth graders are struggling to understand Augustine's *City of God*." Literature has faced extinction in our own era, but in a way different from the past. In the ancient world, rare manuscripts were destroyed; in our age they have been crowded out by the abundance of technology and paper and by philosophies of education that have undermined books and knowledge. But in Christian school and home school settings, books have been rediscovered.

There have been some useful textbooks written in the past several decades since the Christian education movement emerged. But more important than the textbooks are the classic works that students are reading. My students are now reading books in the junior high and high school levels that I never read even in college. I repeatedly learned about the *Federalist Papers*, but only after I taught in a Christian school did I begin actually studying the *Federalist Papers*. At its best, much of my education seemed better suited to train me to watch "Jeopardy" or to play "Trivial Pursuit" than to think.

In this modern reformation, Christian educators debate whether it is best to read the ancient pagans or the early church fathers. Further debates occur between those who favor Cromwell's secretary, John Milton, and those who favor the Italian Catholic poet Dante; advocates for Shakespeare lock horns with devotees of Spenser; and some even assign Hemingway and Faulkner to the disgust of those who prefer Tolkien and Lewis. We more eclectic types try to assign and read them all. But the debates continue amongst Christian educators. Among language teachers, disagreements break out over whether to teach Greek, Hebrew, Latin, or some modern language. Even logic teachers differ over whether you begin with fallacies or focus instead on syllogisms and validity. My response to these intramural debates is: Isn't this great? Isn't this fun?

In the Christian education community, we are producing a generation of graduates who are well-read in Greek and Roman classics, Patristic theology, Reformed treatises, the Great Books tradition, the Medieval Trivium, and much more. There is no uniformity imposed by a statist decree telling these students what to read and telling teachers what to teach. Instead, we are experiencing the rise of a generation of thinking students who have traveled all over the intellectual globe. They will have achieved Mortimer Adler's ideal of having read the best ideas that men have thought and written. In one sense of the word, they will be Renaissance men and women. But in another sense, because they are viewing these books through Scriptural lenses, they are Reformation men and women.

Imagine an iron-sharpened generation of people who go beyond "Trivial Pursuit" to actually discuss issues. Imagine political debate where Christians grounded in Hamilton's and Madison's views of the Constitution are sparring with other Christians holding to Patrick Henry's objections to the Constitution. Imagine your children fighting over whether Calvin or Augustine was the greatest theologian. Imagine young people who will be in awe of us who lived in the same era as Rushdoony, Van Til, and Bahnsen.

Some of us struggle to resist watching the evening political talk shows. When we give in to the temptation and watch the shows, we rejoice in seeing conservative Christian spokesmen locking horns with liberals in debate. Such a witness and voice is good, but a few Christian ideas touted by talking heads squeezed in between toothpaste commercials in a national debate will not change the culture. Books will do that.

Today's Monasteries

Likewise, churches will change our culture. Churches should strive to be the monasteries of today. Monasteries are not well understood in our culture. We picture drab, dark places where hooded monks went about reciting chants. Instead, monasteries were centers of Christian activism. J. O. Westwood describes monasteries as

> ...schools, all the way from kindergarten to university, hospitals, hotels, publishing houses, libraries, law courts, art academies, and conservatories of music. They were houses of refuge, places of pilgrimage, marts for barter and exchange, centers of culture, social foci, newspaper offices, and distilleries. A score of other public and practical things were they: garrison, granary, orphan asylum, frontier fort, post office, savings bank, and general store for surrounding agricultural districts. We carelessly imagine the early monasteries as charnel-houses of cant and ritual—whereas they were the best-oiled machines for the advancement of science, the living accelerators of human thinking, precedent to the University of Paris.[7]

---

[7] J. O. Westwood, quoted in James Westfall Thompson and Edgar Nathaniel Johnson, *An Introduction to Medieval Europe 300-1500* (New York: W. W. Norton & Company, Inc., 1937), 213.

Referring to the works of the monks in the Middle Ages in his book *The Making of Europe*, Christopher Dawson said, "The greatest names of the age are the names of monks—St. Benedict and St. Gregory, the two Columbas, Bede and Boniface, Alcuin and Rabanus Maurus, and Dunstan, and it is to the monks that the great cultural achievements of the age are due, whether we look at the preservation of ancient culture, the conversion of new peoples or the formation of new centres of culture in Ireland and Northumbria and the Carolingian Empire."[8]

Christian churches actually are doing the work of monasteries today, without the baggage of the more noticeable errors of the Medieval time. Christian churches and voluntary agencies provide the best social services for our society today. Without endorsing President Bush's program for aiding faith-based organization, it is reassuring that the national debate recognizes that Christian organizations are the most effective means of dealing with poverty, drug abuse, and family problems. Christians are the ones providing the real educational reforms (at no cost to taxpayers), music instruction, marriage counseling, English language instruction, and other needs of society.

There remains those churches that are merely stained glass edifices open to the public only for a few hours on Sunday mornings. But, some great Christian works are being done in places that do not look like traditional churches. The news coverage of the hurricane relief efforts in Louisiana and surrounding states in the fall of 2005 could not help but highlight Christian ministries to the evacuees.

The greatest events going on in our day are not happening in cabinet meetings at the White House or in caucuses on Capital Hill or in executive board rooms on Wall Street. Civilization is being saved by faithful pastors, dedicated Christian teachers, moms and dads who are teaching their children about Jesus, small name book publishers, newsletters, magazines, and web sites dedicated to Christian causes, and to a host of other Samaritine-type works happening across the land.

Thomas Cahill contrasted the Romans, who were unable to save or salvage their once grand civilization, with the Irish saints, who changed the direction of history. Cahill says, "The twenty-first century, prophesied Malraux, will be spiritual or it will not be. If our civilization is to be saved—forget about our civilization, which, as Patrick would say, may pass 'in a moment like a cloud or smoke that is scattered by the wind'—if *we* are to be saved, it will not be by Romans but by saints."[9]

---

[8] Christopher Dawson, *The Making of Europe* (New York: Barnes & Noble Books, 1994), 17.

[9] Cahill, 218.

We could spend a lot of time bemoaning the legion of dangers to our republic, our civilization, and our way of life. Hilliary or Obama just might get elected in 2008, the economy might implode, and gay marriages might become the rage. Congress might not pass and the President might not sign some mythical piece of legislation ending all bad things and promoting all good things. Don't despair. Instead, teach a Sunday school class, support a Christian school or mission work, buy some Christian books, give away some Christian books, go to prayer meeting, witness to someone, encourage a faithful minister, and pray for God's will to be done on earth as it is in heaven.

Arend van Leeuwen's book *Christianity in World History* ends with this note: "We live in a time of crisis: and *krisis* is a biblical word. In the Bible it signifies 'judgment', but along with that, 'justice' and 'salvation'. The Servant of the Lord 'will not fail or be discouraged till he has established justice (*krisis*) in the earth; and the coastlands wait for his *torah*,' (Is. 42.1ff.; Mt. 12:18ff.)."[10]

Holding on to a few acres of rocky and jagged islands, Christians once persevered for a century, laboring to see the faith spread. We here in this land have so much more.

---

[10] Arend Th. Van Leewen, *Christianity in World History* (New York: Charles Scribner's Sons, 1964), 439.

Chapter Fifteen
Some Not So Good Ole Days

> When He opened the fourth seal, I heard the voice of the fourth living creature saying, "Come and see." So I looked, and behold, a pale horse. And the name of him who sat on it was Death, and Hades followed after him. And power was given to them over a fourth of the earth, to kill with sword, with hunger, with death, and by the beasts of the earth.
> —Revelation 6:7-8

> No age is tidy or made of whole cloth, and none is a more checkered fabric than the Middle Ages.
> —Barbara Tuchman[1]

    Being a history teacher, I'm occasionally asked the following question: "If you could be born at any time in the past, when would it be?" My answer: "Yesterday." My life revolves around great heroes and epochs of the past, but I am content to know them through books.

    I would like to have known Winston Churchill, but have no interest in dodging German Stutkas on the sands of Dunkirk or the streets of London. The Reformation was a glorious revival of God's saving truth, but I prefer friendly disagreements with Catholics today to burning at the stake for the teachings of Luther and Calvin. And it's not just the heat of fire, for the cold of the Delaware River in 1776 or of winter at Valley Forge makes me more of a sunshine soldier than a committed patriot. As a Southerner, I glory in the heritage of Robert E. Lee and Stonewall Jackson, but cringe at the contemplation of charging straight toward the barrels of Yankee-held Springfield muskets or being mercifully saved by amputations from the saws of Confederate surgeons.

    Even those most blessed days of the Apostles and early Church Fathers remind me of how comfortable I am sitting in a pew, freely worshipping,

---

[1] Foreword to *A Distant Mirror: The Calamitous 14th Century*, (New York: Bollantine Books, 1978) xvii.

rather than contending for the faith in those birthing days and infant years of the Christian Church.

I am content to be living in this glorious era, even with the threats of terrorism and irritations of telemarketers. But if I were forced to live in some distant era of the past, it certainly would not be the late Middle Ages of the 14th and 15th centuries.

I have visited those centuries—many times in my readings and teachings. More memorable intellectual visits have included journeying to Canterbury with Geoffrey Chaucer and a host of pilgrims telling tales. Longer visits to the past have included reading Barbara Tuchman's *A Distant Mirror: The Calamitous 14th Century*. Tuchman's book, first published in 1978, was written to mirror the upheavals of the calamitous 20th century. Having to choose between calamitous times, I am glad to have lived in the latter difficult times rather than during the late Medieval centuries. Nuclear proliferation in the last century was frightening, but not any more so than dentistry of the Middle Ages.

Spiritually, politically, and personally, the 14th and 15th centuries seemed to herald the end of time to those who lived then. They experienced an eschatology of catastrophe, more grounded in their circumstances than in biblical exegesis. Indeed, the despair of that age was well founded and the only seeds of hope that we historically can see were just beginning to germinate. As Tuchman says, "The pessimism of the 14th century grew in the 15th to the belief that man was becoming worse, an indication of the approaching end."[2] The problems of that age were woven together in the fashion of Medieval tapestries at their best. War and brigandage, plague and social uprisings, heresies and corruptions, and immoralities and cruelties all combined to darken the spirits of a whole civilization. The more frightening images from John's Revelation were seemingly being fulfilled in that age.

Little things, like the bacilli attached to fleas that infested rats, erupted into the Black Death, which stripped the population by thirty to fifty percent. The Bubonic Plague was exceeded only by the combination of madmen kings, vainglorious knights, political pawns, and religious charlatans who occupied or infected thrones, political principalities, and church offices.

The first great problem was the Hundred Years War between England and France (1337-1453). The war began over English claims of dynastic rights to the throne of France. England started the war and often seemed to have the upper hand, winning battles, such as Crecy, Poitiers, and Agincourt. English armies occupied key ports and land areas of France throughout the

---

[2] Tuchman, 588.

war. Struggling to maintain some sense of unity of the different regions, France endured incompetent and insane kings, political betrayals, peasant revolts, and military defeats. The war itself stretched and tugged the once unifying and workable fabric of Medieval feudalism, ripping it to shreds. That France emerged from the war as one nation, that France even survived the war, that France—in some sense—won the war was due to endurance rather than brilliance. Like World War I, this was a war of attrition, but the attrition was of leadership rather than of human life. In other words, France won because English stupidity exceeded their own.

But wars, even short ones, tend to bring out the worst in mankind—both incompetence and brutality. Many are the testimonies of man of this truth. Channing said, " Under its standard gather violence, malignity, rage, fraud, perfidy, rapacity, and lust…It turns man into a beast of prey." Sidney Smith was not far from accurate when he called war the greatest curse on mankind and said, "God is forgotten in war; every principle of Christianity is trampled upon." Dwight D. Eisenhower correctly noted, "[T]he essence of war is fire, famine, and pestilence. They contribute to its outbreak; they are among its weapons; they become the consequences." To this could be added thousands of other testimonies to war's evils, but as Ernest Raymond noted, "As men of reason we scoff at war; as men of business we fear it; as men of religion and good-will we loathe it; and as artists we love it."[3]

Artists and history teachers, as well, cannot help but love war, in part because wars display human skills and courage. Some brilliant lights lit up the French landscape. Bertrand du Guesclin, or Bertrand of Brittany, was an effective military leader, cut from the same cloth as William Wallace or Nathan Bedford Forrest. When his mother first saw him as an infant, she responded by saying, "He's a monster." But Bertrand overcame his childhood rejection and apparent physical unattractiveness to rise to leadership during the second phase of the Hundred Years War. His efforts almost completely expelled the English from French soil. His brilliant military skills and chivalric stature have caused him to be called the "last flare of the chivalric knight of the old days."[4] Much better known is Joan of Arc. Joan proved adept at rallying the French cause, propping up the spineless Dauphin, and forcing the English

---

[3] Quotes found in *The New Dictionary of Thoughts: A Cyclopedia of Quotations,* originally compiled by Tryon Edwards and revised and enlarged by C. N. Catrevas, Jonathan Edwards, and Ralph Emerson Brown (Standard Book Company, 1959), 714.

[4] Bertrand Du Guesclin is almost forgotten in our day. His story, referenced above, can be found in Roger Vercel's *Bertrand of Brittany: A Biography of Messire Du Guesclin* (New Haven, CT: Yale University Press, 1934).

into their worst long-term public relations act ever—burning a saint.[5] Her religious impulses continue, to our delight, to baffle secularist historians.

England had her days of glory during those same years. Edward, Prince of Wales, 'the Black Prince,' won glory at the battles of Crecy and Poitiers, where his army captured the French king. Edward's brother, John of Gaunt, enjoyed political fame rather than military success. In a later phase of the war, Henry V gained glory for his victory at Agincourt and the political alliance he affected with the French king. Many years later, Shakespeare's play, *Henry V,* further enhanced his glory, which was all lost under his son Henry VI. Besting all these nobles and besting the knights of both England and France were the unnamed English archers whose longbows leveled the French cavalry on many occasions.

Shakespeare's character, Henry V, at the start of the battle of Agincourt exclaimed in his St. Crispin's Day speech rallying his troops, "And gentlemen in England now abed shall think themselves accursed they were not here...." But putting powerful poetic rhetoric aside, it was the war itself—with its seeming inability to end, its dynastic rivalries, its political ruthlessness, and countless manifestations of human depravity—that was accursed. The Anglo-French hostility did not completely abate until the Twentieth Century World Wars. And even then, the French quipped that the English would fight the Germans down to the last Frenchman.

Parleys were often conducted. Peace was often proposed, and sometimes actually achieved for a season, upon the bases of reason, or dynastic marriages, or upon a common desire to unite in a crusade against more distant enemies. Reasonable men on both sides could have halted the war at many points, but such reasonableness rarely happens in history. So for over a century, a conflict over rival claims to the throne of France settled one issue: This war would be ranked by name and duration as history's longest military conflict.

But a threat greater than the war engulfed all of Europe during the 14th and 15th centuries. Like the armies at war, it attacked, then withdrew, but then would come back to attack again. Four times it swept through Europe. It was the Black Death, or the Bubonic Plague. The plague is horrible to read about no matter how it is viewed: whether by the astronomical death tolls, the shocking percentages of the population destroyed, or the anecdotes, grim humor, art, and personal testimonies that remain. The plague resulted in

---

[5] R. J. Rushdoony told the story of a British historian who was almost totally unfamiliar with the American War of 1812. When told that the British burned Washington in that war, he exclaimed, "Oh my, I knew we burned Joan of Arc, but I had no idea we burned George Washington too!"

insanely silly actions, as in the case of villagers who danced to drums and trumpets believing it gave them immunity. It also resulted in insanely wicked actions, such as killing Jews.

Just as there is a ripple effect to war and battles, so there are ripple effects of diseases and plagues. Amidst the Black Death, some people looked to God for answers, and some people resorted to lawlessness and debauchery. The depletion of the population reconfigured the working class, land ownership, and the make-up of society at all levels. It spawned some good effects. Universities, a Medieval development, were advanced by the desire to preserve learning and save civilization from annihilation amidst the plague. But on the negative side, the fear of sin and death caused the sale of indulgences to skyrocket. Many of the paintings of the time reflected the horrors of the disease and the morbidity of a people plagued in mind and body.

Those spared by the war and plague still faced roving bands of outlaws or brigands. These brigands were generally soldiers, yes, even knights, who maintained a profession of arms even during the lulls in the war. Decrees from both church and government officials warned against brigandage, but the idleness between wars, the callousness toward life caused by war, and the lure of goods caused the brigands to ignore the decrees. Knights all too often lacked shining armor, chivalry, or virtue.

On the other hand, the commoners, the peasants, were not morally much better than the brigands. Happy serfs, tilling the land, harvesting crops, and celebrating the seasons may have existed, but the historical records more often depicted a darker side to the lower classes. Peasant uprisings generally had two bad results. The first was extreme violence. Peasants grabbed whatever implements they worked with in the fields or shops and wielded them as weapons in the streets. The governing officials often chose to deal with the peasants, making promises of tax relief and other benefits. The Wat Tyler rebellion in England was one such example where the king himself, the boy Richard II, rode in amongst the rebels and promised to lead and protect them.

Government promises —even those granted by the king—were then immediately forgotten and the rebel leaders were soon left hanging from gibbets about the land. The bloodshed and sacrifices of such peasant uprisings did make a long-term contribution to human freedom and eventual participation in the affairs of government by common men.

The Christian Church had great opportunities to minister to a civilization reeling between war and plague. But rather than being salt and light, the Church was filled with corruption and darkness. Medieval Catholicism had its glorious moments, but the 14th and 15th centuries are more often remembered for spiritual decay. As always, there were faithful churchmen. This was the age of John Wycliffe, Jan Hus, Gerard Groote (founder of the Brethren of the Common Life), and Thomas á Kempis. Chaucer highlights a faithful parson and a godly knight who stand in marked contrast to his many portrayals of ungodly, hypocritical, and licentious church leaders on the road to Canterbury. Chaucer's art reflected a stark spiritual reality that many noticed, but few endeavored to change.

We Protestants take notice of and oppose Medieval Catholicism from a particular set of premises based on the Bible and restated in the theologies of Luther and Calvin. But on the basis of Medieval Catholicism's premises, one can argue against the practices found, and all too often, tolerated in the Catholic Church of that time. Chaucer and Dante both strongly portrayed and condemned church abuses. Besides a host of problems ranging from wicked and immoral clerics to political wheeling and dealing by the prelates, the Roman Catholic Church's highest office, the papacy, seat of the supposed Vicar of Christ on earth, lost honor and authority. The French captured the papacy in 1303, moving the Pope and his See to Avignon so as to guarantee French control. This event turned further south in 1379 when political and religious maneuverings resulted in two rival claimants to the papacy. Political states and entities lined up behind one pope or the other based on previous conflicts and alliances. Hence, England supported the pope in Rome, while France backed the pope in Avignon.

It might have helped matters if either of the original popes in the Papal Schism had buttressed his claims to the office with displays of any godliness. That was not to be. The Avignon pope, Clement VII, came to office with the nickname "Butcher of Cesena" as a result of events in his life prior to being pope. His rival, Urban VI, was both insane and vicious, which is illustrated by his hiring of mercenaries to protect him by force. Both popes promptly excommunicated each other. Tuchman writes, "When each Pope excommunicated the followers of the other, who could be sure of salvation?"[6] In time, a council would depose both popes and appoint a new man as pope. Rather than solving the problem, the result was that now three men laid claim to being the sole ruler of Christ's church.

As a way of uniting the factions of Europe divided by war and religion, some church leaders resorted to calling for a crusade. The need was there and was great. By the early 1400s, the Ottoman Turks were battering down the last vestiges of the Byzantine Empire and were advancing into Europe. A coalition of Serbs, Rumanians, and Moldavians had been crushed in their efforts to stem the Muslim tide at Kossovo.[7] The Muslim Turks, under a

---

[6] Tuchman, 335.

[8] Hence explaining why American foreign policy in the 1990s was, as often the case, historically blind and misguided.

Sultan named Bajazet, advanced into Bulgaria on the Danube River and were poised to take Hungary. King Sigismund of Hungary appealed to the rest of Europe for help. An army, largely French, advanced into eastern Europe to deal with the Muslim threat. This coalition was well provisioned with silks and wines, but neglected such less important details as carrying along siege equipment and catapults.

Great confidence in the glories of the French cavalry led the leaders to plunge into battle with a frontal assault. The result was defeat of the crusaders and the capture of many of their leaders by the Muslims. Europe was saved only later when Mongol-Turkic forces under Tamerlane diverted Sultan Bajazet's attention from his conquest of Europe.

In the year 1453, with an English defeat in battle at Castillon, the Hundred Years War came to an end. The war's end did not undo the century of damage to Christendom. Tuchman says, "The Hundred Years' War, like the crises of the Church in the same period, broke apart medieval unity. The brotherhood of chivalry was severed, just as the internationalism of the universities, under the combined effects of war and schism, could not survive."[9] England's peace was short-lived, for soon after continental hostilities ceased, King Henry VI's madness became so intense that rival factions began vying for his throne. The result was the civil war in England known as the War of the Roses. In that same year of 1453, Constantinople fell before the Turkish Muslim armies of Mahomet I.

God was not yet through with Europe. (I believe He is still not yet through with Europe.) This same time, roughly 1453-1454, was when a German devised a movable type printing press and produced his first document from it. Gutenberg's invention would pave the way for a new age. Within the next fifty to one hundred years, Columbus would discover the New World and Luther would rediscover the New Covenant. The greatest products of the 14th and 15th centuries, particularly the poetic works of Chaucer and Dante and Thomas á Kempis, would be preserved and disseminated. The Tudors would emerge as the leading family of England and provide political stability and provoke religious reform.

The wars, plagues, rebellions, insanities, and evils of the calamitous late Middle Ages would be seen in time as simple stepping-stones on the rocky paths of God's providential dealings with His people. A Reformation was being born.

---

[8] Tuchman, 594.

Chapter Sixteen
The Great Siege Then and Now

Many more difficult victories have fallen to your scimitar
than the capture of a handful of men in a tiny
little island that is not well fortified.
—Viziers of the Divan to Soleiman the Magnificent, October 1564[1]

It is the great battle of the Cross and the Koran, which is
now to be fought. A formidable army of infidels are on the
point of investing our island. We, for our part, are the chosen
soldiers of the Cross, and if Heaven requires the sacrifice of
our lives, there can be no better occasion than this.
—Jean Parisot De La Valette, Grand Master of the Knights of Malta[2]

In one instance at least, I wish that Voltaire, the French atheistic philosopher, were right. He said, "Nothing is better known than the siege of Malta." In this dark age of historical ignorance, with abysmal historic mental lapses and pandemic historic amnesia, the siege of Malta in 1565 ranks as one of the most forgotten events ever.

The island of Malta, located in the Mediterranean Sea just south of Sicily, has been a hinge upon which the tide of history has turned on several occasions. In the first case, in Acts 28, Malta served as a refuge for the Apostle Paul and all his fellow ship passengers after their ship struck a reef. After the friendly Maltese saved Paul and ministered to him, God opened the door for Paul to return their kindness by preaching the Gospel to them. Malta is a springboard to Italy, and from there Paul went to Rome where he wrote several of the New Testament epistles.

---

[1] As quoted in Jack Beeching, *The Galleys at Lepanto* (New York: Charles Scribner's Sons, 1983), 79.
[2] As quoted in Ernle Bradford, *The Great Siege: Malta 1565* (Hertfordshire, Great Britain: Wordsworth Editions, 1999), 57.

Malta again played a crucial role in World War II, over a hundred years after the British had gained control of the island in the early 1800s.[3] Domination of the Mediterranean was a key issue in World War II. Nazi Germany, Fascist Italy, and Vichy France controlled most of the land and territories of Europe and North Africa bordering the Mediterranean. Rommel's Afrika Korps and his less than stellar Italian divisions were poised to capture Egypt and the Suez Canal. That "what-if victory" would have toppled the dominoes of the Middle East into the Axis camp, leading to an encirclement of the beleaguered Soviet Union.

Perhaps as important as the valiant campaigns of Montgomery's Eighth Army, perhaps as heroic as the Royal Air Force in the Battle of Britain, the British garrison on the island of Malta kept the Axis powers from winning the war. Rommel's tanks were left without fuel, replacement parts, and personnel in large part because the British air and naval units striking out from Malta were sinking Axis supply ships. Franklin Roosevelt heralded Malta's role in World War II, saying, "Under repeated fires from the skies, Malta stood alone but unafraid in the center of the sea, one tiny bright flame in the darkness—a beacon of hope for the clearer days which have come."[4]

Roosevelt's words about Malta standing alone and being one tiny bright flame in the darkness could have been applied to an earlier time. In between the events of Acts 28 and World War II, Malta played its greatest role in history where its people and defenders (to quote from FDR again), "in the cause of freedom and justice and decency…rendered valorous service far and above the call of duty."[5] The earlier time was 1565, when much of the attention of Europe was focused on the religiously and politically fractious events of the Protestant Reformation. Within the inner circles of Christendom, theologians and bishops, kings and priests, Reformers and Catholics battled with pen and sword. Critical doctrines were at stake. The rhetoric was inflamed, but the battle was for the soul of man and of Christ's Church. While all these matters were being hammered out—not always very nicely—inside Europe, a threat loomed outside.

The threat was Islam. Under Suleiman (or Soleyman) the Magnificent, Sultan of the Ottomans, Islamic forces possessed the power, the will, and the desire to conquer all of Europe. Islamic theology gave an ideological drive to the Seljuk (also called Ottoman) Turks, who from the year 1071 combined fanatical faith and military might with the ambition and will to rule. This

---

[3] See James Holland, *Fortress Malta: An Island Under Siege 1940-1943* (London: Orion Books, 2003).
[4] Holland, 387.
[5] Holland, 387.

power vanquished the once great Byzantine Empire in 1453. The fall of Constantinople broke the last barrier between the forces of Islam and the Christian West.

By the 1500s, Ottoman expansion already reached deep into Europe. The Balkan Peninsula was Ottoman territory. In 1529 the Ottoman forces were stopped only at the gates of Vienna. That defeat was not the end of Ottoman expansionism. Brandon Rogers said, "Every Ottoman Sultan was expected to bring at least one foreign state under Islamic rule during his reign."[6] Under Suleiman, this was accomplished when the Ottoman Turks added thousands of square miles to their possessions. Among his conquests was the island of Rhodes, captured in 1522.

Rhodes had been defended by a holy order of monks, known as the Knights of St. John. This religious and military order dated back to the time of the Crusades. Their primary calling was hospital ministry to Christian pilgrims. This holy order of nurses dropped their bedpans and bandages for the sick only when the occasion called for the sword and shield. They refrained from battle when Christian fought Christian, but took up the sword readily when the enemy was Muslim.

After a valiant and hard-fought defense of Rhodes, they were defeated, but were granted the honors of war by being allowed to leave. From Rhodes the knights wandered about Europe for several years. Since they owed fealty to the Pope alone and no monarch, the kings were little interested in them. Since they were forbidden by oath to fight against other Christians, their resumes were further hindered among monarchs.[7] Emperor Charles V of Spain gave the Knights the island of Malta in 1530. Losing Rhodes and having to resettle in the smaller and less attractive island of Malta was a depressing event for the warrior monks, who were now increasingly becoming relics of obsolete medieval Christendom. The spirit of nationalism of the 1500s had little regard for a military force that was united by faith and not by a geographic or a political identity.

By 1565, there were about five hundred and fifty knights on Malta, along with about four thousand Maltese men capable of bearing arms. Suleiman recognized that possession of Malta and the final liquidation of the Knights of St. John would provide the base from which to conquer Sicily and Italy, and from there, the rest of Europe. Beeching said,

---

[6] Brandon Rogers, "The Background" from *Lepanto by G. K. Chesterton with Explanatory Notes and Commentary,* edited by Dale Ahlquist (Minneapolis, MN: American Chesterton Society, 2003), 48.
[7] Beeching, 69.

The rocky little island might be barren of crops and short of water. But if only the Turks could take Malta quickly, its great harbour would serve as the base for yet another leap forward—a landing, for instance, on the wheat-growing island of Sicily, only sixty miles to the north.….From Malta it would be feasible to land directly on the southern shores of Italy, or even to cross over to Spain.…With Malta taken, the Turks next year could keep the whole Western Mediterranean on the jump.[8]

Suleiman marshaled a force of nearly two hundred ships, bearing ample arms and powder, and somewhere between thirty and forty thousand troops. Malta was all that stood between the Islamic East and the Christian West. In a practice that European leaders have honed to perfection in the twentieth and twenty-first centuries, the European sovereigns—narcissistic, greedily nationalistic, and strategically blind—did nothing. Francis I of France was allied to the Sultan Suleiman, even though many of the Knights were Frenchmen. (Imagine that: France—allied to the enemies of Europe and Christendom! France—doing nothing to stem the threat to Europe!) Along with diplomatic perfidy, France had its own internal religious and political divisions.

The German states and Elizabethan England were entangled in internal matters and the more consuming issues did not reach much beyond their own borders. Germany had been divided by religion for nearly fifty years. England under the Elizabethan Compromise was straddling its own tensions, with foreign powers eager to court or depose the queen. Spain, under Phillip II, had the power and the interest to act, but also did nothing. Spain was struggling with imperial overreach, for its dominions included parts of France and Italy and what are now Belgium and the Netherlands. Spain, with the Inquisition, was attempting to control religious dissent and had its own Muslim faction in the southern part of that land.[9] Hence, Malta stood alone.

The Siege Begins

The military battle that ensued at Malta fulfills all the drama and vicissitudes of war that have lured historians, poets, filmmakers, and armchair soldiers from Homer's time to our own. As Robert E. Lee said, "It is well that war is so terrible less we grow too fond of it." The battle for Malta had no lack of the blood, gore, and carnage of war, with the heroism and superhuman actions of men in warfare, as well.

---

[8] Beeching, 76.
[9] Rogers, 46.

The initial key to the defense of Malta was the fortress of St. Elmo. The Turks anticipated capturing it in a few days time, with a minimal cost. In the end, it took over thirty days and 8,000 Muslim dead before the Turks could raise their banners over this one fortress. After that, the Knights and Maltese still held two well-defended peninsulas from which they were never removed.

The great Christian hero of this story was Grand Master Jean La Valette. The capital of Malta is now named after him. Seventy years old at the time, he was, in the words of Ernle Bradford, "that rarest of human beings, a completely single-minded man."[10] He had endured and survived the siege of Rhodes, naval battles with the Turks, the miseries of being a galley slave under the Turks, and physical wounds from battle. His rhetoric in war-time was like that of Churchill; his religious zeal like that of Cromwell; his strategic and tactical gifts like those of R. E. Lee and Stonewall Jackson; his personal bravery and example to the men like that of Washington.

Like all commanders in wartime, he took actions that cause the more prissy historians (to borrow a term from R. J. Rushdoony) to blanch and faint. When the decapitated bodies of four brave knights were nailed to crosses and sent across the channel to the shore defended by the knights, Valette responded forcefully. He took his Turkish prisoners, beheaded them, and fired their heads from his cannons into the enemy camp. This action sent a message of defiance to the Turks, but also told his own men that this fight was to the death. There would be no exit strategy.

When the Turks sent a miserable underling to Valette to offer surrender terms, Valette coldly responded, "Hang him." The messenger begged for his life. Valetta showed him a huge ditch on the edge of the Knight's defensive perimeter. "Tell your master that this is the only territory that I will give him. There lies the land which he may have for his own—provided only that he fills it with the bodies of his Janissaries." At this point, the poor messenger, according to those present, "dirtied his breeches."[11]

The Knights' methods of warfare are amazing for both personal gallantry and technique. Their combat gear consisted of suits of armor weighing about 150 pounds. This metal encasement from head to toe shielded them from nearly all enemy blows and added weight to their own jabs and thrusts. Their weapons were large two-handed swords. When confronting the long robed Turkish Janissaries in man-to-man combat, the Knights were most often successful.[12]

---

[10] Bradford, 32
[11] Bradford, 150-151.
[12] Beeching, 84-85.

Not only did the Knights fight bravely for their faith and their island, the native Maltese, little noticed in the chronicles of the battle, earned their laurels for courage and dedication. Along with the image of the Knights clad in their full armor of by-gone eras, one must picture the hardy Maltese swimmers, stripped to the buff, dashing into the water with knives in the mouths, going after the Turks who were attempting to dismantle the off shore defenses.

The battle for Malta raged from May to September of 1565. For a time, one Maltese defense line after another was reduced to rubble. But each Turkish victory exacted a high cost. After the siege of St. Elmo, which took the Turks thirty one days and eight thousand casualties to capture, the Muslims faced yet more obstacles. Still standing across the water was the fort at St. Angelo. Mustapha Pasha, one of the Turkish leaders, thus exclaimed, "Allah! If so small a son has cost us so dear, what price shall we pay for so large a father?"[13] They discovered the price on the Senglea peninsula. Here, boatloads of Janissaries were hit with shot and shell before they reached land. Those who did reach land found Maltese women and children, aiding the Knights, by hurling stones and artificial fire and pouring boiling cauldrons of water upon the attackers. When the five hour attack by land and sea was called off, the Turks had lost three thousand troops to the two hundred and fifty Christian dead.[14]

In time, help came from Sicily. But by then, the Turkish juggernaut had already been blunted, with that enemy having been bled white, ravaged by death and disease, and broken in morale. Beeching says, "The Turks had lost 31,000 men there, or three-quarters of their force—and all the survivors had to show for it were epidemic sickness and wounds."[15] The Turkish fleet limped back to Istanbul with the miserable news of their defeat to present to the Sultan.

The war ended with many of the Knights dead and wounded. Those who had sent no aid at least now had the decency to issue proclamations of thanks to the defenders of Malta. Donations were collected and sent to rebuild the shattered island.[16]

Valette spent his later days rebuilding the defenses of Malta. His knights resumed their works of medical mercy and built a great hospital where "the sick and wounded of every religion and condition, Catholic, Protestant, Orthodox, Moslem, or Jew, slave or free, might be nursed back to health on

---

[13] Bradford, 140-141.
[14] Bradford, 161.
[15] Beeching, 96.
[16] Beeching, 96-97.

terms of equality."[17] The Knights advanced medical knowledge. They were the experts in diseases of the eye, and they were among the first to recognize the value of combating plagues by quarantines. They also recognized mental illnesses for what they were, and they understood the need for such hospital comforts as separate beds for patients and clean dishes for food.[18]

For Further Reading

The greatest account of the Siege of Malta and one that is unlikely to be surpassed is Ernle Bradford's *The Great Siege: Malta 1565*. It is the main background book I have used. A good many exciting episodes and details have been left out of my account. Bradford's book is still in print and readily findable in the new and used book markets. Another Bradford book, *The Knights of the Order,* tells the story of the Knights from their beginnings to the battle of Rhodes, with a brief account of Malta. Bradford was a British historian who wrote many historical studies and biographies. In World War II, he was a naval officer who spent some time in Malta. After the war, he spent a good many years living near and sailing on the Mediterranean Sea. His histories that pertain to the Mediterranean excel in their geographic detail as well as in narrative excitement. He teaches history quite well in his writings.

Jack Beeching is also an English historian. His book *The Galleys at Lepanto* focuses upon the historical sequel to Malta and that was the naval battle at Lepanto in 1571. It was this battle which clearly and completely stopped the long threatened Turkish invasion of Europe. Beeching, however, does not merely deal with Lepanto. He devotes a whole chapter to Malta (and borrows heavily from Bradford). He also devotes attention to the Spanish Empire, and in particular, to the hero of Lepanto, Don John (or Juan) of Austria. With digressions into events in the Netherlands, which was Spanish held and was in a battle for independence, and references to the other upheavals relating to the Reformation, this account gives a good, bigger picture of the European scene after Luther and before the 1700s.

Dale Ahlquist's book of notes and commentaries on G. K. Chesterton's poem "Lepanto" is a useful work on this same time period and on both the poem and the history surrounding it. The poem, no doubt, helped memorialize the naval battle. We wish Chesterton had also written a poem about Malta.

---

[17] Beeching, 97. Any sick deemed heretical, schismatic, or pagan were segregated from Catholics by the Knights.
[18] Beeching, 97.

The Great Siege and Us

Europe in the 1500s faced a culture war within and an external threat on the outside. As Shakespeare character Claudius in *Hamlet* says, "When troubles come, they come not in single spies, but in battalions."[19] The problems and challenges of the Reformation were enough for the powers of church and state to attend to. Both church and state failed at many points in addressing the issues raised by the Reformers. But there was that real outward threat: The advance of the Muslim Turks. Eastern Europe was vulnerable, disunited, partially occupied by Turks, and weakly defended. The Mediterranean was up for grabs. Southern Spain was partially occupied. Islamic forces once again were on the move.

Western Civilization today again has a culture war within and an external threat from the outside. Time has restructured the battle fronts and shifted the geography and politics, but essential similarities remain between our century and previous eras. Christianity could be written off as dead and buried in Europe based on many cultural indicators. There is just one problem with penning the obituary: Christianity has a odd habit of resorting to resurrections. Tombs just seem to be minor obstacles to our Faith. Hope is essential for Christians—hope for God's victory in time and history as well as eternity. But along with hope, realism is needed. Realism about the threats within and without.

The Western world does not seem to understand history and the nature of real war. We seem to have imbibed a twisted Freudian view of history that somehow our subconscious past is filled only with guilt and wrongdoing on our collective European and Western part. The Christian West has been victimized by shame over our past, particularly the Crusades. After all, we are told, Middle Eastern people are still angry over the hypocritical and brutal Crusades. All the problems of the Middle Eastern people today, excluding the Israelis, are traceable to European imperialism. Poor Muslims, poor Arabs, poor Middle Easterners—all victims of bad, white European Christendom.

Before you order your 'sackcloth and ashes kit' off the web, you might better rethink and restudy the Crusades. Also, we need to consider the fact that Islamic forces threatened the future of European Christendom in the early 700s, until turned back by Charles Martel and the Franks. When the Ottoman Turks combined Islamic fanaticism with military power in the Eleventh Century, they threatened the future of Europe again. It was the defense of Malta and the latter sea battle of Lepanto which finally halted this Islamic threat in the 1600s.

---

[19] Shakespeare, *Hamlet,* Act IV, Scene V, Line 78-79.

Imperialism and territorial conquest were not invented or monopolized by white Europeans. It can be argued that Europeans made imperialism more perfect or did it more efficiently or made it more beneficial to all parties involved. Victor Davis Hanson's *Carnage and Culture* suggests that free institutions and higher views of the common man enabled Europeans to develop social institutions and war machines that have and will best anything the non-Western world puts against them. He contends that non-Western countries, even when armed with Western weaponry, are no match for the heirs of the Greco-Roman and Judeo-Christian culture. Niall Ferguson's *Empire* suggests that all parts of the world where the British flag once flew are much better off as a result of European, particularly British, culture. Whether military prowess or cultural superiority can be defended as adequate grounds for imperialism is not the point here. World history is the story of a long war for territorial control. Cain no doubt added Abel's livestock to his own possession after killing his brother. Europeans invaded Islamic held Middle Eastern territories during the Crusades. In turn, when Islamic peoples had the might, they rallied forth in search of lands to conquer.

The militaristic Islamic ideology is still around. Islam is a world-view; it is dominion oriented; it is fanatical; it rests on the concept of Jihad, or holy war. What modern Islam lacks is military and political power. The Islamic world is largely parasitic. The West is only one effective non-gas combustion engine away from reducing most of the Middle East to the economic equivalent of Antarctica. Technologically, we can get there in less than a generation. The West has the theology—mostly stored away in its attic—and the technological know-how to win the outward war. No Islamic country could field an army that could stand against the West for a solid day, and no Western country has an ideology—buttressed by a theology—that can match a suicide bomber.

Even in the time of Suleiman, the best Turkish soldiers were the Janissaries. The Janissaries were an elite unit of soldiers, consisting of boys conscripted at age seven from Christian homes and molded into Muslim soldiers. Bradford says they were "Christian by birth, Spartan by upbringing, and fanatical Moslem by conversion." (I refrain from commenting here on the absolute necessity of Christian education.) Politically, modern Islam has only puppet states, third world countries, and sheiks basking on oil reserves. Instead of the armies of the Sultan, they rely on the terrorist camps of Osama Bin Laden and company. Their weapons of war—car bombs, plane hijackings, terror networking—have changed. Their objectives are the same.

Europe is rather passively evolving into an Islamic continent. Europeans are depopulating themselves, while the Muslim population is growing by both begetting and immigrating. George Weigel's book *The Cube and the Cathedral: Europe, America, and Politics Without God* is must reading on this topic. Spain was train-bombed into pacifism. Germany shed Nazism, but picked up pacifism and appeasement. France, well, is still France. By a mercy from God, Tony Blair, former Labor Party Prime Minister of Britain, seems to have contracted a Churchillian virus from somewhere in the halls of Parliament.

While the Knights fought a war not for land but for faith, modern Europe has little or no Christian faith. Searching European cities for true Christianity makes the pilgrim long for an American Bible belt city like Boston or San Francisco. Europeans have shed their Christian clothing with a brash zeal that would make a stripper blush. Europeans cannot halt immigration from Muslim countries and will not match population growth among Muslims in Europe.

Even in America, which Ronald Reagan called mankind's last and greatest hope, many are blind to the lessons of history and the dangers of the future. All too many American leaders on the left seek to fulfill Neville Chamberlain's destiny. The Left still believes Chamberlain's mantra: "We shall have peace in our time." Americans still tend to politicize our conflicts, with a greater notice of upcoming elections than of civilization's survival. Americans go to war against an ideology that has tormented the world since 610 A.D., and we wonder why we can't tame it in time for the 6:00 evening news. But remember that until the time of Ronald Reagan, most American leaders thought only in terms of peaceful—and cowed—coexistence with the Soviet Union. Only after Reagan's vision succeeded did the political world acknowledge that Communism was vulnerable.[20]

Valette was a man who knew how to identify an enemy and how to fight a war. He also knew the only options for peace: Victory or death. Since American Christianity is often so effeminate and passive, we assume that most Muslims are really nice 'love-your-neighbor' type people, too. If only we could just trade our Precious Moments Christian figurines (or are they theologians and pastors?) for sturdy Amish farmers, at least we would have a vision of Christian manhood. I wish for Scottish Covenanters, for English Puritan Roundheads, for Washington's Continental Army, or for Robert L. Dabney, but that is too much.

Something Medieval is needed in this culture war. Our President falters in details and particulars, but he seems to instinctively understand the long war. Something that happened between that west Texas upbringing and the

---

[20] At which point, many gave credit to Mikhail Gorbachev.

new birth gave him a vision of a God bigger than the Washington beltway or the U.N. His advisors falter, but most of them at least understand what guns are for. When the Christian West fulfills Voltaire's statement, "Nothing is better known than the siege of Malta," I think the war will be won.

Chapter Seventeen
Light on the Enlightenment
A review of *The Roads to Modernity*
by Gertrude Himmelfarb

> The Enlightenment has been truly formative in history and has engaged in cultural disclosure—also beyond the area of natural science and technology built on it. In the economic sector it opened the way towards development of individual initiative, which...greatly developed economic life. In jurisprudence it untiringly pleaded for the individual rights of man which form the foundation for our civil law today....The Enlightenment has laid many cornerstones for the modern constitutional state....Without ceasing it pleaded for freedom of public expression of opinion and freedom of religion. In all these areas the Enlightenment could indeed work formatively in history because here it followed the line of genuine cultural disclosure.
> —Herman Dooyeweerd[1]

> [N]atural law became the order of the day, and thus there was born the Age of Enlightenment. In its fantastic faith in the infallibility of the scientific method, this new age created for itself a new trinity of reason, nature, and humanity and proceeded to worship this secularized or naturalized god with a devotion which would have been much more fitting for the worship of the God revealed in the Scriptures.
> —C. Gregg Singer[2]

I have long since given up on learning anything. My self-educational efforts are now devoted simply to realizing how little I know. I could take consolation in comparing myself with that great philosopher Socrates, but I also realize how little I know about Socrates.[3] For many years, the problem has been that of relearning everything I once thought I knew. Now I realize

---

[1] As quoted in *Contours of a Christian Philosophy: An Introduction to Herman Dooyeweerd's Thought*, by L. Kalsbeek (Toronto: Wedge Publishing Foundation, 1975), 142

[2] *From Rationality to Irrationality*, 70.

[3] Perhaps I need to see Peter Kreeft's *Philosophy 101 by Socrates* (San Francisco: Ignatius Press, 2002).

that not only do I have to relearn what I thought I once knew, I also have to relearn what I had already relearned.

To illustrate what I first learned, the following is a part of the consensual catechism of American education:

> - Neanderthals evolved from frogs billions of years ago;
> - Greeks and Romans were good, creating democracy and ruling the Ancient World;
> - The Middle Ages were Dark Ages, in which freedom and science were suppressed;
> - The Church supported the Inquisition, the Crusades, and superstition;
> - The Renaissance was a great time of art and creativity,
> - But the Reformation produced Luther the anti-Semite and Calvin, who burned Servetus; the Church opposed science and free thought;
> - Puritans were witch burners, but Roger Williams and Anne Hutchinson were good;
> - Democracy is always good, but Theocracy is dangerous to even consider;
> - Americans had a revolution, and then the French had one just like ours;
> - All Southerners in the War Between the States were bad, for they fought for slavery;
> - FDR ended the Great Depression that Hoover started;
> - Joseph McCarthy was a bad man who saw a Communist behind every bush;
> - Kennedy ushered in Camelot;
> - Vietnam proved the failure of America as a military power;
> - Ronald Reagan was a B-grade actor and worse as a President;
> - Freedom of the press is the American ideal, but conservative talk radio is Fascism;
> - Government programs are good, but private free enterprise economics is bad;
> - And the list goes on.

Such a litany of historical facts is the product of textbooks, documentaries, and movies that have dominated the classrooms, airwaves, and mental images of most of us educated in the 20th century. But God delights in remodeling projects. Like a segment off of HG/TV, sometimes in short order while the occupants are preoccupied, God completely remodels a culture, ripping out the old worn cultural edifices and installing something brand new, which is actually not new at all. At least since the 1960s, such a modern reformation has been happening in our culture. At least three movements, perhaps more, began to change the way Americans worshipped and used the Bible. The three movements were the rise of the charismatics, the rediscovery of Reformed theology, and the Bible Church movement.

With all of their differences, with all of their disparities, with all of their oddities, these three movements all dragged Christians out of the established comfortable settings of stained glass windows and pews and put believers in a circle, often with little more than a guitar and an open Bible (or maybe for the Reformed, an overhead projector with theology outlines and an open Bible). God's most simple revival technique always begins with a rediscovery of the Bible. Erasmus saw the value of the Biblical text in the pre-Reformation in the early1500s, but fell short of application; however, Luther lit the fuse to the weapon Erasmus discovered. The Bible, at all times, is revolutionary, life changing, and culture changing. It led to a series of changes in Europe in the 1500s and 1600s. Similarly, it is doing so in our time.

First comes the Bible, and then comes a reexamination of history. The revival since the 1960s that began with little Bible groups led to an intellectual rebirth of Christian thought and activism. Men such as R. J. Rushdoony and Francis Schaeffer lectured to small groups, wrote books read by small cadres, and suggested courses of action heard by only a few. But those few came to occupy pulpits and classrooms. And they wrote books, reprinted books, published newsletters, made tapes, and now they post their thoughts and reading on their weblogs (blogs).

It was largely from those two men, Rushdoony and Schaeffer, that I learned history for the second time. Add a third name, C. Gregg Singer, author of *A Theological Interpretation of American History*. This triumvirate of Presbyterian thinkers taught me, not the facts of history, but the way to view the facts of history. Many a page of their books in my library is underlined, highlighted, and annotated. In some cases, the first reading merely dazed me. It took a couple of re-readings for me to understand and accept what was written. Sometimes the first reading was rejected; only later, after some paradigm shifts, did the concepts make sense.

For all practical purposes, after my re-education I might as well have held the standard textbooks upside down as I read, because what I read from the text was not what I believed. Great doubts were cast upon the Greeks. Not only was their democracy not very democratic, but also their worldview was humanistic and pessimistic. After emptying the Greeks of glory, the grandeur of Rome quickly crumbled. The Romans were the ultimate Statists, one-world government people, proclaiming as gods, mortal decaying Caesars, who were mere pawns in the hands of the true Triune God. It was the Son of God, Jesus Christ, whose birthplace and sentence of death were directed, but unnoticed, by the Roman Empire, who redirected history back to limiting Caesar's renderings to his mere, often debased coinage. The Middle Ages had problems, and Christianity during this time underwent radical contortions and distortions. Yet the Middle Ages, overall, was a great frontier age of light and conquest for the faith. The cathedrals still stand as monuments and symbols of the best of that era.

The Renaissance was, with all its artistic and philosophical beauty, a rebirth of much of the worst of the true dark ages, the Ancient World. While some in the Renaissance rediscovered the true place of man in this world, others rediscovered the false Greek idea of man being the measure of all things. The Reformation accented the light of Scripture and the amazing grace of God. Luther and Calvin had their failures in both theology and life, but the legacy they left was the open pages of the Bible, which alone can correct and direct all men. Democracy, I learned to my shock, was highly questionable, and strongly abhorred by many of our Founding Fathers, while Theocracy was not something to be so easily dismissed. Both the Puritans and the Founding Fathers agreed upon the depravity of man and hence limits to the extent of either government or suffrage. The American and French Revolutions were contrasting, not comparative, events. To even try to link the driving cause of a George Washington with the agenda of Robespiere is warped. Even the American War Between the States was rethought and refought. The Southern Confederacy fought more to preserve the genius of the federal system against centralization than to preserve the failed institution of slavery.

While Hoover certainly did not cause the Great Depression, both he and FDR prolonged rather than shortened that event. Austrian economist Ludwig Von Mises had rightly suggested that instead of the New Deal that FDR should have done nothing about the Great Depression and done it sooner. Tail-gunner Joseph McCarthy had fired his guns a bit wildly, but some of the bullets hit true targets. And so the relearning continued.

I was happy marching to a different historical drummer. I could have been happy simply going against all the traditional consensus from my right wing conservative, somewhat libertarian, and strongly Calvinistic vantage point. But then comes the next painful step of relearning what has already been relearned. In the words of the favorite historical maxim of one of my former teachers, Dr. Tom Wagy of Texas A&M at Texarkana, "In history, nothing is simple." As Socrates reminds us, the wise man only knows how little he knows. And yet, the desire to know is enticingly driven by the elusiveness of knowing all one needs to know.

With this in mind, I recommend a book, titled *The Roads to Modernity: The British, French, and American Enlightenment* by Gertrude Himmelfarb.[4] That there is such a thing or time as Modernity and that it was birthed by the Enlightenment are both quite acceptable notions. In my own experience, I would expect studies of the Enlightenment to fall into two categories. The establishment view marks it as a grand and glorious movement. After all, the name given to it tells us that in the 1700s, enlightened men, not God, said, "Let there be Enlightenment," and it was so. Baron von Holbach, a spokesman for the Enlightenment, wrote,

> Let us endeavor to disperse those clouds of ignorance, those mists of darkness, which impede Man on his journey...which prevent his marching through life with a firm and steady step. Let us try to inspire him...with respect for his own reason—with an inextinguishable love of truth...so that he may learn to know himself...and no longer be duped by an imagination that has been led astray by authority...so that he may learn to base his morals on his own nature, on his own wants, on the real advantage of society...so that he may learn to pursue his true happiness, by promoting that of others...in short, so that he may become a virtuous and rational being, who cannot fail to become happy.[5]

In a college history book, titled *Western Civilization*, historian Edward McNall Burns says, "No other movement, with the possible exception of humanism, had done more to dispel the accumulated fogs of superstition and illogical restraint that still enveloped the Western world. The rationalism of the Enlightenment helped to break the shackles of political tyranny and to weaken the power of conscienceless priests."[6]

But before I could ever join the parade celebrating the end of ignorance and superstition, I had to go back to my sources. So turning to my most favored Calvinist and revisionist and historian, Rushdoony, in *This Independent*

---

[4] Gertrude Himmelfarb, *The Roads to Modernity: The British, French, and American Enlightenment* (New York: Alfred A. Knopf, 2004).

[5] As quoted in Bruce L. Shelley, *Church History in Plain Language* (Dallas: Word Publishing, 1995), 312.

[6] Edward McNall Burns, *Western Civilization* (New York: W. W. Norton & Company, Inc., 1973) Eighth edition, 508.

Republic, he says of the Enlightenment, "The three major expressions of the philosophy of the Enlightenment have been, first, the French Revolution; second, Darwin and the mythology of evolution; and, third, the Russian Revolution and its Marxian theories."[7]

Francis Schaeffer, in *How Should We then Live?,* says "The humanistic elements which had arisen during the Renaissance came to flood tide in the Enlightenment. Here was man starting with himself absolutely. And if the humanistic elements of the Renaissance stand in sharp contrast to the Reformation, the Enlightenment was in total antithesis to it."[8]

Gregg Singer credits the Enlightenment with creating a whole new religion of humanity where man worships himself and his own achievements. The new religion of humanity failed, and in its wake, produced the French Revolution, which Singer says was "the greatest political catastrophe yet experienced by the Western world."[9]

Looking both forward and backward, these three Christian scholars portray a movement totally at odds with Von Holbach's and Burns' glorious interpretation of the Enlightenment.

Gertrude Himmelfarb's book edges right in between the extremes of the interpretations of the Enlightenment given above. She views it as a period of real enlightening, without ignoring its darker elements. Her main thesis is that the Enlightenment has too often been viewed as an almost totally French affair, hence her metaphor of there being three roads of the Enlightenment. Her aim is to restore to prominence the British and American thinkers, who were on the one hand, the products of the Enlightenment, but on the other hand, were proponents of ideas far to the opposite shore of the French philosophes. As if this stirring of the mixture was not mentally challenging enough, Himmelfarb examines each country and highlights both clear and muddled thinking in each case.

The first of the three roads to Modernity was the British road. The key result of the British Enlightenment was the focus put upon what Himmelfarb calls the "sociology of virtue."[10] Adam Smith and Edmund Burke were both Enlightenment thinkers. Simply put (for my sake, not yours) Adam Smith formulated the concept of free markets, and Edmund Burke clarified the concept of free governments. Burke saw fundamental moral issues in the revolt staged by the American colonies, leading to his role as writer and speaker

---

[7] Rushdoony, *This Independent Republic,* 137.
[8] Schaeffer, *How Should We Then Live?,* 121.
[9] Singer, 70-86.
[10] Himmelfarb, 23-146.

inside Parliament for the American cause. Shortly afterwards, when the French stormed the Bastille, Burke saw a different strain at work, leading to his writings analyzing the dangers of the French Revolution.

Englishmen like philosopher David Hume and historian Edward Gibbon were both opposed to Christianity, as were most French philosophes. Yet, there was an acceptance or at least accommodation to Christianity in England. Never did the vehement anti-clericalism develop in England as in France. In an amazingly bold assertion, Himmelfarb presents John Wesley and the Methodist movement as key components of the British Enlightenment. The Methodists in their day were as scorned by the intellectual elite as evangelicals are scorned in our own day. In the histories that followed, many historians relegated the Methodist revival to sidelines and footnotes. The writings of such evangelicals as Wesley were as ignored then as such writings often are now. But, Himmelfarb points out approvingly, it was this Methodist movement that was credited by a 20th century French historian, Elie Halevy, with having prevented England from having a bloody, nasty revolution like the French had.

English Enlightenment thinkers who might never pass a test of orthodoxy still had brilliant insights into the importance of religion. A quote from Adam Smith's *Wealth of Nations* explains our own cultural and moral divide as brilliantly as anything I've read:

> In every civilized society, in every society where the distinction of ranks has once been completely established, there have been always two different schemes or systems of morality current at the same time, of which the one may be called the strict or austere; the other the liberal, or if you will, the loose system. The former is generally admired and revered by the common people; the latter is commonly more esteemed and adopted by what are called people of fashion.[11]

Looking at the second road to Modernity, the French road, one finds the more degenerate aspects of the Enlightenment. The survey of the French philosophes brings in the usual suspects, such as Voltaire, Diderot, and Rousseau. And they were just as nutty as I imagined. These men believed in the perfectibility of man, but rejected the faith that has done more than any other to improve man, Christianity. Voltaire did not want to abolish Christianity for others. He said, "I want my lawyer, my tailor, my servants, even my wife to believe in God, because it means I shall be cheated and robbed and

---

[11] As quoted by Himmelfarb, 45.

cuckolded less often...If God did not exist, it would be necessary to invent him."[12]

In the place of faith, the philosophes placed reason. They defined reason by a quite interesting comparison, saying, "Reason is to the philosopher what grace is to the Christian. Grace moves the Christian to act, reason moves the philosopher."[13] They sought to crystallize the tenets of their beliefs in their *Encyclopedie*, which contained, catalogued, and clarified man's accumulated knowledge that gave him the promise of true enlightenment. The philosophes wanted to bring about a perfect society and a perfect world. In this, as Rushdoony, Schaeffer, Singer, and many others have noted, they failed. The descending line from the French Enlightenment to the Reign of Terror is quite short. Robespierre and Napoleon are the true sons of the philosophes.

The third road to Modernity was America. Early America in its colonial and early national stages produced its own brilliant cadre of Enlightenment thinkers and men of action. Even more than the English accommodation of religion was the American Enlightenment's embracing of religion. Our Enlightenment thinkers include such Christian thinkers as Jonathan Edwards and John Witherspoon, transplanted here from Scotland, and such political thinkers as the authors of the *Federalist*. Unlike the French who worshipped at the throne of Reason, the Americans cultivated Enlightenment thought in search of the idea of liberty. Especially in the Constitution and the essays found in the *Federalist,* the Americans were concerned about the precise balance of government and liberty, not just for themselves, but also for the long-term future.

Alexander Hamilton professed, "I never expect to see a perfect work from imperfect man." His sometimes partner-in-politics, James Madison, in *Federalist* #51, wrote that government was needed because men were not angels or governed by angels. He added to this, saying, "You must first enable the government to control the governed; and in the next place oblige it to control itself." The Constitution itself never promised a perfect union, but rather a more perfect one, modestly meaning, simply better than what existed before.

Our Enlightenment heritage is alive and well. *The Federalist* is still assigned in political science courses and is quoted by all sides of the political spectrum. (Finally, after years of teaching about *The Federalist,* I have read the work and been able to teach from this weighty classic.) Biographies of our Founders, particularly Adams, Hamilton, and Washington, are best sellers.

---

[12] Himmelfarb, 155
[13] Himmelfarb, 152.

The greatest of the French Enlightenment thinkers, Alexis de Tocqueville, had a greater impact on American thought than on his native France. Himmelfarb says, "No one knew better than he that it was precisely a belief in human *imperfectability*, and the civil and political arrangements deriving from that belief, which sustained the country—a united country—through all the turmoil of its history."[14]

America made even better use of the British Enlightenment than did the British. More from Himmelfarb: "If America is now exceptional, it is because it has inherited and preserved aspects of the British Enlightenment that the British themselves discarded and that other countries (France, most notably) never adopted." And "Americans take for granted what Europeans regard as an inexplicable paradox: that the United States is the most capitalistic and at the same time the most moralistic of countries." [15]

Lest anyone falsely assume this discussion of the Enlightenment is arcane, historical trivial pursuit, Himmelfarb concludes her study saying, "We are, in fact, still floundering in the verities and fallacies, the assumptions and convictions, about human nature, society, and the polity that exercised the British moral philosophers, the French philosophes, and the American Founders."[16] Lest anybody missed it, President Bush's second inaugural address of January 2005 was packed full of the better features of Enlightenment thought.

I am forever grateful for the personal, spiritual, intellectual "enlightenment" given to me by Rushdoony, Schaeffer, Singer, and others. A great part of that education was not just learning the facts or interpretations in their books. It was, to use Dorothy Sayers' phrase, "learning how to learn." Gertrude Himmelfarb does not share the theological perspective of my original mentors. Like other great modern thinkers, such as Paul Johnson, Victor Davis Hanson, and Jacques Barzan, she brings great depth and insight to a host of historical issues that are as relevant as today's headlines. That Transcendental fruitcake, Ralph Waldo Emerson, said, "There is a time in every man's education when he arrives at the conviction that envy is ignorance." Wrong again, Waldo. I envy the insights of those who helped me relearn what I learned and those who help me relearn what I thought I had already relearned.

---

[14] Himmelfarb, 229.
[15] Himmelfarb, 233.
[16] Himmelfarb, 233.

Chapter Eighteen
The Crooked Road from Darwin to Hitler
A Review of *From Darwin to Hitler: Evolutionary Ethics, Eugenics, and Racism in Germany* by Richard Weikart

> The Darwinian revolution was not merely the replacement of one scientific theory by another, but rather the replacement of a worldview, in which the supernatural was accepted as a normal and relevant explanatory principle, by a new worldview in which there was no room for supernatural forces.
> —Ernst Mayr, zoologist[1]

> The commonest question asked of historians by laymen is whether history serves a purpose. Is it useful? Can we learn from the lessons of history?
> —Barbara Tuchman[2]

I hope it is obvious from this book that I like to read, and I especially enjoy reading history. Yet sometimes reading is a grim burden. There are those books, subjects, and studies, which fulfill an intellectual curiosity, but depress the spirit. All centuries and eras have their dark clouds, but the twentieth century was especially known for human horrors and evils. From concentration camps to gulags, from Nazis to Communists, from aerial bombing to genocide, the means and extent of the human capacity for evil seemed boundless in the last century. Technology and human accomplishments seemed to herald a golden age in 1900. Even after World War I, some remained optimistic about the century. James Harvey Robinson concluded his three volume study of history, titled *The Story of Our Civilization,* in 1926 with these shockingly premature observations:

---

[1] "Evolution and God," *Nature* 248 (March 22, 1974) 285, as quoted by Nancy Pearcey, *Total Truth: Liberating Christianity from its Cultural Captivity,* 221.
[2] *Practicing History: Selected Essays* (New York: Alfred A. Knopf, 1981), 247.

> Were there space here I think I could make out a fair case for the guess that the World War which began in 1914 may prove to be the last of its species.

And

> To judge from the way in which witchcraft, slavery, and active religious persecution disappeared—all ancient and sanctified and seemingly permanent human institutions—the doom of war may possibly be near at hand. At any rate the forces making against war are far more potent than ever before.[3]

This Pollyanna did admit that one more lesson, resulting in the shattering of New York, London, Paris, Berlin, and Rome, might be needed before the lesson against war sunk in.[4] His failed vision, no doubt, sprung from his belief in what constituted progress. He celebrated secularization, in particular, noting, "Education has to a great extent escaped from the control of the churches….Legislative assemblies may still be opened with prayer, but rarer and rarer are the appeals made to the Bible by lawgivers."

 The history of the golden age that was suppose to occur during the twentieth century was mired up in the trenches of World War I, the tramping feet of soldiers in the dark valley of World War II, and the iron and bamboo curtains of Communism lasting throughout much of the century. The horrors of that First World War are examined in Niall Ferguson's *The Pity of War: Explaining World War I*.[5] The millions killed, the millions more wounded, and the yet more displaced and traumatized certainly call for study and result in sadness. That terrible decade leading to the Second World War is amply portrayed in Piers Brendon's *The Dark Valley: A Panorama of the 1930s*.[6] The decade which contained the reigns of Hitler, Mussolini, and Stalin, and the rise of Japanese militarists and the Spanish Civil War was undoubtedly dark. The only consolation is that some of the evils were defeated in the next decade. Yet even with the defeat of the Nazis, Fascists, and Japanese militarists, in some cases, the change was no better. For this reason, *The Black Book of Communism: Crimes, Terror, Repression* is a worthy study.[7] Covering the worldwide

---

[3] James Harvey Robinson, *The Story of Our Civilization,* Volume III From Napoleon to Today (New York: William H. Wise & Co., 1934), 747-748.
[4] Robinson, 746-747.
[5] (New York: Basic Books, 1999).
[6] (London: Jonathan Cape, 2000).
[7] Compiled by Stephane Courtois, Nicolas Werth, Jean-Louis Panne, Andrzej Paczkowski, Karol Bartosek, and Jean-Louis Margolin, and translated by Jonathan Murphy and Mark Kramer (Cambridge, MA: Harvard University Press, 1999).

scope of Communism, this study documents and attempts to quantify the countless evils inflicted on the world by Marx's children.

The Christian teacher and writer must confront these evils. Like Dante's journey through the Inferno, he must descend from depth to depth examining the evidences and artifacts of human depravity practiced by wicked regimes. We are compelled to better understand what turned a Catholic choirboy and an Orthodox seminary student into Hitler and Stalin. And they did not act alone, so we have to figure what dynamics created Goebbels and Himmler, Beria and Molotov. What sycophantic forces create legions of immoral monsters to surround such men as Hitler and Stalin? And to what degree did the average man in the streets of Berlin or Moscow know or care that such atrocities were taking place? We also have to read the accounts of those who suffered. The victims, immortalized in the writings of Solzhenitsyn and the diaries of Anne Frank, must be remembered. Those of us who live our lives in great comfort must still confront the uncomfortable subject of human suffering. Yes, even the good guys, even the good countries, like the United States and Great Britain, have their dark secrets. Aspects of the Boer War waged by Great Britain and racial atrocities in America cannot be ignored just because they dint our pristine armor.

Grim books must be read. One such recent reading of mine was *From Darwin to Hitler—Evolutionary Ethics, Eugenics, and Racism in Germany* by Richard Weikart.[8] This book, sober and academic, focuses on root causes of the Holocaust. It examines ideas, academic communities, intellectual ponderings, arcane journal studies, and obscure (to us now) scientific, political, and ethical trends among the educated elite. This survey of German thought in the late 1800s and early 1900s would be useful only to academic specialists (meaning, Ph.D. candidates in search of a minor point) were it not for the sequel to the story. The story itself is the initial impact of Darwinian thought on issues of ethics and morality. Darwin's works caused an awakening, an enlightenment, for his readers, for many found a liberation in Darwinism from the restraints of the older Christian-natural law consensus. The sequel was the rise of the Third Reich and Hitler in the 1930s. The issue is this: Was there a connection between the student in the early 1900s reading Darwin and asking, "How should we then live?" and his son attending a rally at Nuremberg thirty years later?

Linking your enemies to Hitler is an overused and much abused tactic. I have seen pictures of both President Bill Clinton and President George W.

---

[8] Richard Weikart, *From Darwin to Hitler—Evolutionary Ethics, Eugenics, and Racism in Germany* (New York: Palgrave Macmillan, 2004).

Bush, presented by their enemies, showing them caught in the midst of a wave looking like they were giving Nazi salutes. Any position, any viewpoint, any program can be superficially discredited by linking it to Nazism. People are also discredited for opposing Darwinism. Opponents to Darwin in our day, whether committed Creationists or supporters of Intelligent Design, have frequently been dismissed out of court for lacking scientific credentials and intellectual seriousness, in spite of advanced degrees from major universities. Meaning, if you doubt Darwinism, you are by definition stupid. The author of this study, Dr. Richard Weikart, by the way, is an associate professor of history at California State University, but that is irrelevant if Darwin is questioned. With so much at stake, academically, what is the value in this debate of using the Hitler card?

First, we need to note where we are in the long-term battle between proponents of evolution and believers in some form of creation. The battle of Yorktown took place two years before the Treaty of Paris was signed. Likewise opponents of evolution have won some decisive victories, even though the war continues. Surely, there have been hard-fought skirmishes along the way. Chesterton and Spencer debated in England over a century ago. William Jennings Bryan and Clarence Darrow duked it out in Dayton, Tennessee, in the 1920s. Science faculties fought state legislatures, clergymen railed against scientists, parents protested against textbooks, and so on the battle has raged.

We so often assume the Darwinists have won the day. Public school textbooks tow the party line, regardless of what stickers are affixed to the book or what verbal tricks are used to tone down the language. College professors hold to Darwinism with the tenacity of a medieval monk reciting his prayers. Endless scientific documentaries, especially those featuring animals, regale us with evolutionary dogma. Even most Christian colleges blush when a freshman gullibly mentions six-day creation in mixed (that is, secular and Christian) company. We know the catechism question: "What do all credible, educated scientists believe?" Answer: "Evolution is our god and Darwin is his prophet."

Yet, we as Christians do not notice that the enemy has pulled behind its academic Maginot Line and made concessions on the implications of Darwinism to ethics and public policy. The biology professor might not allow for any objections to Darwinism inside the confines of his classroom and thus Darwin rules the biology lab. But don't take the biology book to sociology class or to political science class or to an ethics class. Like a body part in a Picasso painting, Darwinism is not to be attached to the rest of the body of human thought in a rational, traditional way. This refusal to apply Darwinism to all of life was not always the case. First it was necessary that the university be replaced by the multiversity.

Darwinism was dangerous in the day of the university. When Ernst Haeckel (1834-1919), the German zoologist, or Herbert Spencer (1820-1903), the English philosopher, read Darwin, their minds—still a product of a fading Christian consensus—adhered to a unity of truth. Therefore, men sought for a university education, a universal search for truth, a unifying principle of reality. For this reason, many people were "born again" upon accepting Darwin. Darwin offered not just biology, but philosophy, a worldview. At last an alternative to Christianity was offered. Darwin's book was a best seller to a world longing for liberation. Darwin's early disciples grasped the implications of his gospel quite quickly.

Sparks were flying in the academic circles, especially in Germany. Germany was brimming with brilliant minds and a nationalistic will-to-power. The higher critics were leading the world in theological studies, leading even the most conservative branches of Christian churches to send its best to Germany to study theology. Some of these same higher critical theologians were furiously undermining the foundations of Christianity. "God is on life-support and the Bible contains errors" was proclaimed in the theology department, while across the walkway in the science department, similarities were noted between the embryos of frogs and the students' baby brothers.

There was a German propensity for producing the best, for accentuating the finest. This resulted in amazing technology and craftsmanship, and when this tendency wedded science and social policy, the proto-Third Reich was born in the minds of men. But for the time, it was only words and paper competing against the older ethic, once carved on stone. A new science, in a new country, with a new worldview created the genesis of a new ethics and a new version of what constitutes a healthy society. We are all bothered by the sufferings and miseries of the incurably ill, the elderly, the infirm, and the hopelessly insane. Such people, such social misfits, are inconvenient. They tie us down. They do not produce anything for the common welfare. The new ethic suggested that it was more moral to dispose of such people than to be inconvenienced. The older Genesis account proclaimed man made in God's image; the new Genesis divided man into categories of fit and unfit.

Slower, sicker, weaker animals die in the pack. Either they are killed as prey, or they are unable to kill prey. This benefits the herd or the pack, and so surely benefits the human tribe, as well. Of course, all this was academic debate: The meanderings of scholars were loosed upon the pages of a journal or in the company of his fellows at conferences. Still iron sharpens iron. One scholar influenced another. Each book sparked another flurry of articles. Each lecture raised questions of further implications and applications. Just the merry life of professors—debating and arguing—and passing on to their students the findings of their research.

World War I upset many of these scholars. Although in one sense, the killing of thousands by the incessant machine gunning and poison gas might seem just another phase of the fit eliminating the unfit, still the war was troublesome. As Weikart says, "... what they found objectionable about modern wars was that the *wrong* people were being killed—the strong and the healthy rather than the weak and sickly."[9] Merely disposing of useless individuals and inferior races was helpful, but white Europeans slaughtering one another was unacceptable. Then out of the ashes, the destruction, and despair of Germany's defeat, Hitler arose. Hitler was not a scholar, although he was not stupid either. Like many of us, he picked up the major parts of his worldview second and third-hand. Whether he ever read Darwin or Darwin's pupils is irrelevant. Ideas have consequences and intellectuals change nations and arcane philosophies translate into political agendas. Many followers of Darwin opposed Hitler, and some died under his regime. Still as Weikart points out, "No matter how crooked the road from Darwin to Hitler, clearly Darwinism and eugenics smoothed the path for Nazi ideology, especially for the Nazi stress on expansion, war, racial struggle, and racial extermination."[10]

This crooked road wound through the university. Thankfully, for a season, that institution no longer exists. Fragmentation of reality has replaced universal truth, and multiversities have replaced universities. Just suggest to your biology professor that our race (any race) is superior. Propose to your political science professor that we purify the land. "Don't you dare apply Darwinism to politics," they will angrily reply. Did you forget that politics and religion don't mix? We live in an age that wants the pleasure of sex to be uninterrupted, but it wants the Darwinian imperative of sex—a superior race—politely ignored.

Yes, we still have our expendables. Aborted children are dispensed with by denying them the rights of "life, liberty, and the pursuit of happiness." The sick and mentally incapable are at risk in our nation. The ethics of the university campus still reach the grammar school classrooms all too quickly. Yet, the Darwinists, who are many in number, are tightlipped when it comes to ethics. It is absurd, they protest, to link the truth of "Survival of the Fittest" with horrors of the Third Reich. Their silence about the implications of Darwinism says too much.

---

[9] Weikart, 164.
[10] Weikart, 6.

Richard Weikart's book is filled with many brilliant insights, quotes, and references. Scholars out there, like Weikart, are doing in academic circles what bloggers are doing to the media. This is not pleasant reading. This is not the delightful read to have at the bedside. Not a lot of people will read this book. But for those of us who teach, who preach, and who pound away at our computers, this is a book we need to know.

Further Reading

The scientific world changed in 1961. While the proponents of evolution were reigning supreme in the academies, their allies were echoing the same message with such things as the film and drama versions of *Inherit the Wind,* which was released in 1960.[11] This play and movie mocked the Christian and Creationist positions in the famed Scopes Trial. Most Christian educational institutions had already become committed to accommodationist positions, meaning, that they would be diligent to modify the Bible in the light of scientific findings.

Then a scientist, Henry Morris, and a theologian, John Whitcomb published *The Genesis Flood,* a book upholding the Bible's account of Creation and the Noahic Flood.[12] The word flood in the title is ironic, because, in time, the books of Morris, Whitcomb, and other creationists became a flood. The Creationist in the early 1960s would have had a small section of his bookshelf stocked with books. By the late 1960s, his collection would fill several complete shelves. Now, with books by committed Creationists, advocates of Intelligent Design, and critics of Darwinism who take no particular religious stance, a whole room can be filled with books, journals, magazines, film documentaries, and other materials.

Any of Morris or Whitcomb's books are useful reading. As a history teacher, I find Morris's *The Long War Against God* to be particularly useful in understanding the key figures in the debate.[13]

Phillip E. Johnson helped change the direction of the evolution/creation debate and helped raise the volume of hysteria from the Darwinists

---

[11] Gary North, *The War on Mel Gibson* (Powder Springs, Georgia: American Vision, 2004), 7-8.

[12] John C. Whitcomb and Henry M. Morris, *The Genesis Flood: The Biblical Record and Its Scientific Implications* (Phillipsburg: Presbyterian and Reformed Publishers, 1961). Amazingly, the book is still in print. That it was published in the first place was due in large part to two committed, long-range Christian thinkers, R. J. Rushdoony, who read the manuscript and then promoted its publication, and Charles Craig, who owned Presbyterian and Reformed Publishing Company.

[13] Henry M. Morris, *The Long War Against God: The History and Impact of the Creation/Evolution Conflict* (Grand Rapids: Baker Book House, 1990).

with his books, such as *Darwin on Trial* and *Reason in the Balance*.[14] Mr. Johnson's training was in law, not science. His approach was to focus on the logical fallacies of Darwinism. Of course, the Darwinists howled. After all, Johnson had no scientific credentials and implying that Darwinism was illogical was unfair. But scientists did weigh in. Two key scientific thinkers who critiqued Darwin are Michael Behe, a professor of biochemistry, who wrote *Darwin's Black Box: The Biochemical Challenge to Evolution,* and Michael Denton, an Australian scientist, who wrote *Evolution: A Theory in Crisis*.[15] Scholars have lined up to punch the Darwinian model in such books as *Uncommon Dissent: Intellectuals Who Find Darwin Unconvincing*.[16]

Two of the best works taking on the Darwinian worldview have been written by two brilliant women. Nancy Pearcey's *Total Truth: Liberating Christianity from Its Cultural Captivity* covers much more than just Darwinism. Her book covers both the general problem of the loss of the Christian mind and then shows how Darwinism was able to gain its ascendancy. She deals quite forcibly with the negative effects of modern day evangelism (modern as in, since the late 1700s) and shows how the Christian faith tended to exalt experience over reason and emotion over theology. When Christians abandoned the academic fields, the enemies of the faith were ready to take over.

Ann Coulter's *Godless: The Church of Liberalism* topples quite a few idols of our current religious, political, and social scene. Along with castigating the liberal ideology for its detrimental effects on education and government and for its war against the unborn, she devotes five chapters to science, in particular, to evolution. Her book is quite saucy and inflammatory, but it has been perhaps the first bestseller that has contained such a devastating critique of Darwinism.

Studies on the Third Reich, including books about Nazism, the Holocaust, and Germany during the 1930s, are incredibly numerous. The classic work, William Shirer's *Rise and Fall of the Third Reich,* still stands as a major source for understanding that era.[17] Weikart quotes approvingly from Richard J. Evans' *The Coming of the Third Reich,* and Evans, in turn, endorsed Weikart's

---

[14] Phillip E. Johnson, *Darwin on Trial* (Washington, D. C.: Regnery Gateway, 1991) and *Reason in the Balance: The Case Against Naturalism in Science, Law & Education* (Downers Grove, Illinois: Intervarsity Press, 1995).

[15] Michael Behe, *Darwin's Black Box: The Biochemical Challenge to Evolution* (New York: The Free Press, 1996) and Michael Denton, *Evolution: A Theory in Crisis* (Bethesda: Adler & Adler Publishers, Inc., 1985).

[16] William A. Dembski, editor, *Uncommon Dissent: Intellectuals Who Find Darwinism Unconvincing* (Wilmington, Del.: Intercollegiate Studies Institute, 2004).

[17] William Shirer, *The Rise and Fall of the Third Reich* (New York: Simon and Shuster, 1960).

book.[18] More studies like Weikart's are needed to show the historical and intellectual impact of Darwinism. Such works may not be popular or enjoyable to read; however, history is constantly reaffirming that ideas have consequences. It should be no surprise that evil ideas have evil consequences.

America came perilously close in the early part of the twentieth century to the same evils as Nazi Germany, with court cases approving sterilization of those deemed "unfit." The story is brought out in the taped lecture series by Dr. Gary North, titled "The Unknown History of the Twentieth Century." Parts of this lecture series are taken from North's book *Crossed Fingers*.[19]

Living in a fallen world, the study of history can be quite grim and even depressing. But in that great Advent hymn, we affirm that Christ came to make "His blessings flow far as the curse is found." The horror chambers of history, including Darwinism and Nazism, will also be reckoned with by the Risen Lord of History.

---

[18] Richard J. Evans, *The Coming of the Third Reich* (New York: The Penguin Press, 2004).
[19] The lecture series is distributed by American Vision, Powder Springs, GA.

Chapter Nineteen
The Saved Generation

Still, I wonder if we shall ever be put into songs or tales.
We're in one, of course; but I mean: put into words, you know,
told by the fireside, or read out of a big book with red and
black letters, years and years afterwards. And people will say:
"Let's hear about Frodo and the Ring!' And they'll say:
'Yes, that's one of my favorite stories.
Frodo was brave, wasn't he, dad?"
—Samwise Gamgee to Frodo in *The Two Towers*

Why Sam, to hear you somehow makes me as merry as if the story
was already written. But you left out one of the chief characters:
Samwise the stouthearted. "I want to hear more about Sam, dad."
—Frodo Baggins to Sam in *The Two Towers*[1]

The last war, during the years 1915, 1916, 1917, was the most
colossal, murderous, mismanaged butchery that has ever taken
place on earth. Any writer who said otherwise lied. So the
writers either wrote propaganda, shut up, or fought.
—Ernest Hemingway[2]

In the early 1920s, Ernest Hemingway and F. Scott Fitzgerald were dubbed 'the lost generation.' During these years, they lived for a time in France, formed a friendship, nurtured each other's literary careers, and traveled about Europe. Across the channel from Hemingway and Fitzgerald, J. R. R. Tolkien and C. S. Lewis were beginning their careers as teachers and scholars at Oxford University. In time their famed literary friendship began around an informal group called the "Koalbiters" where they gathered to read Old Norse myths in the original languages.

---

[1] J. R. R. Tolkien, *The Two Towers*, Second Edition (Boston: Houghton Mifflin Company, 1982), 321-322.
[2] Introduction to *Men at War*, edited by Ernest Hemingway (New York: Wing Books, 1999), xiii.

Hemingway, Fitzgerald, Tolkien, and Lewis all enjoyed popularity from the books they wrote. Most of their works remain in print with sales remaining quite high. Books of all four writers have been made into movies. The influence of these authors and their books lives on.

Even though all four men were contemporaries, several factors separated Hemingway and Fitzgerald from Tolkien and Lewis. While the first pair were Americans and the second British, more than geography and history separated them. And while the first two devoted themselves almost entirely to being writers (aided with lots of pretty heavy drinking), the second two were primarily university professors whose writing careers were secondarily pursued amidst lectures and grading exams. But more than academic robes separated the two pairs.

The main gathering spot for Hemingway and Fitzgerald was the apartment of a writer named Gertrude Stein. More remembered for her influence than for her actual writings, Stein influenced the writers, poets, painters, and other artists—mostly American—who found a literary comradeship in post-World War I France. She directly affected much of modern twentieth century literature and art (Picasso, for example). It was Stein who told Hemingway, "You are a lost generation." Hemingway used the phrase in the opening of *The Sun Also Rises*. The phrase became a description of the entire group.

The main gathering spots for Tolkien and Lewis were a pub called "The Eagle and Child" and their rooms at Magdalen College. As Lewis once put it, "My happiest hours are spent with three or four old friends in old clothes tramping together and putting up in small pubs—or else sitting up till the small hours in someone's college rooms talking nonsense, poetry, theology, metaphysics, over beer, tea, and pipes."[3] It was in these gatherings that Tolkien and Lewis shared their faith and fiction. It was here that they came to be called "the Inklings."

The Contrast

Living in the same era, having literary camaraderie, and penning their early works, these two sets of friends developed two entirely different modes of writing. Hemingway and Fitzgerald were both known for their realism, for the tragic bent of their plots, and for the uprooted, cynical, modern, this-is-all-there-is-to-life heroes who sought some type of this-worldly grace to live under the pressure of existential meaninglessness. Hemingway's heroes faced war and the loss of loved ones; they accepted death or life on its own terms

---

[3] Walter Hooper, *Through Joy and Beyond—A Pictorial Biography of C.S. Lewis* (New York: Macmillan Publishing Company, 1982), 73.

with resignation and stoicism. Fitzgerald's heroes struggled to find life in the parties and opportunities for wealth during that era known as the 'Jazz Age.' Their heroes usually died with the same vigor with which they lived. These were fictional characters without roots, for the past was irrelevant. They were characters without futures, for the future had been lost somewhere out on the battlefields of the First World War.

Tolkien and Lewis rejected modernism and realism in literature. The main characters in the fiction of Lewis and Tolkien—children, talking animals, Hobbits, and elves—fought against magical and mystical forces in fantasy worlds. The issues were clear, the battle lines plainly drawn: Lucy and Edmund, Bilbo and Frodo all faced evil forces and battled for the good. They battled for Narnia and Middle-earth, found strength in the supernatural and fantastic, and faced death with courage and honor.

To read *The Lion, the Witch, and the Wardrobe* and then pick up *A Farewell to Arms*, to read *The Return of the King* and then read *The Great Gatsby*, to try to find a common thread between these two sets of writers is most disconcerting. One is reminded of G.K. Chesterton's comments about fantasy. He said that fantasy reminds us "the universe is wild and full of marvels. Realism means that the world is dull.... In the fairy tale, the cosmos goes mad, but the hero does not go mad. In the modern novels the hero is mad before the book begins, and suffers from the harsh steadiness...of the cosmos."

To assess the importance of these writers, one must go beyond style; they were all master stylists. One cannot demean Tolkien and Lewis by saying that they wrote "children's stories." As a matter of personal experience, I read a fair bit of Hemingway and Fitzgerald in my teenage years, but did not read Tolkien and Lewis until many years later. Some critics see realism as superior to fantasy because it is more representative of life; that is, as Aristotle talked about literature as imitation, so realism is imitation. The problem is that Samwise Gamgee acts more like people we know than does Jay Gatsby. Likewise, Eustace Scrubb's transformation into a dragon in Lewis's *Voyage of the Dawn Treader* is a better picture of man's character and need for change than Fredric Henry's fatalistic nihilism in Heminway's *Farewell to Arms*.

The real point of demarcation between these two sets of writers concerns their different worldviews, or you could say philosophies or even religions. Both Tolkien and Lewis were dedicated Christians whose theologies permeated their fiction. Their religious experiences and doctrinal convictions were different. Lewis comments on his early friendship with Tolkien, saying, "Friendship...marked the breakdown of two old prejudices. At my first coming into the world I had been (implicitly) warned never to trust a Papist, and at my first coming into the English Faculty (explicitly) never to trust a philologist. Tolkien was both."[4] In time, Tolkien and Owen Barfield would discuss with Lewis the importance of believing in Jesus Christ as the true God/Man and the True Myth. After Lewis's conversion, the friends began sharing their writings. From their friendship sprung the worlds of Middle-earth and Narnia. While Lewis was more obvious with his Christian symbolism and themes, Tolkien was strongly committed to Christian themes and symbols in his fiction.

Besides the events that caused Hemingway and Fitzgerald to abandon the Christian culture of Midwestern America and the events that caused Tolkien to be a committed Catholic and the events that would later bring Lewis to the Christian faith, the key event in all their lives that they shared was participation in the military in the First World War.

World War I

The experience of World War I and its aftermath impacted them all. The experience of this war is one of the underrated events of the twentieth century. World War I, more directly than anything else, caused World War II. It also caused the Great Depression in the United States and the world, the rise of Communism in Russia, and the rise of Nazism in Germany. Perhaps even greater than the military and political effects of the war were the social, cultural, philosophical, and theological effects.

The clumsy film images of young men, brightly uniformed, being cheered by huge crowds give a foreboding image of the naivety toward the horrors that would soon face the youth of Europe in 'No Man's Land' in the trenches of France. Some particular battles, like the Battles of the Somme and the siege of Verdun, produced casualty counts that exceeded whole wars of the past. In some cases, the first hours of an attack destroyed more young men than whole campaigns from previous centuries.

The grim futility of the war can be found in the anti-war novel *All Quiet on the Western Front* by Erich Marie Remarque. His story takes a group of young men, Germans in this case, and traces their lives in the trenches, their struggles with fear and death, their momentary flings with youthful fun, through the war until the last one dies. In one sense, it would only be "all quiet on the Western Front" when all were dead. The grim futility of World War I still begs for an explanation, a reason why, that can never be found by mere men.

The causes of World War I were vague. History books might list causes, both immediate and long-term. None of the causes seems to explain the

---

[4] *Surprised by Joy* (New York: Harcourt Brace and Company, 1955), 216.

extent of the effects. Some years back Barbara Tuchman's *The Guns of August* eloquently described the course of events in the August of 1914 that led to the outbreak of war and the first month of battle that initially saved France. Her book chronicles the tensions in the European capitals in that last peaceful summer of 1914. Leaders all seemed to be blindly, obstinately, and foolishly gravitating toward a course of events that finally set armies to marching. Tuchman's book covers but one month out of a war that would last for nearly four years.

The course of the war was insane, with ever increasing casualties remedied only by the development of ever-more shocking weapons; the results of the war displayed a blinded greed on the part of the winners and guaranteed a desire for revenge by the losers, particularly Germany. After the Versailles Peace Treaty was signed, French General Ferdinand Foch rightly prophesied that the peace treaty was nothing more than a twenty-year armistice.

The Wartime Experience

The British went to war in 1914, so Tolkien and Lewis were quickly drawn into it. It was 1917 before America declared war on Germany. Americans went into that war with the idealistic promise that "this was a war to end all wars" and a "war to make the world safe for democracy." Our comparative casualty count was low (over 100,000 killed and over 200,000 wounded), since we entered the war late and at that point in time when the last German offensive was grinding to a halt. By 1918, the German army was reduced to large numbers of old men and boys. Still lots of Americans died; others survived shell-shocked, gassed, and scarred for life. The optimism of youth, the promise of a bright century, the certainties of life were gone.

Fitzgerald said in his novel *This Side of Paradise* that the men returned from the war to find "all gods dead, all wars fought, all faiths in man shaken." Disillusioned by the war, rejecting belief in God or any creeds, pained over his past and lost youth, Fitzgerald's character says at the end of the book, "I know myself, but that is all."

In *A Farewell to Arms,* Hemingway's character, Frederic Henry, faced the death of his lover, Catherine, and her son and of his wartime comrades with the thought, "That was what you did. You died. You did not know what it was about. You never had time to learn. They threw you in and told you the rules and the first time they caught you off base they killed you…. You could count on that. Stay around long enough and they would kill you."

Plenty of British writers experienced the same despair, unbelief, and existentialism. Some, like the poet Wilfred Owen, died in battle; others like

Siegfried Sassoon survived to continue his writing career.[5] It is in this same cultural context that T. S. Eliot published his famous poem *The Waste Land*.

But not all who experienced World War I emerged with philosophies of despair. Both novelists and historians have often written about the unbelief and the existential reaction to World War I. What have been less often explored have been the stories of the boys of 1914-18 who left the war with a greater vision of life. There were many. While he was not converted until some years after the war, Lewis avoided the cynicism of so many. In his autobiography, he spoke of "the frights, the cold…the horribly smashed men still moving like half-crushed beetles, the sitting or standing corpses, the landscape of sheer earth without a blade of grass.…"[6] But the war itself was forgotten and other events had greater impacts on Lewis's mind. Two Southern literary scholars who served in the war, John Crowe Ransom and Donald Davidson, returned to Vanderbilt University in Tennessee and proceeded to give the world a great body of Southern literature, especially poetry, and the Agrarian movement. Eugene Rosenstock-Huessy conceived his vision of history at the Battle of Verdun where he was serving in the German army and from that began his work *Out of Revolution*.[7]

Tolkien and World War I

Most important from our perspective, from the experience of the Battle of the Somme and the trenches of France, J. R. R. Tolkien resolved to fulfill the vision of his university chums, most of whom perished in battle, and he put together vital pieces of his epic creation of Middle-earth. The way the war affected Tolkien the man and ultimately how it effected the creation of Middle-earth is the theme of an important book on Tolkien, called *Tolkien and the Great War: The Threshold of Middle-earth* by John Garth. The author says, "Without the war, it is arguable whether his fictions would have focused on a conflict between good and evil; or if they had, whether good and evil would have taken a similar shape."[8]

Garth's story begins with the comradeship and scholarship of four young men at King's College. These men were certainly among Britain's finest. Their education embodied the best of the older Classical education model—a later

---

[5] God was gracious: Sassoon's conversion is chronicled in Joseph Pearce's book *Literary Converts* (San Francisco: Ignatius Press, 1999).

[6] C. S. Lewis, *Surprised By Joy* (New York: Harcourt, Brace and Company, 1955), 196.

[7] Eugen Rosenstock-Huessy, *Out of Revolution: Autobiography of Western Man* (Providence, RI: Berg Publishers, Inc., 1993).

[8] John Garth, *Tolkien and the Great War: The Threshold of Middle-earth* (Boston: Houghton Mifflin Company, 2003), 309.

casualty of the 20th century. They performed Greek plays in the original language; they fellowshipped together as members of the Tea Club and Barrovian Society (TCBS); they played spirited games of Rugby against school rivals; they pursued various academic disciplines, with Tolkien being ever drawn to the field of Philology and the writings of Norse legends.

This fellowship was disrupted by the outbreak of the war. College educated men were prime candidates for the officer corps. Off they went to training and later to battle, carrying along copies of *Paradise Lost* along with their own poetry and dreams of bright future lives as men of letters. As officers, their risks were great, and their casualty numbers were high. Like the characters in *All Quiet on the Western Front*, they soon began to die in battle.

After the first member of this fellowship was killed (Rob Gilson was his name), another one, G.B. Smith, wrote to Tolkien, "I am safe but what does that matter…Now one realizes in despair what the TCBS really was. O my dear John Ronald what ever are we going to do?"[9] Gilson was not the only one to die. Looking back years later, Tolkien said, "One has personally to come under the shadow of war to feel fully its oppression; but as the years go by it seems now often forgotten that to be caught in youth in 1914 was no less hideous an experience than to be involved in 1939 and the following years. By 1918 all but one of my close friends were dead."[10]

As the scythe of war swept more men away, Tolkien was providentially blessed by contracting trench fever. This disease, fatal for some, was life saving for Tolkien.

Victor Davis Hanson points out in his book *Ripples of Battle* that battles produce consequences far beyond the immediate effect of which sides wins and which side loses on the battlefield. Garth's book certainly illustrates some of the far-reaching ripples of the Battle of the Somme. As Tolkien created the battles for Middle-earth, he used his visual memories of WWI to construct the settings. Garth says, "Middle-earth, I suspect, looks so engagingly familiar to us, and speaks to us so eloquently, because it was born with the modern world and marked by the same terrible birth pangs."[11]

Tolkien was not unique in falling back on his war experiences for his fiction. Tone, subject, and attitudes from the war affected the literature of the next generation, but what was unique about Tolkien was the perspective he had on the war. In the last chapters of Garth's book, he brilliantly examines the ways different writers reacted to the war. This portion is worth the

---

[9] Garth, 168.
[10] Foreword to the second edition of *The Fellowship of the Ring* (Boston: Houghton Mifflin Company, 1965), 7.
[11] Garth, 309.

price of the book. Garth says, "...writers such as Graves, Sassoon, and Owen saw the Great War as the disease, but Tolkien saw it as merely the symptom." [12] A bit earlier he pointed out, "In a century when revolutionaries dismissed the whole concept of good and evil as a delusion of the weak or deviant, this became a substantial issue, and already during the Great War it was an urgent one. For Tolkien's mythology, 'the memory of good and evil' is the keynote."[13]

So the battlefields of France merge into the fictional battle for Middle-earth. A real war with indefinite causes and unclear moral realities helps create a mythical war with an all-powerful ring as the cause and good and evil as the unmistakable alternative outcomes. A historical human tragedy becomes a fantastic epic. Tolkien insisted that his trilogy was not an allegory of World War II, which was taking place while the book was written. Tolkien said, "I cordially dislike allegory in all its manifestations....I much prefer history, true or feigned, with its varied applicability to the thought and experience of readers."[14] His result was a book more allegorical to the human experience than merely a twentieth century war. Tolkien's "feigned history" is chocked full of applicability to our own current thoughts and experiences.

Tolkien ended the war with a pen in hand and a vision in mind. Unlike the Lost Generation, for Tolkien, God was very much alive; for him, faith was strengthened; and for him, all wars were not fought—there would be more wars, the shires would need scouring, but the ultimate victory was sure. Gertrude Stein was more right than she realized in referring to Hemingway and Fitzgerald and company as 'the lost generation.' What we can now see is that they have been way surpassed by their contemporaries who were or were to be 'the saved generation.'

---

[12] Garth, 300.
[13] Garth, 292.
[14] Tolkien, 7.

AMERICAN HISTORY—
A CALVINIST'S INTERPRETATION

Chapter Twenty
The Protestant Reformation—
American History, Chapter One

> It was not from Greece or Rome that the regeneration of human life came forth; that mighty metamorphosis dates from Bethlehem and Golgotha; and if the Reformation, in a still more special sense, claims the love of our hearts, it is because it has dispelled the clouds of sacerdotalism, and has unveiled again to fullest view the glories of the Cross.
> Abraham Kuyper, *Lectures on Calvinism*[1]

The story of the discovery of the Americas in the 1500s and the founding of the American colonies in the 1600s is often told in terms of the accomplishments of various explorers. Along with the primary explorations of Columbus, the claiming, mapping and settlement of North America is ascribed to a familiar list of mysterious, solemn men, such as DeSoto, Champlain, Marquet and Joliet, La Salle, Henry Hudson, Sir Walter Raleigh and others. Their discoveries were geographical points: rivers and lakes, settlements, and future cities, named after them or their sovereign kings. Upon discovery of a territory, the explorer would stake his country's flag in the soil and proclaim the land as part of his sovereign's dominion. Countries, such as Spain, with the wealth to fund explorers and the military might to maintain their claims were able to carve out large portions of the Americas. Weaker countries, such as Sweden, laid claim to smaller tracts of land for a short time that were later consumed by other powers.

Is the story of America's founding a story of power politics, military might, and economic virulence? Or are there other dimensions to the story that led to the establishment of the United States? What are the theological roots of the founding of America? The question seems odd, history is rarely approached as the unfolding of theological currents, but a theological interpretation of history is vital to the Christian historian or student. As C. Gregg

---

[1] (Grand Rapids, MI: William B. Eerdmans Publishing Company, 1931),

Singer noted, historians have rarely given theology its proper place as a determining factor in history.[2] But theology must be placed on the witness stand to explain the development of the Americas.

America had been discovered numerous times prior to the Asian-seeking quest of Columbus. Both from Europe and from Asia, explorers had found the two huge landmasses separating the two great oceans. Evidence abounds that the ancient world, in the centuries before Christ, had discovered, mapped, and settled many parts of both North and South America.[3] History is not social evolution from simple societies to complex civilizations. Rather, civilizations have risen and fallen throughout history. What Phoenicians and Carthaginians most likely knew well was forgotten in the centuries following the Punic Wars.

What had changed in European thinking that caused the 1492 re-discovery to trigger a chain reaction that resulted in a massive migration to and development of the Americas? What caused the North American settlements to far outpace and overwhelm the South American settlements, when the latter seemed initially to contain the better resources? Along with abundant resources, the South American lands were not lacking in the mettle of the settlers, since the Spanish Conquistadors proved to be brilliant warriors, able administrators, and either enlightened colonizers or brutal empire builders, depending on the need or the character of the leader.[4] Just as the Catholic theology of the Spaniards proved vastly superior to the pagan, idol-worshipping, blood-thirsty religions of the Aztecs and Incas, so did the Protestantism of the Northern Europeans who settled North America prove superior to Roman Catholicism as a colonizing motive.

Simply put, North America was discovered geographically as a result of the combined efforts of Spanish, French, Dutch, and English explorers, but the real origins of America are found in the theological fires of the Protestant Reformation. Theologians rather than cartographers are the key to America's founding. Martin Luther and John Calvin must be ranked along with, if not above, Christopher Columbus and John Smith when the founding of America is considered.

---

[2] C. Gregg Singer, *A Theological Interpretation of American History*. (Nutley, N.J.: The Craig Press, 1974), 5.

[3] See Barry Fell. *America B.C.: Ancient Settlers in the New World* (New York: Pocketbooks, 1986) and *Saga America* (New York: Times Books, 1983).

[4] See Bernal Diaz, *The Conquest of New Spain* (New York: Penguin Books, 1963). See also Phillip Powell *Mexico's Miguel Calderas and the Taming of America's First Frontier* (Tucson: The University of Arizona Press, 1977) and *Tree of Hate* (Vallecito: Ross House Books, 1985).

Referring to the roles of Luther and Calvin in later American history, Page Smith has commented:

> The American Revolution might thus be said to have started, in a sense, when Martin Luther nailed his 95 theses to the church door at Wittenburg. It received a substantial part of its theological and philosophical underpinnings from John Calvin's *Institutes of the Christian Religion* and much of its social theory from the Puritan Revolution of 1640-1660, and, perhaps less obviously, from the Glorious Revolution of 1689.[5]

Rarely in history have two former law students had such an impact on the world as did Luther and Calvin. Rarely have two men of conservative bent so radically changed the world's landscape. Rarely have two more complementary personalities and intellects effected in tandem a cultural and ultimately geographic shift in the world. Both changed the way that Europeans thought about God, the Bible, the Church, and society; almost as important, both changed the way Europeans approached thought and action itself. Both saw themselves as loyal churchmen with a desire to change the church from within. Both effected the greatest schism in Christian history. Beyond the shores of Europe, these two men determined the shape of the land they knew little about.

Some historians have relegated the Reformation to a sub-heading, a northern European sideshow, of the broader movement known as the Renaissance. While the Reformation, as a movement, grew out of and was heavily influenced by the Renaissance, it developed enough distinctive differences to qualify as a separate movement. The Reformation and the Renaissance produced different approaches to the issue of authority and the role of government. Another misunderstanding of the Reformation would be to assume that it was only a religious movement, a church squabble, or an intramural debate among professing Christians. The Reformation affected more than the name on the door of the church and the order of service inside the church. The theological battles of the Reformation affected more than the nature and meaning of the bread and wine used in the communion service. The theological changes had far reaching consequences and the sociological, political, and economic changes brought further changes in European thought and society, before spilling the mixture over into North America.

---

[5] Page Smith, editor, *Religious Origins of the American Revolution*. (Missoula, Montana: Scholars Press, 1976), Introduction, 2.

The Reformation was arguably the major factor in the established of the North American settlements. German historian Ranke said that John Calvin was the virtual founder of America.[6] The same could be said for Martin Luther. A case can be made for John Knox's influence in the establishment of the colonies, and the English Puritans certainly played key roles in the political and religious battles of England that were part of what spilled over into the New World.

The history of the Reformation can be initially simplified, and arguably oversimplified, as being the work of Martin Luther and John Calvin. Of course, a more detailed study would include the contributions of men and movements during the Middle Ages, such as John Wycliffe and the Lollard Movement and John Hus and the Hussites. It would include the theological, political and economic forces contributing to the social and religious revolution wrought by the Reformation. The roles of lesser known men, such as Philip Melancthon of Germany, Martin Bucer of Strasburg, and Hugh Latimer and Thomas Cranmer of England would be highlighted. All historical studies tend to greater and greater complexity, and all simplifications are oversimplifications in some sense, yet there is a place for the survey, the scanning for significant details, and the reduction of great events to a list of causes and a small number of people. Therefore, this examination of the Reformation will focus initially upon the lives and works of Luther and Calvin.

Martin Luther has oftentimes been portrayed—both favorably and unfavorably—as a rebel against Roman Catholicism. Yet, rather than a rebel, Luther can be more properly viewed as a loyal son. The Roman Catholic Church professed to uphold true Christianity, and as such, it offered an explanation of ultimate truth concerning spiritual matters. In Acts 16, the Philippian jailor, realizing that an eternal issue outweighed his present crisis, asked Paul, "What must I do to be saved?" This is one of the most profound and fundamental questions of human existence. It was not rebellion for Luther to have asked that same question. Paul told the Philippian jailor to believe on the Lord Jesus Christ. A millennium and a half later, the theological garden had grown so thick with weeds that Luther could barely see Christ. Rites, rituals, man-made ordinances, and outright heresies had put the pearl of great price at the bottom of the sea. Both Protestant and Catholic theologians and historians, with the benefit of five hundred years hindsight and a more civil atmosphere, have questioned the extremes both Luther and his opponents went to in rhetoric and faith to draw the battle lines of the sixteenth-century brawl.

---

[6] As quoted in Loraine Boettner, *The Reformed Doctrine of Predestination*. (Philipsburg: Presbyterian and Reformed Publishing, 1975) 389.

Luther may have been psychologically a little too vexed over sin and righteousness. Perhaps he could have taken consolation in the affirmation of the Apostles' Creed that Christians believe in "forgiveness of sins." But his anxiety has become our consolation. At what point a distorted and obscured gospel ceases to be the gospel is no idle question.

Luther charged into the late Medieval plan of salvation. If ever zeal and fanaticism alone could have saved a soul, his would have been saved. He responded to what had by then become the Church's answer with a zeal that would have frightened the Pope. Luther pushed Roman Catholic soteriology, that is, their doctrine of salvation, to the limits. A look a Luther's life will illustrate this.

Luther was the son of a German coalmine worker who had long envisioned his son attaining a higher station in life than he had. Young Martin would be a lawyer–a respectable profession with worthy economic benefits even in the late Middle Ages. An encounter with God via God's hand in nature during a lightening storm abruptly caused Luther to drop his law studies and commit his soul to a monastic life. Despite his father's anger, Luther entered a monastery intent on winning God's favor. Luther's religious sensibilities were extremely delicate. He found administering the Mass tremendously unnerving. His soul was overly vexed about appeasing God's wrath. As his spiritual struggle developed, Luther tried typical Roman Catholic cures. His priests grew tired of his incessant, overly detailed and petty confessions, yet Luther feared the consequences of even the smallest unconfessed sins. Luther punished his body, tormented his soul, and wracked his mind for spiritual consolation.

His superiors recommended that Luther journey to Rome, the seat of the church, to find answers. After having traveled to Rome, Luther attended masses in the Holy City, saw the then current Pope, climbed the steps that supposedly Jesus had climbed when taken to Pontus Pilate, and did all the acts sacramental and otherwise that the ritual-laden capital of Catholicism had to offer. In his words, "I came to Rome smelling like an onion, and left it smelling like garlic." This was hardly the result his spiritually tortured soul had longed for.

The next step Luther's superiors took was fatal to European Roman Catholic hegemony. Luther was directed upon a course of study with the goal of earning a doctorate in theology and of obtaining the position of teacher or professor of theology. Students of theology–whether Luther, Augustine, Calvin, Marx, or Stalin–have tended to be world movers and shakers in one direction or the other. Luther's studies set him to the task of painstakingly examining the text of the Scripture. While some characterization of the suppression of the Scriptures during the Middle Ages are exaggerated, of a truth, Biblical theology was not the most prominent feature of the age.

In Luther's day the Scriptures were available–though not in mass quantities–but were not generally widely read, known, or applied. Of course, in our time we have learned that mass production does not result necessarily in greater understanding. Luther's theological awakening seemed to have begun with his studies in the book of Psalms around the winter of 1512-1513. This collection of theocentric songs–intensely personal in character and Messianic in message–separated Luther from the world of ritual and man-made sacraments and showed him the themes that would characterize the Reformation. In other words, the Book of Psalms unveiled the themes of God's glory, the work of Christ, the regenerating work of the Holy Spirit, the nature of faith, and the life of joy–mixed with travails–that characterized the Christian.

If the Book of Psalms was the bombardment before the battle, the Book of Romans was the invading force. In the first chapter of Romans, the issue that would rip Christendom was shown to Luther. Romans 1:17 states, "For in it (the gospel of Christ) the righteousness of God is revealed from faith to faith; as it is written, 'The just shall live by faith.'"

Luther described it years later:

> After I had pondered the problem for days and nights, God took pity on me and I saw the inner connection between the two phrases, "The justice of God is revealed in the Gospel" and "The just shall live by faith." I had begun to understand that this "justice of God" is the righteousness by which the just man lives through the free gift of God, that is to say "by faith."...Thereupon I felt as I had been born again and had entered Paradise through wide-open gates. Immediately the whole of Scripture took on a new meaning for me.[7]

The language, immediacy, and directness of being saved by faith in Christ, as common as the notion seems in modern evangelicalism, was so radical in Luther's time that it sent the papacy, the sacraments, the priesthood, the relics, the indulgences, and the rituals of Catholicism crashing down throughout much of Europe. Luther was personally changed, and so his teaching and preaching changed. Reformation is always proceeded by a change in rhetoric.

---

[7] As quoted in E. Harris Harbison, *The Age of Reformation* (Westport, Connecticut: Greenwood Press, Publishers, 1982 reprint), 49.

When Luther later confronted the issue of indulgences by posting his ninety-five theses on the church door in Wittenberg, he probably hoped, at best, for a rousing and spirited debate between scholars to be followed by a post-game analysis over a stein of beer at the local tavern. The church door was not only the message board for a Medieval community, but also the equivalent of the academic journal for scholars like Luther. He was hotly pursuing a debate, and he got it.

The bombshell that exploded with the ninety-five theses exceeded Luther's expectations. Europe had been spiritually longing for this cathartic release. The Reformation had now begun in earnest. Pope Leo X, the artistically minded, spiritually defunct Vicar of Christ in Rome, responded with the typical blindness and obstinacy of entrenched leadership. Leo said the theses were simply the babblings of a drunk German. The problem was that Luther never sobered up.

Luther tried to remain in the Roman Catholic fold. He joined that long list of reformers past and future who would attempt to reform an entrenched institution from within. Luther debated, wrote books, preached sermons, and prayed and agonized over the conflict that had erupted. The historic showdown for Luther came at the Diet of Worms in 1521. Into the grand hall where representatives of the Pope and the political and religious rulers joined with the Holy Roman Emperor, the German monk and religious doctor armed with a pile of books gave one of the most powerful defenses in all of history.

William Manchester described the pageantry of the assembly and the contrast they were with Luther:

> The diet setting was spectacular: the monk, appearing in his simple plain robe, faced his inquisitor, Johann von der Ecken, a functionary of the archbishop of Trier, and behind him, the court. This body comprised, first, a panoply of prelates in embroidered, flowered vestments and, second, secular rulers and their ambassadors in the most elaborate finery of the time—short furred jackets bulging at the sleeves, silk shirts with padded shoulders, velvet doublets, brightly colored breeches…Titled laymen wore coronets, tiaras, diadems; young Charles, presiding on a throne as supreme civil judge, wore his imperial crown; prelates wore miters, and burghers furred and feathered hats. Luther's head was uncovered and tonsured.[8]

---

[8] William Manchester, *A World Lit Only By Fire: The Medieval Mind and the Renaissance* (Boston: Little, Brown and Company, 1992), 171-172. While written in an engaging narrative style, Manchester's views on Luther, the Medieval Era, and the Reformation are not completely reliable.

This simple monk held his own quite well against the august and powerful assembly of church and state. The inquest began with von der Eck asking Luther if the books on the table were his and if yes, then did he still stand by the contents of the books.[9] Luther proved himself to be spiritually discerning, but also practically wise–a rare combination in Christian circles. First, when the Diet called for him to recant, he asked for time. Luther did not want to burn at the stake having second thoughts of what he might have said.

Second, Luther spoke to the international body in his native German tongue as well as in Latin. While this excluded some from understanding his message, it strengthened the feeling of the German princes and rulers toward one of their boys who was standing strong against the powers around him. Luther's powerful speech signaled the shift in the ultimate base of authority for society. The social order would not find its meaning and center in the institutional and centralized Roman Catholic Church and the political Holy Roman Empire. Rather truth would be determined upon the authority of Scripture, interpreted by the individual. Conscience, not papal decrees or church counsels, would guide the individual in his decisions. Luther's speech before the Diet would become one of the center-pieces of Protestant thought:

> Unless convinced by the testimony of the Scriptures or by clear reason (for I do not trust either in the pope or in councils alone, since it is well known that they have often erred and contradicted themselves), I am bound by the Scriptures I have quoted and my conscience is captive to the Word of God. I cannot and I will not retract anything, since it is neither safe nor right to go against conscience. I cannot do otherwise, here I stand, may God help me, amen."[10]

With the confidence that comes from the Word of God, Luther, upon leaving the room, raised his arm in a gesture that German knights traditionally used when they had unhorsed their opponent.[11] Luther was confident, but he was in danger.

Luther's allies wisely kidnapped him and took him to a castle called Wartburg to protect him until the imminent threat was over. While in hiding, Luther grew a beard and assumed the name and title Knight George and

---

[9] Gene Edward Veith, Jr., *A Place to Stand: The Word of God in the Life of Martin Luther* (Nashville: Cumberland House, 2005), 68.

[10] As quoted in Veith, 70.

[11] Otto Scott, *The Great Christian Revolution*, 92.

translated the Bible into his native German.[12] His dream of Germans reading God's Word in their own language began to be fulfilled. The remainder of Luther's life consisted of continuing to preach and write, influencing men both around him and throughout Europe, and marrying, which for a former monk was a radical thing to do. Luther died in 1546, having changed the world around him, and the forces he set in motion continued. His intended scholars' debate over the ninty-five theses ultimately led to the settlement of North America as a fulfillment of that debate. The commitment to the Word of God, the role of the individual conscience, and the unwillingness to bend to the will of popes, councils, and kings all became hallmarks of the theology of the colonists.

The historian E. Harris Harbison aptly summarizes Luther's work as giving these answers to four key questions in Christian history:

> To the question how is a man to be saved, Luther answered: not by works but by faith. To the question where does religious authority lie, he answered: not in the visible institution known as the Roman Church, but in the "Word of God" contained in the Bible. To the question what is the church, he answered: the whole community of Christian believers, since all are really priests and since every man must be "a Christ to his neighbor." To the question what is the essence of Christian living, he replied: serving God in one's calling, whether secular or ecclesiastical, since all useful callings are equally sacred in the eyes of God.[13]

John Calvin

If Luther seemed to be an unlikely revolutionary, John Calvin was certainly more unlikely. Calvin was the sort whose heart rate increased with excitement at the thought of a day in the library. A life of study would have fulfilled all of his needs for adventure. Calvin, when freed from his father's insistence that he study law, turned to classical studies. His first work, a study of the Roman author Seneca, might have established him as a leading scholar in humanist studies in his day and resulted in his total obscurity outside of a few little known footnotes in our day. But God purposed other things in the life of this Frenchman. His conversion experience, never fully explained, only alluded to in the preface to his commentary on the Psalms, was of a quiet nature. He said, "God by a sudden conversion subdued and brought to

---

[12] Veith, 73-74.
[13] Harbison, 53.

my mind a teachable frame, which was more hardened in such matters than might have been expected from one at my early period of life."[14]

Calvin the humanist scholar became Calvin the Bible scholar and teacher rather quickly. In his account, he said, "Having thus received some taste and knowledge of true godliness, I was immediately inflamed with so intense a desire to make progress therein, that although I did not leave off other studies, I yet pursued them with less ardor."[15] Because of his university training and intellectual gifts, Calvin quickly emerged as a teacher to others seeking to know about these new theological matters. He also collaborated with another scholar and Protestant sympathizer named Nicholas Cop. When Cop delivered his inaugural address as rector of the University of Paris, the Protestant content of the message implicated both Cop and Calvin. The political climate became so dangerous for Calvin that he was forced to flee from Paris. After traveling through France in disguise, he stopped for a brief respite in Geneva, Switzerland. There he met another key Protestant Reformer named William Farel.

Farel is largely remembered for one sermon he delivered in his ministerial career. It was his summons to Calvin to stay in Geneva and help him. Calvin explained to Farel that he was just passing through on his way to find a quiet university setting in which to study. By threatening God's wrath and curse upon him if he left, Farel prevailed upon the young French scholar to stay in Geneva and work for the ongoing reformation there. Calvin's ministry became identified with this city where he preached and taught and wrote for much of the rest of his life. Historian J. E. Neale said that Calvin did two outstanding things:

> [F]irst, he wrote the bible of the new protestant movement, his *Institutes of Christian Religion,* published in Latin in 1536 and afterwards in French and other languages; secondly, he founded at Geneva the Protestants' New Jerusalem, the City of God on earth.[16]

Calvin would probably chuckle at the thought of Geneva being "the City of God on earth." His experiences there were quite exasperating. The city itself was a microcosm of the Reformation. Having dispensed with the Roman Catholic order, the city longed for freedom. But freedom as a concept was disputed between those who wanted the freedom of the Reformed

---

[14] John Calvin, *Commentary on the Book of Psalms,* Volume 1 (Grand Rapids: Baker Book House, 1993 reprint.), "The Author's Preface, xl.

[15] Calvin, xli.

[16] J. E. Neale, *The Age of Catherine de Medici* (New York: Harper Torchbooks, 1960), 16.

faith, that is, freedom within the bounds of God's order, and those whose penchant for personal and social freedom earned them the name Libertines. This group, desiring the freedom from all restraint, cursed Calvin but rejoiced in the benefits that developed from a Christian order. Calvin's life, apart from his scholarly pursuits, was consumed with political and religious battles with the Libertines. Both Calvin and the Libertines rejoiced when Calvin was expelled from Geneva. Moral anarchy being what it is, in a few years, the city officials called Calvin back. No doubt, only his belief in a joyous afterlife enabled him to return to the ungracious city.

He battled for church, political, and social reforms against a host of opponents. He endured curses and insults, many too profane to repeat. People sang bawdy songs outside his window at night and even dogs tried to attack him. The church and state issues were often foggy, leading many historians to wrongly surmise that Calvin ruled the city as a tyrannical theocrat. Yet, he was not even a citizen there until late in life. Much of what is now better understood as proper roles and demarcations for church and state grew out of Calvin's experiences and writings.

In spite of the hardships he endured in Geneva, it was from this small Swiss city, and from Strasburg where he lived in exile for a time, that Calvin penned his *Institutes of the Christian Religion,* his commentaries on almost the whole Bible, scores of letters to evangelicals across the continent, and a number of religious tracts. Initially the *Institutes* had the objective of educating a political ruler, Francis I of France, in sound religion by showing that the Protestant religion was both the biblical and historic Christian faith. While failing to win over King Francis I, this theological masterpiece crystallized the message of the Reformation. Far from being a dated piece of historical theology, Calvin's *Institutes* maintains a theological freshness and applicability to this day. Its presence and continuing relevance in recent decades is a story yet to be fully told.

The countries of Europe poured a steady stream of sons and daughters into Geneva to be taught by Calvin during his tutorial reign there. John Knox referred to Calvin's theological teaching as "the most perfect school of Christ." Calvin's Academy had two levels of instruction, one for Geneva's youth and the other for the training of ministers.[17]

David Hall comments on the impact of Calvin's Academy:

> From 1560 onward, the Genevan Academy also doubled as the ministerial training ground for France and other international

---

[17] Hall, *The Genevan Reformation and America's Founding,* 89.

centers. In time, scholars from Paris and Lausanne flocked to this leading educational center. Those original students would go forth to draft influential confessions of faith, serve as political advisors in Scotland, Germany, France, Holland, and England, and teach at leading universities....Moreover the Academy exported missionaries. The Genevan church sent over 100 missionaries to France, Brazil, Italy, Holland, and England before 1562....Geneva became an enormous source for reform, acting at times like the best of resistance movements. Its influence in Europe, England, and Scotland was enormous.[18]

The theological, political, cultural war of the Reformation revolved around Geneva, rather than Wittenberg. Luther's work had been to ignite the Reformation; his theology was inadequate for the next stage, and his immediate successors only consolidated Luther's gains. It remained for Calvin to carry the Reformation through to the next stage. Calvin's vision has never been consolidated, and his successors still labor to fulfill the job. W. Fred Graham comments on how Calvin's work differed from that of Luther:

Luther felt God's law primarily as the threat which drives us to God's mercy, and that was the end of its Lutheran usefulness. For Calvin, the law had a further purpose, that of guiding the believer after he had accepted God's mercy and forgiveness. This meant that the Calvinist was a more "driven" Christian—driven to live a life more in harmony with stern biblical morality, and thus driven to change society in this direction. This helps explain why Calvin was more concerned than Luther to tell soldiers how they must fight—no rape, pillage, or harassment of noncombatants—and also more concerned to tell the Geneva city council how it should govern. Luther turned over such legal questions to the political arm, and this in no small measure helped produce in Germany and Scandinavia a more peaceful, less revolutionary movement, when compared with the government-toppling cadres issuing from Geneva.[19]

What were the results of the lives and ministries of Luther and Calvin? They shattered the world they were born into. Roman Catholicism repre-

---

[18] Hall, 89.

[19] W. Fred Graham, *The Constructive Revolutionary: John Calvin and His Socio-Economic Impact* (Richmond, Virginia: John Knox Press, 1971), 20-21.

sented a religious, political, and social corporate world resistant to change. Its great strength was its unity and its stability. Like many united and stable institutions, it created an atmosphere that stifled the mind and ensnared the soul. Luther and Calvin changed the debate about the issue of authority. Not the Church, as the Roman Catholics had said, not reason or experience as later philosophies would say, but Scripture, Sola Scriptura, in fact, was the basis of authority and truth. Philosophically, they shifted the basis of epistemology from the thinking of Aquinas back to the Scriptures.[20] Practically, they stripped the priest of his robes and placed them on the backs of every believer. The two Reformers freed the individual from the group. Man must follow his conscience. They broke the yoke of soul-tyranny without unleashing licentiousness,[21] for man was bound by covenant not only to God, but to the church and the historic creeds and confessions of the church, as far as they adhered to Scripture. Neither the individual, nor the group was ultimate. The philosophical problem of the One and the Many as posed by the ancient Greeks was resolved socially by the individual Christian man within the covenant body of the church.[22]

Luther and Calvin, both personally men of great scholarship, ushered in a new wave of scholarship. Harbison said, "The Protestant Reformation began in a scholar's insight into the meaning of Scripture. It was to a large extent a learned movement, a thing of professors and students, a scholars' revolution….There is no better age than the Reformation in which to study the Christian scholar and his *vocatio*, divine calling and professional occupation."[23] The Protestant minister had to be a man of learning to master the Scriptures; his congregation needed learning to double-check the preaching and to carry out God's dominion mandate into the world. It was this worldliness of Calvinism, a worldliness predicated upon other-worldliness, that so baffled Calvin's critics. Christopher Dawson marveled over this saying, "It is one of the paradoxes of religious history that a theology which centered in the doctrines of predestination and reprobation and denied or minimized the freedom of the human will should have developed an ethos of personal responsibility which expressed itself in moral activism."[24]

---

[20] W. Andrew Hoffecker, "Augustine, Aquinas, and the Reformers," found in *Building a Christian Worldview*, 235-258.

[21] This is not to say that all who imbibed their theology applied it in complete and balanced ways.

[22] See R.J. Rushdoony, *The One and the Many* (Fairfax, Virginia: Thoburn Press, 1971), 243-264.

[23] E. Harris Harbison, *The Christian Scholar in the Age of Reformation* (New York: Charles Scribner's Sons, 1956), Preface vi-viii.

[24] Dawson, *The Dividing of Christendom*, 12.

The Catholic insistence that the spiritual life found greatest fulfillment in the monastery or the convent was overturned by both Calvin's and Luther's marriages and delights in such a carnal thing as marriage. The family as a strong institution, far from being a constant fixture in the history of our world, was revived by the Reformation. In his excellent study on family life during the Reformation, Steven Ozment points out:

> Protestants were faced with what they considered to be a crisis in domestic relations, one that could be traced to the institutions of medieval religion. To correct the situation, they exalted the patriarchal nuclear family as the liberation of men, women, and children from religious, sexual, and vocational bondage....The Protestant reformers were...the first to set the family unequivocally above the celibate ideal and to praise the husband and the housewife over the monk and nun in principle.[25]

Scholars have been puzzled, confused, hostile, and often terribly wrong in their efforts to understand the social impact of Luther's and especially, of Calvin's thought. For Max Weber and Richard Tawney, the worldly success of Calvinism could only be explained by the warped notion that the lonely adherent to Calvin's theology was driven psychologically to make money to affirm God's election. Such notions have no foundations in either the written texts of Calvin's writing and his successors or in their worldly activities.

The political implications of the Reformation, especially of Calvin's variety should fill several volumes in any series of political science texts. The most fundamental doctrine affecting and limiting the power of government was Luther's, but even more so Calvin's emphasis on the doctrine of the sovereignty of God. If the sovereignty of God is asserted, then the sovereignty of the state (totalitarianism) is prohibited, the sovereignty of the individual (autonomy) is denied, the sovereignty of "the people" (democracy) is discounted, and even the sovereignty of the institutional church (ecclesiastical tyranny) is checked. As Gregg Singer noted, "Calvin's political thought represents the only satisfactory safeguard against despotism in that it refers all true sovereignty to God alone and constantly affirms that all rulers are merely His regents."[26] Where Calvin's ideas spread, governments were made more free and open. While historian Edward McNall Burns described Calvin

---

[25] Steven Ozment, *When Fathers Ruled—Family Life in Reformation Europe* (Cambridge, Mass.: Harvard University Press, 1983), 6-7.

[26] C. Gregg Singer, *John Calvin: His Roots and Fruits*. (Philipsburg, N.J.: The Presbyterian and Reformed Publishing Company, 1967), 40.

as ruling Geneva with a rod of iron, he noted that Calvinism opposed tyranny and despotism wherever it took root.[27] Harbison concurs saying, "One of the key factors in the development of modern constitutional government was the resistance of Calvinist minorities to the exercise of arbitrary power by monarchs."[28] Calvinism and political tyranny were and are incompatible.

The political implications of the Reformational adherence to Scripture are also manifold. First, the Scriptures contain many commands and examples regarding civil government. The thirteenth chapter of Romans gives the rationale for obeying governments (even wicked pagan governments, such as Rome under the Caesars), and thirteenth chapter of Revelation describes tyrannical, God-hating governments (characteristic of Rome and its successors even into the 21st century). The Scriptures also establish one of the most profound governmental concepts in its development of the concept of the covenant. Covenant theology provides a basis for the notion of the compact theory of government. From this developed the idea of government by constitution, preferably a written constitution. Calvinistic people were theologically trained to think covenantally. When one party breaks the covenant, then the other party is freed from the demands of the covenant. Calvinism posited an equality of the people before God that did not exempt kings from the law. In a later age that rejected the Calvinistic worldview, Americans still insisted that presidents were not above the law. Divine right of kings went to the chopping block and rolled with the divine heads of kings. The cutting edge of Scripture effectively severed 17th century tyranny, at least in England.

There are some great studies on the political impact of Calvinism in history. David Hall's book *The Genevan Reformation and the American Founding* has been referenced and will be examined in more detail later. Douglas Kelly has written one of the best studies of the topic in *The Emergence of Liberty in the Modern World: The Influence of Calvin on Five Governments from the 16th Through 18th Centuries*. Abraham Kuyper's classic *Lectures on Calvinism* and N. S. McFetridge's *Calvinism in History* both include sections on Calvinism's political history and implications. These are not all the books on the topic, but still not enough study has been done on the question of why Calvinists refuse enslavement as a people.[29]

---

[27] Burns, *Western Civilization,* 416-419.
[28] Harbison, *The Age of Reformation,* 78-79.
[29] David Hall, *The Genevan Reformation and the American Founding;* Douglas Kelly, *The Emergence of Liberty in the Modern World* (Philipsburg, N. J.: Presbyterian and Reformed Publishing Company, 1992); Abraham Kuyper, *Lectures on Calvinism;* N. S. McFetridge, *Calvinism in History* (Edmonton, Canada: Still Water Revival Books, 1989 reprint).

Calvinism also affected the area of law. Calvinists insisted on the political application of God's Law. While theologians struggled with and disagreed over the pertinent applications of God's Law, they alike insisted on its relevance in some sense. Any views that law was rooted in "nature," the people, the legislature, or the king were rejected. Jurisprudence was founded upon Scriptural norms. Singer says that Calvin "was convinced that the basis of all sound social life was to be found in the Ten Commandments and that the last six are the norm for all correct social relationships."[30] This Calvinistic emphasis on Biblical law in the political realm brings up the often cited charge of Calvin and his followers imposing Theocracy upon their subjects. In the historical efforts to balance the proper roles of both church and state, abuses of power can be found on both sides. Clear lines of demarcation between church authority and state power did not emerge in Calvin's time with the clarity we might wish.

Our political freedoms and ecclesiastical liberties grew out of the Reformation. The concept of separation of church and state emerged slowly. Our age is certainly much freer in many respects than the era of the Reformation and the centuries that preceded and succeeded that time. But the challenges of pluralism, which is really polytheism, and the evils of the purely secular and ever-encroaching state, and the threat posed in our time by Islamo-fascism all force us back to realizing our own political and theological inadequacies. A humble study of Calvinist political theory is needed.

The Calvinistic emphasis on Biblical law can be found in such documents as the Westminster Larger Catechism's questions pertaining to the Ten Commandments. In American colonial history, John Cotton proposed the *Massachusetts Body of Liberties,* which was, according to its author, a model of Moses' judicial law. It gleaned from the entirety of the Old Testament, and especially the Pentateuch, laws to govern the colony. In the late twentieth century, several Reformed theologians and writers began re-exploring the political implications of God's Law. These men were not content to argue for posting a copy of the Ten Commandments on a government building, but advocated the wide-scale application of God's law in the civil realm, social realm, church, family, and individual life. The two cornerstone books were R. J. Rushdoony's *Institutes of Biblical Law* and Greg Bahnsen's *Theonomy in Christian Ethics.*[31] Quite a few other books followed in the wake of these two major treatises, along with much controversy. The "Theonomy Debate"

---

[30] Singer, 62.
[31] Rushdoony's *Institutes* came out in 1973 and Bahnsen's *Theonomy* in 1977. Both were originally published by Presbyterian and Reformed Publishing Company.

The Reformation Spreads

The Reformation spread throughout most of Europe during the 1500s. In some places, such as Italy, small groups adopted Reformed theology, but were unable to change the culture or even survive. In France, the Reformed Christians, called Huguenots, developed into a powerful group with upper middle class economic strength and significant political strength. Events such as the St. Bartholomew's Day Massacre diminished the Reformed movement in France. Both the high and low points for the Reformation in France occurred when the religious wars and internecine strife for the crown ended with Henry of Navarre taking the throne. Henry, previously a Protestant, embraced the Catholic Church with the famous comment, "Paris is worth a mass." Now as King Henry IV, he published the Edict of Nantes over the protests of Catholic clergy and many of the governing officials in France. This edict granted to Huguenots liberty of conscience and freedom of worship, with certain restrictions.[32]

In the Netherlands, the Reformed movement was more successful. The Netherlands had been ruled over and was part of the realm of the Hapsburgs of Spain and Austria. Dutch Calvinists and their political allies ousted the Roman Catholic Spanish overlords, and the small, low-lying nation achieved a power status out of proportion to their size. The spread of Calvinism in the Netherlands, which had been preceded by Lutheran and Anabaptist influences, caused Spanish authorities to clamp down on what they considered heresy. Their repressive measures pushed the people of the Netherlands toward a great hatred of religious persecution and furthered the growth of Calvinism. For quite a few years, war was waged throughout the Dutch provinces. Not all of those in rebellion against the Spanish were Calvinists; for example, the leader who emerged out of the conflict, William of Orange, was not a Calvinist, but he found his Calvinist allies to be a dedicated and determined lot. The revolt in the Netherlands lasted from 1566 to 1648; it involved not just Spain and the Netherlands, but also England and France. Not all of the Netherlands achieved independence: the southern provinces remained under Spanish and Catholic influence. The part of the Dutch Netherlands that became a free country went on to experience "their most glorious age of commercial prosperity, naval glory, and cultural achievement in the seventeenth century."[33]

---

[32] Harbison, *The Age of Reformation,* 111.
[33] Harbison, 119-120.

While Lutheranism spread from northern Germany into Denmark, Norway, and Sweden, Lutheran ideas in England only served as a bridgehead for the more thorough-going Calvinistic theology that would follow. Calvinism achieved great prominence in the British Isles. The English story is one of struggles, persecutions, political schemes, religious devotion, and a theological-political pendulum. Out of the struggle emerged some great theological writings, greater concepts of political freedom than the world ever knew before, the Puritan movement, and the colonization of America. The story of the political and religious travails of England—and Scotland—from the time of Henry VIII, whose reign began in 1509, to the Glorious Revolution of 1688 has to be among the most thrilling two hundred events in history. With such figures as the Tudor monarchs (Henry VIII, Edward VI, Mary, and Elizabeth), the great Protestant martyrs (Latimer, Ridley, Cranmer, and others), the English Sea Dogs, the Stuarts of Scotland and England, Cromwell and the Puritans, Knox and the Scots to the north, and Shakespeare, Milton, and Donne, the whole age shines with drama, romance, war, love, tragedy, and beauty. Our few paragraphs will not even serve as an adequate outline of the times.

The Reformation entered England through the unlikely channels, not of the church, but of the King's palace and bedroom. Love, or lust, and power began the process that would break Roman Catholicism's shaky tie with England. King Henry VIII, determined to sire a male heir to the throne, proceeded to divorce his lawful wedded wife Catherine of Aragon. For reasons more political than theological, the pope refused to grant the divorce, and so Henry divorced the papacy, Parliament granted his divorce to Catherine, and the Catholic Church lost its tenuous hold on England.

Henry, a brilliant man, though only a lowly pawn in God's purposes, sought to establish himself as the head of a theologically Roman Catholic, yet Anglican Church. Once given the title "Defender of the Faith" by the pope for his opposition to Luther, Henry had none of the spiritual motivations of Luther and Calvin. While his immediate objective had been to marry Anne Boleyn, who was already seven months advanced into a pregnancy, his actions created opportunities for changes far beyond his theological expectations.

Forces for church reform, which were seeping into England through scholars and sailors, gained momentum. In time an English Bible, translated at the cost of William Tyndale's life, reached the English people. Archbishop Thomas Cranmer compiled and produced *The Book of Common Prayer,* which along with Calvin's *Insitutes* and Luther's *Bondage of the Will,* is one of the classic and defining works of the Protestant Reformation. Because of Henry's unchanging Catholic convictions and frequent changing of wives, the progress of the Reformation had many starts and stops. Protestants in his court were often displayed stealth, pragmatism, and less than pure means of achieving what they believed were godly ends.

Church reforms reached a high pitch when Henry's physically weak, but theologically committed Protestant son, Edward VI, succeeded his father to the throne. England swung forcefully toward the Reformation. Upon Edward's death in six years, his sister Mary, a hard-core Roman Catholic with a vengeance toward her mother's enemies, literally tried to burn out Protestantism in England. But when the heat increased, so did the mettle, and Protestantism lost some good men at the stakes, but gained the heart of England. The martyrdoms of men such as Bishop Ridley, Bishop Latimore, and Archbishop Cranmer all contributed to a determined mettle in the Reformed movement that became the substance of yet another Protestant classic, John Foxe's *Book of Martyrs*. Mary's death brought Elizabeth to the throne and brought many exiles who had been living in Geneva and elsewhere on the continent back to England.

Elizabeth proved to be the master of political expediency and pragmatism. Her Elizabethan Compromise pleased neither the growing factions of Puritans nor the remaining Roman Catholics. But her compromise held England together, protected Elizabeth's throne and life, enabled her country to defend itself against Spain's invasion force, and aided in the establishment of a New World colonial empire. The Age of Elizabeth is characterized by a certain power and energy surging out of the English island. Harbison characterized her religion and politics as follows:

> Elizabeth was first a patriot and second (or third) a Protestant Christian. She said she had no intention of opening windows into men's minds, and all her life she consistently concerned herself with men's acts, not their opinions. This meant that as long as Catholics did not commit treason and so long as Puritans did not infringe upon her royal prerogatives, they might think as they pleased.[34]

The word "Puritan" would be applied to a large varied group who agreed on the principles of reformation of the church and state, although they held to a number of varying beliefs on what that would mean. In spite of later contemptuous treatment by some historians and commentators, the Puritans exhibited remarkable tenacity, intellectual ability, and piety. They were the shock troops of Calvinism who would change the civilization of England

---

[34] Harbison, 121.

and mold the English colonies. The impact of Puritanism remains to this day.

After Elizabeth's death, her cousin James Stuart, James VI of Scotland, would be hailed in England as James I, a Protestant king. James, one of history's most pitiful failures and degenerate and stupid leaders, succeeded mainly in two ways. He called for and got his name attached to a remarkable translation of the Bible. The King James Bible, or Authorized Version, published to offset the anti-tyrannical Geneva Bible, gave the English-speaking world an outstanding work of inspired literature. His other accomplishment was to strengthen the power and determination of the Puritans and other factions in Parliament. Government leaders change the world probably most often in ways they did not intend. His son, Charles I, advanced his father's work by provoking Parliament to a point where arms were raised for war.

The English Civil War of 1642 to 1649, sometimes referred to as the Puritan Revolution, resulted in the execution of Charles I, who had proved to be totally untrustworthy, and the establishment of the English Commonwealth under Cromwell. An unexpected result of this war was the calling of the Westminster Assembly in 1643 with the express purpose of establishing a church government that would be "more agreeable to God's Word and bring the Church of England into a nearer conformity with the Church of Scotland and other Reformed Churches abroad."[35] The 121 divines, with others, met from 1643 to 1649 and produced the Westminster Confession of Faith, the Larger and Shorter Catechisms, the Form of Church Government, and the Directory for Public Worship (all commonly called the Westminster Standards).[36] These theological bombshells never became the spiritual constitution of the Anglican Church, but they became one of the most lucid explanations of Reformed theology in the world. Presbyterians in England, Scotland, and later America would adopt the Westminster Standards. Other Christian groups, such as the Congregationalists and Baptists, would model their confessions after the Westminster Confession.

After the brief and tumultuous reign of the man who would not be king, Lord Protector Oliver Cromwell (1653 to 1658), England restored the monarchy under Charles II, the son of the dead king. Charles was a weak ruler who was in the pay of the French and whose religion changed with the political winds. During his reign, the Puritans, at this time in history often called Dissenters, were considered a political threat and were harshly subju-

---

[35] Adam Loughridge, "Westminster Assembly" from *The New International Dictionary of the Christian Church*, edited by J. D. Douglas. (Grand Rapids: Zondervan, 1978), 1039.
[36] Loughridge, 1039.

gated. After Charles' death, his brother James II became king. While Charles kept his Catholic beliefs a secret until his deathbed confession, his brother James was openly a Catholic. Parliament, which had basically become the kingmaker in England, was content to let James live out his days as a Catholic king with limited powers. But James pushed for Roman Catholic policies and then fathered a son by his Catholic wife. James's heir before this was his Protestant daughter who was married to the King of the Netherlands, William. Now this Catholic baby boy would be in line to inherit the throne.

This led to the Glorious Revolution of 1689 when Parliament reminded the monarchy that the old days of divine right of kings were over. England reached a stage where laws of state and laws of church could not change the commitment of people's hearts. Parliament, not the monarchy, the church, or the papacy, would determine who was truly the king.

Calvinism Among the Scots

To the north, the rugged country of Scotland played out a religious drama with far reaching effects. The key figure, John Knox (c. 1514-c. 1572), played major roles in the theological and political upheavals of England, Geneva, and Scotland. After having converted to the Reformed faith in Scotland, Knox was exiled in the midst of the religious struggles of his country. He studied under Calvin, calling his Geneva school, the "most perfect school of Christ, since the Apostles." Knox pastored Reformed churches both on the continent and in England. As a result of his time in England under Queen Mary, Knox earned the enmity of Queen Mary of England, Queen Mary of Scotland, Queen Elizabeth of England, and feminists to this very day, with his book, titled *First Blast of the Trumpet Against the Monstrous Regiment of Women Rulers*. Knox would be remembered, and both loved and hated, for his fiery confrontations with Queen Mary Stuart of Scotland. Mary, Roman Catholic, tyrannical, and unscrupulous, could never hold her own in arguing against the astute, quick thinking, Bible-grounded John Knox. She once said that she would rather face an army of 10,000 invading soldiers than a Calvinist convinced he was right.

If Luther's gift was initiating Reformation, and Calvin's was in clarifying and defining Reformation, then certainly Knox was best at implementing Reformation in church, state, and culture. The cultural effect of combining Celtic hardiness with Reformed theological exactness and determination enabled a poorly placed, sparsely populated country to impact the world with books, missionary activities, settlements, and well-noted Scottish hardiness and perseverance.

Knox's theological successor was Andrew Melville, who is best remembered for lecturing the king of Scotland, James VI (or James I of England), and calling him God's silly vassal. In contrast to modern clerics who fawn before world leaders, with the exception of the late Mother Theresa, Melville warned the king that there were limits to his rule in the state and even more limits to his role in the church. Melville told King James, "There are two kings and two kingdoms in Scotland: There is King James, the head of this commonwealth, and there is Christ Jesus, the King of the Church whose subject James the Sixth is, and of whose Kingdom he is not a king, nor a lord, nor a head, but a member."[37] In other words, in God's kingdom, James had no more standing than the most miserable convert.

Another great Scottish Calvinist was George Buchanan. Buchanan had one great failure and one great success in life. Rather than breaking even, the effects of his success far outweighed his failure. As private tutor to the boy, young James VI, Buchanan tried to instill his sharp, but evil student with a Calvinistic combination of classical education and Biblical theology. James emerged from his studies perverted morally and intellectually. His hatred of Presbyterianism stemmed in large part from his school experience.[38] Buchanan's success came in his political theology which appeared in a book called *The Rights of the Crown in Scotland (De Jure Regni Apud Scotos)* and which was considered to be one of the most influential political essays of the century.[39] Buchanan's phrase, "Rebellion to tyrants is obedience to God," became a key idea in Thomas Jefferson's political thought and was proposed for the official seal of the United States.[40] David Hall said, "Historians concur that the political contributions of Buchanan and other late sixteenth-century Scottish thinkers were instrumental in spawning freedom movements in Holland, England, and America."[41]

One of those other late sixteenth-century Scottish thinkers was Samuel Rutherford (1600-1661) whose book *Lex Rex,* whose title means law is king, has had a recurring influence in history. Rutherford was one of the Scottish commissioners at the Westminster Assembly in London when the book was published in 1644. The most recent renewed interest in this book came from Francis Schaeffer's recommendations for it during the late 1970s.[42] This

---

[37] As quoted in J. Marcellus Kik, *Church and State: The Story of Two Kingdoms* (New York: Thomas Nelson and Sons, 1963), 96.

[38] Otto Scott, *James I: The Fool as King.* (Vallecito: Ross House Books, 1986).

[39] David Hall, *The Genevan Reformation and the Founding of America,* 243.

[40] Hall, 251-252.

[41] Hall, 252.

[42] Francis Schaeffer, *How Should We Then Live?,* 108-109.

masterpiece of political philosophy captured the key Calvinistic concepts of government that were being fought over throughout Europe. The pen, even mightier when backed by the sword, proved effective. David Hall says that *Lex Rex* is helpful for understanding the Calvinistic mindset of Colonial America.[43] Along with this political treatise, Rutherford's letters show a high level of spiritual devotion matched only by his intellectual devotion to God.[44]

Around 1579, an unknown Calvinist writer in France produced a political writing similar to the Scottish treatise. This work, called *Vindicia Contra Tyranos*, meaning claims against tyrants, also presented the Reformed answer to tyranny. This work of a Protestant revolutionary showed how governments could be changed within, resisted, or even overthrown. R. J. Rushdoony said that *Vindicia Contra Tyranos* was "held by John Adams to be the most influential book in America on the eve of the Revolution."[45] Rushdoony states the central teachings of the book as follows:

> First, any ruler who commands anything contrary to the law of God thereby forfeits his realm. Second, rebellion is refusal to obey God, for we ought to obey God rather than man. Third, since God's law is the fundamental law and the only true source of law, and neither king nor subject is exempt from it, war is sometimes required to defend God's law against the ruler. A fourth tenet also characterized this position: legal rebellion required the leadership of lesser magistrates to oppose, *in the name of the law,* royal dissolution or contempt of law. All these doctrines were basic to the colonial cause.[46]

Along with the political developments, much could be said about the literary outpouring of the Reformed groups. Their classics ranged from Calvin's *Institutes* to Luther's *Bondage of the Will* to thousands of Puritan sermons that exhaustively studied and applied Biblical texts. Other works included such writings as John Bunyan's *Pilgrim's Progress* and John Milton's *Paradise Lost*. If Calvinism separated church and state, it joined church and university. Calvinism was one of the world's most powerful educating forces in history. The economic impact has been touched upon, and the impact on the

---

[43] Hall, 255.

[44] Samuel Rutherford, *Letters of Samuel Rutherford* (Edinburgh: Banner of Truth, 1984, reprint.).

[45] R. J. Rushdoony, *This Independent Republic* (Philipsburg, N.J.: Presbyterian and Reformed, 1973), 24-25.

[46] Rushdoony, 25.

family has been mentioned. Calvinism was obviously a tremendous influence both in church and individual application of Christianity. Calvinism changed the face of northern Europe. Calvinism was the force that resulted in much of the settlement of North America, and it provided the defining characteristic of the North American colonies.

It remains only to hear now the testimony of some additional witnesses to the influence of Calvinism in history.

> The historian Froude said, "Calvinism has produced characters nobler and grander than any which republican Rome ever produced."

> The historian Merle D'Aubigne said, "Wherever Calvinism was established, it brought with it not only truth but liberty, and with all the great developments which these two fertile principles carry with them."

> The historian Motley said, "To the Calvinists more than to any other class of men, the political liberties of Holland, England, and America are due."

> The Frenchman Guizot said, "Calvin's *Institutes,* in spite of its imperfections, is, on the whole, one of the noblest edifices ever erected by the mind of man, and one of the mightiest codes of moral law which ever guided him."

> The historian John Fiske said, "The promulgation of Calvin's theology was one of the longest steps that mankind has taken toward personal freedom."

> The historian George Bancroft said, "They (Calvinistic doctrines) infused enduring elements into the institutions of Geneva, and made it for the modern world, the impregnable fortress of popular liberty—the fertile seed-plot of Democracy."[47]

The testimony having been considered, the jury now has spoken.

---

[47] Quotes all taken from *The New Dictionary of Thoughts,* 73.

For Further Reading

Books on the Protestant Reformation, Luther, Calvin, Huguenots, England during the age of the Tudor monarchs, Knox, the Puritans, Cromwell, the Scottish Covenanters, and other aspects of this time are legion. The footnotes only hint at the many good resources. Highland Books, a division of Cumberland House, has a series called Leaders in Action. These biographies are usually around two hundred and fifty to three hundred pages; the subjects of the biographies are Christian leaders; and the goal of these books is to acquaint readers with the chosen historical figure, their historical challenges and circumstances, and the ways they exhibited good and godly leadership in word and action. This series includes biographies of three of the leaders of the Reformation. David Hall has written a biography of Calvin, titled *A Heart Promptly Offered: The Revolutionary Leadership of John Calvin*. This work is a simplified account of his greater work on the impact of Calvin's thought on America. Gene Edward Veith penned *A Place to Stand: The Word of God in the Life of Martin Luther* and Douglas Wilson wrote *For Kirk and Covenant: The Stalwart Courage of John Knox*.

Other key biographies of the Reformers include Roland Bainton's *Here I Stand: A Life of Martin Luther* and T. H. L. Parker's *John Calvin: A Life*. Bainton and Steven Ozment are both modern scholars whose works on the history of the Reformation are highly acclaimed. Older Protestant historians, particularly Philip Schaff and J. H. Merle D'Aubigne, have written some of the standard and classic accounts of the Reformation. Deborah Alcock's *The Romance of Protestantism: Tales of Trials and Victory* is a good simple account written for young people over a century ago, which means it is readable by adults today. Some of the more academic publications focus on the interplay between political, economic, and theological forces. Other authors have focused upon the Reformation in terms of the spiritual dimensions. Whatever the angle, whatever the approach, the Protestant Reformation never ceases to thrill both the mind and the soul.

Chapter Twenty-One
The Reformation in America

The Shorter Catechism: Question #7: What are the decrees of God? Answer: The Decrees of God are His eternal purpose, according to the counsel of His will, whereby, for His own glory, He hath foreordained whatsoever comes to pass.

Among other things, they (the American colonies) had become the most thoroughly Protestant, Reformed, and Puritan commonwealths in the world. Indeed, Puritanism provided the moral and religious background of fully 75 percent of the people who declared their independence in 1776
—Sidney Ahlstrom[1]

Calvinists are well known for our belief in the doctrine of predestination. It is a point of emphasis, and sad to say, contention, in regard to soteriology, or the doctrine of salvation. The particular emphases on election and a chosen people of God are broad Biblical concepts and language. The doctrines that are distinctively Calvinistic are not necessarily exclusively Calvinistic. All Christians acknowledge some sort of a doctrine of predestination and election; after all, the terms are biblical.

Predestination affects more than just personal salvation. There is a cosmic aspect to the doctrine. Again, all Christians recognize some greater cosmic control of the world by God; therefore, all Christians acknowledge a doctrine of providence. An understanding of God's control over all the minute particulars of this world, including events both evil and tragic, have perplexed believers from the time of Job to the present. We cannot understand all the details of life in this world from our earthly perspective, but we recognize that God rules the world. And this God who controls the world, we confess is both omnipotent and good.

This emphasis on God's rule, specifically, the sovereignty of God, has long been a Calvinistic emphasis. God's sovereignty is acknowledged as

---

[1] Sidney Alhstrom, *A Religious History of the American People*. (New Haven: Yale University Press, 1973), 124.

absolute and total, but not arbitrary and capricious. Twice in the Book of Genesis, Joseph appeals to God's sovereignty over history as an explanation of the evils he endured at the hands of his brothers. When Joseph reveals his true identity to his brothers, he tells them:

> "Please come near to me." So they came near. Then he said, "I am Joseph your brother, whom you sold into Egypt. But now, do not therefore be grieved or angry with yourselves because you sold me here; for God sent me before you to preserve life. For these two years the famine has been in the land, and there are still five years, in the which there will be neither plowing or harvesting. And God sent me before you to preserve a posterity for you in the earth, and to save your lives by a great deliverance. So now it was not you that sent me here, but God; and He has made me a father to Pharaoh, and lord of all his house, and a ruler throughout all the land of Egypt." (Genesis 45:4-8)

Later after Jacob, the father of Joseph and his brothers, had died, the brothers, still feeling guilty, began fearing the retribution for their having sold their brother into slavery. Joseph responds to their plea for forgiveness with these words: "But as for you, you meant evil against me; but God meant it for good, in order to bring it about as it is this day, to save many people alive." (Genesis 50:20)

This same doctrine of God ruling history for His own purposes is emphasized in the Book of Daniel. That book is a compendium of history and prophecy concerning God's rule over the past, present, and future. Nebuchadnezzar testifies to God's sovereignty over men, nations, and kings when he makes this great affirmation following a seven year bout with insanity:

> And at the end of the time I, Nebuchadnezzar, lifted my eyes to heaven, and my understanding returned unto me, and I blessed the Most High, and I praised and honored Him who lives forever:
> For His dominion is an everlasting dominion, and His kingdom is from generation to generation.
> All the inhabitants of the earth are reputed as nothing;
> He does according to his will in the army of heaven,
> and among the inhabitants of the earth.
> No one can stay His hand,
> Or say to him, 'What have You done?
> (Daniel 4:34-35)

Prior to Nebuchadnezzar's recovery from seven years of grazing with cattle and thinking of himself as an ox, he had a dream of a great statue. His dream, which only Daniel was able to interpret, was a political and historical commentary on the future. The humanistic and divinized states of the ancient world were destined to reign powerfully for a time, but would then be supplanted by a spiritual kingdom, the reign of Christ, the Rock not hewn by human hands. All the great kingdoms of the ancient world—Babylon, the Medo-Persians, Greeks and Macedonians, and Romans were simply marching in place until the advent of Christ. The underlying theme again: God rules history.

God's sovereignty over events in the life of Christ are most powerfully displayed in Acts 4:27-28 where the following words appeared in a prayer:

> For truly against Your holy Servant Jesus, whom You anointed, both Herod and Pontius Pilate, with the Gentiles and the people of Israel, were gathered together to do whatever Your hand and Your purpose determined before to be done.

Here we have a recognition that the wicked and unjust crucifixion of Christ, done in evil concert by both Romans and Jews, was done in fulfillment of the purposes and plan of God.

These passages, and many more, all affirm the sovereignty of God over history. Without such a doctrine, the past has no meaning, the present is indecipherable, and the future is uncertain. The fact that historians who reject a belief in God teach and write history and do so quite well is an evidence of the insuppressible nature of God's truth. Unbelieving historians borrow from God's truth. In some cases, they make economics, geography, the nation-state, the culture or chemical make-up to be the predestinators, rather than God. Historians might personally hold beliefs like Picasso, but they cannot teach or write history with the disorder and chaos and ugliness of a Picasso painting.

Christopher Dawson, a Christian historian of Catholic persuasion, echoes the belief in God's providential rule over history in words sounding most Calvinistic:

> Whatever else is obscure, it is certain that God is governor of the universe and behind the apparent disorder and confusion of history there is the creative action of the divine law. Man is a free agent and is continually attempting to shape the world and the course of history to his own designs and interests. But behind the weak

power and the blind science of man, there is the overruling purpose of God which uses man and his kingdoms and empires for ends of which he knows nothing and which are often the opposite of those which man desires and seeks to maintain.[2]

God's purposes are established in time and history. We do not know all the inner workings of events or the meaning of all details, for the secret things belong to God (Deuteronomy 29:29). But Moses says in the passage referenced that the things that are revealed belong to us and to our children forever. The Incarnate Christ is revealed, the Bride of Christ—the Church—is revealed, and the ultimate triumph and glorification of the Triune God and His people are revealed. Scripture reveals enough of God's purposes and man's nature and destiny for us to make sense of history. Macbeth's existential despair concerning life—"a tale told by an idiot, full of sound and fury, signifying nothing"—need not weigh down our approach to history. We can see the hand of God in the past.

To look at it another way, we can say that if we believe in *pre-destination,* as our spiritual forefathers Luther and Calvin (and Augustine before them) taught us, we also believe in *post-destination.* A look at history reveals what God had planned and purposed. And while we cannot always know the correct interpretations of historical events, we can still affirm a meaning and a design to God's work in history.

The events we discover and the meanings we interpret are for our instruction. Simply put, history edifies, history sanctifies. Even the pagan historian Livy noted this when he commented on the need to study history. He said,

> The study of history is the best medicine for a sick mind; for in history you have a record of the infinite variety of human experience plainly set out for all to see; and in that record you can find for yourself and your country both examples and warnings; fine things to take as models, base things, rotten through and through, to avoid.[3]

Livy's point is good, and its message is needed in our time where culture as a whole has a sick mind, but his approach is not enough. He sees history only as a man looking at other men. Without a Christian view, history can just

---

[2] Christopher Dawson, *The Movement of World Revolution.*
[3] Livy as quoted in Michael Grant, *Readings in the Classical Historians* (New York: Charles Scribner's Sons, 1992), 296.

as likely bring greater sickness rather than health. History cannot cure society or the individual; only the Gospel can changes lives. As Christians, we need history for growth in godliness. That's why the Bible contains so much of it. Just as a Christian approach to science always beckons us to look at Creation and Origins, so a Christian approach to history beckons us to look at Genesis itself, and then to look at subsequent geneses, or beginnings, throughout history. Isaiah exhorted his listeners to do this very thing when he said, "Look to the rock from which you were hewn, and to the whole of the pit from which you were dug" (Isaiah 51:1).

It is imperative that Americans look back to our founding. We are in a culture war; we are battling over the meaning of civilization; and history is a key battlefield in this greater conflict. The revival of interest in our Founding Fathers of the Independence Era is an encouraging sign.[4] But America did not begin in 1776 with the signing of the Declaration of Independence, nor did it begin one year earlier at Lexington and Concord. John Adams said, "The Revolution was effected before the war commenced. The Revolution was in the minds and hearts of the people; a change in their religious sentiments of their duties and obligations."[5]

Certain of the political and military factors leading to the war can be found in the French and Indian War of 1756-1763. Even more roots of our nation's origins can be discovered in the Great Awakening of the 1740s—1760s. But even these starting dates are well past the earliest experiences in the North American colonies. Far better is it to look back to the 1600s to reach the bedrock of the American experience. Specifically, we must consider the following:

> The establishment of the Jamestown, Virginia settlement in 1607
> The landing of the Pilgrim-Separatists at Plymouth in 1620
> The Great Puritan Migration to New England in the 1630s
> The further settlement of the colonies
> The settlement of the frontier by the Scots-Irish in the 1700s

God's Timing

The European roots of the American story begin with the Age of Exploration and the Protestant Reformation. Columbus and his successors charted the land and opened the door toward exploration, and Luther and

---

[4] Again, we urge the reader to consider David McCoullough's books *John Adams* and *1776* and Joseph Ellis' *Founding Brothers: The Revolutionary Gentlemen* and *His Excellency: Washington*.

[5] John Adams, as quoted by Gertrude Himmelfarb, *The Roads to Modernity*, 193.

Calvin and their successors charted the theology that would supplant exploration with colonization. The Reformation itself occurred in the 1500s in Europe and in the 1600s, and from growth of renewed biblical theology, God transplanted various species of Reformed thinking to America.

God's timing in these events is clearly seen. First, by the time the American colonies began to be settled in great numbers, key Bible doctrines had been contested, sharpened, and applied for a century in Europe. Questions regarding the authority of Scripture, the government of the Church, and the saving grace of Christ, along with many other applications of Reformed theology to society, the individual, and politics had all been debated, disputed, and well defined by the time ships began embarking to the New World carrying Pilgrims and Puritans. The foundations for the Reformation having been established, the colonies were then able to begin with a high degree of theological maturity. The colonists were emerging out of a theological culture, based largely on books and scholarship. The theological wheel did not have to be invented; it only needed directions in which to go.

Second, neither Roman Catholicism nor an Anglo-Catholic Episcopacy were able to gain monopolistic control over the colonies. There were Catholics and high church Anglicans. Maryland was a refuge for Catholics and some other colonies, like Pennsylvania, were open for Catholic settlement. Yet even in Maryland, the Protestant Christians were numerous and the Catholic establishment was quite open in their willingness to allow non-Catholics to participate in colonial worship and civic affairs. The high-handedness of the Stuart kings in England and Scotland was not effectual in controlling colonial events. Many colonists came because they opposed Stuart policies back home, and they came from regions of England that were strongly in the Roundhead tradition.[6] The very hint or rumor or fear of the appointment of an Anglican bishop over the colonies was itself a major factor in motivating many colonists, particularly New England Congregationalists and Scots-Irish Presbyterians, to join the Patriots.

Third, the American colonies provided a haven for religious refugees and a laboratory for theological experiments. Pastors in Europe recognized the confining strictures of church and society. The Reformation occurred in Europe in concert with nationalistic forces. This resulted in the authority of the pope and Catholic bishops often being replaced more by the authority of princes than by Scripture. The Reformation had changed Europe drastically, but true reformation has to be ongoing. Strict denominational definitions do not always fit the colonial congregational species. Congregationalist churches

---

[6] See David Hackett Fischer, *Albion's Seed* and Kevin Philips' *Brother's Wars*.

had strong presbyterial tendencies, and Presbyterians had streaks of independency in their practices. Sweet referred to the New England churches as being "Presbyterianism in embryo."[7] Churches learned how to redefine ministerial roles, congregational government, and parish life. Of course, the American penchant for theological splintering and innovation finds its roots in these times. Church history is never a neat, clean, and totally wholesome experience.

Fourth, America became a melting pot for Reformation theologies. Some of the best and brightest men and ideas from the different strands of European Reformed thought made their way to the American shores, and many gifted pastors and theologians sprang from the American experience that blended these different traditions. Interaction of congregations and exchanging of books and ideas will result in quite hardy varieties of Reformed Christianity. Some branches of Reformed theology will be fitted within the Anglican tradition, some in the more moderate Presbyterian and Congregational traditions, and many branches will be offshoots of Pietist and more radical movements. The gifts were often distributed unevenly. Revivalism tended to unduly attack church government. The churches with the best emphases on educated ministries were hindered in mission works in the western reaches. Mission works on the frontier often lacked the deeper theological groundings, but were brimming with zeal in reaching the lost. Hymnody, religious training, voluntary societies, and even church architecture all benefited from the theological melting pot. Evangelist George Whitefield perhaps personified this American experiment. He was an Anglican minister, an ardent Calvinist, a revival preacher, and the patron of mission works for orphans. This tradition continued well past the Colonial Era with such figures as Philip Schaff, a Reformed theologian and historian who combined his European educational experiences with the Calvinistic conditions in America in the nineteenth century.

Waves of Reformation Hit the Atlantic Coast

In the providence of God, not every work dedicated to the glory of God succeeds. The first attempt by Calvinistic Christians to create a settlement in the New World failed. Established in Rio de Janiero in 1555 as a refuge, this mission was the dream of French Huguenots and the famous French Huguenot leader, Admiral Gaspard de Coligny. Shortly after the colony was established, the leaders sent word to France and Geneva requesting that

---

[7] William Warren Sweet, *Religion in Colonial America* (New York: Charles Scribner's Sons, 1942), 245.

ministers be sent to them. John Calvin and other pastors supported the effort by sending fourteen men to the colony, including Pierre Richier and Guillaume Chartier, the first Protestant ministers to cross the Atlantic. This colony also had the distinction of conducting the first Protestant worship service in the New World on May 10, 1557. The colony failed when the man in charge, Nicholas Durand de Villegagnon, abandoned all pretense of holding to Protestantism, deported the Calvinists back to France to be charged with heresy, drowned the few that were left, and dismantled the colony.[8]

A second effort to start a colony, again influenced by de Coligny, took place along the Florida coast under Jean Ribaut in 1562. This experiment also failed when the Spanish, consistent foes to the Protestants, exterminated the colony in 1565.[9]

A third effort of French Calvinists took place in Canada, more specifically at Port Royal in Nova Scotia. This settlement was led by a Huguenot nobleman named Pierre du Guast, Sieur de Monts. The community consisted of a mixture of both Calvinists and Catholics. In fact, the Calvinist minister and the Catholic priest were often, as expected, in dispute. Being egged on by both their fellow Frenchmen and local Indians, the two spiritual leaders all too frequently sought to settle their theological differences with fist fights.[10] De Monts also influenced Samuel de Champlain to establish Quebec in 1608. New France was controlled by an uncle and his nephew both named de Caen. The nephew, Emery de Caen, attempted to establish Huguenot prayer and psalm singing in Quebec, but all such efforts to root Calvinism in New France were suppressed by the Jesuits (who arrived in 1625) and later by the governing authorities of New France.[11] The Huguenots "had no liberty to worship or organize, and their religion survived only in a few families, to the English conquest of 1759."[12]

There were, back in France, large numbers of Protestant Huguenots. In the midst of a long period of religious, social, and political turmoil in France, it never seemed to occur to the French monarchy that encouraging resettlement of the Huguenots in French Canada was a viable option. McNeill notes that historians have pondered how history might have been different. He writes, "The historian [Francis] Parkman thought it probable that if they had

---

[8] John T. McNeill, *The History and Character of Calvinism* (New York: Oxford University Press, 1957), 331.
[9] McNeill, 331.
[10] Still preferable and arguably more gentlemanly and Christian than modern day Internet squabbles.
[11] McNeill, 332.
[12] McNeill, 332.

been permitted to settle in New France, the French occupation would have been, through their numbers and energy, expanded over the areas that were, instead, to be slowly peopled by the New England Puritans."[13] It certainly raises one of the more fascinating "what if's?" of history to imagine how the world would have been different with the presence of a strongly Calvinistic French Canada.

Throughout their years of occupying the lands north of the Great Lakes and along the Mississippi, the French never established colonies that were much more than outposts for trade and military occupation. Fur traders and soldiers rather than families populated the French settlements in New France. By the time of the French and Indian War, the population of the English colonies, made up of families and communities, was about ten times that of the French.

The vision for the settlement of English colonies can be traced in part to a clergyman and lawyer named Richard Hakluyt. In his youth, he was shown a map of the world and a Geneva Bible opened to Psalm 107:23-24, which says, "They that go down to the sea in ships, that do business in great waters; These see the works of the Lord, and his wonders in the deep." From that experience, Hakluyt began envisioning the English colonization. He published a book in 1584, the shortened title is *Discourse of Western Planting*, at the request of Sir Walter Raleigh, which was presented to Queen Elizabeth. Hakluyt's *Discourse* contained accounts of English voyages to the New World. The work called upon Queen Elizabeth, as a premier Reformed monarch[14], to support colonization which would aid in the spreading of the Gospel to savages and provide a refuge for those who were persecuted. His own words were "that this westerne discoverie will be greatly for the enlargement of the gospill of Christe, whereunto the princes of the refourmed religion are chiefly bounde, amongst whome her majestie ys principall."[15] Along with the evangelistic opportunities and the creation of a refuge for religious dissenters, colonies would enable England to defeat Spain, England's primary enemy, and thwart efforts of Catholics to proselytize the natives. In subsequent works advancing colonization, Hakluyt criticized those who had "a preposterous desire of seeking rather gain than God's glory."[16] Hakluyt captured in almost

---

[13] McNeill, 332.

[14] Queen Elizabeth, a Reformed monarch? Yes, she held the official position of a Reformed monarch as the leader of the Protestant Church of England and queen of Protestant England. Her personal beliefs were, politically, secondary.

[15] As quoted in William Warren Sweet, *Religion in Colonial America* (New York: Charles Scribner's Sons, 1942), 3. Sweet is one of the premier historians on American religion from the mid-twentieth century.

[16] As quoted in McNeill, 333.

prophetic language, a more Christian version of the Emma Lazarus stanza on the Statue of Liberty, what became the American colonial experience. He said,

> Wee shall by plantinge there inlarge the glory of the gospel, and from England plante sincere religion, and provide a safe and a sure place to receive people from all parts of the worlde that are forced to flee for the truthe of Gods worde.[17]

Jamestown

England had several failed efforts to establish colonies, the most notable being the Roanoke settlement. Then in 1607, a fleet of three ships, the *Susan Constant,* the *Godspeed,* and the *Discovery,* carrying 104 men, sailed up a body of water they named the James River and established Jamestown, with both the river and establishment named in honor of the king who had chartered the expedition. The Jamestown story is well known. They nearly starved to death on several occasions; Captain John Smith was the key leader who saved the colony from starvation; Pocahontas was an Indian maid from a neighboring tribe that befriended the colonists; the long hoped for gold was never found in the region, but they discovered in tobacco a cash crop that enabled the colony to thrive.

The worldly motives and experiences of the Jamestown settlers are often contrasted with the theological motivations of the Pilgrims and Puritans who settled New England. The contrast, while containing a modicum of truth, has obscured more than it revealed. Jamestown, in its charter and the character of some of its settlers and in its laws, was a Christian colony. Perry Miller notes that in a sermon given by William Crashaw to the members of the Virginia Company, the basic doctrines of "election, faith, perseverance, and assurance of salvation" were proclaimed, along with the warning that if the aim of the company were mere profit, God would defeat it.[18] The settlement of Jamestown, established by the Virginia Company, was in many respects as Calvinistic and as Protestant and as Puritan as any colony in New England. McNeill says, "The Anglican Church was established in Virginia at a time when its ministry in England was prevailingly Calvinistic in theology."[19]

The First Charter of Virginia, drawn up by the chief legal officers of the Virginia Company, evidenced this same strongly Calvinistic flavor. It outlines

---

[17] As quoted in Sweet, 7.
[18] Perry Miller, *Errand Into the Wilderness* (New York: Harper Torchbooks, 1956),106.
[19] McNeill, 334.

the task of the colonizers as a "Work, which may, by the Providence of Almighty God, hereafter tend to the Glory of His Divine Majesty, in propagating ...the Christian religion...."[20] The charter goes on to support the true worship of God and the evangelization of the "Infidels and Savages" in the New World. Such language is often discounted because it was a commonplace way of writing and speaking. References to God's Providence and to reaching the lost with the Gospel was perhaps more an idiom of speech rather than personal convictions of all. But the fact that such Biblical language and concepts had become the social foundation of language and law reveals the underlying presuppositions of the society of that time.

In our own time, we commonly and flippantly use words like freedom, liberty, and justice. All politicians echo these concepts. Sometimes the language is used to back things that are the opposite of what that language should mean. Still, because the concepts of freedom, liberty, and justice are the bedrock of American thinking, we keep reverting back to them and we keep rediscovering what those terms meant by those founders who passionately believed in them. For that reason, as Americans, we need to rejoice in the re-reading of our founding documents, and as Christians, to rejoice when the historic creeds are still recited by those who have yet to rediscover the meaning of them. Language has consequences.

The Christian legal language of the Charter may have had a minimal impact upon the piety of all of the original Jamestown settlers. Still, the Jamestown experience as a whole was one to push the inhabitants back to fundamental presuppositions. Neither socialistic egalitarianism nor gold hunting was putting food on the table. It took the leadership, heavy-handed as it was, of the Christian explorer John Smith to bring order to the colony. The fundamental Biblical principle implemented was from 2 Thessalonians 3:10, which says, "If anyone will not work, neither shall he eat."

Due to the backing of the Virginia Company, the Puritan element became a part of the Jamestown experiment. The Puritans in England were a wide-ranging group of theological activists. They were not one party, one group, one single set of theological convictions: They were, after all, mostly Calvinists. People of varying Protestant positions and convictions today still rightly claim to be the true heirs of the Puritans. By definition, a Puritan was one who wanted to purify the Church of England of its theological and usually Roman Catholic-inherited corruptions and faults. Some Puritans desired to maintain bells, candles, robes, the Book of Common Prayer, and the Bible—

---

[20] As quoted in Gary DeMar, *Building a City On a Hill* (Powder Springs, Georgia: American Vision, 2005), 111.

faithfully read and taught. Others desired to cast away all the other features—all thought to be relics of popery—and focus just on the Bible and the faithful exposition of its precepts. The battles and perspectives of 16th and 17th century English church life are still with us today and can be found in the books and worship styles of American Christians.

So the Puritan fathers of Jamestown never had quite the same motivations of the Puritan fathers of Massachusetts Bay Colony. It might be like comparing two Christian men in college. One chooses as his academic major the field of theology and trains for the ministry, while the other majors in business management and trains for work in the corporation. Both love the Lord and believe His Word, but their studies, and in time, their careers look different. It is a matter of emphasis, rather than of sacred versus secular.

Because of the distance of English governing institutions, the absence of societal restraints, and the tenuous family and community structure, colonial life was always threatened with chaos. Like communities struck by disaster, law and order and civil decorum were often threatened in Jamestown. The legal codes that were put in place by Puritan Christians echoed, if not actually exceeded, the legal codes in New England. Penalties were enacted against blasphemy, adultery, Sabbath-breaking, and sacrilege. It was as theonomic as anything Dr. Greg Bahnsen ever imagined.[21] It made the modern Christian political right look like a convention of the National Organization for Women. Perry Miller comments upon these laws,

> Ministers were to hold services every Sunday; attendance was compulsory; the moral law was enacted into statute; idleness, gaming, drunkenness, excess in apparel were heavily fined; ministers and church wardens were instructed to present "all ungodly disorders...as suspicions of whordoms, dishonest company keeping with woemen (sic) and such like" to the judgment of the church, and if an offender did not amend, he was to be excommunicated and his goods confiscated. Further legislation in the next two decades made the code still more drastic: observance of the Sabbath was enforced by laws as rigorous as those of New England, in fact even more rigorous, and persons could be presented for such minute violation as carrying a gun, shelling corn, or fetching a pair of shoes.[22]

---

[21] Greg Bahnsen, *Theonomy in Christian Ethics* (Nacogdoches, TX: Covenant Media Press, 2002). See pages 525-550.

[22] Perry Miller, *Errand Into the Wilderness* (New York: Harper Torchbooks, 1956), 105.

Calling attention to such laws in Christian communities is not to give us smug satisfaction in our own age of moral laxity. It is not so we can react with horror at such "legalism" or forcible imposition of Christianity. Neither is the goal to advocate a return to Jamestown's legal code. A society that punishes a person for "fetching a pair of shoes" on the Sabbath has its own problems, but that does not compare with a society that readily allows the murder of unborn children. In our age, we need to shut our mouths, suspend our judgments, and humbly learn from the past. Miller shows the pervasiveness of the culture of that time. He says, "If we are astonished to find in Virginia the legislation of a New England 'theocracy,' it is only because we forget that both communities were legatees of the Reformation, and that much we consider distinctly Puritan was really the spirit of the times."[23]

A significant leader in Virginia was Alexander Whitaker, dubbed the Apostle of Virginia. He was the son of a prominent Calvinist, William Whitaker of Cambridge who authored the Calvinist Lambeth Articles. Alexander Whitaker labored in Virginia for six years from 1611-1617 until he drowned. He was an Anglican, but of the low church variety, and he gave the colony a theology that was Episcopal, Reformed, and evangelistic. Like many a pastor, he lamented the condition of his parishioners. Historian Sidney Ahlstrom said of Whitaker:

> His *Good Newes from Virginia* declared that some of the company's leaders were "miserable covetous men," while the settlers they sent out were often drawn from the dregs of society. Too many, he said, "had not been reconciled to God nor approved of Him."[24]

On the more positive side, Whitaker was the man who baptized Pocahontas.[25] Her true story, often obscured in movies and tales, is an amazing testimony in and of itself. John Rolfe was in love with Pocahontas, but could not marry her since she was not a believer. So he prayed earnestly for her salvation, and when she was converted and baptized, he then married her.[26]

Seeing Virginia as a vital mission field, Whitaker labored to persuade more ministers to come to the colony. This effort failed due in part to opposition of the royal governors and the confines of the parish system. Ahlstrom notes, "Virginia never felt the shaping power of institutional Puritan nurture,

---

[23] Miller, 105.
[24] Ahlstrom, 190.
[25] McNeill, 335.
[26] Miller, 107-108.

even in the early days."[27] Colonial Virginia had the benefit, then, of being started with certain Puritan law codes and influences, and these were implemented within the traditional Anglican parish system. By the early 1700s, only about half the churches had ministers. Lacking the ongoing drive for reformation, religion in Virginia lagged behind until the influx of Presbyterians and Baptists in the Great Awakening.[28]

The Pilgrims of Plymouth Rock

More than any other story in American history, the story of the Pilgrims of Plymouth Rock has very much defined the American experience. The sheer audacity of their undertaking, the courage of boarding and enduring the trip on the *Mayflower*, the political wisdom of their *Mayflower Compact,* their cooperation with the local Indian tribes, and their institution of the celebration of the harvest, now celebrated as Thanksgiving, are all vital parts of the American story. But even this most Christian segment of our history has been occasionally marauded by secularists. The first Thanksgiving, as now sometimes taught to elementary children, was when the Pilgrims were giving thanks to the Indians. I suppose they sang, "Praise Indians from whom all blessings flow."

No doubt the Mayflower settlers appreciated both the help local Indians provided and the venison they brought to the feast, but all the documents attest to the spiritual zeal for God that characterized these Christians. The Pilgrims are more accurately termed Separatists, meaning that they desired not merely to purify the Church of England, like Puritans, but to separate from it and start a new, purer church. In the turmoil of religious strife in England in the late 1500s and early 1600s, some congregations found that leaving was the better option over conforming against conscience or being persecuted. The congregation from Scrooby, England, the group from which the Plymouth Pilgrims came, went across the English Channel to the Netherlands. The Dutch nation was both strongly Calvinistic and relatively free in its toleration of Christian sects.

Opportunities for exercising theological convictions were limitless in the Netherlands, but English Christians were still Englishmen and the society of the Netherlands was Dutch. The English settlers would have gone to their graves speaking English and worshipping according to their convictions, but their children were already picking up the accents and idioms of their Dutch

---

[27] Ahlstrom, 191.
[28] Ahlstrom, 190.

playmates. All traces of English heritage would have vanished by the third generation. For this reason the Separatists began looking for other options, and they decided on the New World. They set out in 1620 on two ships, and after the first proved not to be seaworthy, they crowded into the *Mayflower.* Their destiny was the northern portion of the Virginia Colony. Due to weather and navigational problems they landed further north than they intended at the place now known as Plymouth Rock. The distancing from Virginia, another providential blessing, enabled them to develop their own colonial community where it would not be subsumed into the already existing Virginia colony.

Before they left the Netherlands, they were given a charge that would not only define them, but would characterize the greater Reformed work still just beginning in the New World.

Pastor John Robinson had charged them:

> The Lord has more truth yet to break forth from His Holy Word. I cannot sufficiently bewail the condition of the reformed churches who are come to a period in religion and will go at present no further than the instruments of their reformation. Luther and Calvin were great and shining lights in their times, yet they penetrated not the whole counsel of God....Be ready to receive whatever truth shall be made known to you from the written word of God.

This hardy band of Pilgrims have endeared themselves to future generations for several reasons. They were not the first to celebrate thanksgiving in the New World, for a thanksgiving service had taken place in Virginia two years before the famed Plymouth celebration. Still, it was the Plymouth gathering that defined what would in time become an American holiday. It was the Christian grace of including the Indians and the common grace of Indian participation that portrayed the better part of a relationship that was not always good. The Pilgrims helped define the American economic spirit. They tried a communal or socialist system of farming and nearly starved before resorting to something more akin to the free market and private ownership. Governor William Bradford attributed this failure to spiritual pride and blindness. He said, "We thought we were wiser than God"—an admission all too rare among political leaders. Bradford himself immortalized the Plymouth adventure in his book *Of Plymouth Plantation,* one of our nation's earliest Christian histories.

The Puritans of Massachusetts Bay Colony

Much of history is approached in the same fashion as impressionist painting is made. Instead of clearly distinct trees, flowers, and people, there are splotches and globs of paint that then—at a distance—appear to be trees. Our knowledge of history likewise can consist of scattered images, blobs of impressions, and splotches of facts that then form—at a distance—a picture of an historical era. Such is the case with the Puritan roots of American history.

Of course, we have heard that the Puritans burned witches; of course, they wore black and frowned a lot; of course, they were harsh and narrow-minded, self-righteous, and hypocritical. Aren't the sins and failings of the Puritans made clear by the author Nathaniel Hawthorne in his historical document *The Scarlet Letter*? Add to that, a hundred Hollywood images reinforcing the same scowling countenances, bigoted theology, and harsh condemnations of free thought, science, and religious conscience. Add to that, H. L. Mencken's quip that the Puritan was haunted by the thought that somewhere, somehow, someone was happy.

Left out of all these images are the stories of Puritan feasts (and food fights), of the complexities and varieties of the New England Puritans' experiences, of the sheer precariousness of holding on to life and community constantly threatened by the howling wilderness, and of the richness of the theology of the Puritans. Truly, Puritans did not have all of our religious and political freedoms, economic opportunities, and social advances, but they contributed to making all the benefits of modern America possible.

Christian history is always a story of sin and grace, of depravity and sanctification, of images of Hell and foretastes of Heaven. So the person in search of hypocrisy, duplicity, and inconsistency can always find vivid examples of such in any era of Christian history or in any local church. The failure to understand the Puritan experiment in America comes from several sources. First, it stems from a presupposition against a vibrant culture-wide Christian faith. Puritanism does not bode well among secularists and pluralists. Those who think Christian or religious convictions ought to occupy only a tiny portion of the human experience find Puritanism's wide embrace troubling. Second, it stems from not understanding the wider historical and political situation the Puritans were in. They fled from certain problems in England, and they did not want to lose the New World opportunity to right what wrongs they had experienced. Having so often experienced life on the losing end of the political machinery of England, they were not about to put their hard-fought convictions on a referendum for all to vote on. Third, the failure to understand the Puritans comes from simply not knowing enough about them, their culture, and the beliefs that motivated them. With knowledge of the Puritans, we still may not like all aspects of their world, but the goal of history is to understand, not necessarily agree. Fourth, Puritans themselves would be the first to acknowledge the prevalence of sin in man's nature and in history. Puritans, like moderns, may have been blinded to certain of their sins, but they were not blind to the existence of sin and its remedy.

Given man's sinful nature, what is amazing is not the prevalence of human depravity constantly bubbling to the surface, but the occasions where godliness and righteousness do prevail. The Christian study of history is never predicated on finding the time when "Christians did things right." That is to fall into the same error as those who want a truly New Testament church, not apparently realizing that Corinth and Laodicea were both truly New Testament churches. The time of the Puritans was not a Christian golden age of untarnished truths, but it was a time of much Christian gold filled with many truths. The impact of the Puritans on both England and America is incredible.

Numerically, the Puritan migrations completely overwhelmed the Plymouth colony. A few hundred people came to Plymouth over the course of time, but over 20,000 came to Massachusetts Bay Colony during the time from 1630 to 1640. This was known as the Great Migration. This was the time of King Charles I in England, and there the conflicts were building up to what would become the English Civil War and what would ultimately result in his execution. His father, King James, had once voiced his dislike of the Puritans and threatened to "harry them out of the land." Many welcomed the opportunity to leave the turmoil of England and, while still living under the crown, live out of reach of effective crown control over church and state. Even Oliver Cromwell, later destined to be the de facto Puritan king (or "Lord Protector") considered relocating to the colonies.[29]

Despite differences over church government between the Puritans and the Separatists, theologically both groups were firmly Reformed. The Puritans, however, not only attracted far more followers, but also different classes of folk. As the historian John T. McNeill has noted, "In 1638 some forty or fifty Cambridge graduates were among the settlers, and these included the great majority of the ministers. The most scholarly of the ministers of the 1630s—John Cotton, Thomas Hooker, and John Davenport—had earned distinctions at Cambridge colleges. These 3 were invited to be members of the Westminster Assembly."[30]

---

[29] Just imagine how that might have changed history.
[30] McNeill, 338.

The Puritans were more highly educated and more attuned to business and economic development. These characteristics gave rise to both the concept of the Puritan Work Ethic and the warped notion of Weber and Tawney that wealth was a sign of God's electing grace. Because of the educational and business motivations, the Puritans not only established churches in which to worship, but also schools and colleges for furthering education. With what was called the "Old Deluder Satan Act" they promoted public or community sponsored schools. Harvard University was also a fruit of their educational zeal.

This Puritan emphasis on education provided both the support of schooling for the youth and the establishment of university training for candidates for the clergy and other professionals. Books were a valued commodity, so the Puritans favored both the importation of the latest and best works from England and the publishing of works in the colonies. The clergy were both spiritual and political leaders, although not political leaders in the sense of holding offices of civil magistrates. The political strength of ministers was a matter of influence. They occupied roles not merely like that of ministers today, but more like a combination of minister, counselor, news commentator, and community leader. In both sermons and lectures, they helped form the body politic, the educational culture, and the theological climate.

It has been noted, "The New England clergy largely controlled the country. They gave it schools, they framed its laws, they shaped the character of its people. From John Cotton to Jonathan Edwards, New England Puritanism passed through an epoch of greatness and produced a type of human being that no just and informed mind can think of without admiration."[31]

The Puritan story in America is lengthy in terms of duration—from approximately 1630 to the 1760s. It is varied in terms of its leaders, emphases, and responses to challenges from both within and without the community. Thomas Hooker and others who settled Connecticut (the only U.S. state settled from west to east) differed at fine points from the Massachusetts community. Puritans who settled north of Boston also had their differences. On the more radical extreme were those like Roger Williams who rebelled against the Puritan establishment, but still adhered to quite a few of the same basic precepts.

A desire for theological preciseness—note that Puritans were originally nicknamed "Precisionists"—is a good and godly attribute that usually goes awry. The only thing worse than being overly dogmatic is being completing lax on theological matters; in other words having a creed whose basic premise

---

[31] McNeill, 340-341.

is "Whatever." The Calvinistic desire to search the Scriptures, to fine-tune the key theological features, to apply each jot and tittle carefully, yielded much fruit in New England and also much subsequent strife. The Puritans were masters of human psychology—without its modern Freudian perversity. Their heavily Biblical sermons were microscopic probes into the recesses of the soul, "piercing even to the dividing asunder of soul and spirit, and of the joints and marrow, and is a discerner of the thoughts and intents of the heart" (Hebrews 4:12).

This introspection often led to personal crises of assurance. Such spiritual doubtings—and who doesn't doubt his salvation when reading the best of the Puritans?—led them to seek radical spiritual experiences to confirm the presence of grace.[32] To this day, Christian groups struggle with and even go to war over questions relating to how a person can know himself to be a true Christian. J.I. Packer, whose experiences include knowing both the dry climate of modern Anglicanism and the emotionalism of modern day evangelicalism, calls modern Christians spiritual dwarfs. He urges a reexamination of the Puritans to both size up ourselves with a more fervent Christianity and to press us to attain what they had.[33]

Modern Christians desperately need a large dose of Puritanism. Always remember that we have to read discerningly, read widely, and balance things Biblically. For the purpose of teaching history, we need to reckon with the great spiritual heritage our country gleaned from the Puritan fathers. Historians of all stripes have recognized the contributions of the Puritans to the American success story.

The arrival of Scots and Scots-Irish

Not all of the settlers in the Thirteen Colonies were New England Puritans or southern Anglicans. Quakers, whose theology sprang from Reformational impulses and then dove off the deep end, established key colonial settlements in Pennsylvania, New Jersey, and Delaware. The Quaker tradition is a mixed lot that is characteristic of the splintering effects of Protestantism. Instead of struggling with developing a theology from the Bible, Quakers opted for a still, small voice speaking inside them. Hence, Quakers got in lots of trouble in Puritan Massachusetts for such things as appearing naked in worship services and shouting, "New England stands naked before God."

---

[32] See Edmund Sears Morgan, *Visible Saints: The History of a Puritan Idea* (New York: New York University Press, 1963). This is an excellent study of how a Puritan strength —the search for a real and experiential faith—warped into an unbiblical pattern.

[33] J. I. Packer, *A Quest for Godliness: The Puritan Vision of the Christian Life* (Wheaton: Crossway Books, 1990). Introduction.

Puritans didn't quite cotton to such visual aids and disruptions to formal worship. When William Penn obtained title to the lands of Pennsylvania, Quakers had their refuge, which they developed quite successfully. The Quaker theological laxity and extreme imprecision worked in the providence of God for great good.

To the west of the Quaker settlements was the frontier—the region of the northern portions of the Appalachian Mountains. Out there were the warring Indian tribes. Quakers were pacifists and were exemplary in their treatment of Indians at many points. Still, the frontier—being a part of this fallen and not so Edenic planet—was no fit laboratory for pacifism, and Indians lived up to only the latter part of the Rousseau's concept of Noble Savages. In short, the Quaker colonies needed people on the frontier and needed protection.

German Christians went to those frontier regions. Some were from the different branches of the German Reformed Churches, particularly refugees from religious strife in the Palatinate; some were Lutherans; and some were members of various Germanic pietistic and Anabaptist sects. German colonists gained the reputation for being expert farmers.[34] The Germans were content with the more dominant British culture, and they devoted themselves to minding their plows and furrows and to maintaining more self-contained communities.

A more restless and vigorous group began arriving by the early 1700s. These were the Scots and the Scots-Irish. The Scottish people that colonized were parts of three groups. Lowland Scots came to America as individuals or in families. Having already partially assimilated their lives to English ways, they became skilled tradesmen, farmers, and professionals in the wider English colonial setting. They were attracted to the economic opportunities in the colonies. Driven even more by economics, particularly the dire conditions at home, Highland Scots also came to the colonies. They tended to gather along frontier river valleys; hence, the Cape Fear River in North Carolina, the Mohawk River in New York, and the Altahama River in Georgia were areas of settlement for them. The Highlanders tended more to maintain the Gaelic language and Celtic customs.[35] They were attracted to both the land and the danger of the American frontier. Alan Taylor quotes a Scots Highlander as saying,

---

[34] According to Thomas Sowell, farming skills have characterized the Germans wherever they have migrated.

[35] Alan Taylor, *American Colonies* (New York: Viking, 2001), 316-317.

They launched out into a new World breathing a Spirit of Liberty and a Desire of every individual becoming a Proprietor, where they imagine they can still obtain land for themselves, and their flocks of Cattle at a triffling Rent, or of conquering it from the Indian with the Sword, the most desireable holding of any for a Highlander.[36]

The third wave of Scottish immigrants were the most prominent, due to their numbers. These were the Ulster Scots, the descendants of Scots who had immigrated to north Ireland in the late 1600s. Violence between them and the Catholic Irish and terrible economic conditions convinced many to go to the colonies. Some came as indentured servants. Others came in groups, typically whole church congregations organized by their pastors.[37] As McNeill has noted, "About 1710, large numbers of the Ulster Scots, who had suffered economic distress and political and religious disabilities under Queen Anne's government, began to arrive in New England and Pennsylvania."[38] Upon arriving from Ulster, they resented being lumped together with the Irish. In time, they became known as Scots-Irish.

Somewhere around 145,000 Scots came to the colonies in the 1700s. The Scots who initially settled in New England were not warmly received, so they began moving toward the frontier regions. They gained a reputation for stubbornness with a strong tenacity toward defending their lands. Those descending from Scottish clans and bloods have never been prone to pacifism. From that most barren and rugged land of Scotland and from the hostile environs of north Ireland, the colonial frontier was merely just one more set of rocks and trees to be settled and Indians were no more a threat than rival clans and English interlopers had been for centuries.

William Warren Sweet describes the spread of the Scots-Irish:

No single racial group coming to the colonies scattered so widely as did the Scotch-Irish, and by the middle of the century (1750) they were to be found in every colony in sufficient numbers to make their influence felt, culturally as well as economically and politically....Hanna estimates that all told there were more than five hundred distinct Scotch and Scotch-Irish communities in the American colonies at the end of the colonial period, and they

---

[36] Taylor, 316.
[37] Taylor, 317.
[38] McNeill, 345.

constituted the stuff out of which American colonial Presbyterianism was chiefly made.[39]

The American experience is the story of a vast frontier offering land and opportunities far beyond the imagination of the Old World. Early in colonial history, the coastlands were dotted with thriving cities and the fields were the domains of colonial gentry replicating the English patterns with phenomenal acreage. The Celtic peoples were more often drawn to the more limitless opportunities to the west. The story of the Scots in America is a popular one, told with self-deprecating humor and pride. Whatever personal characteristics the Scots had—sometimes portrayed as fierce independence and sometimes as intractable stubbornness—has been portrayed in a number of good books.

Our emphasis is on the theological beliefs of the Scots and the Scots-Irish. The frontier in America was not a safe place to go for spiritual solace. Just as it is easy for the individual Christian to fall out of the habits of Bible reading, prayer, and church attendance, so the Scots on the frontier often found themselves distanced from their spiritual roots. Being fallen men they strayed at many points, but God continually revived them and recalled them back to their Scottish Presbyterian roots.

Presbyterianism as a denominational and theological branch of Christianity is attributed in part to John Calvin himself and more particularly to John Knox of Scotland. In fact, if our theological Mount Rushmore were to feature Luther and Calvin, it would need to feature Knox as well.[40] His life and struggles are a fascinating latter chapter of the Protestant Reformation in Europe. He prayed from the depths of a galley slave ship for God to give him Scotland, and God heard his pleas. The Scots became hearty and bold Presbyterians. Their Celtic nature gave them a propensity for risks and adventure, and their theology gave them a comfort in hardship and grit to persevere.

Look at a map of the eastern part of the United States and notice the Appalachians running from north to south on what would have been the limits of settlement. The Scottish colonists generally moved into the western portions of Pennsylvania and from there toward the southern colonies. Later when the British imposed the Proclamation of 1763 and closed off the frontier to settlement, this was especially irksome to the Scots-Irish and others who viewed the west as synonymous with opportunity.

---

[39] Sweet, 253-254.
[40] The fourth great theological founding father would be George Whitefield, the first of several George W.'s who impacted this country for good.

Portions of the story and heritage of the Scots-Irish will be discussed in the chapter on the South. As a people, they were Calvinistic Presbyterians who never shucked off a heritage of resisting English control. The blood feud tracing back to Bannockburn and erupting again at Colloden continued to fester in Scotland's sons and daughters in the colonies. Even before the colonies rose up against the British, conflicts arose between those living on the western and less settled portions of the colonies and the more gentry-controlled eastern seaboard portions.

And Yet More Reformed Christians

New York was originally New Amsterdam, a Dutch colony. In this colony Christians from the Dutch Reformed Church began the first of several Dutch migratory waves that would contribute to the settlement and growth of America. In 1609, just two years after the settlement at Jamestown had begun, a Dutch community was started on Manhattan Island. In 1623, a group of Walloon Calvinists, who had found refuge in Holland just as the Pilgrims had, settled near Albany. Even though economic interests predominated in the New Netherlands, there was a Calvinistic element from the earliest times. The Dutch West India Company established but gave little attention to a Dutch Reformed Church in the colony. Peter Minuit, a director of Manhattan Island and New Amsterdam, was a Huguenot. Worship in the colony was conducted by Jonas Michaelius, who organized a church of the 270 people there. Later another church was started in Albany by Johannes Megapolensis, who also labored to bring the Gospel to the local Mohawk Indians.[41] Later, Waldensian refugees and Huguenots would find friendly refuge in the area.

It would be a Dutch Reformed pastor, Theodore Jacob Frelinghuysen, whose preaching in the Raritan Valley of New Jersey in the 1720s and onward would spark the Great Awakening. McNeill described him saying, "Frelinghuysen preached with evangelical passion, called his hearers to repentance and renewal of life, charged his colleagues in the ministry with being unconverted, warned the ill-disciplined and careless from the Lord's Supper, and pronounced damnation upon hardened sinners."[42] Although the Anglican Church would supplant the Dutch Reformed Church as the official state church after the English conquest of the New Netherlands, the Calvinist influence would remain in the area. The Roosevelt's of New York were of Dutch Reformed heritage, of which more evidence showed up in Theodore than in his distant cousin Franklin.[43]

---

[41] McNeill, 342; Ahlstrom, 203-204.
[42] McNeill, 344.
[43] George Grant, *Carry a Big Stick: The Uncommon Heroism of Theodore Roosevelt* (Nashville: Cumberland House, 1996).

When the Edict of Nantes was revoked in 1685, a tumultuous history of a Reformed movement in France began coming to a close. Huguenots had negotiated with English authorities ever since the early part of the 1600s, but they would not have a large settlement in the colonies until 1680 in South Carolina.[44] Erskine Clark's extensive study of Calvinism in South Carolina includes the influence of the Huguenots in South Carolina. He points out both the negative and positive impact of France's expulsion of the Huguenots:

> In 1685 the Edict of Nantes was revoked and there began a mass exodus of French Protestants, perhaps 200,000. Their exodus was a blow to France and its economy—although not the catastrophe once thought—for the Huguenots represented much of the nation's rising commercial and entrepreneurial classes. Many went to Switzerland and Germany; others went to Holland and England. Some dared to cross the Atlantic and to settle in the British North American colonies. Among these were some who settled in the young colony of Carolina.[45]

The Huguenots who came to the colonies were spread out in terms of geography and influence. Among the more prominent descendants of the Huguenots were Paul Revere, a dedicated church member and Calvinist Christian,[46] and Elias Boudinot, the original president of the American Bible Society.[47] In time, most Huguenots blended into the more established forms of Reformed Christianity, meaning that many became Presbyterians or Congregationalists.[48] Significantly, the Huguenot Church of Charleston, South Carolina, maintained its distinctive French Reformed character on through the colonial period and the next two centuries. Clarke comments on its survival:

> By the end of the colonial period, this congregation had set a pattern that it would follow for the next two centuries: the church

---

[44] Sweet, 25.

[45] Erskine Clark, *Our Southern Zion: A History of Calvinism in the South Carolina Low Country*, 1690-1990 (Tuscaloosa, Alabama: The University of Alabama Press, 1996), 13.

[46] David Hackett Fischer, *Paul Revere's Ride* (Oxford University Press). For a detailed study of Revere's life and times, culminating in his famous ride, consider my audio lecture series "Paul Revere: Calvinist on Horseback", which is largely derived from Fischer's book. The lectures are available from Covenant Media Foundation: www.cmfnow.com.

[47] David W. Hall, *The Genevan Reformation and the American Founding* (Lanham, Maryland: Lexington Books, 2003), 388 and 429.

[48] Clarke, 42.

would survive through the dedication of a few members, a substantial endowment, and the support of others of Huguenot descent. The congregation would be marked, however, not so much by the old theological vitality and passion of the French martyrs and exiles as by a memory of and genealogical pride of those who, as refugees to a new land, helped shape a distinct colonial society.[49]

This characteristic, what might be called Genealogical Calvinism, helps explain not just a particular church in Charleston, but the greater Calvinistic experience in America where the downtown portions of both large cities and smaller towns are noted by the high steeples, grand architecture, and stately forms of Presbyterian, Reformed, and Congregationalist churches where the gospel in either Reformed or evangelical form has not been heard in decades.

Not enough notice is given to the German Reformed Christians from the Palatinate who settled in America. Also, Lutherans fit into the broader definitions of Reformed Christianity. Moravians and other groups also came to the colonies. Also, a major study of colonial Calvinism entails the Baptist experience in America.

Baptists groups, both then and now, were divided between what is sometimes called Particular Baptists, meaning Calvinistic Baptists, and General Baptists, meaning more Arminian-type Baptists. There were both Baptists who came to this country and colonists who became Baptists by convictions. Of the latter group was Isaac Backus, a neglected Founding Father and Baptist leader. Far more than the theologically unstable Roger Williams, Backus was a key leader in American Baptist history of both the colonial and independence eras.

Baptists were often found on the rich mission fields of the American frontiers. Later, they shared this mission and revivalistic zeal with the Methodists. Especially after the American War for Independence, zealous Baptists and Methodists evangelized the ever-expanding frontiers of America. From this the famed circuit riding preacher legends arose. Straggling behind both groups were Presbyterians, who were hindered on the frontier by the theological rigor of their system and the ministerial requirements for ordination.[50] In short, and especially in regard to the Southern portions of the United States, Baptists and Presbyterians agreed largely on Calvinism, but differed

---

[49] Clarke, 42.
[50] See Gary North, *Crossed Fingers: How the Liberals Captured the Presbyterian Church* (Tyler, Texas: Institute for Christian Economics, 1996). See Appendix B: "How to Immunize Presbyterianism," 972-973.

over church government and baptism. Presbyterians and Methodists agreed over the mode and subjects of baptism, but both Presbyterians and Baptists stood opposed to the Arminian theology of the Methodists.[51]

The Great Awakening

We often question what happened to the Reformed, Puritan, and generally vibrant Christianity in colonial America. Why was it that the New England region, the ground planted and fertilized by Puritan theology, later produced crops of Unitarianism, Deism, Transcendentalism, and modern day theological and political anti-Christian Liberalism? The question certainly calls for Christian study, both as a historical question and as a theological concern. Covenantal faithfulness in future generations is a vital concern for Christians, and that is why we are now so zealous for Christian schools. Presumptive Christianity, excessive doctrinal bickering, rationalism, hypocrisy, and a host of other dangers contributed to both past and recent apostasies of Christian youth. None of us want Deistic or Hindu or apostate Christian grandchildren.

Douglas Wilson has pointed out that to grow weeds in a garden, all that has to be done is simply do nothing. Weeds naturally spring up, even after years of careful hoeing and tilling. Likewise, it is not unusual for a Christian community to stray after a generation or two. Nominal Christianity, that is, people who are Christian in name only and not in commitment, doctrine, and life, plagues all denominational varieties of the faith.

The Christian experience in America—as in every other culture—is not a static experience. The Christian church is always facing losses and dangers, is always threatened by theological drifting, and is always endangered by the next generation's loss of theological memory. Genealogical Calvinism takes pride in the still-standing edifices and worships the memories, but lacks the saving power of Christ. The church is never to be a museum of the past. It admires and builds upon the past, but cannot be sustained by genealogical records.

The American Christian experience has included dark periods and times of indifference and decay, but God has continued to graciously revive His people and His church in this land. George Weigel has issued a warning in

---

[51] On religion on the frontier, see Ross Phares, *Bible in Pocket, Gun in Hand: The Story of Frontier Religion* (Lincoln: University of Nebraska Press, 1964); Charles A. Johnson, *The Frontier Camp Meeting: Religion's Harvest Time* (Dallas: Southern Methodist University Press, 1955, 1985); Walter Brownlow Posey, *Religious Strife on the Southern Frontier* (Baton Rouge: Louisiana University Press, 1965); and John B. Boles, *The Great Revival: Beginnings of the Bible Belt* (Lexington, Kentucky: The University of Kentucky Press, 1972).

our time about the religious apostasy of Europe and the danger of America seeking to emulate Europe's secularization.[52] Europe will not, in fact, remain a secular culture: Either it will reclaim its Christian heritage or it will be a Muslim annex to the Middle East. America is still far from being a secular culture. Certainly there is a battle for the soul and future of this country. Portions of the Hollywood community, elements of Washington, D.C., and many communities in the northeastern urban regions of the country may reflect a strongly anti-Christian thrust in our time, but there is a vast Christian heartland, more pervasive than the red county election maps indicate. In our own time we have been experiencing our own version of a Great Awakening.

That first event dubbed the Great Awakening is one of the key transition points in the later colonial period. No doubt the Great Awakening contributed to the colonial uprising against British control in the Independence Era. No doubt the Great Awakening both revived Calvinism and ushered in an era of religious individualism. No doubt it spotlighted several key theological leaders in America, particularly the home-grown theologian Jonathan Edwards and the English preacher George Whitefield. No doubt that many people came to either know Christ as Savior during this time or else came to realize their faith more experientially. No doubt the Great Awakening led to the subsequent revivalistic tradition in America, including the far less Calvinistic and far more theologically unstable Second Great Awakening. No doubt the Great Awakening destablilized the older ecclesiastical structures of the colonial seaboard communities and fertilized the more spontaneous frontier varieties of religious experience.

With all of these "no doubts," we have to also notice that questions have been raised as to whether or not the Great Awakening ever really happened. In other words, was it a real culture changing event that marked a change in the American Christian experience, or was it more a part of a process that did not start with either Whitefield or Edwards? The good effects of the First Awakening, Calvinistic though it was, have been questioned by no less an authority than Princeton theologian and Calvinist Charles Hodge.[53]

---

[52] George Weigel, *The Cube and the Cathedral: Europe, America, and Politics Without God* (New York: Basic Books, 2005).

[53] Charles Hodge, *The Constitutional History of the Presbyterian Church in the United States of America* (Philadelphia: Presbyterian Board of Education, 1851, reprinted in 1983). Nancy Pearcey, in *Total Truth*, also points out ongoing weaknesses in American Christianity, particularly in its emphasis on emotion to the exclusion of the intellect that are the result of both the First and Second Great Awakenings. See *Total Truth: Liberating Christianity from Its Cultural Captivity* (Wheaton: Crossway, 2004), 251-293.

There is a place for the analysis of the Great Awakening for both our theological and historical understanding. But a study of the events related to it, for our purposes, confirm the abiding Calvinistic theology and traditions in America. Edwards was indisputably a Calvinist theologian. William Tennent, the founder of the Log College, was a revivalist preacher and a Calvinist. George Whitefield, in his many trips to the colonies, called upon all hearers to believe on Christ alone for salvation, and Whitefield was a thorough-going Calvinist.

The story of Calvinism in America does not stop with the colonial era. With different degrees of belief and influence, it continues on throughout American history. Faults and failings have abounded in the Calvinistic theological circles, and they still do. But if Calvinism is far more than the ideas of John Calvin and his followers; if Calvinism represents Biblical truths reaching from our vision of a Sovereign God to our lives in both time and eternity, this Calvinistic heritage is worth continually rediscovering and reapplying. Historian Christopher Dawson was a Catholic and not a Calvinist. His understanding of Calvinism is marked both by insight and limitations. Yet, he rightly diagnosed America's plight without Calvinism by saying, "[W]hen this religious inspiration has evaporated, American civilization without Calvinism, like modern European civilization without humanism, becomes a body without a soul."[54]

How Should We Then Study?

Loraine Boettner's study of Calvinism, titled *The Reformed Doctrine of Predestination,* has taught several generations of pastors, teachers, and laymen the historic doctrines of Calvinism. While his book has rarely been equaled in extent and thoroughness, it has been surpassed by his students in recent years in the publications of books that are more readable, meaning among other things—shorter, and more apt at reaching a wider reading public. Like all great writers and teachers, part of Boettner's accomplishment was in collecting bits of wisdom that hooked his readers into doing more personal study and research. Loraine Boettner sent many of us to both the Bible and the library. A notable example of this impact is found in a quote contained in his section on the history of Calvinism: "John Calvin was the virtual founder of America, according to the German historian Leopold Von Ranke."

American history texts include discussions of the religious impulses in early America. In particular, they nearly all emphasize the fleeing to America

---

[54] Christopher Dawson, *Christianity and the New Age* (Manchester, New Hampshire: Sophia Institute Press, 1988), 16.

to escape persecution and the development of free and secular institutions in America. But it is not unusual to find history textbooks that never reference Luther, Calvin, and Knox, and even George Whitefield is occasionally excluded. History texts have scrambled to include every contribution by minorities and women in the American story, but religion, in particular in its Protestant, Reformed, and Puritan varieties, has often been treated more like childhood allergies that were outgrown in the post-Enlightenment American experiences.

The history student and teacher wanting to understand the Calvinist history of America has often had to read widely and cut and paste the themes together. Thankfully, both Calvinist and secular scholars have been putting the random pieces of the puzzle together, thus making the picture more coherent and the teacher's task easier. Now after having to endure so many textbooks that denied, distorted, or minimized the picture, the full story is much more easily accessible, and the case is proven.

How our country was founded will impact discussions concerning where it ought to be headed, especially in light of the nature of covenantal succession and blessings and cursings. Some scholars teach that our Founding Fathers were predominantly Deists, and no doubt elements of freethinking and skepticism can be noted in many of the later colonial leaders. Students are frequently catechized about the influence of the Enlightenment on our country. Concepts such as "pluralism", "separation of church and state", and "secularism" have all been lodged in my mind by repeated exposure to the academic establishment. Oh sure, we are told, the Founding Fathers were church members, but that was all form and tradition.

We are told that Thomas Paine, the infidel, molded the American mindset. Thomas Jefferson, the Deist, formulated the American ideal. John Locke, the secular thinker, fashioned the principles of the Revolution. We had Sons of Liberty, Patriot armies, signers of the Declaration of Independence, creators of the Constitution, and superb individuals like Washington, Madison, and Adams, all of whom operated in a religious vacuum.

The ideals of the American Revolution seemingly sprang out of the soil even though the colonies had a long and rich history of ideas, largely cultivated by political sermons, preceding 1776. There had been Puritans, but they simply burned witches and persecuted such progressive thinkers as Roger Williams and Anne Hutchinson. There were colonial legislatures, but they restricted the suffrage to white, landowning males and clashed with royal governors over tax policies. There were pamphlets and broadsheets, but they were economic responses related to mercantilism. There was the Great Awakening, but it was religious fundamentalism and emotional frenzies over fear of God's wrath.

A secularized presentation of American history with theological figures pushed to the sidelines and theological ideas ignored was the primary interpretation presented to students for many years. Then the Christian school movement began, even though it started with a paucity of curriculum. Thankfully, Christians in the 1970s and 1980s did not wait until God provided every provision before they obeyed God. Sometimes, the little academies consisted of secular textbooks with prayer added. But God answers prayers, and the books began to appear that have created a reformation of historiography.

In 1977, while the nation was still recovering from the Vietnam debacle and the Watergate disaster, Peter Marshal and David Manual published *The Light and the Glory*. This book was a study of the beginnings of American history from a decidedly Christian viewpoint. It was aimed at a popular audience and filled with stories, first hand testimonies, and narratives illustrating Christian people and ideas in early America. Columbus, who was increasingly viewed as an imperialistic invader seeking gold and fame, was reinterpreted according to his Christian presuppositions and motivations. His *Book of Prophecies* had not at that time been translated into English.[55] His desire was to fulfill his name as a Christ-bearer, which he, with all his inconsistencies and flaws, accomplished. The Puritans, long the stereotyped targets of both history and fiction, were portrayed as a godly and even fun-loving lot. The Founding Fathers were, with some exceptions, men who had a theological outlook on the world and the events they faced.

The Light and the Glory, as a historical study, was light reading, superficial at points, and prone to exaggerate the Christian influences found in early America. Lots of Christians bought and read the book, and it has remained in print and is still used in Christian schools. It helped change the approach to our heritage for Christian students. It helped spawn an interest in American history that resulted in books both at the popular and scholarly levels. Just as its authors had searched and gleaned both the primary and secondary sources, so it caused others to begin obtaining original sources, older out-of-print studies, and scholarly works that recognized Christian contributions. A whole library of books, along with videos and reference works, has followed in the last several decades enabling Christians to rethink and reclaim our heritage. Some of the books are outstanding; some overstate the case, for example by virtually elevating the Constitution to the level of Scripture; some of the recent books simply quote from the other of the recent books with little depth or original research.

---

[55] Peter Marshall and David Manuel, *The Light and the Glory* (Old Tappan, New Jersey: Fleming H. Revell Company, 1977), 360.

Marshall and Manuel merely popularized an interpretation of American history that had other adherents. R. J. Rushdoony's *This Independent Republic* (originally published in 1964) and *The Nature of the American System* (1965) and Gregg Singer's *Theological Interpretation of American History* (1964) were heavyweight studies that preceded *The Light and the Glory*. Both Rushdoony and Singer, whose works are reviewed earlier in this book, wrote interpretive scholarly essays that presupposed certain knowledge both of the narrative of American history and of theology. Calvinist scholars in the 1960s were often better at coaching Olympic divers than in teaching beginners how to tread water. Rushdoony's and Singer's taped lectures are evidence that both were quite informative and entertaining speakers. Their books, however, were aimed more at scholarly, rather than popular audiences.

The ongoing revival of both Reformed theology and increasing interest in Christian education have worked together to spur both Christian historical scholarship and book publishing. When I was in college doing research papers on Calvinism, I had handy a half dozen or more resources written by Reformed Christians. Now from both Christian and scholarly secular publishers, the number of books for such topics is legion. Whether one is searching for whole books or simply references, the research is growing.

In 2003, pastor, theologian, and author David W. Hall completed his magnum opus, titled *The Genevan Reformation and the American Founding*. This book opens the floodgates that should change or confirm the way we view America's roots and future. At least it will change or confirm it for those of us that read the book and faithfully teach its core content to others. It should, at the more scholarly level, have the same impact that *The Light and the Glory* has had at the popular level.

As Christian students of history have discovered that America's founding was Christian, it is now increasingly evident that these same roots were Calvinistic. As shown above, people of Reformed and Calvinistic persuasion largely colonized America. Let's hear from the historians once again on this note.

Gregg Singer stated this as follows:

> Calvinism was not confined to England and the continent, for it quickly spread to the English colonies of America. Not only was it the theology of the Puritans of New England, but it was also held by the Dutch of the Middle Colonies, as well as by the Presbyterians who were numerous in the Middle and Southern Colonies. In 1729 the Presbyterian Synod officially adopted the Westminster Confession of Faith as the doctrinal standard for the Presbyterian

Churches in the colonies, following the example of the Puritans of Massachusetts Bay, who as early as 1648 had taken a similar stand in the Cambridge Platform, although they omitted the paragraphs dealing with church government. In 1708 the Congregational Churches in Connecticut adopted the Saybrook Platform which continued the same general principles. The German Reformed Church, which was strong in New Jersey and Pennsylvania, held to a Calvinism which was somewhat modified by the federal theology of Coeccius. It is also of great importance to note that the early Baptists in the English colonies were decidedly Calvinistic in their thinking, although they, like the New England Puritans sought to eliminate the Presbyterian form of government in favor of one which was designed to guarantee the independence of each congregation.[56]

Historian Kenneth Scott Latourette labeled the theological groups that broke with the Anglican Church as radical Protestants. Here is how he described the American religious climate:

In 1750 the most compact and the most numerous influential group of churches was not the Church of England but New England Congregationalism.

In general, the radical Protestants were of the Reformed tradition. Whether Puritans, Independents, Separatists, Baptists, or Quakers, they were either distinctly of it or had been profoundly influenced by it, even when, like the Quakers, they had rebelled against it. New Englanders had a large share in the founding Presbyterianism in the Thirteen Colonies. They were closely allied in spirit and in some instances in personnel with the more widely spread Presbyterianism. The New England churches held to the Westminster Confession as standard. Usually those who moved away from New England to other colonies organized themselves into Presbyterian churches. The Reformed strain from England was reinforced by Reformed from Holland and Germany and by Scotch-Irish Presbyterians.[57]

---

[56] Singer, *John Calvin: His Roots and Fruits.* 22-23.
[57] Kenneth Scott Latourette, *A History of Christianity: Volume II: A. D. 1500—A. D. 1975—Reformation to the Present* (Peabody, Massachusetts: Prince Press, 1997) Revised Edition, 954.

Focusing more on the South, John Boles notes the commonality of doctrines that even included the Methodists, who were more Arminian than Calvinistic in theology:

> This idea of man's position, whereby he in life was stranded somewhere between God and a hell of eternal punishment, was accepted in detail by the proponents of evangelical Protestantism in the South, as elsewhere in the nation. Furthermore, the Baptists, Methodists, and Presbyterians all held depraved man to be in a state of absolute dependence upon God for aid in salvation. Man could not by his own free will turn aside from his sinful condition. God had to initiate within man the faith that recognized Jesus Christ. That this was a general belief common to Methodists as well as Presbyterians, Separate Baptists as well as Regulars, is indicated by their doctrinal statements. On this extremely important theological point, each denomination was in total agreement.[58]

The fact that so many of the early colonists, so many of the earliest churches, and so many of the earliest colonial institutions were Calvinistic is often not so much suppressed, as simply ignored. Since church membership and profession of faith are so often superficial today, historians and teachers assume such superficiality in the past. Colonial America included lots of well-read and theologically educated people. Their bookshelves may have been scanty, but typically the books they contained were weighty and theological. Easily found would be Bibles. Along with that, such works as Bunyan's *Pilgrim's Progress* and the Westminster Standards were commonplace. Calvin's *Institutes of the Christian Religion* and Foxe's *Book of Martyrs* would not have been rare. Still, not every Colonial American was a theologian, but all would have been directly and subtly influenced by theologians, especially through sermons and tracts.

There are many of us today who do not own a single compact disk (or album) by Elvis Presley, the Beatles, and Simon and Garfunkel. But we still recognize and are familiar with the tunes, because their music permeated (with continuing popularity) the culture for more than a generation.[59] In the same

---

[58] John Boles, *The Great Revival: Beginnings of the Bible Belt* (Lexington, Kentucky: University of Kentucky Press, 1996), 132.

[59] Of the three, I have the music only of Elvis, who is as much a part of the country music tradition as of rock and roll music. My son Nicholas has works of all these artists.

way, the Calvinism of Colonial America had an abiding impact, even on those who were not believers or Calvinists. Benjamin Franklin's *Poor Richard's Almanac* and his autobiography echo strong Puritan emphases even in a man who rejected orthodox Christianity most strongly. Statements from Franklin about God's sovereignty over nations and Thomas Jefferson's recognition of God's justice both evidence Calvinistic influences.[60]

This Calvinistic impact was especially strong when events began coalescing into the American War for Independence. Hall makes this point the central thesis of his work. He says,

> My argument is that the American logic of liberty did not arrive *ex nihilo* in 1776 or spring self-evident from an Enlightenment Deism, but was built on a specific legacy of institutional arrangement—following on well-known precedents formulated earlier in Geneva—which properly constrained hierarchy and power.[61]

America did not invent a new order of the ages in 1776. It continued a process of refining a Biblical and Reformational theory of government that acknowledged the sovereignty of God and not kings. Jean Calvin of Geneva, not Jean Rousseau of Geneva, created the mindset that governed this country. And Calvin was not alone. Such theologians, writers, and pastors as William Farel (Calvin's co-pastor in Geneva), Peter Viret of Geneva, Theodore Beza (Calvin's successor), John Ponet of Strasbourg, the anonymous author of *Vindiciae Contra Tyrannos* in France, and Johannes Althusius (the author of *Politica*) all weighed in on the theological implications of governmental tyranny, persecution of the Christian faith, and the limits of obedience to ungodly rulers.

If these continental Reformers did not say enough, from the British Isles came another regiment of political and theological thinkers. John Knox, Andrew Melville, and other Scots put their theology in action during the turbulent reigns of the Stuart queens and kings of Scotland. Scotsmen George Buchanan and Samuel Rutherford penned great treatises on government. As those same ideas were accepted and reformulated among the Puritans in England, they carried these theological and political convictions with them in their trek across the Atlantic to the New World.

William Bradford, John Winthrop, John Cotton and others set the norms for Biblical and covenantal civil government in Colonial America. By the

---

[60] R. J. Rushdoony, *This Independent Republic*, 5-6.
[61] Hall, Preface, page viii.

time of the American War for Independence, the war for the hearts and minds of the people, the true revolution, had been completed by scores of pastors who had faithfully preached election sermons for generations. The language of the colonial charters, the resolutions preceding the Declaration of Independence, the ongoing sermons and theological pamphlets all testify to the Reformed heritage in this country's founding and the extent to which Calvinism sparked our independence. Presbyterian and Congregationalist pastors and laymen filled the ranks of both officers and soldiers in the Continental armies. The War for Independence was truly a Presbyterian Rebellion.

Dr. Hall begins his survey with a most brilliant coup. His first major witness called to testify before the court is a surprise. Surely Cotton Mather or John Witherspoon or George Whitefield might testify to America's Calvinistic heritage. They are all examined later on in his book, but the first witness is Thomas Jefferson, the 'creator' of the wall of separation of church and state, the arch-Deist and unbeliever among the Founding Fathers, the primary secular and Enlightenment thinker of his age. Jefferson's motto was "Resistance to tyranny is obedience to God." As in the case of the Declaration of Independence, Jefferson was not so much a poetic creator as a wise scholar and compiler, meaning that he cultivated his ideas from others. That motto was not of Jefferson's devising. It was a summary, a Cliff's Notes version, of a long theological heritage worked out by the Reformers, the Covenanters, the Huguenots, and the British and American Puritans.

As a further proof of Jefferson's wonderful inconsistency, Hall cites the case of Jefferson's efforts to move the entire faculty of the University of Geneva to the United States. Jefferson knew that this faculty was Calvinistic, yet like the careful botanist he was, he knew that they would flourish in this land if transplanted.

Hall's book is weighty, long, heavily documented, filled with analyses of theological tomes, devoid of anecdotes, plodding in its lining up the proofs of the thesis, scholarly and academic. In other words, it is the kind of book to make a Calvinist's heart throb with excitement. This is certainly no easy read; it will not fit at your bedside or near your fattest easy chair. This book calls for a desk, a notepad, strong coffee, and quiet children. I had to read it in the quietness of early mornings.

The bibliography alone can provide a wonderful list of books to satisfy the wanderlust for more knowledge of the Calvinistic heritage in both Europe and America. Dr. Hall has marshaled and referenced scores of books by pastors and scholars we all recognize, as well as books from others, many of whom are secular scholars, whose labors are common grace blessings to us.

Further Reading

A narrative history that straddles between the scholarly level of Dr. Hall and the popular level of *The Light and the Glory* is the series titled *To Pledge Allegiance,* published by American Vision in Atlanta, Georgia. The principal author of this series is Gary DeMar, the president of American Vision, and the author of a number of books on America's Christian history and Christian worldview issues. The second volume in this series, titled *Building a City On a Hill* and co-authored by DeMar, Fred Douglas Young, and Gary L. Todd, surveys the history and religious foundations of each of the colonies. The third volume, titled *On the Road to Independence* and co-authored by Demar and George Grant, covers events from the Great Awakening through the early Federalist Era.[62]

These books are the distilling of the Reformed studies of Christianity geared to both young and older students. I have used these materials in teaching junior high. They are a challenging reach for younger student, but quite full of Christian insights, humor, and stories. These books include study questions and tests, so they are especially geared toward classroom use. DeMar's book *America's Christian History: The Untold Story* includes some useful original sources, including colonial charters, that document the influence of Christianity in general and Reformed Christianity in particular all throughout American history.[63]

The study of the Puritans has two major sources in our times. The first is the scholarly work of Dr. Perry Miller, a historian whose writings appeared from the 1930s until the 1960s. When Miller first set out to study the impact of the Puritans, his professors attempted to dissuade him on the grounds that there was nothing to learn from them. Miller persevered and not only produced a number of great studies of his own, but he also published collections of Puritan works and inspired other scholars to study the Puritans. Ironically, Miller was not a Christian and his interpretation of the Puritans has to be viewed carefully. Still, he is a major resource for Puritan and colonial American studies. His many books are still available in both new and used editions. An older contemporary of Miller, Samuel Eliot Morison, one of America's all-time great historians, wrote *Builders of the Bay Colony* and *The Intellectual Life of Colonial New England,* both useful works on the Puritan influence. Books by Alan Heimart and Edmund S. Morgan on Puritans and colonial America are also beneficial.

---

[62] The first volume, *A New World in View*, gives extensive coverage to Columbus and to Cortes' conquering of Mexico and other events relating mostly to exploration of Central and South America.

[63] These works and many others are available through American Vision, P.O. Box 220, Powder Springs, Georgia 30127 (www.americanvision.org).

The other major source for Puritan studies has been the neo-Puritan Calvinistic presses that have reprinted Puritan works. Beginning with Banner of Truth Publishers in Britain, and largely influenced by Martyn Lloyd-Jones and Ian Murray, old Puritan books and sermons have been rescued from obscurity and reprinted in large numbers. Many of these reprints have focused upon the English Puritans, but American and colonial Puritan works have also been included. Sometimes it is easier to scan the books just to get a sense of how incredibly deep and detailed the Puritans were than to try to wade through the small print and exhaustive wordiness of the Puritans. A most intimidating case in point is Cotton Mather's *The Great Works of Christ in America* (or *Magnalia Christi America*), which was the earliest Calvinist and Puritan history of America.[64]

Two indispensable studies that topically and favorably study Puritan ideas are J. I. Packer's *A Quest for Godliness: The Puritan Vision of the Christian Life*[65] and Leland Ryken's *Worldly Saints: The Puritans as They Really Were*.[66] Both books survey Puritans' writings and actions in areas of church, society, and family. Both books seek to answer modern stereotypes and distortions of the Puritans with a call to emulate rather than castigate these Christians. A very favorable survey of Puritanism can be found in John Adair's *Founding Fathers: The Puritans in England and America*.[67] This book covers the Puritan experience in its beginnings and in the migration to the colonies and ends with a study of the on-going influence of the Puritans.

Two useful books on the Scots-Irish are *The Scotch-Irish: A Social History* by James G. Leyburn[68] and *Born Fighting: How the Scots-Irish Shaped America* by James Webb.[69] Leyburn's book is one of the most referenced and definitive sources on the Scots-Irish experience in America.[70] Leyburn's three sections are "The Scot in 1600," "The Scots in Ireland," and "The Scotch-Irish in America." The American portion covers roughly half the book. Webb's

---

[64] Cotton Mather, *The Great Works of Christ in America* (Edinburgh: Banner of Truth Trust, 1979). Two volumes reprinted from 1702.

[65] J. I. Packer, *A Quest for Godliness: The Puritan Vision of the Christian Life* (Wheaton, Illinois: Crossway Books, 1990).

[66] Leland Ryken, *Worldly Saints: The Puritans As They Really Were* (Grand Rapids: Academia Books, 1986).

[67] John Adair, *Founding Fathers: The Puritans in England and America* (London: J.M. Kent & Sons Ltd., 1982).

[68] James G. Leyburn, *The Scotch-Irish: A Social History* (Chapel Hill: The University of North Carolina Press, 1962)

[69] James Webb, *Born Fighting: How the Scots-Irish Shaped America* (New York: Broadway Books, 2004).

[70] Scots-Irish or Scotch-Irish? Far be it from me to intervene in a battle betwixt the clans. One Scotsman explained it to me saying that Scotch was a drink and that Scots are the people.

book is a fun and spirited celebration of Scots-Irish ethnicity and eccentricity going all the way up to the present. It has a certain Celtic and generally Southern pride and humor to it. Still, it celebrates a key contribution to the experience of colonization and independence made by the Scots-Irish.

Two books containing puzzle pieces for the influence of Calvinism in America are David Hackett Fischer's *Albion's Seed: Four British Folkways in America*[71] and *The Cousins' Wars: Religion, Politics, & the Triumph of Anglo-America* by Kevin Phillips.[72] Fischer's book, which is widely quoted and respected, details the cultural and religious beliefs found in England that were then transplanted to the New World where they continued to reflect the battles and social mores of the Old World. Phillips, whose sources include Fischer, covers three wars: the English Civil War, the American War for Independence, and the War Between the States. He amply references the religious causes of each of these wars. In particular, he notes the transplanting of Calvinistic theology and politics—rooted in the Cromwellian struggles of England—to the ideology and participants of the American War for Independence.

More than just pieces of the puzzle, in fact a coherent picture of a part of the colonial story, is found in Erskine Clarke's *Our Southern Zion: A History of Calvinism in the South Carolina Low Country, 1690-1990.*[73] This book is especially useful since so many colonial studies focus upon either Virginia or Massachusetts (and New England). The Carolinas were dominated at certain levels by Anglicans, but Reformed colonists, including Presbyterians, Huguenots, and Congregationalists also were there. As Clarke points out, "If members of the Reformed churches were not as politically dominant as members of the Anglican community, they more than held their own with the Anglicans in the intellectual leadership they provided the colony."[74]

Time and energy would fail us in trying to merely list all the useful original sources, scholarly studies, and biographies that contribute to the Reformed emphases in America's history. Most of the books listed above, especially David Hall's work, contain bibliographies that can aid the scholar and economically break the incurable book buyer. And even with the extensive resources available, the story is still not complete. This essay has focused primarily on those groups that were self-consciously Reformed or Calvinistic in

---

[71] David Hackett Fischer, *Albion's Seed: Four British Folkways in America* (New York: Oxford University Press, 1989).

[72] Kevin Phillips, *The Cousins' Wars: Religion, Politics, and the Triumph of Anglo-America* (New York: Basic Books, 1999).

[73] Erskine Clarke's *Our Southern Zion: A History of Calvinism in the South Carolina Low Country, 1690-1990* (Tuscaloosa: The University of Alabama Press, 1996).

[74] Clarke, 57.

theology. Other Christian groups helped settle the country, contributed to our independence, and helped define our nation's beginnings. The heirs of Europe's religious wars often served shoulder to shoulder in the trenches and legislative assemblies of America.

Looking at the post-destination of America's earliest years can only lead to praise of the Sovereign God of history.

Chapter Twenty-Two
The Presbyterian War

> He that will not honor the memory, and respect the influence of Calvin, knows but little of the origin of American independence.
> —George Bancroft[1]

> Religion was a big factor, as it was and is in everything connected with America.
> —Paul Johnson[2]

Introduction: On the Banks of the Watuga

For several days men gathered along the clearing of the banks of the Watauga River at a place called Sycamore Shoals. Already on these late September mornings, a chill was in the air. Campfires blazed and men gathered around for coffee, a bit of warmth, and talk. At some fires, whole oxen or deer were being roasted.

Harvesting was well under way. Fall and winter hunting was soon to come. Plenty of talk centered around crops and game. Just passing through the camp, glancing at the men talking with hands, you could judge the height of corn stalks, the size of fish, the breadth of a deer's antlers, and other details of life over the mountains.

The men ranged in ages. Some were still boys, who were careful to show no signs of fear or childish behavior. Their still smooth faces visible under hats pulled low gave them away. Many of the older men wore beards; in some cases, just a few days growth marking their time away from home. Their faces also showed years of work in the sun, just as their gnarled and rough hands showed years of work with ploughs, axes, and hoes.

Dressed in buckskins, hunting shirts, and pants, the men had no uniformity in dress. They were a clan, not an army. This was a gathering, similar to

---

[1] From *The New Dictionary of Thoughts*, 73.
[2] Paul Johnson, *A History of the American People* (New York: Harper Collins Publishers, 1997), 172.

a camp meeting, a mustering of the frontier soldiers, not a military drill. These were neighbors, kinfolks, and frontiersmen, not regiments and battalions.

Theodore Roosevelt described these men as "wild and fierce people, accustomed to the chase and to warfare with the Indians. Their hunting-shirts of buckskin or homespun were girded in by bead-worked belts, and the trappings of their horses were stained red and yellow."[3]

About sixteen hundred or more were gathered there in 1780. Quite a few had pitched in local battles a time or two before. Up to now, the battles had been with the Indian allies of the British. Off and on, they banded to fight the Creek, Cherokee, and Shawnee Indians, who had menaced them and been menaced by them around their settlements. On occasion the problem was the government back east, in the coastal lowlands.

Now it was a different enemy. The English army and a motley collection of Tories and others had been ravaging homes and farms across the mountains in the clay hills of South Carolina. Some of them had family or friends there; others had been born there. For some time, word had drifted in of the war going on throughout South Carolina. Word had reached them of a British colonel named Ferguson. This Ferguson had allowed that if the settlers across the mountains did not prove their loyalties to the king, his men would invade their homes, burn their villages, and hang their leaders.[4] Loyalty was not gained or earned by threat for these frontiersmen.

These men did not keep up much with news, certainly not daily happenings, but on occasion, they heard news of happenings at least a month sometimes as much as a year old. Since current events were not important, they valued the past. There were stirrings in their souls and minds when they heard of the trials of their kinsmen. Bits and pieces of stories drifting over the mountains mingled with memories of the old country. Some of the old men had been born in the old country. A few had known Scotland—the moors and hills of that northern land. A few others had known Ulster. They remembered the hard years there and the journeys by ship that took them away.

Quite a few others remembered the back country of Pennsylvania, Maryland, and Virginia, and the continual search for new land. Down from the western frontier they had drifted along the Appalachians through Virginia and the Carolinas. There was so much land. So much good land—filled with

---

[3] Theodore Roosevelt and Henry Cabot Lodge, *Hero Tales: How Common Lives Reveal the Heroic Spirit of America* (Nashville: Cumberland House, 2000), 67. This chapter, titled "King's Mountain," was written by Roosevelt.

[4] Theodore Roosevelt, 65-66.

tall trees—oaks and hickories, full of game—deer and turkeys, flowing with rivers and creeks filled with bass and crappie fish and catfish.

There was always some better land out west, beyond the next range of hills. It was there beyond the range that they had settled. It was beyond the present boundaries of the Carolinas, but such boundaries would be settled later. It was not yet a state, that would come later, and that state would be called Franklin for a time, and later Tennessee.

As the men gathered together to organize, they voted to pick their leaders. Every man's voice and vote was as good as every other man's, but they all knew that some had been born to lead and some to follow. Among their leaders were men named Sevier, who later became governor of Tennessee, Shelby, who later became governor of Kentucky, and Campbell, who died fighting in the War for Independence.

The frontiersmen looked to the ones that had led back home to lead them now. In some cases, they were the ones with a bit more education than the rest. Many of the leaders were well read in the Bible and the Confession of Faith. They were leaders back over the mountains in the churches and community. Some had served in war before. They had fought Indian and Frenchman; or maybe they had fought the English themselves back over the seas. Andrew Nelson Lytle said, "Officers were important and obeyed, so long as they did right and fought well."[5] The leaders were speakers too. They had the right words for the cause. Their words had drawn them out of the fields and onto the banks of the Watauga River. Their words banded them here today.

But it was the words of another that would fill this day. The Reverend Samuel Doak stood out in the mixed gathering of men. His black Genevan robe identified him as a clergyman. In his hand, he carried his Bible. For a time, he mingled with them, swapped stories and laughed at the jokes. Then for a while he walked off by himself beyond the clearing.

There alone, he read the text from his Bible again. He knew it well, but he read it slowly, pausing to think about each word. Occasionally sitting on a log, and alternately pacing back and forth with his hands lifted up to heaven, Pastor Doak could be heard talking out loud.

At some points, one could hear the voice of preaching. He was practicing his lines, rehearsing his sermon. At other points, the voice dropped and in the tone of a suppliant, he could be heard, asking for boldness, for grace, and help in proclaiming God's Word.

---

[5] Andrew Nelson Lytle, *A Wake for the Living* (Nashville: J. S. Sanders & Company, 1992), 74.

When he returned to the camp, the officers had already formed the men up in a group. Muskets and shotguns were seen all around. Some of the hunters had the long rifles that had already proved so successful in the woods and on the battlefields. Historian Don Higgenbotham describes these men, "Such veteran Indian fighters and hunters could travel far without provisions. They could perform remarkable feats with the rifle, allegedly hitting targets 200 yards away, whereas musketmen were ineffective at only half that distance."[6] Along with their guns, they all had knives. A man couldn't live out here without a knife. It had too many good uses in both war and peace.

The camaraderie around the fires, with pipes and swigs from jugs of corn liquor, concealed for the time some of the tensions that riled these men from time to time.

Sometimes a wrestling match for fun turned mean. Sometimes a horse race ended with a fistfight. Like the army of Agamemnon's and Achilles' Achaians, some men had killed or nearly killed each other over women. Land boundaries or too much whiskey or loud boasts had brought about many a quarrel. But today all were bound together.

With knives and guns and axes a-plenty, with a bit of liquor on the breaths of many, with minds contemplating killing and being killed, at this moment, they were quite peaceful.

One warrior stood out amongst them and that was Pastor Doak, a minister of the Gospel of peace and pastor of a church in the Holston settlement in what is now Tennessee. For a text, he turned to the Book of Judges, certainly a less than peaceful book of the Old Testament. From Judges, Pastor Doak began telling the story of Gideon.

They knew the story. Bibles were not plentiful, but neither were they rare. Those who could read had read the story; those who could not read, had listened to it many times. The rhythms and cadences of Bible stories had been heard, prayed, sung, and chanted all their lives. Another blessing of being far from news and happenings and close to the earth itself, they knew something of the warp and woof of the Bible. Many bore names right out of the Bible. Many had been catechized since the days of infancy. For some, the Bible was the first book or the only book they had read.

Gideon could have been a neighbor or a kinsman from across the hills and valleys. Still Pastor Doak told the story. He told of Gideon's call. He recounted Gideon's anguished reluctance to serve God's call—his casting the fleece before God and seeking a special sign.

---

[6] Don Higgenbotham, *War and Society in Revolutionary America* (Columbia, S.C.: University of South Carolina Press, 1988), 135.

Then Pastor Doak talked of the colonies. He told of happenings way off in Massachusetts and Pennsylvania. The men heard tales of other farmers and workers who had been shouldering rifles for several years now. All that had, for a time, been too far off, but now Boston folk were neighbors in this conflict.

Quickly Pastor Doak turned to the Carolinas. It was there that the British army, under General Cornwallis and his minions, like Captain Huck and Major Bannistre Tarleton, were ramping about killing folks, burning their churches and houses, and taking away their lands and freedom. It was there at a place called Camden that distant kinfolk and old acquaintances had been killed and a whole army destroyed.

From there Pastor Doak reminded the men of another old story, a story that almost seemed itself to rise out of the Old Testament. It was a story of a another group of mountain men and women. Another group that gathered on hills and slopes and listened to the Word of God.

There it was that Redcoated Dragoons had ravaged the countryside, killing the parsons, threatening the people. Prayerbooks and bishops, imposed by the English crown, were forced upon the proud people of Scotland.

Outnumbered, outmanned, usually out-trained, and even disorganized, these Scotsmen had banded together and signed the National Oath and Covenant.

God's Covenants are binding, they believed. Prayers long since offered up and oaths long since taken, were still heard and honored by God in heaven. Geography might change. At one point, it might be the land of Canaan, at another point it might be the hills of Scotland, and at this point it might be the mountains in western Carolina. Enemies might change. For Gideon, it was the Midianites. For the Covenanters, it might be English Dragoons. For these men, it was the sons of those same Dragoons, wearing the same hated red-coated uniforms. But covenants do not change.

The Declaration of Independence had been signed a few years back. As usual, some had heard of it. Some had paused their planting and plowing long enough to ponder it a moment, but it was only important when the fighting came near. And the Declaration itself was but an add-on to the original National Covenant.

Pastor Doak continued to preach, his voice rising and his arms raised in passion. The themes merged: "Our fathers, our lands, Gideon, the Covenant, the Declaration, our neighbors, the English, the Midianites, King George, the Devil himself and his red-coated minions," and so on.

The men listened intently. Men who worked alongside death and faced death at the hands of Indians and weather and sickness, still paused when Death approached.

Men who had listened to God's Word now listened more carefully and considered their own souls, their own sins, and the call at this time. If they fought, they knew they should be fighting for God.

Closing with what was a prayer, an exhortation, and a benediction, Doak sent them off in battle with the words, "Go forth, my brave men, and may the sword of the Lord and of Gideon go with you."[7] From that point, their battle cry would be, "The sword of the Lord and of Gideon."

After that prayer meeting and revival, the men rode off, their colonels leading the way, in search of Ferguson and his army. They marched for twelve days to the place where they would rendezvous with other men from the Carolinas.

Major Ferguson, having heard of the approaching enemy, was at this time leading a column of 1,200 men through the region of the headwaters of the Broad and Catawba Rivers toward Charlotte, where Cornwallis was. South Carolinians, led by James Williams, an elder in the church of Little River, with other men from the Watuga River country, had already been skirmishing with Ferguson's troops. In a captured dispatch, Ferguson's fate was ironically stated: "I am on my march towards you (Cornwallis), by a road leading from Cherokee Ford, north of King's Mountain. Three or four hundred good soldiers, part dragoons, would finish the business. Something must be done. This is their last push in this quarter."[8]

Ferguson decided to set defenses on King's Mountain, described by Roosevelt as "a wooded, hog-back hill on the border-line between North and South Carolina."[9]

After a forced march, the Patriot army also reached King's Mountain and was able to surround Ferguson before he had time to acquire reinforcements. On October 16, the two almost equally numbered forces met on King's Mountain. A last general order was given to the frontiersmen: "When you reach your position, dismount, tie your horse, roll coats and blankets and tie them to the saddle. Put fresh primes in your guns. Every man resolves to fight until he dies."[10]

From all surrounding sides, the frontiersmen began their attack uphill. The British and their Tory allies were hardly prepared, but by the skillful use of the bayonet, which they had and the Patriots lacked, they were able, for a time, to repulse the attacks.

---

[7] Henry Alexander White, *Southern Presbyterian Leaders*, 151.
[8] Lytle, 74.
[9] Roosevelt, 67.
[10] Lytle, 77.

But the frontiersmen persisted. After each repulse, they attacked again and again until they reached the peak of the hill. Colonel Ferguson rallied his men by blowing his silver whistle and waving his sword. He made himself an easy target for men skilled with the long-rifles. Soon he lay dead with seven bullet holes in him. The King's regulars and Tories all huddled together and surrendered. A whole British unit had been killed or captured.

Back home across the mountains the families of the Patriot soldiers were lacking in protection from the dangers of Indian attacks. The victors of King's Mountain had to get back to watch over their own homes and hearths.

The Presbyterian War

> Religion, always a principle of energy, in this new people is no way worn out or impaired; and their mode of professing it is also one main cause of this free spirit. The people are Protestants, and of that kind which is the most adverse to all implicit submission of mind and opinion.
> Edmund Burke, Speech on Moving His Resolution of Conciliation with the Colonies, March 22, 1775

> The first voice publicly raised in America to dissolve all connections with Great Britain came, not from the Puritans of New England, nor the Dutch of New York, nor the Planters of Virginia, but from the Scotch-Irish Presbyterians.
> George Bancroft

Each year on the Fourth of July, we celebrate our nation's victory in the War for Independence. We celebrate, in particular, our Declaration of Independence, addressed to the world, about the British government—a government that protected the colonies for over 150 years before provoking them for about twelve years.

The thirteen colonies revolted against the most liberal (in the best sense of that word) government of its day. They revolted over a tea tax with rates so low as to make any modern libertarian green with envy. They separated themselves from the land of their mother tongue, cultural heritage, and religious background. Some of the actual causes were so principled as to baffle us in our age of pragmatism. The risks and improbabilities of success were so great as to as astound us in our age of careful calculations. The degree of internal colonial dissent is perplexing to us in an age where political polls are used to determine truth. The number of Patriot leaders that emerged—

political, military, and theological leaders—seems mythical to us in an age of mediocrity. The rhetoric of freedom and the political acuity amazes us in our age of political banality.

From our school days and from some famous paintings, we as Americans share some common images of the war, some slightly distorted by the facts. We hear the galloping horse and Paul Revere's voice, breaking the midnight calm, announcing, "The Redcoats are coming."[11] We see Gen. Washington, standing at the stern of a boat, surrounded by the boatmen-soldiers, crossing the Delaware River. We have images of Sons of Liberty, gathered in taverns with tankards of brew and pipes, joined in impassioned discussions of "No taxation without representation." We remember a room filled with solemn men, with powdered wigs and finely tailored jackets, signing the Declaration of Independence on July 4.[12] We picture three ragged and tattered soldiers with drum and fife and flag embodying the Spirit of '76. We picture Betsy Ross intently sewing stars on the flag.

New books continue to be written extolling the leadership qualities of the Founding Fathers. Numerous accounts of George Washington have recently been written that counter the trend of some decades back to diminish his standing as a leader. David McCullough's biography of John Adams, somewhat epic in proportion, brought this less remembered, but not less important, leader back to the forefront.[13] Ron Chernow's biography of Alexander Hamilton was also a bestseller, and a number of books have highlighted other leaders, helping Americans renew an interest in the war and early days of the Republic. Thanks to Mel Gibson's movie *The Patriot* in the late 1990s, the vast public that learns history at the box office imbibed some of the images and complexities of the southern campaigns of that war. (Where were the critics warning of potential violence and prejudice against the English when the movie first aired?)

Still, we know little about our War for Independence. It was twice as long as that other long war, the War Between the States. It was seven years after the signing of the Declaration and eight years after the firing of the first shots of the war before the war ended. It also was, in a true sense, an actual civil war, with the colonists divided three ways: a large portion of the colonists—the Patriots—fighting for independence, another large portion—the Tories or Loyalists—fighting just as fiercely against independence, with the remaining colonists straddling the fence.

---

[11] Revere was one of many riders on that night. He would not have said, "The British are coming." The colonials were British.

[12] Even though we celebrate on July 4, most of the actual signing took place on other dates.

[13] David McCullough, *John Adams*.

George Washington, having once aspired to be a British officer, led the Continental Army, but lost far more battles than he won. For those keeping score, Washington lost six major battles and won three.[14] In fact, Washington and his army were not even present at the victorious Battle of Saratoga, usually proclaimed to be the turning point. Someone who was present and who played a key role in America's success in that battle was Benedict Arnold, usually remembered only as a traitor.

That same battle not only netted the Patriots a great victory, but it turned the war into a World War. France, believe it or not, actually sided with the U.S. France, believe it or not, sent supplies, soldiers, and naval support that helped secure our victory. Spain, the Netherlands, and Russia also supported the Colonial cause.

Britain, so long blessed with so many talented leaders in the halls of government and the fields of battle, spawned a host of political incompetents and military imbeciles. America, thought to be backward and rustic, produced not only a war-winning first string of leaders, but also a second and third string of brilliant men. British historian Paul Johnson notes, "[T]he British strategy made no sense. Indeed it is arguable that Britain had no discernible, and certainly no consistent, strategy from beginning to end. It is a mystery that the British, with their political genius, and their very uncertain touch with military affairs, should have rejected a political solution and put all their trust in a military one."[15] Many of their military leaders were also incompetent. The most brilliant British politician of that day, Edmund Burke, defended the American cause before Parliament.

In this war, the British issued an 'emancipation proclamation,' but the slaveholders, like Washington, Jefferson, and others—denounced by no less than Samuel Johnson—won the war fought in the name of human freedom. In this war, the secessionists—their justification presented in the Declaration of Independence—won. This war resulted in the world, as many knew it, being turned upside down.

This war secured the American Northwest Territory—the area from the Ohio River Valley to the Mississippi River—which kept the fledgling United States from being a narrow coastal nation comparable to Chili. This opened a new frontier that enabled the nation to fulfill its Manifest Destiny. This was due to the victories at such places as Kaskasia by one of the less known heroes, George Rogers Clark.

In this war German-speaking Hessian mercenaries did battle against German-speaking Patriots at such battles as Trenton. Highland Scots donned

---

[14] Johnson, 159.
[15] Johnson, 161.

Red Coats and raised the musket against Ulster Scots and Scots-Irish uniformed in American homespun at such battles as Moore's Creek. Americans faced fellow Americans, neighbors against neighbors, brothers against brothers, and uncivilly used bayonet and torch against the lives and properties of each other.

Like so many wars within the confines of historic Christendom, men who read the same Bible, recited the same creeds, and prayed the same prayers to God, shouldered muskets and marched off to battle and killed each other with ruthless abandon.

The Patriots were not perfect or blameless; the war was not neat and pretty; the causes were not altogether as clear-cut as one might wish. In a world of wars and rumors of war, war itself creates its own momentum, and what might have initially been the main cause is superseded by circumstances outside of the cause. 'Why do men fight?' is a question that baffles the philosopher as well as the military general.

In this mix of shared images, forgotten details, and complexities, we have much neglected the religious aspects of this war. Carl Bridenbaugh, in his book *Mitre and Sceptre,* presented a viewpoint about the cause of the war that is not always emphasized or understood. He said, "Religion was the cause of the American Revolution."[16] What has been sometimes slighted by modern historians and largely forgotten in the public mind was well known by the participants in that war.

The Presbyterian Rebellion

Congregationalists in the New England colonies were the descendants of the Puritan Roundheads, those who raised the banner with Cromwell and Hamden against the Royal forces under King Charles I. Scots-Irish on the frontier were the descendants of the Covenanters who, in the tradition of John Knox and Andrew Melville, opposed the imposition of Anglican Prayer books and bishops. In our day, we still have enough cultural memory of our fathers' wars against Nazi and Japanese aggression and against Communist expansion to rile us anew against the tyranny of modern terrorism. In colonial America, the memories of fighting for the Crown Rights of King Jesus, for a free church, and religious freedom were not forgotten. British suppression of the rights of Englishmen and British imposition of taxation apart

---

[16] Carl Bridenbaugh, *Mitre and Sceptre: Transatlantic Faiths, Ideas, Personalities, & Politics* (New York: Oxford University Press, 1962). Bridenbaugh's thesis was adopted and supported by R.J. Rushdoony in his writings and lectures on the American War for Independence. Kevin Phillips' *The Cousins' Wars: Religion, Politics, and the Triumph of Anglo-America* also referenced and supported Bridenbaugh.

from representation dovetailed naturally with the fear of a British-appointed Anglican Bishop to the colonies. Sweet says, "Bishops were denounced as 'Apostolical monarchs,' or 'right reverend and holy monarchs,' who, once established in America, would introduce 'canon law—a poison, a pollution.'"[17]

So the spiritual sons of Calvin and Knox and the Puritans from New England through the Middle Colonies to the Southern frontier all armed for battle. Or as Pennsylvania loyalist Joseph Galloway stated it, the British government's chief opponents were "Congregationalists, Presbyterians, and Smugglers."[18]

A Hessian captain wrote in 1778, "Call this war by whatever name you may, only call it not an American rebellion; it is nothing more or less than a Scotch-Irish Presbyterian rebellion." In Parliament, Horace Walpole agreed, saying, "There is no use crying about it. Cousin America has run off with a Presbyterian parson." In particular, he was referring to the Reverend John Witherspoon, a key Founding Father, and immigrant from Scotland who signed the Declaration of Independence. King George III, who reportedly called the war a Presbyterian War, also reportedly exclaimed after reading the Declaration of Independence, "The Calvinist churches in the colony have gone wild."[19]

From the colonies, an Episcopalian from Philadelphia said, "A Presbyterian loyalist was a thing unheard of." There actually were Presbyterian loyalists, but they were rare. More often Presbyterians were divided in the earlier stages of the conflict between those who hoped for a modified British rule granting the colonies greater local autonomy and those who more strongly favored greater independence due to greater grievances with the British government and the colonial ruling classes. The more moderate Presbyterians have been called the conservatives and those demanding independence have been called radicals.[20]

After efforts to achieve some sort of accommodation with the British failed, more colonists, and in particular, more Presbyterians moved toward favoring independence. As Trintirud says, "Once the colonists had decided to declare their independence, the conservative Presbyterians swung behind

---

[17] William Warren Sweet, *The Story of Religion in America* (New York: Harper & Row, Publishers, 1950), 174.

[18] Sweet, 178.

[19] Roy A. Clouser, *The Myth of Religious Neutrality* (Notre Dame: University of Notre Dame Press, 2005), 299.

[20] Leonard J. Trinterud, *The Forming of An American Tradition*. (Philadelphia: The Westminster Press, 1949), 242.

the Congress almost to a man."[21] Writing several months after the Declaration of Independence had been signed, an Anglican clergyman from New York commented on this:

> I have it from good authority that the Presbyterian ministers, at a synod where most of the middle colonies were collected, passed a resolve to support the Continental Congress in all their measures. This and only this can account for the uniformity of their conduct; for I do not know one of them, nor have I been able, after strict inquiry, to hear of any, who did not by preaching and every effort in their power, promote all the measures of the congress, however extravagant.[22]

Ambrose Serle, a representative of Lord Dartmouth wrote from New York in November 1776: "The war is…at the Bottom very much a religious War; and every one looks to the Establishment of his own Party upon the issue of it. Indeed, upon the Issue, some one Party ought to predominate, were it only for the Conservation of Peace. It is perhaps impossible to keep the ecclesiastical Polity out of the Settlement, without endangering the Permancy of the civil."[23] This blending of theological and ecclesiastical issues with political issues was further brought out in a letter Serle wrote in 1777. He wrote, "When the war is over, there must be a great Reform established, ecclesiastical as well as civil; for though it has not been much considered at Home, Presbyterianism is really at the bottom of this whole Conspiracy, has supplied it with Vigour, and will never rest, till something is decided upon it."[24]

John D. Sergeant, a member of the Continental Congress from New Jersey, speaking favorably of the Presbyterians, credited the Scotch-Irish as being the main pillar supporting the Revolution in Pennsylvania. A New Englander, who took the opposite view of the war, called the Scotch-Irish "the most God-provoking democrats this side of Hell."

A monarchist wrote:

> You will have discovered that I am no friend of the Presbyterians, and that I fix all the blame of the extraordinary American proceed-

---

[21] Trinterud, 250.
[22] As quoted in Trinterud, 250.
[23] As quoted in Trinterud, 250.
[24] As quoted in Trinterud, 250.

ings on them. Believe me, sir, the Presbyterians have been the chief and principal instruments in all these flaming measures; and they always do and ever will act against government from that restless and turbulent anti-monarchial spirit which has always distinguished them everywhere when they had, or by any means could assume, power, however illegally.[25]

British wags caricatured the colonials in print with the character 'John Presbyter,' an ingrate, filled with deceit and pride against the pure maiden mother country.

The Black Regiments

The British and colonials did not just imagine this vast Calvinistic conspiracy. Alan Heimert says, "When the time came for action, moreover, the Calvinistic ministry were the first and longest in the field."[26] Fellow historian Henry F. May said, "The most important emotional reservoir for radicals was that provided by radical religion, and radical religion was as yet usually Calvinistic….Tories, for their part, knew well that the 'black coated regiment' of the Calvinist clergy, particularly in New England, was one of the most unified and effective supports of sedition."[27] The black robes of ministers became, in effect, their uniforms or insignia in this war.

As an example of Calvinist ministers engaging in the war, Heimert cites the case of Benjamin Pomeroy, who, at the age of 71, rushed to serve in the Battle of Bunker Hill.[28] Other examples abound. Calvinist John Cleaveland served on Washington's staff. Calvinist Thomas Allen was described by Washington Irving as "a belligerent parson, full of fight." Missionary David Avery fought at Bunker Hill and Ticonderoga (where a musket ball passed through his eye) and Saratoga. David Jones, a Baptist Calvinist in the tradition of Isaac Backus, nearly died at the hands of Tories in New Jersey. He went on to serve in the military from 1776 to 1781. Some years later, in the War of 1812, at the age of 76, he enlisted for his second war with Britain.

---

[25] W. P. Breed, *Presbyterians and the Revolution* (Decatur, MS: Issacharian Press, 1993 reprint), 15.

[26] Alan Heimart, *Religion and the American Mind* (Cambridge, MA: Harvard University Press, 1966), 474-475.

[27] Henry F. May, *The Enlightenment in America* (New York: Oxford University Press, 1976), 160.

[28] Alan Heimert, *Religion and the American Mind*, 475-477. Credit Heimert with being a most insightful and truthful historian.

Dr. Thomas Smyth cited numerous cases of Presbyterian elders who joined the Patriot cause:

> The battles of Cowpens, of King's Mountain, and also of the severe skirmish known as Huck's Defeat, are celebrated as giving a turning-point to the contests of the Revolution. General Morgan, who commanded at the Cowpens, was a Presbyterian elder. General Pickens, who made all the arrangements for that battle, was a Presbyterian elder, and nearly all under their command were Presbyterians. In the battle of King's Mountain Colonel Campbell, Colonel James Williams, Colonel Cleveland, Colonel Shelby and Colonel Sevier were all Presbyterian elders, and the body of their troops were from Presbyterian settlements. At Huck's Defeat, in York, Colonel Bratton and Major Dickinson were both elders in the Presbyterian Church. Major Samuel Morrow, who was with Colonel Sumpter in four engagements and took part in many other engagements, was for about fifty years a ruling elder in the Presbyterian Church.[29]

In one episode of the war, the Reverend James Caldwell in New Jersey was away from home when British soldiers killed his wife (whether intentional or not is not clear) and burned his home. With a price on his head and filled with desire to punish the enemy, Caldwell joined to meet the Patriot army in battle. At a point when the soldiers were running out of the paper wadding needed to hold the powder and ball in place in their muskets, Caldwell gathered up copies of Isaac Watts' *Psalms and Hymns*. Ripping out pages, he passed them out to the soldiers, saying, "Put Watts into 'em, boys! Give 'em Watts!"[30]

Henry Alexander White tells the following story: "A call for soldiers to fight in the Revolutionary army was sent out by the Virginia legislature. When the people of Rockbridge County met together to consider this call, they were addressed by [Pastor] William Graham. He urged the men to offer themselves for the battle, but only a few stepped forward. Then Graham walked out from the crowd and offered himself as a soldier. A large number

---

[29] Dr. Thomas Smyth, as quoted in W. P. Breed. In regard to Daniel Morgan, he was not a Presbyterian elder at that time, but became a committed Christian later in life. See Don Higginbotham, *Daniel Morgan: Revolutionary Rifleman* (Chapel Hill: The University of North Carolina Press, 1961), 212.

[30] Quoted in Peter Marshall and David Manuel, *The Light and the Glory*, 291.

of men followed him; the company of men were made up at once and William Graham was chosen as captain."[31]

When the British General Cornwallis entered Mecklenburg County, North Carolina, the men of seven churches congregated and formed a unit to oppose him. After confronting this assembly in battle, Cornwallis referred to this area as "the Hornet's Nest." He wrote, "It is evident…that the counties of Mecklenburg and Rowan are more hostile to England than any in America."

James Hall, the pastor of three Presbyterian congregations in Iredell County, North Carolina, preached to his congregations about the wrongs that had been inflicted upon their South Carolina countrymen, and then he called upon the men to take up arms and fight.

The men then called upon Pastor Hall to lead them. White tells us, "He put on a three cornered hat, buckled a long sword about him and rode away into the field. Whenever his men went into camp he preached to them the gospel of grace and liberty."[32]

This pattern of pastoral leadership in the pulpit and field was common throughout the colonies. Alan Heimert points out, "In the spring of 1775 whole Calvinist congregations, often in response to a single sermon, followed their preachers into battle, and for eight years members of the household of faith served at Valley Forge and Bennington, at Cowpens and Eutaw Springs."[33]

Even the young men studying in the classical Christian academies of that day joined in the cause. In the Prince Edward Academy, it is told, "After July, 1776, all of the students over sixteen years of age, about sixty-five in number, were organized as a military company. John Blair Smith was chosen captain. Each of the young soldiers wore as a uniform a hunting shirt colored with purple dye. The next year (1777) they answered the governor's call and marched to Williamsburg to meet the British."

Pastor Samuel Doak prayed for the men who were marching off to the battle of King's Mountain and exhorted them saying, "Go forth, my brave men and may the sword of the Lord and of Gideon go with you."

Henry Alexander White summarized the war on the Southern frontier (arguably where the war was won) by saying, "And who were the men who destroyed Ferguson's force and caused the plans of Cornwallis to fail? They were mounted riflemen from the Presbyterian congregations of the Carolinas, Virginia, Tennessee, and Georgia."

---

[31] Henry Alexander White, *Southern Presbyterian Leaders*.
[32] White, 149.
[33] Heimert, 476.

Kevin Phillips comments on the Presbyterian and Scots-Irish participation:

> This fierce combination—of long rifle, kirk, and academy—had dozens of parallels elsewhere on the frontier. And where it prevailed, Scotch-Irish Presbyterians were, literally, the Minute Men of the Piedmont and foothills. Consider what happened at Rowan County, North Carolina, on a Sunday in January 1781 as Lord Cornwallis's troops were trying to overtake patriot forces. General William L. Davidson, for whom Presbyterian Davidson College was thereafter named, sent couriers to the Rowan Presbyterian churches, Fourth Creek, Centre, Thyatira, and Hopewell, asking for men. Three hundred came from the Centre Church area, accompanied by their minister, and at Fourth Creek, the Reverend James Hall, in the midst of his sermon, stopped, read the message, enlisted much of his congregation, was elected captain, and joined Davidson on the Catawba River where the crossing British were to be stopped or slowed. Where the Scotch-Irish were church-driven, they were pillars of the Revolution.[34]

War is…well, not very nice

Pastors and congregations paid a severe price for their commitment. Trinterud comments on the commitment of the clergy:

> Though many a heroic deed is now forgotten, records do remain of significant participation in the struggle for independence of over one third of the clergy. Their services range from active duty in the line of battle, on through service in the chaplaincy, in colonial and state assemblies and conventions, in the Continental Congress as chaplains, and into such fields as recruiting, buoying up the morale of civilian and soldier, and the work of propaganda…[M]any Presbyterian ministers served tours of duty with the Army. Some of the leading clergymen of the Church, such as John Rogers, as well as young ministers ordained in haste for the purpose, shared the hardships of field and camp in the army.[35]

---

[34] Phillips, *Cousins' Wars*, 185.
[35] Trinterud, 252.

The Presbyterian War

British soldiers burned the house and books of Pastor John Simpson in Chester County, South Carolina. Pastor Simpson, meanwhile, was with the fighting men of his congregation, preaching to them.

More from Trinterud's study of Presbyterians:

> A number of the clergy lost their lives during the war. James Caldwell and John Rosbrough were murdered while on noncombatant duty. Both were known as ardent patriots...No less than forty commissioned officers during the war are said to have come from Caldwell's congregation.[36]

While Pastor Charles McKnight died while suffering from imprisonment by the British, even death did not spare Ebenezer Prime from British wrath. He had died while the British occupied his Long Island parish, but the British commander, Count Rumford, so hated this Presbyterian pastor that he put his headquarters in the church cemetery and made Prime's tombstone his doorstep. Rumford's reasoning was that he wanted "to have the pleasure of treading on the old rebel as often as [I] went in and out."[37]

British soldiers burned the home of Elder John James of Indiantown, South Carolina; also they burned his church and other homes. White says that they "flung into the fire every copy of the Bible and of the Scotch version of the Psalms that they could find. The British regarded the war in this region as against Presbyterians, and in revenge they destroyed houses of worship and books of devotion."

Cornwallis's army destroyed the Waxhaws church in the Carolinas. At an earlier point in the war, this church had served as a field hospital for the wounded. The vicinity of the church was a staging area for some time for the frontier militia. This was the home region and church of a teenage frontiersman and soldier named Andrew Jackson.[38] While he had his rough and rowdy years, he never forgot the Presbyterian faith of his youth; neither did he forget his bitterness toward the British. In his later years, he was known for being a faithful believer. A visitor to this region in 1767, the Anglican missionary, Reverend Charles Woodmason, had described it as "a very fruitful Spot", but he lamented that it was "occupied by a Sett of the most lowest vilest Crew breathing—Scotch-Irish Presbyterians from the North of Ireland."[39]

---

[36] Trinterud, 253.
[37] Trinterud, 253.
[38] Walter Edgar, *Partisans and Redcoats: The Southern Conflict That Turned the Tide of the American Revolution.* (New York: Perennial, 2003).
[39] Edgar, 1.

The Presbyterian War

Henry Alexander White tells of another attack on a church. He says, "Some of the British solders went to Hugh McAden's church at the Red House, and encamped in the house of worship, and burned all of McAden's books. The main body of the British army encamped for a time on Caldwell's plantation; some of the officer's drove out the preacher's family and made their home in his house. Moreover, they burned his Bible and Psalm-books, and with them all the rest of his library and his papers." [40]

In his book, *Presbyterians and the Revolution,* W. P. Breed states "more than fifty places of worship throughout the land were utterly destroyed by the enemy during the war."[41] Quoting from another source, Breed writes,

> As might be expected, religion suffered greatly throughout the entire period of the war. The church edifices were often taken possession of by an insolent soldiery and turned into hospitals or prisons, or perverted to still baser uses as stables or riding schools. The church at Newport had its steeple sawed off, and was used as a prison or guard-house till it was torn down and its siding used for soldiers' huts. The church at Crumford was burned to save its being occupied by the enemy....The one at Princeton was taken possession of by the Hessian soldiers, and stripped of its pews and gallery for fuel.[42]

The Scots-Irish minister William Martin was imprisoned and taken before General Cornwallis. He most aptly and succinctly defended the cause and conduct of the Christians in the war.

He was told, "You are charged with preaching rebellion from the pulpit—you, an old man and a minister of the gospel of peace—with advocating rebellion against your lawful sovereign, King George III!"

Pastor Martin replied, "I am happy to appear before you. For many months I have been held in chains for preaching what I believe to be the truth. As to King George, I owe him nothing but good will. I am not unacquainted with his private character...As a king, he was bound to protect his subjects in the enjoyment of their rights. Protection and allegiance go together, and when one fails the other cannot be expected. The declaration of Independence is but a reiteration of what our [Scotch] Covenanting fathers have always maintained."[43]

---

[40] White, previous citations found on pages 144, 147, 160, 161.
[41] W.P. Breed, *Presbyterians and the Revolution*, 31.
[42] Breed, 31.
[43] White, 156.

Preaching and Theology

Pastors did not neglect the office and duties of actual preaching. Sermons and publications were given to shore up the American commitment, to strengthen morale at home and in the battlefield, and to rebuke, warn, and exhort all hearers in regard to basic Christian duties. Chaplain Hugh H. Brackenridge warned his soldier congregation, saying, "What will it profit [an American], if he escape the taxation of Great Britain; but in the meantime, must lie down in sorrow, and pay the debt, due to God's justice in the flame of hell." He then closed, exhorting the hearers to "fly swiftly to the rock Christ Jesus, and seek for refuge, in the merit, and peace speaking blood of a redeemer."[44]

These sermons were not always delivered in the safest of circumstances. In Reverend George Hays' history of Presbyterians, he noted the following travails of pastors:

> Duffield, when preaching at a point opposite Staten Island, was interrupted by the whistling balls from the enemy. The forks of a tree were his pulpit, and undisturbed by the danger, he bade his hearers retire behind the hill and then he finished his sermon. Joseph Patterson, one of the fathers of the Presbytery of Redstone, had just knelt to pray under a shed when a board in line with his head was shivered by the discharge of a rifle. Stephen B. Balch once preached a sermon on "Subjection to the Higher Powers" while General Williams, with loaded pistols in his belt, protected him from the Royalists who were present.[45]

David Hall called the clergy the "prime educators in resistance theory grounded in theology."[46] Both Hall and Stohlman have taken notice of the labors of Reverend John Witherspoon, who was a pastor, theologian, and political leader. Stohlman said, "Witherspoon's solid contribution in this pre-Revolutionary era lay in his writing, his speaking, and his understanding that great events of all kinds begin in the minds of men."[47]

---

[44] Trinterud, 254.

[45] Reverend George P. Hays, *Presbyterians: A Popular Narrative of their Origins, Progress, Doctrines, and Achievements* (New York: J. A. Hill & Co. Publishers, 1892), 117.

[46] David Hall, *The Genevan Reformation and the American Founding*, 363.

[47] Martha Lou Lemmon Stohlman, *John Witherspoon: Parson, Politician, Patriot*. (Philadelphia: The Westminster Press, 1976), 107. See Hall, 367-375.

Witherspoon's political influence included involvement in the debate in the Continental Congress over independence. His writings included his "Pastoral Letter" of 1775, which urged Presbyterians to show respect both to King George III and to the resolutions of Congress. Witherspoon even wrote appeals to the British people to hear the colonial cause. Most notably, Witherspoon was the only clergyman to sign the Declaration of Independence. He expressed the depth of his commitment to the cause by saying, "For my own part, of property, I have some; of reputation, more; that reputation is staked, that property is pledged on the issue of this contest. I would infinitely rather my gray hairs descend into the sepulcher by the hand of the executioner than desert at this crisis the sacred cause of my country."[48]

His actions and role in the war resulted in his being burned in effigy by the British. Witherspoon, declared a British officer, was a "political firebrand, who perhaps had not a less share in the Revolution than Washington himself." Another Englishman said that he trembled at the thought of Adams, Franklin, and the 150,000 or so rebels "with Johnny Witherspoon at their head."[49]

Witherspoon also influenced his students at Princeton. John Adams spent time with Witherspoon at Princeton and was favorably impressed with Witherspoon's preaching, but noted that the students "sang as badly as the Presbyterians of New York." Musical talent aside, Witherspoon assured Adams that all the students were "sons of liberty."[50] Among Witherspoon's students were soldiers of whom eleven became captains, six majors, four colonels, and ten lieutenant-colonels. Four of these men died in the war. Seven out of eleven of Witherspoon's students who became chaplains also died in the war.[51]

Sermons played as central a role in this war as did gun powder, perhaps an even greater role. Of the sermons in America's founding era in general, Ellis Sandoz has written, "Preachers interpreted pragmatic events in terms of a political theology imbued with philosophical and revelatory learning. Their sermons also demonstrate the existence and effectiveness of a popular political culture that constantly assimilated the currently urgent political and constitutional issues to the profound insights of the Western spiritual and philosophical traditions."[52]

---

[48] As quoted in Reverend George P. Hays, 120.

[49] Jeffrey H. Morrison, *John Witherspoon and the Founding of the American Republic* (Notre Dame, IN: Notre Dame University Press, 2005), 76-77.

[50] Hall, 369.

[51] Morrison, 77.

[52] Ellis Sandoz, *Political Sermons of the American Founding Era*, 1730-1805. (Indianapolis: Liberty Press, 1991), Foreward, page xiv.

Sandoz's point is aptly supported by the more than 1,500 pages of sermons he includes in his collection, *Political Sermons of the American Founding Era,* but also by the quote at the beginning of his book from John Wingate Thornton: "To the Pulpit, the Puritan Pulpit, we owe the moral force which won our independence." As Paul Johnson noted, "The English church and state lost the political and military battle because they had already lost the religious battle."[53]

David Hall's study of the influence of Calvinism on America's founding also highlights the key influence of sermons. He wrote:

> Thus, it becomes clear that between the Great Awakening in the 1740s and the Declaration of 1776, the pulpit in America was prominent in shaping American notions of liberty, a liberty that was rooted in a divinely created order. We cannot fully understand early orations on this vital topic without understanding their biblical roots. These sermons were not only proclaimed but were also frequently published and distributed to civil magistrates and ministers.[54]

Calvinism and Presbyterian theology were congenial to the cause of American independence.[55] On the one hand, many of the Patriots were the offspring of those who had fought against the English crown and its imposition of Anglicanism upon her subjects. Trinterud gives three convictions held by Calvinists in colonial America.[56] First, traditionally, Calvinists had often asserted the right of a people suffering under a tyrant to resist such tyranny through properly constituted representatives. In Calvin's *Institutes,* book four, section twenty, the issue of opposing lawful authorities was addressed with attention being given to the rights of lesser magistrates (such as colonial legislatures) to oppose the higher authorities. The type of revolution sponsored by mobs in the street, which characterized parts of the French Revolution and others growing out of it, were disapproved by a Calvinistic theology. In contrast colonial legislatures and representative congresses had such a right to resist.[57] The second principle was that no lawful government

---

[53] Johnson, 173.
[54] Hall, 363.
[55] Trinterud, 251.
[56] Trinterud, 252
[57] See David Hall. The classic Calvinistic work on the right to resist an evil tyrant was *Vindiciae Contra Tyrannos*, an anonymously written Huguenot tract of the 16th century. See also Douglas Kelly, *The Emergence of Liberty in the Modern World* (Philipsburg, N.J.: Presbyterian and Reformed Publishing, 1992).

exists without a mutual compact freely entered into by the king and the people. This concept can be found at the root of such events as the signing of Magna Charta, the Puritan Revolution, and the Glorious Revolution of 1688. It is built upon the biblical idea of covenants and of covenant theology.

Gary North wrote, "So common was the covenant-compact theory in the eighteenth century that Jefferson's words in the preamble induced little enthusiasm, pro or con. The idea was taken for granted by patriots and Tories alike; the focus of the debate centered on the legitimacy of the Declaration's claim that King George III had actually violated social compacts with the thirteen colonies.[58] The third concept was that government must be based on a fundamental written law. This concept, like the others, was rooted in much of the history of Britain and the Christian tradition.

Sometimes the influence of Christian theology has been neglected when examining our nation's founding. Locke, whose Christianity is suspect and at the very least highly secularized, and Jefferson, who orthodoxy is highly questionable, were tremendous influences on the founding of our nation. But they do not exist in a secular vacuum. Page Smith has written, "It is a scholarly commonplace to point out how much Jefferson (and his fellow delegates to the Continental Congress) were influenced by Locke. Without disputing this we would simply add than an older and deeper influence—John Calvin—was of more profound importance (or that Locke's consciousness, like Jefferson's was a consequence in large part of the Reformation)."[59]

On to Victory

In the classroom and in the political assembly, America's War for Independence still impacts our political and historical debates. Economic historians have tried to make the case that colonial plantation owners from the southern colonies and merchants from the New England colonies pressed the claims for independence due to the economic straits Britain had them in. Such interpretations are useful, but unconvincing. Sometimes the case is made that the war was fought for such vague concepts as "liberty" and "freedom." When the more political libertarian thinker cites these words, he has in mind liberty and freedom from taxes, mercantilism, and quartering troops. The more social libertarians see the concepts in terms of freedom of the individual to do whatever he wishes with his life and body.

---

[58] Gary North, "The Declaration as a Conservative Document," *The Journal of Christian Reconstruction: Symposium on Christianity and the American Revolution*. (Vallecito, California, Summer 1976), 112-113.

[59] Page Smith, editor, *Religious Origins of the American Revolution*. (Missoula, Montana: Scholars Press, 1976), 185.

The Presbyterian War

The Christian can benefit from the many histories of the American War for Independence. But since man is a theological being—always acting either in direct obedience to God or in rebellion against God—and since the Christian faith was a strong influence in early America, Christians must recover and uncover the Christian influences, people, and directions of our nation's beginnings.

The hodge-podge of an army that peppered and pounded Cornwallis' troops all through the Carolinas and inflicted defeats at Cowpens, King's Mountain, and Guilford Courthouse was largely manned by Presbyterian laymen-soldiers and led by Presbyterian elders and officers, often holding both titles. This same army pursued Cornwallis and his British army to the fateful village of Yorktown. Here they were joined with the Congregationalists from New England and other Presbyterians of the Middle Colonies. Led by the Anglican vestryman George Washington and aided by the Catholic French army and navy, this great ecumenical council ended the main British efforts to subdue the colonies.

Presbyterians do not hold a monopoly on participation in the War for Independence. There were Anglicans, like General Washington, who fought against the British. Baptists, like Isaac Backus, were motivated by the same impulses as the Presbyterians and Congregationalists. Dutch Reformed and German Reformed Christians fought for independence. Lutherans and Catholics, once divided by the Reformation, united together for American independence. Without blindly attributing the victory solely to Presbyterians, Scots-Irish, or even Southerners, it has to be recognized that something in the essence of Calvinistic theology made the difference. Along with being a War for Independence, more than being an American Revolution, more than being a war over tea and taxes, it was a Presbyterian War.

Chapter Twenty-Three
1776 and *Washington's Crossing*

> Remember officers and Soldiers, that you are Freemen, fighting for the blessings of Liberty—that slavery will be your portion, and that of your posterity, if you do not acquit yourself like men.
> —General George Washington, 1776

> I was but the humble Agent of favouring Heaven, whose benign interference was so often manifested in our behalf , and to whom the praise of victory alone is due.
> —General George Washington, 1789

On January 1 of 1777, Robert Morris wrote to George Washington, "The year 1776 is over. I am heartily glad of it and hope you nor America will ever be plagued with such another."[1] History has a way of recasting difficulties as triumphs. It is a perspective that only makes sense if there is something transcendent and beyond the experience of the moment. We live in an age that too often assumes that the pronouncements of the evening news or the findings of the latest poll are the final judgment of truth and reality. Robert Morris showed both a recognition of the miseries of 1776 and the expectation that both America and George Washington would go on to better things.

We celebrate the year 1776. We remember one event of that year—the signing of the Declaration of Independence. The year of 1776 was filled with a number of great events from the War for Independence, including the siege of Boston, the capture and removal of the guns from Fort Ticonderoga, defeat of the American raid on Canada, the defense and loss of New York City, the retreat across New Jersey, and Washington's victories at Trenton and Princeton.

That year began with the focus on the siege and subsequent evacuation of Boston. This was an American victory of sorts. Boston carried lots of

---

[1] David Hackett Fischer, *Washington's Crossing* (New York: Oxford University Press, 2004), 363.

psychological weight for the Patriot cause. The British army was basically bottlenecked there. The British capturing of Breed's Hill (the battle better known Bunker's Hill) was a tactical victory for the crown's cause, but this victory was quite costly for the British in terms of the number of lives taken to acquire that height. It gave the American army a sense of satisfaction at having extracted such a price for real estate. From the British viewpoint, it interjected a sense of caution in General Howe, causing him to refrain from further efforts to break out of Boston.

This caution was heightened when the Americans occupied Dorchester Heights, overlooking Boston proper, and trained the newly acquired field guns on the British positions. For the British, evacuating Boston was simply a change of tactical emphasis. The British army and navy continued to amass strength in both numbers and resolve. The wiser course of action was to shift military operations—after a short interlude—to New York. From there the British could use both land and sea to better direct the war effort toward New England to the north and toward the middle colonies of New York, New Jersey, and Pennsylvania.

The struggle for New York tilted the balance of events strongly in favor of the British. Basically, General Washington was out-fought, out-thought, and outmanned. The capture of Long Island and later the capture of Fort Washington and even later the miserable retreat across New Jersey should have ended a short chapter of rebellion in English colonial rule over North America. Washington and Jefferson and others should have been relegated to footnote status and obscurity, as well as infamy.

Several factors prevented this denouement from coming to a completion. First, Washington began conducting his most often practiced and successful military maneuver—a retreat. This is not as simple as it sounds. A retreat puts an army in a spread out and most vulnerable situation. Communications and supplies are generally not in best order, and the ability to respond to an attack is gravely hindered. In terms of morale, it can be even more devastating: Only losers retreat. Yet Washington's retreat from Long Island was successful. A second factor that made it successful was beyond Washington's control.

David McCullough writes, "Incredibly, yet again, circumstances—fate, luck, Providence, the hand of God, as would be said so often—intervened. Just at daybreak a heavy fog settled over the whole of Brooklyn, concealing everything no less than had the night. It was a fog so thick, remembered a soldier, that one 'could scarcely discern a man at six yards distance.'"[2]

---

[2] David McCullough, *1776* (New York: Simon & Schuster, 2005), 191.

Nine thousand American soldiers escaped across the river during the night and during the morning fog without the loss of a single life. After the troops were safely delivered, the fog lifted, revealing the enemy presence on the shore left behind. Throughout the war, the weather did not always so favor the Patriot cause, but from a historical perspective, we can nudge McCullough's speculation toward certainty: This was the Providential hand of God.

God uses means and God uses men. George Washington was one such man used of God. Washington's personal faith and doctrine are disputable. Depending upon the historian, he has been alternately described as an evangelical Christian believer and as a Deist. He was certainly a theist and a man of conviction about God's governance of the universe and moral order. His theological restraint may have been an indication of a lack of personal faith in Christ or it may have been a characteristic of the times. Even today, many political leaders are guarded in their use of religious language. Whatever the status of Washington's soul, he was certainly gifted by God and used by God in the events of 1776.

Washington is an amazing case study in the category of leaders. He excelled and ultimately succeeded both as a military and political leader. Because of this, he exceeds such men of greater battlefield gifts as Napoleon, Robert E. Lee, U. S. Grant, and Hannibal. Washington never lacked personal bravery and devotion to the cause, but as a military tactician, as a strategist, as an on-the-battlefield commander, Washington's abilities seemed limited. He lost far more battles than he won; he retreated more than he advanced; he commanded men who more closely resembled rabble than armies; his military background and training were limited; and even some of his victories seem more like random lottery winnings than calculated strategic military calculations.

His greatest gift was perseverance. He said, "Perseverance and spirit have done wonders in all ages."[3] He was helped by having some very capable commanders serving under him. These included men like Nathaniel Greene and Henry Knox. Likewise, he was hindered by a few who fancied themselves his superiors and who did not hesitate to convey such sentiments. One in particular was General Charles Lee. As Washington retreated across New Jersey, Lee insubordinately moseyed along on his own with his contingent of soldiers. He was content to let circumstances destroy Washington and advance his own career.

---

[3] Quoted in an unnumbered opening page of McCullough's *1776*.

1776 and Washington's Crossing

Here the British stepped in and, in effect, won the war for America: They captured Lee at a tavern. Washington's response was careful and guarded, but inwardly he must have been delighted. The British were thrilled at any rate, for they ranked General Lee above Washington in their estimation.

Washington held an army together that was lacking almost every ingredient of a successful military unit. It is said that an army moves on its stomach; yet the Continental army was malnourished and constantly in need of food. Pay was sporadic; the soldiers' homes and farms were often nearby and as luring as the sirens of ancient myth; with defeats, retreats, and betrayals, the cause usually seemed lost; and the middle colonies were increasingly coming under the sway and flags of the British army. On paper, Washington's army numbered around 18,000 or a little more than half that of the British. But those numbers belied the true situation. Desertions and illness claimed many of the soldiers. In reality, Washington retreated across the Delaware River with only about 3,000 men,[4] and many of these were nearing the end of their enlistments.

On the south shores of the Delaware River, the Patriot cause survived thanks to Washington's command and initiative. From here he launched his famous crossing of the Delaware River on Christmas night, leading to his attack on the Hessian command stationed at Trenton. The crossing was slow, dangerous, miserably cold, and risky. Two of the columns that were to participate in the attack were turned back by delays and weather. The march to Trenton was likewise slow and miserably cold. The attack began sometime after daybreak rather than before as Washington had hoped for. The resulting victory was much greater than he had imagined.

In this short battle, Washington's troops killed twenty-one enemy soldiers, wounded ninety more, and captured approximately nine hundred more. On the American side, the actual casualties in battle were four wounded and none killed.[5] From this initial victory, Washington went on to conduct a spirited defense against a British counterattack. Once again, Washington showed his skill in retreating from the battlefield in the night, leaving the British poised against mere vacated campfires. But rather than simply retreating from battle, he swung his army north of Trenton where he surprised another British unit at Princeton, winning another victory and netting an additional three hundred prisoners. Only then did Washington take his victorious army back across the Delaware River.

---

[4] Larry Schweikart and Michael Allen, *A Patriot's History of the United States*. (New York: Sentinel, 2004) 79.

[5] McCullough, 281.

In this particular campaign, Washington dominated the campaign and confounded his enemy in a manner worthy of such military greats as Hannibal or Stonewall Jackson. Up to this point, his success had consisted of avoiding total defeat and somehow holding his ragged troops together through thin and thinner. But in this case, Washington's offensive kept his army moving swiftly as a sword, keeping the British forces unbalanced at a time when the war was thought to be all but won by the British.

The winter of the American soldiers' discontent turned into the means of victory for the American cause. David Hackett Fischer writes,

> Americans have known many dark days, from the starving times in the early settlements to the attack on the World Trade Center. These were the testing times and the pivotal moments of our history. It was that way in 1776, after the decision for independence and the military disasters in New York. In early December, British commanders believed that they were very close to ending the rebellion, and American leaders feared that they may be right. Then came a reversal of fortune, and three months later the mood changed on both sides. By the spring of 1777, many British officers had concluded that they could never win the war. At the same time, Americans recovered from their despair and were confident that they would not be defeated. That double transformation was truly a turning point in the war.[6]

This story of America's struggle for independence and its triumphs in the face of incredible adversities should never grow dull or dim in the American mind. Our school children should be taught this story repeatedly. Adults need the story as much as children. The ever-present prophets of defeat and 'nattering nabobs of negativism' (to use the late Spiro Agnew's only memorable phrase) can best be countered by recalling our own history. Whether coming from the morally hollowed-out eastern liberal establishment, the cynical and anti-American wings of the media, or even from overly pessimistic conservatives and defeat-oriented Christians, we need to be rescued from such by the perspective of history the year 1776 gives us.

David McCullough's book *1776* and David Hackett Fischer's *Washington's Crossing* overlap in their coverage of the glorious days of our country's beginnings. Both books are excellent and well-written accounts of those times. Both writers have previous works that are related to these topics. McCullough's

---

[6] Fischer, 363.

biography of John Adams is a landmark example of excellent historical writing and of a great, though somewhat overshadowed, Founding Father. Fischer's *Paul Revere's Ride* gives a fuller account of a story that goes beyond Longfellow's poem. He also aptly deals with the greater issues and events, political and theological, which led to the war.

Christian influences in the war are highlighted in both McCullough's and Fischer's recent works. For example, Fischer points out that "the hard core of the Revolutionary movement in New Jersey consisted of English speaking Calvinists." He goes on to reference a comment by Lutheran minister Nicholas Collins who said, "By God there will never be any peace till the Whigs and Presbyterians are cut off."[7] McCullough cites the British General James Grant as saying, "If a good bleeding can bring those Bible-faced Yankees to their senses, the fever of independency should soon abate."[8] No doubt General Grant recognized the connection between the theology found in the Continental Army and the issue of independence.

Dr. Benjamin Rush, a signer of the Declaration of Independence, a member of the Continental Congress, and a physician who set up a field hospital for the American army, spoke quite brilliantly when he said, "Our republics cannot exist long in prosperity. We require adversity and appear to possess most of the republican spirit when most depressed."[9] The history of our country bears out the truth of Rush's statement. Times like 1776 or September 11, 2001 demonstrate that depressed times and events make for the most glorious history and successes of our republic. The glory and success, of course, have to be seen from a historical perspective.

---

[7] Fischer, 162.
[8] McCullough, 179.
[9] Fischer, 143.

Chapter Twenty-Four
A Southern Perspective

> Young men, the God of your fathers is a just
> And merciful God Who in this blood once shed
> On your green altar measures out all days,
> And measures out the grace
> Whereby alone we live;
> And in His might He waits,
> Brooding within the certitude of time,
> To bring this lost forsaken valor
> And the fierce faith undying
> And the love quenchless
> To flower among the hills to which we cleave,
> To fruit upon the mountains whither we flee,
> Never forsaking, never denying
> His children and His children's children forever
> Unto all generations of the faithful heart.
>
> —Donald Davidson, "Lee in the Mountains, 1865-1870"

The men in the book of Nehemiah had to rebuild the walls of Jerusalem. They also had to be armed against the surrounding enemies. And they had a third task, removing the rubble from the then ruined walls of the past. Christian teachers have a similar challenge. We are rebuilding the walls of Christian culture, but our students must also be taught apologetics so that they can defend the faith. Amidst all this work, we have the accumulated educational rubble that has to be removed as well.

Christian education in its different facets must seek to correct the cultural deficiencies of America. It must do so by teaching Christian doctrine, Christian history, and Christian thinking skills. Christian education is all about heritage because it is all about what the future will look like. Whether the return of Christ is in short order, as the belief of many is, or whether it is more long term, as my belief is, we must be faithfully laboring about our duties and occupy until Christ comes.

One of the great deficiencies in our day is godly leadership in the state and church. We long to have leaders like the sons of Issachar (1 Chronicles 12:32), who understand the times and know "what Israel ought to do."

Cultural, moral, and spiritual breakdown in our society demonstrates God's judgment on the unbelief and evil rebellion of our own and recent generations; nevertheless, with this judgment also comes blessings. Herbert Schlossberg said, "There is a sense in which judgment that issues in catastrophe is the only way for good to come, inasmuch as it entails the erasure of evil....Only when judgment falls, said the prophet, will people 'cast forth their idols of silver and their idols of gold'(Isaiah 2:20)."[1] God's judgment brings blessings because it forces Christians to re-examine themselves and their doctrinal standards (1 Timothy 4:16).

Many Christians have discovered that modern-day evangelicalism lacks roots or depth. Pastor and author John MacArthur points out the weaknesses and absurdities of modern churches which rely on "music, skits, multimedia, and other means of communication to convey the message." He continues:

> Almost nothing is dismissed as inappropriate: rock'n'roll oldies, disco tunes, heavy metal, rap, dancing, comedy, clowns, mime artists, and stage magic have all become part of the evangelical repertoire. In fact, one of the few things judged out of place in church these days is clear and forceful preaching.[2]

The waters of me-first, humanistic, entertainment-oriented religion have proven to be shallow and bitter. This is like the days of the prophet Jeremiah when the Lord spoke saying, "For my people have committed two evils: They have forsaken Me, the fountain of living waters, And hewn themselves cisterns—broken cisterns that can hold no water" (Jeremiah 2:13). There are Christians crying out for and rediscovering the fountain of living waters. The Reformation slogan "sola Scriptura," that is, Scripture alone, sounds again in the pulpit and pew with a call for a biblical, authoritative theology. The need is for a theological compass that points to the Word of God.

Such a theology has been part of the Christian church for centuries. We have no need to invent it, but only to rediscover it. So, we must return to the theology of the 16th century Protestant Reformation. The Reformation was

---

[1] Herbert Schlossberg, *Idols for Destruction—Christian Faith and Its Confrontation With American Society* (Nashville: Thomas Nelson Publishers, 1983), 295.

[2] John F. MacArthur, *Ashamed of the Gospel: When the Church Becomes Like the World* (Wheaton: Crossway Books, 1993), 46.

not an innovation or creation of new doctrines, but a reforming according to the pattern or blueprint of Scripture. The theology and polity of the corrupt church of the late Medieval era had to be reformed with biblical theology. The writings of Luther and especially of Calvin which restructured Christian thinking in the 1600s and following are being reprinted and read, and not by sheltered academics, but by pastors and laymen who are applying the ideas in their churches, homes, and society. Confessional Christianity is re-emerging from the ashes of individualism and doctrinal confusion, although the numbers of followers are small. The Westminster Confession of Faith and the Larger and Shorter Catechism, the historic creeds of Presbyterianism, along with related documents from other Reformed groups are shaping the thoughts of a new generation.

The study and rediscovery of Biblical theology leads to the rediscovery of church history. Theology and history are inseparable. Indeed, the ultimate book on theology—the Bible—is a book of history. God revealed Himself in the historical events in the Old Testament. In the New Testament, Jesus Christ, the incarnate Son of God, appeared. As the Apostle John said, "And the Word became flesh and dwelt among us, and we beheld His glory, the glory as of the only begotten of the Father, full of grace and truth." (John 1:14) As King of kings and Lord of lords, Jesus not only was a historical person, He is the Lord of history. The hymn "Crown Him With Many Crowns" rightly proclaims Him "the Potentate of Time." As Gordon Clark noted, "If the second person of the Triune God actually became flesh and dwelt among us, and died on the cross for men, that event would naturally overshadow every other aspect of the world, scientific or historical."[3] And as Clark and many of us affirm, such did happen and history then revolves around Christ's work. History since the New Testament era simply unveils the advance of Christ's kingdom in this world. Church historian Philip Schaff said, "The central current and ultimate aim of universal history is the Kingdom of God established by Jesus Christ."[4]

We are all products of our history, whether we know that history or not. C. S. Lewis said, "The unhistorical are usually, without knowing it, enslaved to a fairly recent past."[5] Reformational theology breaks those chains of enslavement to that fairly recent past and reconnects believers with the strong chain

---

[3] Gordon H. Clark, *A Christian View of Men and Things: An Introduction to Philosophy* (Grand Rapids: Baker Book House, 1981 reprint), 80.

[4] Philip Schaff, *History of the Christian Church, Volume One: Apostolic Christianity*. (Grand Rapids: William B. Eerdmans Publishing Company, 1910, reprinted 1978), 3.

[5] C.S. Lewis, *De Descriptione Temporum*, (London: Geoffrey Bles, 1962), 23. Statement given as quoted in Schlossberg, *Idols For Destruction*, 36.

of historical Protestantism, which reconnected the chain to the Scriptures. Reformed Christians need to be historically, as well as theologically, equipped to give a defense of their position (1 Peter 3:15). They have to know and explain the meaning of the word "Reformed," the issues of the Reformation, and the reasons why the name "Calvinism" came to be attached to the doctrines of grace. Reformed Christians, or Calvinists, must know what they believe and why they believe it, but they also must know the history of that belief.

The study of church history since the Reformation reveals the surges and declines of Calvinistic or Biblical theology. The Reformation itself, the first of these movements, spawned a series of spiritual and political upheavals throughout Europe. In the Netherlands and France, fierce struggles ensued. While the Dutch Calvinists prevailed over their Spanish Catholic overlords, the French Huguenots were subdued or forced to flee from the Catholic religious and political establishment to England, the Netherlands, or the North American English colonies. In England, the Puritan movement arose. This movement led to the translation of the King James Version of the Bible, the Cromwellian Revolution, the settlement of the New England colonies, and the writing of a massive collection of Puritan literary works ranging from John Bunyan's *Pilgrim's Progress* to John Owen's theological works.[6]

To the north, the Scottish Covenanters, following in the footsteps of the intrepid John Knox, proclaimed unto death when necessary, the crown rights of King Jesus. Whereas the Reformers declared against a tyrannical state church that Christ alone saves, the Covenanters declared against a tyrannical king that Christ alone rules.[7] Into the American colonies, a flood of religious refugees were poured from the cauldron of European religious upheavals. John Winthrop, first governor of the Puritan-dominated Massachusetts Bay Colony, spoke of building a city set on a hill for all the world to see.[8] Christians of different denominations commonly united around basically Reformed theological tenets and dominated the landscape from present-day Maine to Georgia.

---

[6] For an excellent account of the political and religious events of the period of the Reformation up through the restoration of King Charles II of England, read Otto Scott's *The Great Christian Revolution* (Vallecito, California, Ross House Books, 1991). Other contributors to this book discuss the theological struggle between Calvinism and Arminianism. Scott's portion covers about two-thirds of the book.

[7] Jock Purves, *Fair Sunshine: Character Studies of the Scottish Covenanters* (Edinburgh: the Banner of Truth Trust, 1982). This book contains exciting historical and devotional reading that stirs the believer to greater faith and works.

[8] Former President Ronald Reagan loved Winthrop's phrase and often used it. Reagan was very postmillennial in his vision of America.

Yale history professor Sidney E. Ahlstrom has been previously cited as saying that "Puritanism provided the moral and religious background of fully 75 percent of the people who declared independence in 1776."[9] Other historians concur. Fred Hood points out that in the middle and southern states, Reformed denominations, specifically Presbyterians, Dutch Reformed, and German Reformed, were the largest sector in 1780. In time, as Baptists and Methodists gained in numbers, the Reformed clergy's educational attainments gained them both national significance and a cultural impact.[10] Paul K. Conkin said,

> Because of the patterns of migration to early America, the largest number of colonists came from the state churches of Britain (Anglican and Presbyterian). Whether orthodox Calvinists or not, they traced their origins back to John Calvin, to his close associates, or to the church order he helped establish in Geneva. Such a tradition informed the four largest colonial denominations, all of British origin (Anglican, Congregational, Presbyterian, and Separate Baptists), and two much smaller continental transplants (Dutch Reformed and German Reformed).[11]

After the colonial settlements, which led to all sorts of theological controversies and arrangements, the next big movement generally noted by historians was the Great Awakening. This was a series of revivals in the colonies that lasted from the 1730s through the 1740s. Two men, strangely contrasting in style, characterized this movement. Jonathan Edwards, Congregationalist pastor from Northampton, Massachusetts, and the descendant of a long line of Puritan preachers, solemnly read his image-packed message entitled "Sinners in the Hands of an Angry God" to a neighboring congregation. The crowd erupted, not from a theatrical performance, for Edwards's style was subdued, but from the Spirit's work of conviction, and revival followed. Edwards, a man devoted to a life of study and philosophical interests, both encouraged the revival and attempted to restrain its more emotional tendencies. George Whitefield, an English preacher who once sought a career on the stage, toured the American colonies repeatedly and drew incredibly

---

[9] Sidney E. Ahlstrom, *A Religious History of the American People* (New Haven and London: Yale University Press, 1973), 124.

[10] Fred J. Hood, *Reformed America: The Middle and Southern States, 1783-1837* (University, Alabama: The University of Alabama Press, 1980), 3.

[11] Paul K. Conkin, *The Uneasy Center: Reformed Christianity in Antebellum America* (Chapel Hill: The University of North Carolina Press, 1995), 32.

large crowds. Whitefield was the more powerful preacher; Edwards the more powerful intellect. Both preached a Calvinistic theology.[12]

The Second Great Awakening of the 1820s and 30s saw less emphasis on Calvinistic theology and more on emotion. It tightened the tensions that were already creating theogical struggles among American Christian churches. One of those struggles was over the balance between intellectual theology and emotional pietism. A greater tension was between Calvinistic theology and Arminianism. The battle was best illustrated by the opposite theologies and revival methods of Calvinistic evangelist Asahel Nettleton and Arminian evangelist Charles G. Finney.[13]

While these theological movements are well known, documented and studied by Christians, another chapter of the story of American Christianity has not received as much attention. That chapter covers Christian influences in the Old South.

Few have known and understood the theological significance and accomplishments of the Old South. For some, the Old South is ignored because of its defeat in the War for Southern Independence. Not only have winners written the history, but also many readers have read only the winners. Any significance Southern history might have lies buried beneath the banners and stacked weapons at Appomattox. Eric McKitrick has stated that "nothing is more susceptible to oblivion than an argument, however ingenious, that has been discredited by events."[14]

For some, Southern Christianity evokes images of a sweaty, red-faced, Bible-thumping fundamentalist preacher pounding a pulpit and screaming at an enraptured congregation of men in overalls and women in bonnets. Or bluegrass gospel groups singing "in the sweet by and by." Or all shapes and varieties of holiness and Pentecostal groups shouting, rolling, and even barking in religious frenzies. Or the extreme example of fanatical believers handling rattlesnakes. In fact, a marvelous story of snake handlers is given in

---

[12]. See the following books: Ian Murray, *Jonathan Edwards: A New Biography* (Edinburgh: The Banner of Truth Trust, 1987) and Arnold Dallimore, *George Whitefield: The Life and Times of the Great Evangelist of the 18th Century Revival,* 2 volumes (Edinburgh: The Banner of Truth Trust, 1975).

[13] George Marsden, *Fundamentalism and American Culture—The Shaping of Twentieth Century Evangelicalism, 1870-1925* (New York: Oxford University Press, 1980), 7. Also, see Keith J. Hardman, *Charles Grandison Finney, 1792-1875, Revivalist and Reformer* (Grand Rapids: Baker Book House, 1990) and J.F. Thornbury, *God Sent Revival: The Story of Asahel Nettleton and the Second Great Awakening* (Grand Rapids: Evangelical Press, 1977).

[14] Eric McKitrick, *Slavery Defended: The Views of the Old South* (Englewood Cliffs, New Jersey, 1963), pp. 1-2. As quoted in James Oscar Farmer, Jr., *The Metaphysical Confederacy—James Henley Thornwell and the Synthesis of Southern Values* (Macon: Mercer University Press, 1986), 1.

Dennis Covington's personal account of being involved with such a group. He writes,

> One night in East Tennessee, a snake-handling preacher came up to us and said, "You boys got any snakes in that car?" We told him we didn't.
> "What? You mean to tell me you don't have any rattlesnakes in your car?"
> "No, sir."
> His eyes widened. 'What's the matter with you boys?' he said. 'Are you crazy?'[15]

Southern religion does seem to have more than its share of craziness. It is hard to know whether the stereotypes or the realities are worse. People tend to think of Southerners as people who are fiercely religious, but just as fiercely anti-intellectual; a people who believes every word of the King James Bible as they believe Jesus spoke it, but who are too illiterate and untheological to read and properly exegete the Bible; a people who know nothing of the Protestant Reformation and who think Martin Luther was a black civil rights leader of the 1960's. Jokes abound of rural Southern Christians rejecting the educated minister who refers to commentators while preaching to a congregation who only knows of "sweet potaters and arsh potaters," and who offends his congregation by referring to exegesis, because they don't believe in "no extra Jesus."

What is the religious history of the South? How central is it to understanding Southern culture? What difference does it make? How do we connect the religious history of the South with its political history and defeat? Richard Weaver in his excellent defense of the culture and ideas of the South titled *The Southern Tradition at Bay*, said, "The Old South may indeed be a hall hung with splendid tapestries in which no one would care to live; but from them we can learn something of how to live."[16] The South has been described as a region "haunted by God."[17]

---

[15] Dennis Covington. *Salvation on Sand Mountain* (Reading, MA: Addison-Wesley Publishing Company, 1995), 1.

[16] Richard M. Weaver, *The Southern Tradition at Bay: A History of Postbellum Thought* (Washington: Regnery Gateway, 1989), 380.

[17] The actual statement comes from Flannery O'Connor, who says that the South is "Christ-haunted" in her essay "Some Aspects of the Grotesque in Southern Fiction." (Found in *Mystery and Manners.*)

Southern thinkers and writers, whether historians, novelists, or theologians, have recognized the deep Christian roots of the Old South. Christianity is as inescapable from Southern life as humidity. No air conditioners of modernity can forever shield the Southerner from a confrontation with the historic faith of Jesus Christ. However much the modern age and the dominance of faddish and alien philosophies seek to root out the vestiges of Christianity, new growth keeps shooting up with the return of spring.

The Pulitzer Prize winning Mississippi novelist William Faulkner said, "In the South, the past isn't history. It isn't even past."[18] And for the Southerner, that past is more than just the Confederacy: it is Christianity. Weaver said the Old South was "the last non-materialist civilization in the Western World."[19] He could have said it was, at least in some respects, the last Christian civilization in the Western world. The subject of the South as a cultural entity with a distinctively Christian worldview must be examined and discussed.

To call the South "Christian" is not meant to imply that all Southerners were or ever have been Christians. Neither is it meant as a description of Southern character and behavior.[20] The South was Christian in its presuppositions or its worldview. As George Garrett has written:

> The primarily Protestant, and certainly Christian, base of the Southern social structure—and thus, also, of the social fabric of Southern life—begins with the assumption and acceptance of the universal equality of original sin....All men are immortal souls, equally fractured by sin....At his deepest level of knowing, the Southerner expects this world—filled as it is with fallen fellow creatures, creatures who are, to a greater or lesser extent, depraved—expects the world to be a violent place, as brutal and savage as conditions will allow.[21]

---

[18] William Faulkner, *Requiem for a Nun*.

[19] Weaver, 375.

[20] For a good description of Southern character and conduct, see Grady McWhiney, *Cracker Culture: Celtic Ways in the Old South* (Tuskaloosa: University of Alabama Press, 1988).

[21] George Garrett, "Southern Literature" from *Why the South will Survive: Fifteen Southerners Look at Their Region a Half Century after I'll Take My Stand* (Athens: The University of Georgia Press, 1983), 138. Nearly every contributor to this collection of essays made reference to the religious nature of the South.

A Southern Perspective

Many assume since the South lost the War for Southern Independence,[22] the South has little or nothing to offer outside of a negative example. Professor Eugene D. Genovese said, "The Northern victory in 1865 silenced a discreetly Southern interpretation of American history and national identity, and it promoted a contemptuous dismissal of all things Southern as nasty, racist, immoral, and intellectually inferior."[23]

Even some Southern politicians, regrettably oblivious to history and pandering for media approval, seek to remove remaining remnants of their Southern heritage found on monuments and flags that testify to their state's involvement in the Confederacy. Even where history is less than honorable or praiseworthy, it should not be suppressed. Whether a person agrees with the goals and conduct of the Southern Confederacy, they should not suppress the history of the events related to it.

Many think of the South as the land that gave America slavery, the nullification crisis, the Secession movement, the worst war in our whole history, resistance to the benevolence of the Federal government Radical Reconstruction program, the Ku Klux Klan, opposition to modern science (as displayed in the Scopes Trial), opposition to Civil Rights, lynchings, shootings, and other types of murders of Negroes, fanatical opposition to racial integration, and chewing tobacco, snuff, and cigarettes. The only good people from the South are those that repudiate the South. Some find the South a social and cultural embarrassment to the world. A meeting of the Arkansas historians I once attended contained many negative comments about the South, in particular Arkansas. Quotes from Arkansawyers upholding the Old South were sneeringly laughed at, but the crowd was quite pleased with the political leadership at that time which hailed from Arkansas.

---

[22] The War fought from 1861 to 1865 has never been completely resolved. Even deciding what to call it is contested. Many Southerners think the name "War for Southern Independence" much more aptly describes it than the name "Civil War." By definition, it was not a civil war. Missouri experienced civil war from 1861-1865 as two factions struggled to control that state's government, but the Confederacy was not interested in controlling the United States government. "All we ask," President Jefferson Davis said, "is to be left alone." (Notice how little regard the current government pays to that request.) The name "War Between the States," that is the Confederate States and the United States, is also a name favored by Southerns, although we have been known to call it "The War of Northern Aggression."

For some enjoyable and thought-provoking reading on this topic, see *The South Was Right* by James Ronald Kennedy and Walter Donald Kennedy (Gretna, Louisiana: Pelican Publishing Company, 1994) and *Southern By the Grace of God* by Michael Andrew Grissom (Gretna, Louisiana: Pelican Publishing Company, 1994).

[23] Eugene D. Genovese, *The Southern Tradition: The Achievement and Limitations of American Conservatism* (Cambridge: Harvard University Press, 1994), preface xi.

The answer is not an inordinate Southern, Celtic, or Confederate pride. Pride, as expressed in political terms, is nationalism. Christians can be patriots, but not nationalists, in the sense of exalting their nation above all things. Nationalism is wrong when directed at the country as a whole ("My country right or wrong.") or at a particular segment of the country ("the South right or wrong.") Salvation is not achieved by clinging to some mythical historical era or some nation-state, but sanctification is not achieved by suppressing the works of God in certain historical eras, even when those works were not totally pure or consistent. No doubt both Joseph and Daniel ruled over realms that were filled with many things inconsistent with their covenant belief in God.

Southerners must reconsider our heritage, not so we can re-fight the battles of the past century, but so we can discover any remnant of the past useful for our own battles of this century. From the anvil of defeat, we can forge the weapons of our future victory.

Richard Weaver said:

> The South possesses an inheritance which it has imperfectly understood and little used. It is in the curious position of having been right without realizing the grounds of its rightness.[24]

It is time to understand and use our inheritance. The time has come to realize the grounds upon which Southern culture was right. Weaver said the South was a "refuge of sentiments and values, of spiritual congeniality, of belief in the word, of reverence for symbolism, whose existence haunts the nation."[25]

In short, the South must return to God, to the Christian faith of its fathers, to the spiritual heritage of the past. The South must become more than a refuge, but rather a stronghold of sentiments and values based on the standard of God's law, and a community of spiritual belief in the saving gospel of Jesus Christ, and a land that reverences the symbols of faith, family and the land. Drew Gilpin Faust said, "The most fundamental source of legitimation for the Confederacy was Christianity. Religion provided a transcendent framework for Southern nationalism."[26] The failure of the South should provide only insights and inspiration for the future.

---

[24] Weaver, 373.
[25] Weaver, 375.
[26] Drew Gilpin Faust, *The Creation of Southern Nationalism: Ideology and Identity in the Civil War South* (Baton Rouge: Louisiana State University Press, 1988), 22.

What about those who are reading this who are not Southerners or even Southern sympathizers? What stake do you have in this? Christians do not all have to have a deep interest in the history and religion of the South, but Christians must be concerned about truth and history. The hope can never be for a Christian South, but for the greater kingdom of Christ wherever it advances, reforms, or revives. Everything said about New England in this book is premised on the hope that Christian churches there will revive and return to their Puritan heritage. The same is true for whatever has been said about Europe, and of course, that same hope is for the South. The hope for a Christian South is a part of a hope for a Christian America, and that is part of a hope for a Christian world.[27]

The eleven states that banded together in 1861 were not the first Southern Confederacy. Another existed centuries before. Like the Southern Confederacy, it received many blessings from God, but also like our Confederacy, its sins were as scarlet. We refer to the southern kingdom of Judah in the Old Testament. The Biblical account of the spiritual revivals and apostasies of Judah inform and instruct us to this day (2 Timothy 3:16). The story of Judah transcends regional and local history. From the tribe of Judah came the Lord Jesus Christ, the Son of God, the Savior of the World. From the South needs to come the message of this same Jesus, who is still Lord of lords, King of kings, and the only Hope of this world.

Weaver says that it is from the South that the "revolutionary impulse of our future" is developing.[28] That impulse must be a new reformation that will build upon the foundations of that greater and previous Reformation. With reformation must come repentance: repentance for our neglect of our spiritual heritage, repentance for our sins against one another (including racial sins committed by all races), and repentance for our many sins as individuals, communities, churches, families, and as a nation. Like the Jews in the book of Nehemiah, we need to remove the rubble, rebuild the walls, defend our-

---

[27] See Psalm 2:8; Psalm 72: 8-11; Daniel 4:35, 44; Daniel 7: 13-14, 27; Zechariah 14: 7; Matthew 13: 24-43; John 3:16-17; and consider the Biblical basis for Postmillenialism, which was a predominant view of Southern theologians in the 19th century. See James Jordan's article "A Survey of Southern Presbyterian Millenial Views Before 1830" as found in *The Journal of Christian Reconstruction: Symposium on the Millenium*, Volume 3, Number 2, 1976-77. The following books are useful for further study: Ken Gentry, *He Shall Have Dominion* (Tyler, Texas: Institute for Christian Economics, 1992) and Ian Murray, *The Puritan Hope: A Study of Revival and the Interpretation of Prophecy* (Edinburgh: The Banner of Truth Trust, 1975), John Jefferson Davis, *Christ's Victorious Kingdom: Postmillenialism Reconsidered* (Grand Rapids: Baker Book House, 1986), and Rousas John Rushdoony. *God's Plan for Victory: The Meaning of Postmillennialism* (Fairfax, Virginia: Thoburn Press, 1977).

[28] Weaver, 375.

selves against our enemies (chapters 1-6), but we also need to re-establish spiritual priorities, develop spiritual leaders (chapter 7), once again listen to and apply the Law-Word of God (chapter 8), and acknowledge God as our Creator, Ruler, Judge, and Saviour (chapter 9). The prayer of the Levites of Nehemiah 9 concludes with a message proper for us:

> Here we are, servants today!
> And the land you gave to our fathers,
> To eat its fruit and its good things,
> Here we are servants in it!
> And it yields much increase to the kings
> You have set over us,
> Because of our sin
> Also they have dominion over our
> bodies and our cattle
> At their pleasure,
> And we are in great distress.
> (Nehemiah 9:36-37)

The Importance of *Southern Presbyterian Leaders* by Dr. Henry Alexander White

Originally this book was published by the Neale Publishing Company of New York in 1911 and it was reprinted in 2000 by Banner of Truth. The front cover of the dust jacket of the original edition described the author, Henry Alexander White, D. D., as the author of *The Pentateuch in the Light of Ancient Monuments, Robert E. Lee and the Southern Confederacy,* and *The History of South Carolina.* He was a well known educator, writer, historian, and minister through the Southern states. He was educated at Washington and Lee University, Union Theological Seminary, and Princeton Seminary. From 1899 to 1902 he was Professor of History at Washington and Lee University, and later held a professorship at Columbia Theological Seminary in South Carolina.[29]

Dr. White was an excellent writer and historian. Simply put, this book is good reading. The content of this book should appeal to more than just those who are Southerners, Presbyterians, or both. Christians of various theological and denominational backgrounds would find this book useful.

---

[29] Found on the dust jacket of the original edition.

Christians outside of the South or the United States would be strengthened to read these accounts of great men of God. Students either homeschooling or attending Christian school would find this useful supplemental reading in American or church history studies. Pastors, ministerial students, historians, and other members of the educated class would profit from this book. Even non-Christians need to read this. They need to know that it was the Christian faith that undergirded the establishment of this nation and the ill-fated Confederacy of 1861-1865.

Southern Presbyterian Leaders recounts the stories of the people who settled the South. Dr. White says,

> Thus came the Presbyterians from Ireland and, also, directly from Scotland to the western borders of the American colonies. *They knew how to use the axe and the rifle. They carried with them the Bible, the Westminster Confession of Faith, and the Catechisms.* [Emphasis added] Just before the American Revolution, houses and churches and schoolhouses were built in what was then the western part of the country among the mountains of Virginia and among the hills near the mountains in the Carolinas and Georgia.[30]

These Scots-Irish and Scottish settlers knew how to "use the axe"; that is, they knew how to work. "Six days shall you labor" was as much a part of their theology as the Sabbath rest.[31] Clearing a wilderness and turning it into farmland is hard work.[32] They expected no government subsidies or handouts and received none. They also knew how to use the rifle.[33] They hunted for food, and no doubt also shot whatever kind of varmints were lurking around the homeplace or in the cornfield. These men knew how to use the rifle to defend their homes and farms against two-legged varmints also,

---

[30] White, *Southern Presbyterian Leaders*, 31.

[31] John Murray, *Principles of Conduct: Aspects of Biblical Ethics* (Grand Rapids: William B. Eerdmans Publishing Company, seventh printing 1978), Chapter 4 "The Ordinance of Labor", 82-106.

[32] On the day I originally wrote this sentence (June 5, 1995), I had worked that morning in my garden, hoeing weeds in the hot summer sun. Every experience like that makes me wonder how men cleared the wilderness and created farmland.

[33] Our political leaders and bureaucrats, or the federal government emissaries, armed and clerical, (to use R.L. Dabney's term as found in *Discussions, Vol. 4*, p. 42) reassure us that they will protect our Second Amendment Right to have hunting rifles. The ownership and use of weapons for hunting forms no part of the Second Amendment. Instead, that falls under the Ninth Amendment. The Second Amendment recognizes the right of the militia, the general population of the states, to have weapons to protect themselves against an oppressive government.

especially the red-coat variety that lurked around under the authority of King George. Originally, men of the congregations, even the ministers, brought their guns to church to protect the group against possible Indian attacks. Later, when the American War for Independence began, Southern Presbyterian men picked up their rifles and followed their church elders into battle. Many a British soldier in the Carolina's felt the sting of Presbyterian lead. White describes Pastor William Graham urging the men of Rockbridge county, Virginia, to enlist in the army. When only a few responded, "Graham walked out from the crowd and offered himself a soldier." [34] A large number of men then signed up and made Graham their captain.

The work ethic and the courage of these people were built upon their belief in the Bible, specifically in the God of the Bible (Nehemiah 4:14). The Westminster Confession of Faith both defined their understanding of the Scriptures and tightly regulated their faithfulness to the Scriptures. As the Confession says in its first chapter:

> The authority of the Holy Scripture, for which it ought to be believed, and obeyed, dependeth not upon the testimony of any man, or church; but wholly upon God (who is truth itself) the author thereof: and therefore it is to be received, because it is the Word of God. (paragraph IV)

> The supreme judge by which all controversies of religion are to be determined, and all decrees of councils, opinions of ancient writers, doctrines of men, and private spirits, are to be examined, and in whose sentence we are to rest, can be no other but the Holy Spirit speaking in the Scripture. (paragraph X)

Ahlstrom says that the Westminster Confession became "the most influential doctrinal symbol in American religious history."[35] The Confession undergirded the thought of the people and their ministers. Matthew Dziennik, commenting on the influence of the ministers, said, "Ministers took on secular appointments as community leaders in a greater way. Churches also became courts and the maintenance of order in a given community was largely contingent on the social constraints by the individual minister and Presbytery."[36] Religious life was not segregated or compartmentalized, but was all encompassing.

---

[34] White, 131.
[35] Ahlstrom, 131.
[36] Matthew Dziennik, "How Can the Term Scotch-Irish be Meaningfully Understood?" Unpublished manuscript.

These people also had the Westminster Larger and Shorter Catechism. The Catechisms were not only used for their own instruction, but for the instruction of their children. They were future oriented. They believed in the covenant blessings of God to their children and children's children as promised in Scripture.[37] They built schools because they wanted educated children. The schools were not identified as Christian, rather, they were assumed to be such. Such schools never were neutral, but were rigorous.

White gives this description of the education of the famed Virginia theologian Robert L. Dabney:

> Soon after attaining the age of seven years he began the study of Latin in a school-house built of logs near his father's house. The teacher was his older brother, Charles William Dabney. The study of Greek was begun in another log building soon after he entered the twelfth year of age. These studies were continued until the year 1835; then a few months of special training in algebra and geometry, under the care of Rev. James Wharey, a Presbyterian minister, made young Robert ready for the sophomore class in Hampden-Sidney College.[38]

Dabney was in college at age 16, already having a background in two foreign languages.[39] Presbyterian ministers were required to be educated; furthermore, they started schools, colleges, and seminaries. In some cases, they privately tutored students. They promoted classical Christian education, which is reviving in popularity among some Christians today. White also recounts how a young man named James Waddell was prepared for the ministry by his teacher John Todd:

---

[37] Robert R. Booth, *Children of the Promise: The Biblical Case for Infant Baptism* (Phillipsburg, New Jersey, 1995).

[38] White, page 382.

[39] Buy and read anything by Robert L. Dabney. *The Life and Campaigns of Lt. Gen. T.J. "Stonewall" Jackson* and *A Defense of Virginia and the South* (both have been reprinted by Sprinkle Publications, Harrisonburg, Virginia) are two of the best books on the War for Southern Independence. Dabney's four volume *Discussions* (also reprinted by Sprinkle Publications) and his work on systematic theology, entitled *Lectures in Systematic Theology,* are also great. In the 19th century, Dabney had almost prophetic insight into the political and theological heresies that would develop in the 20th century.

[40] White, pages 59-60.

[41] Instead of Christians and conservative politicians talking about putting prayer back in government controlled public schools, they should take their children and their tax money out of government controlled public schools.

In that academy in the forest, John Todd trained him (James Waddell) in the Latin, Greek, and Hebrew languages, and in "the sciences of rhetoric, logic, ontology, moral and natural philosophy and astronomy." On these subjects he was examined by the Hanover Presbytery and "on sundry branches of learning" in addition. His examination embraced "divinity" or theology, also. He wrote a thesis in Latin and an exegesis of a portion of the Greek text of one of Paul's epistles; he delivered a popular lecture, preached a sermon and was authorized by the presbytery to try his gifts in the churches.[41]

Too many Americans today lament the decline of our educational system without ever connecting it with the theological decline of our country. Even Christians tend to think that the decline was caused mainly by the removal of prayer from public schools. They do not understand the heritage.[42]

Southern race relations receives interesting attention from this book. During most of the time period this book covers, slavery existed in the Southern colonies or states. The sins of Southern slavery have been well documented and should not be denied or minimized. In fact, Southerners produced some of the most telling critiques of Southern slavery and the Northern slave trade during the antebellum period.[42] What are not often discussed, in fact what is not acceptable to discuss, are the bonds of family love and Christian brotherhood that often existed between Southern whites and blacks.[43] John Adger and later John L Girardeau pastored a Presbyterian church for Negroes in Charleston, South Carolina. Speaking in that church, James Henley Thornwell said, "This building is a public testimonial to our faith that the Negro is of one blood with ourselves."[44] At the general assembly of the Presbyterian Church of the Confederate States of America, Dr. Charles Colcock Jones, who had devoted his ministry to missionary work among slaves, spoke

---

[42] Presbyterian theologians James Henley Thornwell (see *Collected Writings, Volume 4*, Edinburough: Banner of Truth Trust, 1986) and Robert L. Dabney (see *Defense of Virginia and the South,* Harrisonburg, Virginia: Sprinkle Publications, 1977) and others vehemently condemned abuses of Blacks, who they considered as brothers in Adam and Christ.

[43] An outstanding fictional short story by William Faulkner, entitled "Mountain Victory," (*Collected Stories of William Faulkner,* New York: Random House, second printing 1950) illustrates the complexity of racial and social classes in the South. It beautifully shows the mutual affection and concern of a master and his slave.

[44] White, 298.

on the subject of evangelization of the slaves.[45] He said,

> They are not foreigners, but our nearest neighbors; they are not hired servants, but servants belonging to us in law and gospel. They are constant and inseparable associates; whither we go, they go; where we dwell, they dwell; where we die and are buried, there they die and are buried; and more, than all, our God is their God.[46]

The Assembly responded by supporting the evangelistic work. Emancipation and freedom, for all the benefits they bestowed, destroyed much of the fellowship and family-type bonds felt between the races and segregated the churches.

Many of the Presbyterians who served in the Confederate army are highlighted in this book. A chapter is devoted to Stonewall Jackson, D.H. Hill, and Thomas R. Cobb as representatives of Southern elders and deacons. Other chapters emphasize the achievements of men such as R.L. Dabney, Moses Drury Hoge, and Benjamin Morgan Palmer whose primary labors during the War were preaching and teaching the gospel. White describes the task of these and other men:

> The routine of their labors was as follows: To preach to the soldiers twice and sometimes thrice each Sunday; to hold prayer meetings each night of the week; to teach Bible classes almost every day; to distribute Bibles, parts of Bibles, hymn books, tracts and religious newspapers; to visit the sick and talk daily to soldiers about the welfare of their souls.[47]

Presbyterian leaders not only preached the gospel to Southern soldiers, but they also preached a theology of the Confederate cause to their Southern congregations. One of the most famous of these messages is B.M. Palmer's Thanksgiving Day message on November 29, 1860.[48] These men believed in

---

[45] The story of the Jones family is told in two books that consist of their family letters. They are *A Georgian at Princeton* (New York: Harcourt Brace Jovanovich, 1976) and *The Children of Pride* (New Haven: Yale University Press, 1972, 1984). Robert Manson Myers edited both works. These books highlight the godliness, education, and commitment to the Southern cause by this family. In their letters, the family members make frequent reference to "our family, black and white."

[46] White, 325.

[47] White, 342.

[48] Thomas Cary Johnson, *The Life and Letters of Benjamin Morgan Palmer* (Edinburgh: Banner of Truth Trust, 1987), 206-219.

the justness of the Southern cause. Moses Hoge, who previously had opposed the secession of the Southern states, commented after the secession of Virginia in April, 1861:

> With my whole mind and heart, I go into the secession movement. I think Providence has devolved on us the preservation of constitutional liberty, which has already been trampled under the foot of a military despotism at the North. And now that we are menaced with subjugation for daring to assert the right of self-government, I consider our contest as one which involves principles more important than those for which our fathers of the Revolution contended.[49]

With defeat, these men labored not only to preach comfort to their crushed Confederacy, but they continued defending the Southern cause.[50] Palmer spoke of the South saying:

> How dear she is to us now that she sits a desolate widow upon the ashes of what was once her home. All scarred and battered as she is, with the cruel furrows of war traced all over her broad bosom, I would not exchange her for the brightest and wealthiest land upon which the sun shines. Affliction makes her surprisingly beautiful, and I cling to her in her tears as I never did in the days of her laughter and pride.[51]

The men of this book were leaders. Most were pastors, preachers, elders, theologians, and teachers.[52] How rarely in our age, do we see ministers of the gospel as heroes and leaders. Musicians, movie stars, athletes, and even political figures achieve hero status far above theologians. While we can fault the decadent society with blame for these views, we must also blame the church in our age. Ministers are not leaders because all too often they do not lead. They do not exhibit the wisdom, learning, courage, and convictions of their spiritual forefathers. The scandals of television evangelists, the feminization of churches, the mushy theology of many churches, the watering down

---

[49] White, 430-431.
[50] They did not absolve the South of guilt for its own sins. Read, for example, Robert L. Dabney's letter to Major General Howard, chief of the Freedman's Bureau. (Robert L. Dabney, *Discussions, Volume 4* (Harrisonburg, Virginia: Sprinkle Publications, 1979) 25-45.
[51] White, 371-372.
[52] The overlapping and synonymous meanings and the distinctions between these terms can be dealt with elsewhere by others.

of educational standards for the ministry, the decline of some denominations into apostate theological liberalism, and other factors have destroyed the power and prestige once held by Christian ministers in this land.

The men of this book were godly and educated. No false dilemmas existed in their minds between the two. White recounts a letter by the young James Henley Thornwell, who had just graduated from college (at age 19) and was teaching a few private students and at the same time reading Greek, Latin, and German. Thornwell's personal reading plan was as follows: "I have commenced regularly with Xenophon's works…and intend to read them carefully. I shall then take up Thucydides, Herodotus, and Demosthenes. After mastering these I shall pass on to the philosophers and poets. In Latin I am going regularly through Cicero's writings. I read them by double translations; that is, I first translate them into English and then retranslate them into Latin. In German I am pursuing Goethe's works. My life, you can plainly see, is not a life of idleness."[53]

This education was not an end in itself, but was designed to train the mind to think and speak. The spoken message, the sermon, was central to the work of these men. Americans of the 18th and 19th centuries were better trained to listen to in-depth, lengthy messages. John Craig would preach from ten o'clock in the morning until noon. After a meal break, he would continue the message until sunset. The sermon would contain up to fifty-five divisions or points. Once when Thornwell preached for an hour and a half, he stopped and apologized for the sermon length. The congregation shouted, "Go on, go on."

These men preached with great vigor and earnestness. Moses Drury Hoge, a Presbyterian minister himself, wrote concerning Dr. William Plumer's preaching:

> I am hungry to hear him roar once more. I want to see his eyes glare and his hair stand up on end. It will refresh me to see him foam at the mouth again.[54]

Contrasting Plumer as a representative of Southern preaching with his successor, a northerner with a good and highly cultivated mind, Hoge said of the difference in sermons,

---

[53] White, 310
[54] Anne C. Loveland, *Southern Evangelicals and the Social Order, 1800-1860* (Baton Rouge: Louisiana State University Press, 1980), p. 41.

No bursts of passions, no involuntary emotion, no sudden and splendid inspiration, bearing a man from his manuscript and from his commonplaces as in a chariot of fire. Yankees seem to say good things because they have studied them, calculated them out and know it to be a duty to say them. Southern men say good things as if they could not help it.[55]

These were men of courage. Francis Makamie (1658-1708), the father of Presbyterianism in America, boldly stood up to the governor of colonial New York and argued before the courts his right to preach the gospel. Ministers and their congregations formed a large portion of the Continental army in the southern states that pursued and finally defeated British General Cornwallis. All of the colonels in General Washington's army, except for one, were Presbyterian elders, and more than half of all the soldiers and officers in the continental army were Presbyterian.[56] The British singled out and destroyed Presbyterian churches and the libraries of Presbyterian ministers. An elderly minister was hauled before General Cornwallis and charged with preaching rebellion from the pulpit against King George. The old saint told the general, "As a king he [George III] was bound to protect his subjects in the enjoyment of their rights. Protection and allegiance go together, and when the one fails the other cannot be expected. The declaration of Independence is but a reiteration of what our Covenanting fathers have always maintained."[57] As always, these Presbyterian leaders had a good answer (1 Peter 3:15-16).

These men were fighting not only for independence from British rule (political liberty), but for freedom of religion in their own states (religious liberty). The established church in Virginia (the Anglican church) imposed restrictions on Presbyterians, Baptists, and other Protestant groups. Ultimately the First Amendment to the United States Constitution and the disestablishment of the Anglican Church in the state of Virginia were the results of these men's labors.

The Word of God was applied to all areas of life, so these men were not confined to ecclesiastical concerns and personal piety, as important as these things are. They sought to apply the Christian faith into every sphere of life. T.V. Moore spoke of the earthly blessings of Christianity saying,

---

[55] Loveland, 41. Loveland's book is an outstanding study of Presbyterian, Baptist, and Methodist ministers in the South prior to the War.

[56] Loraine Boettner, *The Reformed Doctrine of Predestination* (Philadelphia: The Presbyterian and Reformed Publishing Company, 1975), 384.

[57] Dr. White discusses this in chapter 24. See also W.P. Breed, *Presbyterians and the Revolution* (Mt. Olive, Mississippi: Mount Olive Press, reprinted 1993).

As an agency in the prevention of crime, in fostering habits of temperance, industry, honesty, and peace, and thus increasing at once the wealth of a country, and that which wealth cannot buy, the happiness of its homes, and as a great educational institute which trains men to be good members of society and of the family, by the only process, and supported by the only motives that can be efficient on the masses, it is at once the cheapest and best conservator of a nation's welfare. The pulpit is cheaper than the prison; the Church and Sabbath school less costly than the police and the standing army that would otherwise be needed to prevent the lawless passions of one class in society from bursting out against another.[58]

Thomas Smyth said, "It is not the wisdom of statesmen and legislators; it is not by civil institutions, by the checks and balances of the powers of government, by laws and courts, by armies and navies, that the peace, and order, and happiness of mankind can be secured, and crime and suffering banished from the world." Instead, he proclaimed that the Gospel of Christ was the "true and only panacea for all social and moral ills—the only palladium of all social and political blessings—and the only guarantee for honesty, industry, and prosperity."[59]

The Old South thus provides examples of the some of the kinds of leaders we seek to produce in our day. It is ironic that God would point us to a failed civilization, to a nation that lost its war for independence, to a nation with such obvious flaws to find examples of what we ought to be. It is ironic, but quite typical of our Sovereign God.

"The kingdoms of this world have become the kingdoms of our Lord and of His Christ, and He shall reign forever and ever!" (Revelation 11:15)

Reading About the South and the War Between the States

It is not safe for me to begin discussing books on the South and the War Between the States. I could get started and never stop. Let me make a few specific suggestions for Christian teachers.

1. *Southern Presbyterian Leaders* by Henry Alexander White. Hopefully, the review above is convincing.

2. *The War Between the States: America's Uncivil War* by John J. Dwyer, with George Grant, J. Steven Wilkins, Douglas Wilson, and Tom Spencer.[60]

---

[58] As quoted in Loveland, 110.
[59] Loveland, 110.
[60] Published by Bluebonnet Press in Denton, Texas in 2005.

This is the most comprehensive Christian survey of the war ever. The author and contributors favor the Southern side of the war, but are judicious in their coverage of the many issues and participants in the war. This work will become a standard text for Christian and homeschools.

 3. *Call of Duty: The Sterling Nobility of Robert E. Lee* and *All Things for Good: The Steadfast Fidelity of Stonewall Jackson* by J. Steven Wilkins. Both of these biographies are part of the Cumberland House Publishers' Leaders in Action series. Lee and Jackson were not only outstanding military men, but also both were deeply committed Christians. Along with these two biographies, include *Then Darkness Fled: The Liberating Wisdom of Booker T. Washington* by Stephen Mansfield.

 4. *The Life and Campaigns of Lt. Gen. T. J. "Stonewall" Jackson* by Robert Lewis Dabney. This is a classic work that displays Jackson's life and faith as well as the theological insights of the author, who served on Jackson's staff. Dabney's *A Defense of Virginia and the South,* as well as other writings by and about Dabney are useful.[61] He really was a significant Southern theologian and thinker.

 5. *Southern Evangelicals and the Social Order, 1800-1860* by Anne C. Loveland.[62] This is an outstanding study of the theology, cultural activities, and historical circumstances of Southern Christians.

 6. *Religion and the American Civil War,* edited by Randall M. Miller, Harry S. Stout, and Charles Reagan Wilson.[63] This is a collection of useful and challenging essays on both the northern and southern sides of the war. Not all the essays are complimentary toward the South, but all are worth reading.

 7. *Chaplain to the Confederacy: Basil Manly and Baptist Life in the Old South* by A. James Fuller.[64] Much of my essay above chronicles Presbyterians. This book shows the Baptist involvement in Southern culture and the War.

 8. *I'll Take My Stand: The South and the Agrarian Tradition* by Twelve Southerners.[65] Only one essay actually deals with the war, yet this is a classic defense of Southern culture. To even mention the Agrarians calls for more than we can begin to write.

---

[61] Dabney's works and many other valuable works by Southern Christians have been reprinted by Sprinkle Publications in Harrisonburg, Virginia.
[62] Published by Louisiana State University Press in Baton Rouge, Louisiana.
[63] Published by Oxford University Press in 1998.
[64] Published by Louisiana University Press in 2000.
[65] Reprinted by Louisiana University Press in 1991.

Chapter Twenty-Five
The Greater Depression

> There are two ways open to all men of changing their ways for the better—one is through their own disasters and one through those of others; that involving one's own calamities is the more vivid, but the one involving those of others is less painful. Therefore the former method should never be chosen voluntarily, since it effects its improvement along with great labors and risks; but the latter methods should always be sought out, since in it we can see the better course without being injured. Basing our conclusions on these facts, we must agree that the experience accruing from a study of serious history is the best education for actual life.
> —Polybius, *Histories*[1]

Popular histories usually focus on the wars, the politics, and the personalities of an era. For most people, popular history is history. By that I mean that it is what they remember of history. Often the events of greatest consequence do not happen in the chambers of legislators or the palaces of kings or on the battlefields. Often the greatest events of history are the theological struggles and the intellectual battles that occur. But since the battle of Gettysburg is more exciting than the growth of Nationalism and since the life of Hitler is more intriguing than the rise of Socialism, the attention of readers of history will tend toward the frontline movers and shakers.

In American history, the story from the early 1900s to the mid-1900s generally revolves around the two World Wars and the Great Depression. It would certainly be hard to minimize these three events or to ignore their impact on subsequent history; however, three other events had an impact on this nation arguably as great, if not greater, than World War I, the Great Depression, and World War II.

---

[1] Quoted in Michael Grant, *Readings in the Classical Historians* (New York; Charles Scribners Sons, 1992) 153.

The Summer of 1925

Only one of these three events is well known. This was the Scopes Monkey Trial in Dayton, Tennessee, in 1925. Dayton, Tennessee, was a small Southern town, and John Scopes was a substitute teacher who willingly agreed to confess to having taught the theory of evolution in the classroom. A Tennessee state statute forbade teaching the theory of evolution, so Scopes was guilty as charged. The real story, however, was the media event.

For the first time on a grand scale, a phenomenon occurred which has become a commonplace: The media spin on the story superseded the story itself. The Scopes Trial was an international media event. It did wonders for the local economy of Dayton, Tennessee. And it was great for the media. But the winners of the trial, the defenders of the Genesis creation account, were the losers of the media war.

According to most accounts, William Jennings Bryan—three time Presidential candidate, Presbyterian elder, and opponent of evolution—botched the defense of creation both on and off the stand. In the play and the movie versions of the trial, entitled "Inherit the Wind", the "William Jennings Bryan-like" character was a complete buffoon and simpleton. The defender of Creationism in the film version brags that he never read Darwin, for he only read the Bible. In reality, Bryan read Darwin a good many years earlier and for a time had been sympathetic to a modified Darwinian viewpoint. Bryan and his defense team performed quite well in many of the exchanges in the trial. Perhaps more than many in his time and ours, Bryan saw the ethical and political implications of Darwinism. Nevertheless, his testimony as a witness was badly done and subject to decades of ridicule.

The defender of John Scopes was the lawyer Clarence Darrow. Darrow's scorn for Christianity was monumental. When Bryan accused him of attacking the Bible, Darrow retorted, "I am examining your fool ideas that no intelligent Christian on earth believes."[2] It was a foregone conclusion that Scopes would be found guilty of breaking the law. The intent of the trial was publicity, not an airing of a theological and scientific debate. Darrow had his own definite agenda. In his closing speech he said, "I think this case will be remembered because it is the first case of this sort since we stopped trying people in America for witchcraft. We have done our best to turn the tide...of testing every fact in science by a religious doctrine."[3]

The end result of the trial was not just the publicity stunt itself or the challenge to the state laws of Tennessee or the issue of academic freedom.

---

[2] Edward J. Larson, *Summer for the Gods: The Scopes Trial and America's Continuing Debate over Science and Religion* (New York: Basic Books, 1997), 190.
[3] Larson, 193.

The results of this trial were that Christians lost face, lost influence, lost respect, and lost credibility in the public arena. Larson notes, "After the Scopes trial, elite American society stopped taking fundamentalists and their ideas seriously."[4]

George Marsden said, "Fundamentalists, excluded from the community of modern theological and scientific orthodoxy, eventually were forced to establish their own community and sub-culture in which their own ideas of orthodoxy were preserved."[5]

The media elites and the intellectual elites won the day in 1925. The battle lines for the Scopes Trial had been drawn long before the event. Marsden notes, "In some respects America after 1918 was a new world as compared with America at the end of the nineteenth century. People who had retained the dominant beliefs of the culture in which they were raised now found themselves living in a society where those same beliefs were widely considered out-dated, or even bizarre."[6] The court may have ruled in favor of Bryan's side, but the educated culture as a whole judged Christianity as backward, superstitious, Medieval (meant as an insult!), bound to Dark Age myths, narrow-minded and opposed to science and learning. Darwinism became not simply a view of science, but Science itself. The tenets of Darwinism were the keys to intellectual freedom. Evolution broke the chains of the past and freed the mind to understand the real world. A bright new day was dawning: In an Orwellian mindset, Evolution was Liberty.

This optimistic Darwinism still exists; in a recent edition of "The Griffin," the monthly catalog of the Readers' Subscription, Senior Editor Robert Dreeson said, "Perhaps the best way to understand ourselves, the human species, is to visit the zoo. It's there, rather than in a mirror, that we might get the best view of ourselves."[7]

The Row Amongst the Presbyterians

A second event occurred around 1935. It is less well known than the Scopes Trial; it is less interesting in terms of the excitement generated or the personalities involved. It was, in certain parts of the country, headline news, but it was not a media event of the magnitude of the first event. This was the trial and suspension of J. Gresham Machen from the Presbyterian Church, U.S.A.

---

[4] Larson, 233.

[5] George Marsden, *Fundamentalism and American Culture* (New York: Oxford University Press, 1980) 215.

[6] Marsden, 204.

[7] Robert Dreeson, "The Griffin" (The monthly catalog of *The Readers' Subscription*, June 2004), 4.

God picks the most unlikely candidates to change the world. Such a case was Machen. Machen grew up in a post-bellum Southern family in Baltimore, Maryland. He was educated at Johns Hopkins University and later attended Princeton Theological Seminary. He chose to become a theology professor, rather than pursuing studies in the Greek and Roman classics. He was a rather bookish man (he had his coats tailored so as to fit Loeb classics in the pockets), a life-long bachelor, and a serious scholar and Greek professor.

He could have lived a quiet life of faithful Christian service, but God placed him in the midst of a theological firestorm. Machen became one of the key figures God raised up to battle the forces of Modernism in his day. Modernism can be described as follows: The ideas of Darwinism (Evolution—and its implications), new theories of human psychology, and the Higher Critical movement ("The Bible is the product of man's thoughts, not God's Word"), with a sprinkling of other ideas that were trendy new ideologies being promoted by a host of anti-Christian philosophers and thinkers. Such enemies, all being united in unbelief and hatred of orthodox Christianity, should have been across the trenches from a theology professor's aim. Instead, they were all claiming squatter's rights in the midst of the Christian camp. The historically Calvinistic Princeton Seminary and northern Presbyterian Church had both accommodated the new theologies and philosophies.

Machen's background helped prepare him for his battles. He was nurtured within two strong theological traditions, both with Presbyterian roots. He grew up in Baltimore, Maryland, which despite the fact that it never seceded in 1861, was still a Southern culture. Machen's love of Southern manners, ties with Southern family, and roots in Southern Presbyterianism were powerful forces in his life and personality. Then he went to Princeton, which was still rooted in the historic Calvinistic teachings of its traditions. What really grounded Machen in historic Christianity were his experiences in Germany. At that time, Germany was the center of the most profound and innovative theological scholarship in the world. German theologians were ranked among the most brilliant thinkers. Unfortunately, not all of the German thinkers were being faithful to the teachings of the Bible. German theologians drew many professing Christians further away from the faith. In the case of Machen, his exposure to German brilliance sharpened his own intellect, but led to his reaffirming of the teachings of the Bible.

In time, Machen produced one of the greatest Christian books of the Twentieth Century: *Christianity and Liberalism*. This book became a standard defense of Christianity against those whose commitment to Darwinism, Higher Criticism, modern psychology, and theological liberalism led them to undermining the Bible and redefining Christian truths. The book is still in print and is still having an impact on our Christian culture. As Sean Roberts, a current student at Westminster Theological Seminary recently wrote, "Few books on the shelves of Christianity have as much relevance for the current generation of Christians who seek nothing more than to be on the frontline of the present cultural and spiritual battle for the hearts and minds of mankind than J. Gresham Machen's *Christianity and Liberalism.*"[8] Not only Presbyterians, but Baptists, Lutherans, Bible Church people, and others found comfort and ammunition in Machen's book.

Machen fought to maintain Princeton Theological Seminary as a faithful institution. The seminary's board was reorganized in such a way as to open the doors for liberals to step in. Machen's days there were then numbered. When he left Princeton Seminary, he started Westminster Theological Seminary in 1929, assembling a diverse and brilliant faculty, which included such men as Cornelius Van Til, Ned Stonehouse, and Oswald T. Allis. The plan was to preserve the truth within the northern Presbyterian Church of the USA by carrying on the mission of the older Princeton tradition.

Since a focal point of the liberals had been foreign missions, Machen started the Independent Board for Presbyterian Foreign Missions in 1933. This led the official Presbyterian hierarchy to bring charges against Machen in 1935. After the trial, he was found guilty on six counts and was subsequently suspended from the ministry.

Machen's trial involved no juicy stories. The issues at stake were theological, not moral. Machen contended for a particular theological dogma that was opposed by a faction that held a different theological dogma. Now this may sound like just another case of Presbyterian denominational infighting. As such, it might have been some high stake ecclesiastical wrangling among Presbyterians, but of interest to few others. But once again, bigger issues were at stake.

The theological issues were not fine, obtuse points of theology or scholastic debates or differing theological perspectives on the number of angels that can dance on the head of a pin.[9] Machen's opponents were theological liberals who were denying such essentials as the virgin birth of Christ, the miracles of the Bible, and the resurrection of Christ. Among his better-known opponents was Pearl S. Buck, Nobel Prize winning author and child of Presbyterian missionaries. Miss Buck maintained that it did not matter

---

[8] Sean J. S. Roberts, "A New Look at an Old Classic: J. Gresham Machen's Timeless Christianity and Liberalism (*Christian Culture*, A Publication of the Center for Cultural Leadership, September 2006), 1.

[9] This whole point itself is not irrelevant. See Dorothy Sayers' article "The Lost Tools of Learning."

whether Jesus Christ actually lived or not. What mattered was that 'the spirit of Jesus lived.' D. G. Hart notes that Machen's opposition to the new approach to missions was based on its assumption that Christianity shared basic beliefs common to other world religions.[10]

Machen did not exactly fit the image of the modern, sensitive kind of guy. If he had been such a man, he could have responded to Miss Buck's views by saying, "Hey, it's okay, if that is what works for you, fine, let the spirit of Jesus live. For me personally, I dig the older theology, the real Heilig Geschichte kind of stuff." Or perhaps, he could have allowed that the Presbyterian Church was big enough, inclusive enough, broad-minded enough, to include those whose credo was "I deny…" in the pew right next to those whose credo was "I believe."

Instead, Machen was stubborn, narrow-minded, exclusive, not inclusive, and (forgive this bad language) *intolerant*. Having learned the Westminster Shorter Catechism on his faithful mother's knees, he just could not overlook those Scriptural doctrines affirming the deity of Christ and His resurrection from the dead.

Machen lost to a coalition in the Presbyterian Church U.S.A. made up of a minority of theological liberals and a large number of moderates. The moderates tended to side with Machen's theological preferences, but were guided primarily by their own 11th commandment: "Thou shalt not make waves." In this process—it did not begin or end with Machen—the loss was specifically Princeton Theological Seminary, Presbyterian missions, and more generally, intellectual Protestantism.

Machen went on to found the Orthodox Presbyterian Church. Machen was a popular and well-respected writer and teacher. Still, his leaving the larger Presbyterian Church only drew about 5,000 followers out of some nearly 2 million members in the old church.[11] Even in Westminster Seminary, which he founded, there were some who objected to Machen's unapologetic Calvinism and Presbyterianism. Also, premillennial students objected to Machen's more postmillennial perspective, and fundamentalists opposed faculty members who condoned the use of alcohol and tobacco.[12] To make matters worse, Machen was on the losing side of almost every political cause. His politics was a combination of Jeffersonian democracy with near libertarian tendencies, and he was airing such views in the time of the New Deal.

---

[10] D. G. Hart, "Introduction," from *J. Gresham Machen: Selected Shorter Writings*, 4.

[11] D. G. Hart, *Defending the Faith: J. Gresham Machen and the Crisis of Conservative Protestantism in Modern America* (Grand Rapids, MI: Baker Book House, 1994), 157.

[12] Hart, 163.

In spite of the opposition he faced in his day, in spite of the failing fortunes of the causes he advocated, he never wavered, and the number of his disciples is still growing. His influence and the influence of the institutions he founded have been far reaching. In the long, slow turning of the wheels of history and time, he has already been vindicated repeatedly. Still, the events of his day—his own defeats against the foes—have been quite depressing.

It may be a bit too much of a stereotype, but in the 1800s and early 1900s, Episcopalians controlled the money in the nation, Presbyterians controlled the scholarship, and Baptists and Methodists controlled the numbers, that is, the majority of the Protestants. Baptist theologians like James P. Boyce received their theological training from the Princeton theologians like the Hodges and the Alexanders. Other theologians looked to Presbyterians and admired their scholarship. Taking down a Presbyterian theologian was a hefty coup d'etat.

Machen's fall signaled the defeat of conservative scholarship. It was not, mind you, a defeat in the actual arena of scholarship. Machen's book *Christianity and Liberalism* effectively trounced the arguments of the liberals. The defeat was the loss of institutions and the traditional reigns of power. Machen resorted to what became a tradition in Reformed circles—break away and regroup and hope to recoup the losses. Only the losses are generally never completely recouped and the regrouping group tends to suffer subsequent breaking away.

"Intellectual Bible-believing Christianity" became something of an oxymoron in the halls of academia and among the American intelligentsia. The original publication of the books known as *The Fundamentals* was recognized as a scholarly orthodox response to the theological currents. After Machen was exiled from mainline Presbyterianism into the hinterlands, the only Protestant theologians to be noticed were liberals or neo-orthodox. The most Protestant of nations, the most scholarly of denominations, and the most foundational beliefs—all suffered from Machen's trial and suspension.

School's Out, School's Out

The third event actually began occurring first in the chronology. It is the least known, the least interesting from a popular perspective, and almost completely ignored in terms of media attention or inclusion in the history books. This was the abandonment of classical education. The Founding Fathers of America were all the products of classical education. Pastors, teachers, professors, and all educated people in America were trained in schools that in one fashion or another were classical.

By classical, we mean that the intellectual foundations of education were built upon the study of Greek and Latin languages and that the ethical objectives aimed at producing men of character. This classical strand, tracing back to Homer, Aristotle, Virgil, and others, was reinforced by two millennia of Christian influences. Hence, Augustine and the other church fathers were studied alongside of Homer and Seneca. Educated men were well-versed in what Mortimer Adler would later call 'The Great Conversation.' When educated men wrote books and letters, they freely quoted from the Greeks and Romans in the original languages and did not assume any need to translate the quotations.

This education was being rapidly abandoned in the early part of the Twentieth Century. The greater story of this abandonment is beyond the scope of this essay, but at least a portion of it can be seen by the example of Vanderbilt University in Nashville, Tennessee.

Vanderbilt fit into the tradition of Christian universities that required incoming students to have been classically educated and then advanced that education to an even higher level. Dr. Louise Cowan highlights the case of Southern poet and literary critic John Crowe Ransom:

> In 1908-1909, the year Ransom graduated, all who were working toward a B.A. degree were required to study a year of Latin, a year of Greek (these requirements presupposed four years of Latin and three of Greek in high school), and a year each of mathematics, English, chemistry, history, and philosophy. A major in English literature required two years of Latin, Greek, French, German, two and a half of Biblical literature, and one of Anglo-Saxon.[13]

The purpose of this education was "not to teach vocational skills but to turn out men of good background who could bring to their daily tasks a distinction that derived from superiority of intellect and character."[14] The university was able to complete this educational process only because of the preparatory schools that existed. Such preparatory education enabled Ransom to enter Vanderbilt at age fifteen. Ransom's close associate, Donald Davidson, comments on the school he attended, "They toadied to no educational fashion. Their staple diet was Greek, Latin, and mathematics, with some concessions to history and English. Out of the Spartan necessity enforced by the hard times they made a glory and a moral."[15] Davidson entered Vanderbilt

---

[13] Louise Cowan, *The Fugitive Group* (Baton Rouge: LSU Press, 1968), 33.
[14] Cowan, 33.
[15] As quoted in Cowan, 8.

prepared by four years of Latin, three of Greek, and a vast experience in reading literature. Stanley Phillips Johnson entered handicapped by a public school education, which only gave him three and a half years of Latin and no Greek.[16]

A few years later, when Ransom returned to Vanderbilt to teach, the program had changed. Cowan states, "By 1919, the classical languages had been dropped as requirements, although they were still recommended to English majors."

Cowan says, "Utilitarianism was becoming the controlling attitude at Vanderbilt as it had become dominant even earlier, in most other universities in the nation.... The new philosophy of education shifted this basis, focusing on the recipients of knowledge rather than the disciplines themselves, with a consequent democratization of attitude, so that the aims of education were made subject to timeliness and opportunism, *and standards began their long downward plunge.*"(italics added) [17]

Here around 1915, "standards began their long downward plunge." Long before all of our current education woes, the old school, the proven and tried method, the universal standards, the Greco-Roman-Christian heritage was abandoned.

In 1930, as a professor at the same institution he had attended, Ransom was fighting for the last vestiges of classical education. Chairing a curriculum committee, he noted the "decay of Ancient Languages and Philosophy, which have in the past been the staples of the Arts tradition in the colleges." The committee recommended that the first two years of college include studying either Latin or Greek and formal logic ("the best discipline in abstract thinking"). The recommendations were rejected for "calling for a return along the path which every institution in America has traveled and reinstating regulations that have been universally abandoned."[18] Ransom was told "your scheme presents nothing new" and instead, it simply covered "the same barren and familiar territory" that had already been rejected.[19]

True education and good education was now by definition whatever was new. Trends, fashions, and innovations defined the curricula of education. History was not dropped as a subject, but it was made devoid of any meaning

---

[16] Cowan, 9-12.

[17] Cowan, 32-33. She points out, "In the 1900's, Ciceronian humanism was the ideal at Vanderbilt: the purpose of education was not to teach vocational skills but to turn out men of good background who could bring to their daily tasks a distinction that derived from superiority of intellect and character."

[18] Thomas Daniel Young, *Gentleman in a Dustcoat: A Biography of John Crowe Ransom* (Baton Rouge, LA: Louisiana University Press, 1976), 232-233.

[19] Young, 233.

or use. The past had nothing to teach us. We did not have to have a French Revolution to abolish the calendar and the traditional institutions, for educators created that revolution in the classrooms rather than the streets.

Still, the older education persisted for a season or two. It took time for all the old teachers to die off. Their required courses became electives as their hair turned gray and eyes grew dim. Small, classical academies that had dotted the landscape of Tennessee and other states closed their doors. School consolidation promised to save the day. Learning Latin soon went the way of plowing with mules.

Summary

What dismal history:
1915—the heritage of classical education abandoned.
1925—the authority of Scripture mocked and ridiculed.
1935—Christian orthodoxy and scholarship defrocked.

By contrast, the failed politics of Woodrow Wilson, Herbert Hoover, and Franklin D. Roosevelt seem refreshing. By contrast, the dangers of World War I, the Great Depression, and World War II seem redeeming. By contrast, the writings of Ernest Hemingway and T. S. Eliot seem optimistic. If this story ended here, American history would be a great dark age for the rest of the twentieth century and beyond. But God is gracious. America opened many doors in the twentieth century that could have led to dark periods of decline. No doubt such doors were opened, and all too often, we boldly walked in. But God has been good to us: Every time the lights have gone out for a season, they have come back on again. That obscure historical story is quite exciting.

For Further Reading

All of the books footnoted in this essay are essential reading on these topics. The best overview of the entire time period and cultural changes is George Marsden's *Fundamentalism and American Culture: The Shaping of Twentieth-Century Evangelicalism 1870-1925*. This was a time in which fundamentalists found the culture openly abandoning belief in God. Even secular thinkers noted the problem. Joseph Wood Crutch, for example, said, "There remains no foundation in authority for ideas of right and wrong. Both our practical morality and our emotional lives are adjusted to a world that no longer exists."[20] Bryan and Machen were symbolic of the wide range of styles

---

[20] Marsden, 3.

within Christian circles. Both were Presbyterians, but Bryan represented the more anti-intellectual and populist form of Fundamentalism, while Machen purposely distanced himself from the term Fundamentalist and called himself a Calvinist.

Edward J. Larson's *Summer for the Gods,* which won a Pulitzer Prize in 1998, is a good, recent study of the Scopes Trial. Burton W. Folsom, Jr. offered an able defense of William Jennings Bryan's not-so-able defense in "The Scopes Trial Reconsidered."[21]

There are several great books by and about Machen. *Christianity and Liberalism* should be required reading for anyone in Christian ministry or anyone teaching twentieth century American history. It is both polemical and devotional. It has the stridency of Paul's letter to the Galatians, and it nourishes both soul and mind. The problem of modern liberalism, Machen points out, is that it "has lost sight of the two great presuppositions of the Christian message—the living God and the fact of sin."[22] The whole book is a call for reformation and for the church reclaiming the truths of Scripture. *J. Gresham Machen: Selected Shorter Writings,* edited by D. G. Hart, contains more essays by Machen on the Scriptures, theology, the then-current theological battles, and Christian culture. It also includes some autobiographical sketches of Machen, including his desciption of his favorite hobby, mountain climbing.

Education, Christianity, and the State by Machen is a collection of essays and lectures and a testimony before a Senate committee. These writings, which first appeared in the 1920s and 1930s, contain still brilliant observations about the necessity of Christian education and the hopelessness of abandoning Christian standards. Just as one example among many of brilliant quotes from this work, consider the following: Machen wrote, "The depreciation of the intellect, with the exaltation in the place of it of the feelings or of the will, is, we think, a basic fact in modern life which is rapidly leading to a condition in which men neither know anything nor care anything about the doctrinal content of the Christian religion, in which there is in general a lamentable intellectual decline."[23]

Biographies of Machen include an older work by his colleague Ned B. Stonehouse, titled *J. Gresham Machen: A Biographical Memoir,*[24] and a more critical study by D. G. Hart, titled *Defending the Faith: J. Gresham Machen and the Crisis of Conservative Protestantism in Modern America.*[25] *Reformed Theology in America,*

---

[21] Found in the journal *Continuity: A Journal of History,* Number 12, Fall 1988, 103-127.
[22] Machen, *Christianity and Liberalism,* 69.
[23] Edited by Dr. John Robbins (Unicoi, TN: Trinity Foundation, 2004), 9.
[24] Edinburgh, Scotland: Banner of Truth Trust, 1987.
[25] Grand Rapids, MI: Baker Book House, 1994.

edited by David F. Wells, includes chapters on Machen, Van Til, and a number of other key Reformed theologians associated with Princeton Seminary.[26] Gary North's bicep-building one-thousand-plus pages *Crossed Fingers: How the Liberals Captured the Presbyterian Church* covers the Scopes Trial and the Machen trial, with numerous digressions into American, church, and Presbyterian history. It has much to offer.

For reading on the educational decline, try any biography of any educated person who received their schooling during any time period up to the 1940s. Even after that, thankfully, there were always good teachers, good books, and eager students. Ransom, Davidson, and the others highlighted in Louise Cowan's study of the Fugitive poets, may not have continued exactly the same type of classical training, but they held fast the standards of literary studies in their own classrooms and books.

Machen's last words included a telegraph message he sent to John Murray, saying, "I'm so thankful for active obedience of Christ. No hope without it." Shortly afterwards, on January 1, 1937, he died. The Orthodox Presbyterian Church suffered a host of theological struggles from within, but has survived. Theological liberalism, however, has also survived and still controls many of the older denominational establishments in America. The teachings of evolution now hold sway over most universities and schools across the country. Instead of lawsuits for teaching evolution, teachers and scholars face difficulties for denying it. The rigors of classical education were long since swept away as the teaching methods and the goals of John Dewey captured the educational establishment.

Yet we all have seen plants die in the late fall when the first frost hits. Winter then follows with a bleakness that leaves the spirit most depressed by February. But spring returns. Dormant seeds awaken, new shoots spring up, and the beauty of nature is revived. God reminds us of the resurrection in both natural and special revelation.

We did suffer losses in the early twentieth century greater than the despair of World War I, the hardships of the Great Depression, and the worldwide threats of World War II. But consider Machen's faith. He did not have ultimate trust in institutions, not those he was forced to leave or those he started. He said, "A revival of the Christian religion, we believe, will deliver mankind from its present bondage and, like the great revival of the sixteenth century, will bring liberty to mankind. Such a revival will be not the work of man, but the work of the Spirit of God. But one of the means which the Spirit will use, we believe, is an awakening of the intellect."[27]

---

[26] Grand Rapids, MI: William B. Eerdmans Publishing Company, 1985.

[27] Machen, *Christianity, Education, and the State*, 5.

God has kept the faith alive. Even the Reformed theology of Machen has been blessed with revival. Machen's work of ministry is still pressing on. The doctrine of Evolution and the advocates of Darwinism are under attack. Darrow mercilessly hounded Bryan in his cross examination in 1925. Now those who are attacking Darwinism are paying back this debt with interest. Classical education has suffered, but the message of the great books still speaks. Dr. Louise Cowan, whose book was heavily referenced above, has written widely on literary issues and, in fact, fashioned studies in literature and the humanities that maintain classical ideals at the University of Dallas.[28]

Full-orbed classical Christian education has revived as well. Private Christian academies, home schooling families, and some universities are training a whole new generation in ways that have not been done in nearly a century.

---

[28] Her books are referenced in the bibliography.

Chapter Twenty-Six
The Legacy of Francis Schaeffer

"He dressed like a Swiss farmer. But when he opened his
mouth and began to speak, people were transfixed."[1]
—Nancy Pearcey

The intellect of the wise is like glass; it admits the light
of heaven and then reflects it.
—Hare[2]

    American historians should have had a pretty neat and easy job after the 1970s. Instead, God stepped in and complicated matters, as He so often does. Whether it is turning back the Mongol hordes, turning the corruption of the Renaissance Christianity to the glory of Reformation Christianity, or parting the Red Sea, God seems quite intent on ruling history. This would be okay, if it were not for the fact that God so often uses such odd men and means to do so. Let us consider in more detail the near decline and fall of the United States in the 1960s and 70s.
    The 1960s were a time of great social upheaval and violence. Riots in the streets, protests on college campuses, assassinations of political figures, and a miry Asian war all ripped and tugged the social fabric of America. The establishment, blindly committed to a failed liberalism with an increasingly reactionary approach to the revolution spawned by such liberalism, floundered. Radicalism, representing every shade of leftist political extremism from anarchism to Marxism, punctured the old New Deal Liberalism. The jagged contours of the decade are easy to outline: Camelot arrived in 1960 with John F. Kennedy's election and ended in 1963 with his death; the Beatles arrived just weeks after his death; the Civil Rights Movement began with Blacks being sprayed with fire hoses and attacked by fire hoses and police dogs and climaxed with the riot-filled, hot summer of 1968, following Martin Luther King's assassination; 1968 also saw Lyndon Johnson's last futile at-

---
[1] *Total Truth*, 53.
[2] *The New Dictionary of Thoughts*, 730.

tempts to end the war, the assassination of anti-war candidate Sen. Robert Kennedy, more violence at the Democratic National Convention in Chicago, and the election of Richard Nixon to the Presidency. Large numbers of Southerners and others voted in anger for the fiery Alabama Governor George C. Wallace. Nixon took office with a "secret plan" to end the Vietnam War and by the end of the decade was in the midst of expanding the war to neighboring countries.

The 1970s were worse. Not worse in the sense of the amount of violence or social upheaval, but worse in terms of the reaction. Camelot had been pillaged by marauding Vikings. America's role in Vietnam resulted in a "peace with honor" that lasted long enough for the Communist to snag the whole country. Saigon became Ho Chi Mihn City, and Richard Nixon escaped prison only by the timely pardon by his successor, Gerald Ford. The Watergate scandal further damaged any confidence in politics in America. Protesting college students either grew up or gave up. The energy of the 60s spun out; the lethargy of the 70s set in. Cynicism replaced activism. Drug use for revolution was replaced by drug use by personal gratification. The anti-war movement, the civil rights movement, and the student movement all called for a degree of commitment uninteresting to the apathetic 70s generation. The decadent music grew louder. The Great American Dream did not matter. Inflation ate up the immediate savings, but the older savings account, historic Christianity, was long since depleted. The Supreme Court issued *Roe v. Wade* in 1973 and the evangelical church yawned.

The entire world story was depressing. Communism was advancing. Cuba was securely Communist and close by; Vietnam and neighboring Cambodia and Laos were all Communist. Colonialism was about faded out in Africa, but Russian advisors were there to replace the old British and French colonial forces. Nixon and Ford's Secretary of State, Henry Kissinger, crafted a policy called Détente, which was what Churchill had previously called Appeasement. Prophets of the 1970s may have not been stoned, but Russian Christian and Noble Prize winning author, Alexander Solzhenitsyn, was banished from Russia and refused admittance into Jerry Ford's White House.

Then in 1976 America celebrated its 200th anniversary of our founding, and elected another President. Since 1960, America had a president assassinated; another destroyed by the Vietnam War; another ruined by scandal; another stifled by ineptitude—he (Ford) denied the existence of the Iron Curtain. After four failed and miserable presidencies, America turned to Georgia Governor Jimmy Carter for an even greater and more colossal picture of mediocrity and incompetence. Carter characterized the pathetic state of the nation's spiritual condition when he professed to be a born again Christian, but did so in an interview with *Playboy* magazine.

Yes, the historians' work after the 1970s should have been easy. The downward spiral should have escalated for a short time with a loud crash. Or perhaps the country could have, in W.B. Yeats' phrase, ended with a whimper and not a bang. Yet America revived and survived. The decade was more like a bad cold than a terminal disease. And so the historians' task is a bit more difficult. What CPR method did God use on this country?

The complete answer is quite long and actually not yet complete. A part of the answer is that America revived because of an American Presbyterian missionary in Switzerland by the name of Francis Schaeffer. In particular, America began turning around in 1976 when this missionary produced his greatest book, *How Should We Then Live?* The book had the most unhopeful subtitle: *The Rise and Decline of Western Thought and Culture.* About half of the book was a survey of the history, art, music, philosophy, and politics of Western Civilization from the Romans through the Enlightenment. The other half was a survey of every angle of modernity as found in liberal theologians, radical and totalitarian politics, decadent artists, and prominent—though usually perverse—philosophers. In some ways, the book appeared to be a coffee table book; the kind of oversized books filled with art and illustrations. Accompanying the book was a documentary film series where Schaeffer discussed the sites, the art works, the books, and the issues of the series. The book and the series appeared in some respects to be modeled after Kenneth Clark's *Civilization,* a secular humanist survey of Western culture.

To understand the magnitude of Schaeffer's accomplishment in this book and his other works, one must first see his limitations. Since Schaeffer was a philosophy student and since *How Should We Then Live?* focused heavily on philosophy, I once questioned Dr. Greg Bahnsen, the Christian apologist and student of philosophy, about Schaeffer and his book. Dr. Bahnsen politely replied that he could never give Schaeffer's book to a university philosophy major: Schaeffer's treatment of philosophy was too simplistic. In a discussion some years before, a seminary student commented that no historian could seriously use Schaeffer's historical pronouncements for the same reason.

Some Christian Reconstructionist authors pointed out that although Schaeffer asked, "How should we then live?" his premillennial eschatology and lack of a theonomic Biblical law base prevented him from answering that question. They also pointed out the curious fact that although Schaeffer studied for a time under Dr. Cornelius Van Til at Westminster Theological Seminary and borrowed from his presuppositional apologetic method, he never acknowledged or footnoted this mentor.

In the years of frequently rereading *How Should We Then Live?* and rewatching the series, I have noted a few concerns myself. First, Schaeffer covers the vast domain of Western thought and culture in about 250 pages. Will and Ariel Durant's series on civilization contained ten fat volumes reaching only to the age of Napoleon. Edward Gibbon devoted a few thousand pages just to Rome's decline and fall. Paul Johnson's many volumes number in the thousands of pages. Schaeffer devoted only about seven and a half pages plus some illustrations to cover Ancient Rome.

Like all too many Protestant historians, Schaeffer is a bit shaky concerning the Middle Ages. This thousand-year period is given sixteen pages, but Schaeffer is torn between whether it was an era of Christian gain or of spiritual decline. He praises Dante's *Divine Comedy* lightly, and then dismisses the work for its inclusion of pagan mythology. Music, art, architecture, and the theology of Thomas Aquinas are all introduced, but more questions are raised than answered by his treatment of the Medieval portion of history.

The art of the Renaissance is aptly covered, assuming that Schaeffer's spin on art could pass muster among university art history students. The chapter on the Enlightenment strays off into a discussion of the French and Russian Revolutions. The Reformation receives the coverage of two chapters, with the second focusing on many of the political implications of the Reformation. It was in this second chapter, titled simply "The Reformation—Continued", that Schaeffer reintroduced modern evangelicals to a forgotten political classic, Samuel Rutherford's *Lex Rex*.

With these positive points, we must add that the Reformation issue reminds us of another Schaeffer problem. Schaeffer was a Presbyterian. In fact he wrote a small booklet on infant baptism. But when his collected works appeared, that small work was omitted. Schaeffer was a Calvinist, a one-time student under J. Gresham Machen and Van Til. Yet almost never in his extensive writings did Schaeffer refer to himself as a Calvinist or to his theology as Reformed. Reformed soteriology was re-emerging on the battlefield during the 1960s through the 1990s after a long siege by its enemies. Schaeffer was a key name in the whole battle, and the troops looked in vain for the Reformed banner flying from fortress L'Abri.

Schaeffer's apologetic method lacked the literary grace or style of a Lewis or a Chesterton. His themes from book to book were repetitive. His personal style and appearance were odd, even for a man of the 1960s and 1970s. George Grant remarked that among his first thoughts upon meeting Schaeffer was "What a haircut!" and "What's the deal with the knickers?"[3]

---

[3] George Grant. *The Micah Mandate*. (Nashville: Cumberland House, 1999), 110-111.

Since *How Should We Then Live?* is almost thirty years old, many of the issues and debates of the book are outdated or irrelevant. The Communist threat, which Schaeffer discusses, collapsed over a decade ago. The particular ethical dilemmas, the cultural trends, the movies and music, the manifestations of depravity, and the materialistic fashions of the 1970s are gone. Often replaced with equally bad or worse counterparts, the issues of 1976 are as dated as discussions of Model T Fords and flappers of the 1920s.

Now that I have tossed every flimsy harpoon I can muster at a great white whale, it remains for me to ask the question, how shall we then view Schaeffer the man and his great writings?

There is a logical fallacy called composition. It works like this: Each part of the 747 aircraft is designed to be lightweight. So a 747 must not weigh very much.[4] To find the faults, the missing elements, and the structural weaknesses of Francis Schaeffer is not to demean the man. The accumulation of lightweight parts does not imply a lightweight thinker. How did this man achieve such gigantic spiritual and cultural success?

What Schaeffer Did

The simple answer is that Schaeffer wrote books and people read them. No doubt many people went to Switzerland and personally met the man and many others heard him speak as he traveled about the world, but his main influence came from the books.

Let's examine his legacy a bit closer.

First, Schaeffer enlarged the dimensions of the pastor's study. Traditionally ministers were to be students of the Bible and of theology. Church matters were to occupy their time and attention, but Schaeffer had a holistic view of Christianity. He applied Kuyper's dictum that there was no square inch of the universe where Christ had not said, "This is mine." Now along with theology, the subjects of philosophy, art, music, literature, political science, psychology, economics, and all the arts and academic disciplines were to be the realm of pastoral oversight.

This led to a second effect. Now people who desired or felt called to give themselves to ministry or full-time service of the Lord had an expanded range of options. No longer was church work the only choice, but all those academic and artistic fields were not just open for Christians. All areas of life were, like the Macedonian vision of Acts, crying out to believers, "Come over here and help us."

---

[4] Douglas J. Wilson and James B. Nance. *Introductory Logic: Third Edition* (Moscow: Canon Press, 1997), 110.

This pulled Christian students out of the fundamentalist and evangelical ghettos into the art museums, the concert halls, the libraries, and (brace yourself) the movie theaters. From the Scopes Trial on, the Christian program to conquer the world was through means of retreat. It was the same as Joseph Johnston's method of fighting the invading northern armies in the War Between the States: Dig in, receive the enemy blows, and pull back to another defensive position. Nancy Pearcey testifies, "Here was a Christian talking about modern philosophy, quoting the existentialists, analyzing worldview themes in the lyrics of Led Zeppelin, explaining the music of John Cage and the paintings of Jackson Pollock. You must remember that this was in an era when Christian college students were not even allowed to go to Disney movies—yet here he was, discussing films by Bergman and Fellini."[5]

Schaeffer was not the first, the only, or even the best Christian, cultural critic. There were a host of Dooyeweerdian scholars and students applying Christianity to various disciplines.[6] Schaeffer's fellow Calvinistic Presbyterians, like Rushdoony, Singer, David Freeman, Gordon Clark, and others were lecturing and writing on philosophy, history, science, and other worldview issues. C. S. Lewis, his friends, and his disciples were writing Christian commentaries on issues. Harry Blamires, a student of Lewis's, had penned his book *The Christian Mind* in 1963. Both T. S. Eliot and Dorothy Sayers had written scholarly Christian works before Schaeffer. And one cannot overlook the Catholic scholars like Dawson, Jacques Maritain, and Etienne Gilson, whose writings were respected by Catholics and Protestants alike.

Schaeffer's move to the head of the pack is even more amazing due to the fact that he was in Switzerland during most of the years of his writing and ministry. His success seems to be due to his skills as a popularizer of apologetics, theology, and philosopher. As he viewed himself, he was a pastor, not a theologian or philosopher. In comparison with other pastors or pastor-authors of the time, Schaeffer had more than his share of equals and superiors, but it was more a matter of a niche than a gift. Schaeffer was scholarly enough in his conversations, lectures, and books to talk with the educated community. His communication skills, however, bridged a gap between the scholarly discourse of the educated elite and those needing to hear the gospel preached plainly and simply.

For example, Edith Schaeffer tells the story of a young man of Swiss heritage, named John, who had grown up in New York but was back in Switzerland . A girl invited him to come stay with "a nice American family" in

---

[5] Pearcey, *Total Truth*, 54.
[6] Such as H. Evan Runner and Calvin Seerveld.

Hoemoz, which is where the Schaeffer's mission, called L'Abri, was located. Francis Schaeffer met John and another man at the gate and said, "Let's go for a walk, and talk." John knew nothing of Schaeffer or his theology. Along the way, Christianity came up in the conversation, and he innocently asked, "Oh, I don't think Christianity has a leg to stand on, intellectually, do you?" Schaeffer then gave his future son-in-law a two hour answer.[7]

No doubt many could have fine-tuned or improved his two hour answers. Nancy Pearsey says that Schaeffer's strength was in his " 'bridging' role in leading young people into the intellectual and cultural world."[8] Schaeffer was not lacking in his own exposure to teachers, books, and peers. He studied at Westminster under J. Gresham Machen. He studied apologetics under no less an authority than Cornelius Van Til. He was influenced by Dooyeweerd's thought via his friend Hans Rookmaker, who was himself an art scholar. Schaeffer sidestepped the academic and theological world of point and counterpoint over details. This, no doubt, bothered some, such as Cornelius Van Til. When Van Til challenged Schaeffer in a series of letters, Schaeffer did not respond. On a visit to Westminster Theological Seminary, Van Til sat down with Schaeffer and presented his points one by one, to which Schaeffer nodded in agreement. When Van Til then gave a fifteen minute discourse outlining his own apologetic method, Schaeffer responded, saying, "That is the most beautiful statement on apologetics I have ever heard. I wish there had been a tape recorder here. I would make it required listening for all L'Abri workers."[9]

Whereas Schaeffer's scholarship or apologetic method may have been lacking, there was certainly nothing lacking in the Christian community the Schaeffer's communicated to the world. Schaeffer's books emphasized many aspects of Christian thought and living. Bible study was combined with academic pursuits. Philosophy was mixed with prayer and devotion. Theology concerning God and eternal matters was combined with an awareness of problems like pollution and racial relations. Edith complemented her husband's books with her own works on housekeeping, family life, and an autobiographical accounts of their lives.

Around the Schaeffer's, a whole community of Christian scholars, artists, and disciples gathered. Hans Rookmaker, mentioned above, worked with

---

[7] Edith Schaeffer, *L'Abri* (Wheaton, IL: Cornerstone Books, 1992, revised edition), 132-133.
[8] Pearcey, 400.
[9] Scott R. Burson and Jerry L. Walls, *C. S. Lewis & Francis Schaeffer: Lessons for a New Century from the Most Influential Apologists of Our Time* (Downers Grove, IL: Inter Varsity Press, 1998), 146-147.

Schaeffer and taught art history. Os Guiness, a key writer on Christian issues today, was part of the Schaeffer team. Schaeffer's son Franky produced the film documentary versions of *How Should We Then Live?* and *Whatever Happened to the Human Race?* Nancy Pearcey, herself one of the many who experienced L'Abri, noted that many of Schaeffer's students went on to earn advanced degrees in various areas of scholarship.[10]

God uses means. Luther was not the first to raise questions about indulgences and relics. Calvin was not the first to organize a systematic theology. God uses book sales to effect His will, and so in spite of any deficiencies, Schaeffer's books sold. They were usually shorter works with attractive covers and professional designs. InterVarsity Press reaped a harvest off of Schaeffer's work. Again, it was a case of a niche that was being filled. In this case, the niche was a growing class of conservative and educated young people looking for answers.

In spite of the cultural decline and decadence of the 1960s and 1970s, people were still coming to Jesus. The Jesus People were just one example of how some found Christ even amidst the hippie movement of the time. Many others knew Jesus from their upbringing. Most of us growing up in the 60s and 70s never participated in a riot, a love-in, a war protest, or a drug experience. We went to church weekly, but never to Woodstock. But Jesus was presented as a *personal* Lord and Savior. Even Bible colleges shied away from proclaiming God having spoken in an infallible word. Being a Christian on campus meant trusting Jesus, while still tipping the hat to every vestige of modernity.

Schaeffer preached the gospel to that generation, although he did not do so in conventional terms. Schaeffer read the trendy philosophers; he watched the avant-garde movies; he delved into the liberal theologies; he examined the radical social critics. He acknowledged the Church's failure on race issues. He even sided with the youth protest movement against the establishment. Along with all this, he analyzed historical epochs, raising questions about the Renaissance and the Enlightenment. He ventured into the areas of art and architecture, positing Christian-based interpretations. He was at home with classical music, well versed in literary classics, conversational about Plato and Aristotle, and at home with a world of 'particulars' (to use a favorite phrase of his). Moreover, he did not look like or talk like a preacher!

Meanwhile, he calmly and rationally defended the notion of a living God who speaks to us in His Word and who saved us by sending Jesus to die on the cross. Schaeffer's work is flawed and obsolete at many points. Go back a

---

[10] Pearsey, 400.

few centuries and you will find Calvin prefacing every other paragraph with an indictment against Romanists, or Luther railing against the Holy Roman emperor. Go back beyond that and note that the great Augustine defended celibacy and strayed down many a goofy path. Even the Apostle Paul's writings include a command for his cloak and parchments to be brought to him.

Not every young person in the sixties grew long hair, smoked marijuana, and camped out at Woodstock. Not every child of the seventies bought into the decadence of that era. Since the late 1950s, a conservative movement had been thriving among young people. The Goldwater for President movement, which was a short-term disaster for conservatives, showed the strength of conservative ideas, and that source of strength was found on college campuses. Books and essays by conservatives were pouring off the presses of a few small publishing houses, but most of the conservative movement was based on a coalition of Catholic traditionalists and secular libertarians. Men like William Buckley and Russell Kirk were leaders from within the Catholic circles. The libertarian wing of conservatism included such people as the atheist Ayn Rand and the Austrian economists, like Ludwig Von Mises.

The newly converted Christian walking out of a Billy Graham rally who wanted to affect the culture in bigger ways than handing out evangelistic tracts, had little to choose from in the conservative movement. Even the *Roe v. Wade* decision only roused the Protestant community slightly. It was 1980, seven years after *Roe v. Wade* before the political rumblings of the religious right or the moral majority were even felt.

When Protestants woke up to find the culture spinning about in moral disorder like Phaethon's chariot, the only answer seemed to be figuring out how to best chart the crash and prepare for disaster. Even survival was not very hopeful based on the times. Hence Schaeffer was able to raise a question in his title by asking how Christians should then live, but note in his subtitle that Western thought and culture was in decline. It was a popular era for strategies for surviving the many possible avenues of eminent collapse. The economy was certain to implode into uncontrollable inflation. The next depression was on the horizon. Nuclear proliferation was unrestrained. The Communist one world order was becoming a reality. The liberalism of the churches was a sign of the great apostasy. The degeneracy of the youth foreclosed the future. If some combination of these problems did not destroy the world, then drug abuse, pollution, overpopulation, or racial turmoil would finish off any survivors.

Pessimistic Christians who start trusting God, obeying His Word, applying His order for personal and family living, and praying can turn a culture around. Schaeffer ended his somewhat depressing, Jonah-like sermon-book with a sentence he asked readers to memorize: "To make no decision in regard to the growth of authoritarian government is already a decision for it."[11] Next, he quoted an extensive passage from Ezekiel that exhorts the reader to repent and live. He then closed by expressing a hope that readers would turn from wickedness to the Creator and live.[12]

By 1983, some seven years after *How Should We Then Live?*, Schaeffer wrote *A Christian Manifesto*. This was a political call to action, a rejoinder to Marx and Engel's *Communist Manifesto* of an earlier century. Schaeffer spoke of a window of opportunity that had been provided, a blessed reprieve of God from the deserved judgment. God provided that window partially through the vision of Ronald Reagan. Whether Reagan ever knew of the Schaeffer's or their writings, I don't know. Reagan did for conservative political philosophy what Schaeffer did for Calvinistic worldview thinking: He popularized it and made it workable. Reagan's political base originally consisted of two factions—fiscal conservatives and anti-communists. These two factions brought him within a hair's breadth of winning the Republican nomination away from President Gerald Ford in 1976. But it was a third faction, the social conservatives, that gave Reagan's presidential quest its success and political base.

How Should We Then Live? did not cause the election of Reagan, but it and Schaeffer's other books were certainly factors in changing the political landscape in the US by 1980.

Schaeffer was not the greatest theologian, apologist, writer, speaker, or cultural critic of the age. I don't think he tried to be. He did not seek to give the final word or definitive answer to any question. Perhaps he wanted his students to achieve that goal. America was failing in the 1970s; it has not completely recovered now in this new millennium. But the direction has changed. Mel Gibson's movie and George Bush's 2005 inaugural address both show Schaeffer's influence, even though neither Gibson nor Bush may have ever read Schaeffer. Schaeffer's students have written enough books to fill a library. The college students who read him now fill pulpits, occupy classrooms, write books and articles, and have web sites. Like Beowulf, he slew a few monsters in his day and died still fighting other monsters. He was often a somber prophet, and his agenda reached more toward the past than the future.

Now fifty years after his great mission work in Switzerland was started and thirty years after *How Should We Then Live?* was written, we can begin to access how truly great this servant of God was. Instead of being historians of the decline, we may yet need historians of a new reformation.

---

[11] Schaeffer, *How Should We Then Live?*, 257.
[12] Schaeffer, 258.

Are we ready to chronicle the new reformation? Or are Western thought and culture still in decline? We are still in a culture war. Movies, politics, music, books, educational institutions, and churches are still battlegrounds for the heart and soul of America. Terrorists abroad have to work hard to outdo wickedness at home in the process of tearing our culture apart. Political solutions still fail. Elections all too often indicate that Americans' convictions are located in their pocket books or that moral currency is bankrupt, or that they are, like Gloucester in *King Lear*, a case of blindmen being led by madmen.[13] Societal tensions, when eased, offer no more long term comfort than seismic fault lines in California.

This being a culture war, the solution will not be found until the basis of our societal culture is changed. Schaeffer said, "Christians do not need to be in the majority in order to influence society."[14] Schaeffer's peer, Rushdoony, repeatedly emphasized that majorities never rule history, rather history is ruled by organized minorities who are bound by a common faith. The faith that offers the best answer to the question of how we should then live is Christianity. But that faith has to be presented, not just as an outlet to eternal punishment, but as a present kingdom for this world.

Andrew Sandlin writes, "One reason historic, orthodox Christianity has lost hegemony in the West over the last three centuries, and especially since 1865 in the United States, is that it has become something other than a full world and life view, that is, it has become something less than a real religion."[15] Schaeffer had emphasized the same point in saying, "[P]eople function on the basis of their world view more consistently than they realize. The problem is not outward things. The problem is having, and then acting upon, the right world view—the world view which gives men and women the truth of what is."[16]

Yes, he stumbled; yes, he over simplified; yes, he did not say enough at points. Still Francis Schaeffer played a key role in helping Christians recover that lost hegemony. Better said, he helped us get started in the recovery efforts. Our history classes are filled with eager disciples needing to know how to reach the next step. Francis Schaeffer pointed again to the right world view when he spoke of a Triune God Who is here and is not silent and Who has, in the second person of the Trinity, died for the sins of His people. Night, fog and clouds may obscure parts of a great mountain for a time, but a little bit of sunlight shows us what is truly there.

---

[13] William Shakespeare, *King Lear*, Act IV, Scene 1, Line 46: " 'Tis the times' plague, when madmen lead the blind."

[14] Schaeffer, 256.

[15] Andrew Sandlin, "Afterword: Why We Will Win" from *A Comprehensive Faith: An International Festschrift for Rousas John Rushdoony*, edited by Andrew Sandlin (San Jose, CA: Friends of Chalcedon, 1996), 240.

[16] Schaeffer, 254.

AFTERWORD

> We cannot say the "past is past" without surrendering the future.
> Winston Churchill

I have no interest in surrendering the future. Visionaries like British Prime Minister Churchill, American President Ronald Reagan, and Dutch political leader Groen van Prinsterer were men immersed in history, who then moved their worlds forward. Even the greatest of literary figures, those like playwright William Shakespeare, novelist William Faulkner, and poets and critics like the Agrarians, were grounded in history.

God also reveals His interest in history. Father Abraham has now spent countless centuries in glory with the Lord. While God could have given us an account of Abraham's eternal bliss, He gave us, instead, the account of Abraham's earthly journey, those years of travail and wandering upon the earth, trusting and believing, and sometimes failing, but always persevering. He revealed to us history, not heaven

History is vital to reformation and revival, but it is insufficient. All of life is to be redeemed; every square inch of the universe belongs to Christ. The ministry of churches, the establishment of godly families, the growth of Christian schools, the printing of Christian books, and the advancement of world-wide Christian missions are all components of God's kingdom. "Thy will be done on earth as it is in heaven" remains the most ambitious prayer request ever. As it is fulfilled, we expect our vision to become blurred and our mind's orientation unclear, for we seek a world where the contours of the landscape make us question whether we are here or there, on earth or in heaven.

I would be more than happy if this treatise on history were to have the impact of Augustine's *City of God* or Calvin's *Institutes of the Christian Religion*. I would also be quite pleased if it had the market success of Rick Warren's *The Purpose Filled Life*. I don't expect either to happen, but I do expect some impact.

There are at least four things regarding history that are expressed in the pages of this book. First, it is a call for teachers and students to think Christianly in regard for history. In part, this comes out in the details of a personal pilgrimage, and like many pilgrimages, it is ongoing. Thinking Christianly about history is not like learning to ride a bicycle; that is, a thing once learned and mastered and never forgotten. Rather, it is like learning to master tools of a craft or a musical instrument. Learning provides the foundation for advancing.

Second, this book recognizes Christian historians. While Eusebius, Augustine, Dawson, Scott, Rushdoony, and a few others were noted, many, many more Christian historians still need recognition. I could double the size of this book by adding chapters on Christian thinkers like Merle d'Aubigne, Phillip Schaff, Robert L. Dabney, Herman Dooyeweerd, H. C. Smit, and Paul Johnson. I could triple the size of the book by including the great ancients, like Herodotus, Thucydides, and Livy. I could expand it even more by weaving in the Medieval historians, like the Venerable Bede or Gregory of Tours, and then we might as well envision a second volume highlighting brilliant modern historians who are outside of the Christian orbit. A Christian historiography is much needed for teachers, and I have only scratched the surface.

Third, this book reviews books. Reading useful historical studies and reflecting upon them is the vital work and sheer delight of history teachers. Note that we may call it work, but it is really fun and recreation. Book consumption, book addiction, and book fanaticism form an underlying presupposition of this book. If you love history, but not books, subscribe to cable. If you are really serious about wanting to teach and learn history, get thee to a library or bookstore.

Fourth, this book gives case studies, from Greece, the Medieval Period, the Reformation era, colonial America, and the twentieth century to highlight Christian concerns and interests. Hopefully, these essays also model how Christians can go about the task of applying Christian thought to history. Sometimes in writing Christian history, we err by superficially glossing and romantically idealizing the past. Relying on, rather than evaluating, the judgments of historical documents and romantic chroniclers can unbalance an account. A slavish cutting and pasting of the official rulings of the recognized secondary sources can likewise fail to represent what really happened. Revisionists can be scorned, popularizers can be distrusted, and academics can be dismissed, but they are all ignored to our historical peril. We are saved by grace through faith, but our knowledge of history is through good and difficult work.

Afterword

Our study of history is not the same as the formulating of creeds and confessions, but we must still be careful about our judgments. I can already find parts of this book where my own judgments have been strengthened or weakened or changed since the last revision. God gives the final verdict on history. The events of history—even those of ancient Greece, Rome, and Jerusalem—are all too recent for us to evaluate completely. But the study of history is a dialectical process and hopefully involves dialectical progress.

All of this meandering last word is a way of saying that this book is incomplete. When this baby—meaning this book—is born, perhaps I can envision a hope for another baby brother—meaning another book—to follow. But for now, this odyssey through wars, Punic and otherwise, must stop. *War and Peace* is a very long book, but many of you know Tolstoy, perhaps he was your friend, and you know that I am no Tolstoy.

An Annotated Bibliography
Books and Authors Cited, Reviewed, Quoted, and Prized

> Let me learn, Lord, of human misery. Let me learn the wisdom
> that is born of suffering. Let me learn of illness and infirmity,
> of age and impediment, of wrongful accusation and despair,
> of abandonment and loss. Let me learn of trials of principle
> and tests of faith. Let me learn to endure pain and solitude
> and to sacrifice for right. Let me learn, Lord, what it is to
> be a martyr. Let me learn these things,
> Lord; and let me learn them all *from books.*
> Source Unknown

Adair, John, *Founding Fathers: The Puritans in England and America.* London: J.M. Kent & Sons Ltd., 1982. A choice and favorable study of Puritans.

Alder, Susan, "Education in America," in *Public Education and Indoctrination.* Irvington-on-Hudson: Foundation for Economic Education, 1993. The publisher, The Foundation for Economic Education, is well known for their conservative, somewhat libertarian books on economics and related issues.

Alexander, Benjamin B. Alexander, "The Man of Letters and the Faithful Heart" in *A Defender of Southern Conservatism: M.E. Bradford and His Achievements,* ed. Clyde N. Wilson. Columbia, MO: University of Missouri Press, 1999. M. E. Bradford, the subject of the book referenced above, was a brilliantscholar in the areas of Constitutional history, Southern politics, and Southern literature.

Alexander, Bevin, *How Great Generals Win.* New York: W. W. Norton and Company, 1993. Good selection of military biographies.

Alhstrom, Sidney, *A Religious History of the American People.* New Haven: Yale University Press, 1973. This in-depth survey includesthe history of movements, denominations, and key figures all in the context of America's political and social history. Excellent study of American church history.

Allums, Larry, editor, *The Epic Cosmos*. Dallas: The Dallas Institute Publications, 1992. Understanding epic classics of literature is as vital to understanding history as history books themselves. The introductory essay in this collection of literary criticism by Dr. Louise Cowan, titled "Epic as Cosmopoesis" is a difficult, but highly rewarding study by one of the most insightful literary critics of our time.

Ahlquist, Dale, *Lepanto by G. K. Chesterton with Explanatory Notes and Commentary*. Minneapolis, MN: American Chesterton Society, 2003. Includes Chesterton's poem with historical explanatory notes.

Arbery, Glenn, *Why Literature Matters*. Wilmington, Delaware: ISI Books, 2001. The chapter on *The Iliad*, titled "The Sacrifice of Achilles," is worth the price of the book.

Augustine, *The City of God: An Abridged Version*, edited by Vernon J. Bourke. New York: Image Books, 1958. The advantages of this version are the shortened length, a mere 650 pages, and an excellent introduction by Etienne Gilson.

——*Confessions*. New York: Oxford University Press, 1991. Religious autobiography as a genre grew out of this work. An excellent introduction to a pivotal thinker and to the philosophical rivals of the early church.

——*On Christian Teaching*. New York: Oxford University Press, 1997. Great study for Bible teachers, history teachers, and rhetoric students.

Bahnsen, Greg. *Theonomy in Christian Ethics*. Nutley, NJ: The Presbyterian and Reformed Publishing Company, 1973. Pathbreaking, profound, and weighty study of God's Law and its abiding applications. Much insight on Puritan political thought with applications of both theology and history to ethics.

Bean, W.G., *Stonewall's Man: Sandie Pendleton*. Wilmington: Broadfoot Publishing Company, 1987. Tells the whole story of the man of which my essay is only a portion.

Beeching, Jack, *The Galleys at Lepanto*. New York: Charles Scribner's Sons, 1983. Tells the greater account of events preceding and succeeding the siege of Malta in 1565.

Behe, Michael, *Darwin's Black Box: The Biochemical Challenge to Evolution*. New York: The Free Press, 1996. Major nail in Darwin's coffin.

Billington, James H., *Fire in the Minds of Men: Origins of the Revolutionary Faith*. New Brunswick, NJ: Transaction Publishers, 2003. A detailed scholarly study that shows that revolutionary ideology is basically religious. The goal of revolution was to establish a perfect social order. The results fell far short of that.

Birzer, Bradley J., *J.R.R. Tolkien's Sanctifying Myth*. Wilmington: ISI Books, 2002. One among many useful studies of a key thinker, Tolkien, who is often ignored by the literary establishment.

Blamires, Harry, *The Christian Mind: How Should a Christian Think?* Ann Arbor, MI: Servant Publications, 1978. Originally published in 1963, by a man mentored by C. S. Lewis, this was a wake-up call to Christians to develop worldview thinking.

Blumenfeld, Samuel, *Is Public Education Necessary?*. Old Greenwich: The Devon-Adair Company, 1981. The answer is "No!" and the argument is quite compelling.

Boettner, Loraine, *The Reformed Doctrine of Predestination*. Philadelphia: The Presbyterian and Reformed Publishing Company, 1975. This is a lengthy study of Calvinistic doctrine with a chapter on the impact of Calvinism in history. This is a serious and convincing study.

———*Studies in Theology*. Philadelphia: The Presbyterian and Reformed Publishing Company, 1975. A life-changing book for me personally.

Boles, John B., *The Great Revival: Beginnings of the Bible Belt*. Lexington, Kentucky: The University of Kentucky Press, 1972. The Great Revival marvelously resulted in the saving of many souls. Sad to note, it also contributed to the furtherance of Arminian and individualistic religious attitudes on the frontier.

Booth, Robert R., *Children of the Promise: The Biblical Case for Infant Baptism*. Phillipsburg, New Jersey, 1995. My only claim to scholarly fame: I am footnoted in this book by a wonderful friend.

Bratt, James D., editor, *Abraham Kuyper: A Centennial Reader*. Grand Rapids, MI: William B. Eerdmans Publishing Company, 1998. This is a collection of excerpts of one of the most brilliant worldview theologians ever, the Dutchman Abraham Kuyper. His name has become an adjective; hence, labeling an idea or a writer as Kuyperian is usually a high commendation.

Bradford, Ernle, *The Great Siege: Malta 1565*. Hertfordshire, Great Britain: Wordsworth Editions, 1999. Bradford was a prolific historian and biographer, with *The Great Siege* being only one of his many fine books. He was a storyteller and not an academic scholar. He spent much of his life sailing the Mediterranean Sea, doing historical research.

———*Hannibal*. New York: McGraw-Hill Company, 1981. A great account of a great and ruthless, yet unsuccessful, military leader.

Breed, W. P., *Presbyterians and the Revolution* Decatur, MS: Issacharian Press, 1993. This useful reprint is one of the best sources for the price Presbyterians paid for our freedom in the American War for Independence.

Bridenbaugh, Carl, *Mitre and Sceptre: Transatlantic Faiths, Ideas, Personalities, & Politics* New York: Oxford University Press, 1962. R. J. Rushdoony highly favored this book. The central thesis is that religion, specifically the fear of the appointment of an Anglican bishop over the colonies, was the ultimate cause of the American War for Independence.

Burke, Edmund, "Reflections on the Revolution in France" from *The Best of Burke: Selected Writings and Speeches of Edmund Burke,* edited by Peter J. Stanlis. (Washington, D.C.: Regnery Publishing Company, 1963). Burke is one of the fathers of Conservative intellectual thought. He applauded the American cause in the War for Independence and was critical of the French Revolution.

Burleigh, Michael, *Earthly Powers: The Clash of Religion and Politics in Europe, from the French Revolution to the Great War.* New York: Harper Collins Publishers, 2005. This work builds upon the insights of historian James Billington (cited above) and Christian novelist Fyodor Dostoevsky, especially his novel *The Possessed* (sometimes translated as *The Demons).*

Burns, Edward McNall, *Western Civilization.* New York: W.W. Norton & Company, 1973, 8th edition. A standard college level Western Civilization text. Like many writers of such texts, Burns is quite competent except when in error, and Burns is often in error.

Burson, Scott R. and Jerry L. Walls, *C. S. Lewis and Francis Schaeffer: Lessons for a New Century from the Most Influential Apologists of Our Time.* Downers Grove, IL: Inter Varsity Press, 1998. It is hard to go wrong when Lewis and Schaeffer are your subjects.

Cahill, Thomas, *How the Irish Saved Civilization.* New York: Nan A. Talese, 1995. Reviewed in the text. Cahill's best book and the beginning of his "Hinges of History" series.

———*Sailing the Wine Dark Sea: Why the Greeks Matter.* New York: Nan A. Talese, 2003. Reviewed in the text. Should be subtitled: *How the Greeks Were Perverse.*

Caldecott, Stratford, "Over the Chasm of Fire: Christian Heroism in The Silmarillion and The Lord of the Rings" from *Tolkien: A Celebration,* edited by Joseph Pearce San Francisco: Ignatius Press, 1999. One of many good essays in this collection.

Calvin, John, *Institutes of the Christian Religion,* edited by John T. McNeill. Philadelphia: The Westminster Press, 1960. The defining book of the Protestant Reformation and a classic of Western Civilization. A true blending of profound theological insight with devotional passion.

Carson, Clarence, *The World in the Grip of an Idea.* New Rochelle, NY: Arlington House Publishers, 1979. This book surveys the different shades of collectivism. Communism, Fascism, Nazism, and Fabian Socialism are all covered. Carson's five-volume history of the United States is also a great resource. He is a very conservative, perhaps libertarian, and Christian historian.

Chandler, David Leon, *The Natural Superiority of Southern Politicians.* Garden City: Doubleday, 1977. Very dated book, but still fun political history.

Chesterton, G. K., *The Everlasting Man.* San Francisco: Ignatius Press, 1993, reprint. This is a powerful study of early man based on Christian presuppositions of the origins and destiny of history. Next to Chesterton's *Orthodoxy,* this is my favorite book by this brilliant and often quoted thinker.

Clarke, Erskine, *Our Southern Zion: A History of Calvinism in the South Carolina Low Country, 1690-1990.* Tuscaloosa, Alabama: The University of Alabama Press, 1996. The earlier parts of this history are the best. Plodding, but worthwhile study.

Clark, Gordon H., *A Christian View of Men and Things: An Introduction to Philosophy.* Grand Rapids, MI: Baker Book House, 1981. Chapter 2 of this book, "The Philosophy of History," is essential reading for Christian history teachers. Other chapters cover such equally essential topics as politics, science, religion, and epistemology. One does not have to agree with Clark on every point to profit from reading him. He was a prominent Calvinist worldview thinker of the twentieth century.

————*Historiography: Secular and Religious.* Nutley, NJ: The Craig Press, 1971. I find it puzzling that one can get a degree in history without ever having to study what exactly history is and why it is written and taught. I needed this book in college. It includes studies of both good guys, like Augustine, and bad guys, like Marx.

———*Thales to Dewey.* Jefferson, MD: The Trinity Foundation, 1985. It is unforgivable that people like me were able to get history degrees without having courses in philosophy. But catching up on what I missed is quite fun. This book is one of the most often cited studies of the history of philosophy by a Christian and Reformed thinker.

Clark, Kenneth, *Civilization.* London: The Folio Society, 1999. This is one of those coffee table books, filled with art and illustrations. These types of books are useful for gleaning insights that then need to be filtered through the Christian interpreters, like Schaeffer.

Clouser, Roy A., *The Myth of Religious Neutrality: An Essay on the Hidden Role of Religious Belief in Theories.* Notre Dame, IN: University of Notre Dame Press, 2005. Quite a serious and daunting work by a Dooyeweerdian thinker. His essay "Is There a Christian View of Everything?" is a shorter route to his main ideas.

Coulter, Ann, *Godless: The Church of Liberalism.* New York: Crown Forum, 2006. Miss Coulter's critiques of liberalism have all been best sellers. She takes no prisoners. In this book, she takes aim at the public school system and Darwinism.

Conkin, Paul K., *The Uneasy Center: Reformed Christianity in Antebellum America.* Chapel Hill: The University of North Carolina Press, 1995. The presence, the successes, and the failures of Reformed Christianity in American history are vital topics for Christian study.

Courtois, Stephane and Nicolas Werth, Jean-Louis Panne, Andrzej Paczkowski, Karol Bartosek, and Jean-Louis Margolin. *The Black Book of Communism.* Translated by Jonathan Murphy and Mark Kramer. Cambridge, MA: Harvard University Press, 1999. A worthy and massive epitaph for the Evil Empires of Marx, Lenin, Stalin, and others.

Covington, Dennis, *Salvation on Sand Mountain.* Reading, MA: Addison-Wesley Publishing Company, 1995. Wonderful account of a Southern snake-handling religious group. From even that weird vantage point, the modern secular worldview cannot stand.

Cowan, Louise, *The Fugitive Group.* Baton Rouge: LSU Press, 1968. The Fugitive poets, a group that included John Crowe Ransom, Donald Davidson, and Allen Tate, were literary men who associated with Vanderbilt University in the 1920s and 1930s. From their brilliant and classically trained minds, three key movements were spawned: the Fugitive poetry movement, the Agrarian movement, and the New Criticism school of literary studies. Dr. Cowan knew and studied under these scholar-poets and has furthered their work in the field of literature.

Dabney, Robert L., *Discussions,* Volume II, Evangelical. Harrisonburg, VA: Sprinkle Publications, 1982. This volume includes the essay "Uses and Results of Church History," which is absolutely indispensable for a Christian history teacher. The entire five-volume collection of Dabney's *Discussions* is a thorough examination into the theology, politics, and worldview thinking of one of the South's greatest theologians.

———*The Life and Campaigns of Lt. Gen. T. J. "Stonewall" Jackson.* Harrisonburg, VA: Sprinkle Publications. This work and Dabney's *A Defense of Virginia and the South* are two of the best first hand accounts of the Southern cause. Jackson's faith epitomized the best of the South. His military skills, particularly his Valley Campaign, are still studied in awe. Dabney was a great writer and polemicist for both the Confederacy and Calvinism.

Dallimore, Arnold, *George Whitefield: The Life and times of the Great Evangelist of the 18th Century Revival,* 2 volumes. Edinburgh: The Banner of Truth Trust, 1975. Inspiring account of a man who ought to be listed as a founding father of America and a key figure who helped prevent England from having its own version of the French Revolution.

Dawson, Christopher, *Christianity and European Culture: Selections from the Work of Christopher Dawson.* Washington, D.C.: The Catholic University of America Press, 1998. This work is an excellent introduction to Dawson's writings. I have never found a Dawson book I did not like. He is a model of what a Christian historian should be like.

———*Christianity and the New Age.* Manchester, New Hampshire: Sophia Institute Press, 1988.

——— *The Crisis of Western Education.* Stuebenville, Ohio: Franciscan University Press, 1989. Prophetic.

———*The Dividing of Christendom.* New York: Sheed and Ward, 1965. Fair and balanced survey of the recurring divisions within the Christian faith.

———*Dynamics of World History.* Edited by John J. Mulloy Wilmington, DE: ISI Books, 2002. Sets forth the case for a Christian view of history and examines key historians.

———*The Gods of Revolution.* New York: New York University Press, 1972. Surveys the French Revolution.

———*The Historic Reality of Christian Culture: A Way to the Renewal of Human Life* New York: Harper and Brothers, 1960. This book is contained in *Christianity and European Culture.*

———*The Making of Europe.* New York: Barnes and Noble, 1994.
——— *Medieval Essays.* Washington, D.C.: The Catholic University of America Press. Defining work on Medieval history.
——— *The Movement of World Revolution.* New York: Sheed and Ward, 1959.
———*Religion and the Rise of Western Culture.* New York: Image Books, 1991.
Dembski, William A., editor, *Uncommon Dissent: Intellectuals Who Find Darwinism Unconvincing* Wilmington, Delaware: ISI Books, 2004. This book contains essays by scholars who are promoting Intelligent Design. Great work by co-belligerents fighting the same enemies we are fighting.
DeMar, Gary, with Fred D. Young and Gary L. Todd. *Building a City On a Hill.* Powder Springs, Georgia: American Vision, 2005. Gary DeMar is an important Christian thinker in three areas—the past, the present, and the future. He has rediscovered many key Christian history books and documents from the past century. His work on eschatology is first rate, and his commentaries on current American social, political, and theological issues are sound. He is the president of American Vision and the editor of the magazine *Biblical Worldview.* This book is the second in a series on American history from a Christian perspective called *To Pledge Allegiance.* It covers the colonial era with particular emphasis on the Reformational background to American history.
DeMar, Gary and Fred Young, *A New World in View.* Powder Springs, Georgia: American Vision, 1996. This is the first book in the series *To Pledge Allegiance.* It covers the European background to the discovery of America. The coverage of Columbus's trials, travails, and triumph and of Cortes's brilliant campaign against the brutal Aztec Empire is historical storytelling at its best.
DeMar, Gary and George Grant, *On the Road to Independence.* Powder Springs, Georgia: American Vision, 2005. This volume, written by two of the best Christian historians of our time, is the third volume in the series *To Pledge Allegiance.* It takes the American story through the War for Independence and the making of the Constitution and into the early decades of the new republic.
Denton, Michael, *Evolution: A Theory in Crisis.* Bethesda: Adler & Adler Publishers, Inc., 1985. Yet another nail in Darwin's coffin.
Diaz, Bernal, *The Conquest of New Spain.* New York: Penguin Books, 1963. Diaz was with Cortes in his conquest of the Aztec Empire. Good first hand account to supplement DeMar and Young's *A New World In View,* which is an excellent secondary account.

Dooyeweerd, Herman, *In the Twilight of Western Thought.* Nutley, NJ: The Craig Press, 1990. Dooyeweerd was a Dutch Christian philosopher. Often described as brilliant and just as often described as difficult to understand, Dooyeweerd has influenced some of the greatest Christian thinkers of our age. His writings are built upon the concepts of John Calvin and Abraham Kuyper.

Douglas, Henry Kyd, *I Rode With Stonewall* Chapel Hill, NC: The University of North Carolina Press, 1984, seventeenth printing. It is hard to imagine someone who served with Stonewall Jackson and survived to write about it not writing a great book. Douglas served Jackson well both in serving with him during the war and in composing this autobiographical work.

Douglas, J. D., editor, *The New International Dictionary of the Christian Church.* Grand Rapids: Zondervan, 1978. Excellent resource. With this book, you are always just a few paragraphs away from being able to discuss key figures and events in church history.

Dupoy, R. Ernest and Trevor N. Dupoy, *The Encyclopedia of Military History from 3500 B.C. to the Present* New York: Harper and Row Publishers, 1986. These types of books—encyclopedias, dictionaries, and reference works—even when used sparingly are tremendous tools for the teacher or student.

Durant, Will, *The Age of Faith,* from *The Story of Civilization, Volume IV.* New York: Simon and Schuster, 1950. Will Durant and his wife Ariel wrote a ten-volume history of the world titled *The Story of Civilization.* It goes from the beginnings of man (as the Durant's blindly misunderstood it) to the Age of Napoleon. They understood the role of religion in history and misunderstood most representations of Christianity in history, particularly Calvin. Still, they were brilliant narrators and storytellers. New and used copies of their series show up everywhere.

——— *Caesar and Christ* from *The Story of Civilization, Volume III.* New York: Simon and Schuster, 1944.

Dwyer, John J., with George Grant, J. Steven Wilkins, Douglas Wilson, and Tom Spencer. *The War Between the States: America's Uncivil War.* Bluebonnet Press in Denton, Texas in 2005. There is no one book that covers the War Between the States in a way that aptly defends the Christian and Constitutional elements of the South. But this one is close. Great for use as a textbook, a reference work, or for just reading.

Edgar, Walter, *Partisans and Redcoats: The Southern Conflict That Turned the Tide of the American Revolution.* New York: Perennial, 2003. Sheds light on the Presbyterian involvement in the War for Independence. Good background to the Mel Gibson movie *The Patriot.*

Edwards, Tryon, et. al., compilers. *The New Dictionary of Thoughts: A Cyclopedia of Quotations.* Standard Book Company, 1959. A delightful older collection of quotes.

Eliot, T. S., *Christianity and Culture.* New York: Harcourt Brace & Company. Consists of two lengthy essays by the Nobel Prize winning poet and convert to Anglican Christianity: "The Idea of a Christian Society" and "Notes Toward the Definition of Culture." Eliot's conversion shocked many unbelievers in his day. Insightful and profound thinker, as well as a challenging poet.

Engelmann, Bernt, *In Hitler's Germany: Everyday Life in the Third Reich* New York: Pantheon Books, 1986. Good firsthand account of one who was in the belly of the Nazi beast.

Eusebius, *The Church History: A New Translation and Commentary* Grand Rapids: Kregel Publications, 1999. Reviewed in this book. Eusebius is rightly called the Father of Church History.

Evans, Richard J., *The Coming of the Third Reich.* New York: The Penguin Press, 2004. This is the first of a three-volume history on Nazi Germany. Subsequent volumes are *The Third Reich in Power* and *The Third Reich at War.*

Farmer, Jr., James Oscar, *The Metaphysical Confederacy—James Henley Thornwell and the Synthesis of Southern Values* Macon: Mercer University Press, 1986. Thornwell was a pivotal Southern Presbyterian thinker. His vision for what the Confederacy could have been is inspiring. The best biography of Thornwell is *The Life and Letters of James Henley Thornwell* by B.M. Palmer (yet another great Southern Christian). This study of Thornwell is a useful supplement.

Faulkner, William, *Requiem for a Nun.* I don't know whether overuse of alcohol explains Faulkner's writing style or simply aids the reader in following his stream of consciousness technique. Try as one might, you cannot escape the sheer brilliance of the man. No one can understand the complexities of the South both before and after the War Between the States without reading Faulkner. One had best begin Faulkner readings with his book *The Unvanquished.*

Faust, Drew Gilpin, *The Creation of Southern Nationalism: Ideology and Identity in the Civil War South* Baton Rouge: Louisiana State University Press, 1988. Rightly or wrongly depending upon one's viewpoint, the South's ideology and identity were found in Christianity.

Fell, Barry, *America B.C.: Ancient Settlers in the New World* New York: Pocketbooks, 1986. Fun and convincing study. Columbus was a "Christopher come lately."

———*Saga America.* New York: Times Books, 1983.

Fischer, David Hackett, *Albion's Seed: Four British Folkways in America.* New York: Oxford University Press, 1989. Fischer is one of the best historians in America today. This work in particular shows up in everyone's footnotes. It very aptly shows the influences of Protestant religion in Britain and how it was transplanted across the sea to the colonies.

——— *Washington's Crossing.* New York: Oxford University Press, 2004. Reviewed in this book.

Forbes, Esther, *Paul Revere and the World He Lived In.* Boston: Houghton Mifflin Company, 1942. Miss Forbes's writings breathe the culture and politics of Paul Revere and America, particularly Boston, as they drifted toward independence. This is seen especially in her novel *Johnny Tremain.*

Fuller, A. James, *Chaplain to the Confederacy: Basil Manly and Baptist Life in the Old South.* Louisiana University Press in 2000. Basil Manly is the "man" in "Broadman Press." (John Broadus was the "Broad.") Southern Baptist history includes the glorious story of great Southern Christians who were Calvinists and defenders of the Confederacy. Manly stands right up there with Thornwell and Dabney in his theological rigor and Southern convictions.

Garrett, George, "Southern Literature" from *Why the South will Survive: Fifteen Southerners Look at Their Region a Half Century after I'll Take My Stand.* Athens: The University of Georgia Press, 1983. These essays were written to honor the twelve Southerners of the Agrarian movement.

Genovese, Eugene D., *The Southern Tradition: the Achievement and Limitations of American Conservatism* Cambridge: Harvard University Press, 1994. Genovose is the model of the analytical and fair-minded historian. An economic Marxist and a Northerner, he has provided more solid scholarship on the nature of the Old South than almost any other historian. He aptly understands and strongly defends the Christian convictions of Southerners.

Gentz, Friedrich, *The French and American Revolutions Compared.* The classically trained John Quincy Adams translated this work. Maybe the last word in the title should be *Contrasted* !

Gildersleeve, Basil L., *The Letters of Basil Lanneau Gildersleeve,* edited by Ward W. Briggs, Jr. Gildersleeve was the premier classicist of the 19th century. He was a professor at Johns Hopkins University. One of his students was J. Gresham Machen. He was also an ardent Southerner.

Godawa, Brian, *Hollywood Worldviews.* Downers Grove, Illinois: Intervarsity Press, 2002. Subtitled *Watching Films with Discernment and Wisdom,* this study by a Reformed thinker, movie critic, and screenwriter teaches Christians how to think about the worldly philosophies that show up all over our culture, but most powerfully through film.

Goldsworthy, Adrian, *The Punic Wars* London: Cassell & Co, 2000. Put this one on the top shelf of the Punic Wars portion of your library.

Gonzalez, Justo L., *The Story of Christianity: The Early Church to the Present Day.* Peabody, MA: Prince Press, 1999. Bound as two volumes in one. Most useful and sound history of Christianity by a modern scholar. I have adopted it for my high school classes.

Graham, W. Fred, *The Constructive Revolutionary: John Calvin and His Socio-Economic Impact.* Richmond, Virginia: John Knox Press, 1971. The modern socialistic welfare state is a secularized copycat version of the Christian community envisioned by Calvin.

Grant, George, *Carry a Big Stick: The Uncommon Heroism of Theodore Roosevelt.* Nashville: Cumberland House, 1996. Disagree with Roosevelt's politics at points if you like, still it is hard to escape the enthusiasm and faith enveloped in his character.

——— The *Patriot's Handbook.* Nashville: Cumberland Book House, 1996, 2004. Dr. Grant has compiled an outstanding collection of original documents, poems, and speeches that cover the whole of American history. This includes his summary account of the fourteen forgotten American Presidents who preceded George Washington.

Grant, George and Gregory Wilbur, *The Christian Almanac.* Nashville: Cumberland House, 2000. This book combines the interests, specialties, and wide reading of two true Renaissance and Reformation men. Each day's entry contains suggested Scripture readings, an essay on a key event or person related to the day, a list of famous and important events that happened on that day, and a worthwhile quote. This is a bulky and fun book. Great for classroom use, personal study and devotion, and for guidelines as to what authors, artists, and events Christians should pursue.

Grant, Michael, editor, *Readings in the Classical Historians.* New York: Charles Scribner's Sons, 1992. Grant wrote or edited scores of books on the ancient world. When approaching the Greeks, Romans, and other ancient peoples, his scholarship and insights are constructive. When he slips over into the Christian era and writes of Christian matters, he veers far off the road. The above named collection is the best introduction to the ancient historians.

Gregory, John Milton, *The Seven Laws of Teaching.* Grand Rapids: Baker Book House, 1993. Originally designed for Sunday school teachers, this little pedagogical treatise should be on every teacher's list to read and re-read continually.

Gummere, Richard M., *The American Colonial Mind and the Classical Tradition.* Cambridge: Harvard University Press, 1963. Good anecdotal history. It clearly shows how great the robbery of our educational heritage has been.

Hall, David W., *The Genevan Reformation and the American Founding.* Lanham, MD: Lexington Books, 2003. Reviewed in this book. This book should revolutionize the way Christians view American history.

———*A Heart Promptly Offered: The Revolutionary Leadership of John Calvin.* Nashville, TN: Cumberland House Publishing, Inc., 2006. This is a simpler version of Hall's previous study of Calvin's influence. It is a great starter for introducing students to Calvin's significance.

Hamilton, Edith. *The Greek Way.* New York: Discus Books, 1973. Great survey study of all things Greek.

———*Mythology.* Boston: Little, Brown and Company, 1942. No student of history or literature or theology can afford to be without a good survey of mythology. This survey, which consists largely of stories, focuses largely upon the Greeks and Romans, with a small dose of Norse mythology at the end.

———*The Roman Way.* New York: Discus Books, 1973. This is the companion volume to Miss Hamilton's study of the Greeks.

Hanson, Victor Davis, Carnage *and Culture.* New York: Doubleday, 2001. Hanson is the best military historian in America today. This book is the best work of Hanson's. It surveys battles from the Greeks up through Vietnam and the Tet Offensive. Hanson affirms the superiority of Western culture over all other cultures, due in part, to the ability of the West to defeat all other civilizations in battle. At the center of this superiority is the concept of freedom.

———— *Ripples of Battle* New York: Doubleday, 2003. Battles have winners and losers, but they also have a series of far reaching impacts. Hanson explores such ripple effects of battle in this study of both ancient and modern battles.

Hanson and John Heath, *Who Killed Homer? The Demise of Classical Education and the Recovery of Greek Wisdom.* New York: The Free Press, 1998. This is a great study of the contributions of Greek literature with a resounding call for a return to such classical education. Of course, the foundations surveyed here, being Greek and humanistic, are lacking. But Greek intellectual rubble contains useful stones to used for building Christian educational cathedrals.

Harbison, E. Harris, *The Christian Scholar in the Age of the Reformation.* New York: Charles Scribner's Sons, 1956. Dr. Harbison taught courses at Harvard and Princeton on the Renaissance and Reformation during the early and middle decades of the twentieth century. This fine work includes essays on Erasmus, Luther, and Calvin.

———— *The Age of Reformation* Westport. Connecticut: Greenwood Press, Publishers, 1982 reprint. Great brief survey of the major aspects of the Reformation.

Hart, D. G., *Defending the Faith: J. Gresham Machen and the Crisis of Conservative Protestantism in Modern America.* Grand Rapids, MI: Baker Book House, 1994. Hart is a major Reformed historian on modern American Christianity. Machen is the key Reformed figure in understanding the chasm between Christianity and culture in the twentieth century.

Hastings, Max, *Armegeddon: The Battle for Germany 1944-45.* Large and Homeric look at the convergence of Allied Powers upon the European Axis powers in the last stages of the Second World War.

Hayes, Carleton J. H., *Ancient Civilizations: Prehistory to the Fall of Rome.* New York: Macmillian Publishing Co., Inc., 1983. An unusual college level textbook, in that it deals with ancient civilizations chronologically rather than topically. We sometimes think of ancient civilizations rising and falling as chapters instead of seeing the many simultaneous events of the ancient world.

————*Modern Europe to 1870.* New York: The Macmillan Company, 1957, third printing. Look for copies of Hayes's historical textbooks in used bookstores. He was a sound and thorough historian.

Hays, George P., *Presbyterians: A Popular Narrative of their Origins, Progress, Doctrines, and Achievements.* New York: J. A. Hill & Co. Publishers, 1892. An older and out-of-print work. Worth finding for its often forgotten history.

Heimart, Alan, *Religion and the American Mind.* Cambridge, MA: Harvard University Press, 1966. This is a widely recognized key source on the Calvinistic and Puritans roots of American history.

Higgenbotham, Don. *Daniel Morgan: Revolutionary Rifleman* Chapel Hill: The University of North Carolina Press, 1961. Morgan was the epitome of the frontier military leader. Rough-hewn and unschooled, he excelled at battle. His later years witnessed his conversion to the faith of his forefathers.

———*War and Society in Revolutionary America.* Columbia, S.C.: University of South Carolina Press, 1988. A collection of essays on the War for Independence by one of the leading scholars on that war.

Hill, Samuel S., editor, *Encyclopedia of Religion in the South.* Macon: Mercer University Press, 1984.

Himmelfarb, Gertrude, *The Roads to Modernity: The British, French, and American Enlightenment.* New York: Alfred A. Knopf, 2004. All of Gertrude Himmelfarb's books are desirable for historical study. She is conservative, profound, and entertaining. Of course she is scholarly, for with a name like Gertrude Himmelfarb, you have to be a scholar.

Hodge, Charles, *The Constitutional History of the Presbyterian Church in the United States of America.* Philadelphia: Presbyterian Board of Education, 1851, reprinted in 1983. This hefty work is generally noted for Hodge's criticisms of the effects of the Great Awakening.

Hoffecker, W. Andrew and Gary Scott Smith, editors, *Building a Christian World View.* Phillipsburg: Presbyterian and Reformed Publishing Company, 1986. This is the first of a two-volume set that examines theology, philosophy, and culture from the ancient world to modernity. This is a wonderful introduction to the key names and figures of intellectual and theological history.

Holland, James, *Fortress Malta: An Island Under Siege 1940-1943.* London: Orion Books, 2003. A recent account of a vital, but neglected part of World War II. This obscure island was for a third time a pivot point for Western Civilization's survival.

Homer, *The Iliad* of Homer, translated by Richmond Lattimore. Chicago: The University of Chicago Press, 1951. No one should step into the classroom to teach history without having seriously read and studied Homer's *Iliad.* In this instance, do as I say, and not as I did, for it was only after years of teaching that I met Homer. Richmond Lattimore focused on capturing the poetic meaning of the text, and this war story has to be read as a poem. Of course, after the *Iliad,* the reader is bound to read *The Odyssey* and Virgil's *Aeneid.*

Hood, Fred J., *Reformed America: The Middle and Southern States, 1783-1837* University, Alabama: The University of Alabama Press, 1980.

Hooper, Walter, *Through Joy and Beyond—A Pictorial Biography of C.S. Lewis.* New York: Macmillan Publishing Company, 1982. Hooper has worked with lots of Lewis's writings and has contributed numerous works about his life and beliefs.

Hughes, Philip Edgecumbe, *Christianity and the Problem of Origins.* Phillipsburg, N. J.: The Presbyterian and Reformed Publishing Company, 1974. This is a very short and difficult little booklet. It is one of the most tightly argued works I have ever read. Being assigned in my college Western Civilization class, it helped crystallize in my mind the importance of beginning all thought with Genesis and God's Revelation.

Hyneman, Charles S. and Donald S. Lutz, editors. *American Political Writing during the Founding Era, 1760-1805,* Volume 1. Indianapolis: Liberty Press, 1983. Both volumes in this set are worthy collections of essays by both the better known and more obscure Founding Fathers. You cannot find too many collections of original sources.

Johnson, Charles A., *The Frontier Camp Meeting: Religion's Harvest Time* Dallas: Southern Methodist University Press, 1955, 1985. Southern Christianity and much of American Fundamentalism find their roots in the frontier camp meeting tradition. This is a good source for seeing both the true evangelicalism and the wacky tendencies of American Christianity.

Johnson, Paul, *A History of the American People.* New York: Harper Collins Publishers, 1997. Johnson, an Englishman, gives an appreciative look at the history of America. He credits the Christian faith more than many historians and generally takes a politically conservative approach to American history. Johnson enjoys odd stories that seemingly stray from the traditional historical narrative, yet in his overall scheme even his random points either reinforce or brighten his narrative.

——— *A History of the Jews.* New York: Harper & Row Publishers, 1987. Not Johnson's best book. He falls victim to the usual views of skeptics concerning the Old Testament. But Johnson at his worst is still one of the best historians around.

———*Modern Times: From the Twenties to the Eighties.* New York: Harper & Row Publishers, 1983. This is Johnson at his best. This history of the twentieth century did for historiography what President Reagan did for the political order. Johnson's appraisal of the Great Depression is outstanding.

Johnson, Thomas Cary, *The Life and Letters of Benjamin Morgan Palmer.* Edinburgh: Banner of Truth Trust, 1987. Reverend Palmer was one of that noble cadre of Southern Presbyterian theologians and pastors who defined the best elements of the Old South. Along with reading books by and about James Henley Thornwell and Robert Lewis Dabney, read books by and about Palmer.

Kalsbeek, L., *Contours of a Christian Philosophy: An Introduction to Herman Dooyeweerd's Thought.* Toronto: Wedge Publishing Foundation, 1975. Herman Dooyeweerd is one of the most difficult people to read. This work helps pave the way for the reader to tackle Dooyeweerd. Some of us, however, need an introduction to Kalsbeek's introduction to understand him, as well as his subject.

Kelly, Douglas. *The Emergence of Liberty in the Modern World.* Philipsburg, NJ: Presbyterian and Reformed Publishing Company, 1992. A study of the impact of Calvinism on Europe and America.

Kempis, Thomas á, *The Imitation of Christ.* San Francisco: Ignatius Press, 2005. Ronald Knox, translator. Late Medieval devotional classic by a premier student of the Brethren of Common Life schools. Great primary historical source for Medieval studies; great for the soul and mind.

Kik, J. Marcellus, *Church and State: The Story of Two Kingdoms.* New York: Thomas Nelson and Sons, 1963. Kik is best remembered for his study of Matthew 24 and Revelation 20 titled *An Eschatology of Victory.* This short history of church and state battles is a good summary of one of the key issues of all history and culture.

Kreeft, Peter, *Philosophy 101 by Socrates.* (San Francisco: Ignatius Press, 2002). Dr. Kreeft may not succeed in getting Socrates into heaven (see his wonderful book *Socrates Meets Jesus),* but he is succeeding at getting him into the minds of many readers.

Kreeft, Peter and Ronald Tacelli, *Handbook of Christian Apologetics* Downers Grove, IL: Inter Varsity Press, 1994. While the approach is not Van Tillian, this book and others like it always contain useful and convincing proofs of the Christian faith. I would look favorably on any book that Peter Kreeft authored or co-authored.

Kuiper, R. B., *The Church in History.* Grand Rapids: William B. Eerdmans Publishing Company. This is a wonderful and long used church history textbook. Upper elementary students can use it; however, students of all ages would find it helpful.

Kuyper, Abraham, *Lectures on Calvinism*. Grand Rapids, MI: William B. Eerdmans Company, 1931. This collection of six lectures is valuable for its historical insights into the history of Calvinism. It is also unsurpassed, with its chapters on politics, science, art, and religion, as a resource for a Christian worldview. It is also a primary historical reference showing the then remaining Calvinistic culture in both the United States and the Netherlands at the end of the 19th century.

Lamb, Harold, *Constantinople: Birth of an Empire*. New York: Alfred A. Knopf, 1959. Lamb was a popular historian of some years back. He is known for his novelistic style of writing history.

Larson, Edward J. *Summer for the Gods: The Scopes Trial and America's Continuing Debate over Science and Religion*. New York: Basic Books, 1997. Read this after or instead of watching *Inherit the Wind*.

Latourette, Kenneth Scott, *A History of Christianity: Volume II: A. D. 1500—A. D. 1975—Reformation to the Present* Peabody, Massachusetts: Prince Press, 1997 Revised Edition. Latourette is one of the masters of church history from the twentieth century.

———*The Twentieth Century Outside Europe,* Volume V of *Christianity in a Revolutionary Age* Grand Rapids: Zondervan Publishing House, 1969. If just for reference use, acquire any and all church history sets by Latourette.

Leckie, Ross, *Hannibal: The Novel.* Washington, DC: Regnery Publishing, Inc., 1996. This book is rated R for Carthaginian violence.

Lee, Susan Pendleton, *Memoirs of William Nelson Pendleton*. Harrisonburg, Virginia: Sprinkle Publications, 1991. Originally published in 1893. Pendleton, a Episcopalian pastor and a general in the Army of Northern Virginia during the War Between the States, was a wonderful father, a faithful pastor, and a zealous, but perhaps not overly apt military man. It is well that his daughter wrote his life story.

Leithart, Peter, *Ascent to Love*. Moscow, Idaho: Canon Press, 2001. This is a useful aid to understanding Dante's *Divine Comedy*. Leithart gives useful background, interpretive explanations, and Christian observations on Dante's epic.

———*Heroes in the City of Man: A Christian Guide to Select Ancient Literature.* Moscow, ID: Canon Press, 1999. Leithart has written some brilliant and thought provoking Christian commentaries on such literary figures as Shakespeare, Dante, and Jane Austen, along with this study. His defense of Christians studying of pagan writings is worth the price of the book.

Lewis, C. S., *The Discarded Image*. New York: Cambridge University Press, 1964. Lewis was, by trade, a literature teacher, with a particular emphasis on Medieval literature. This is one of his key works of literary criticism.

———*God in the Dock: Essays on Theology and Ethics*. Grand Rapids, MI: William B. Eerdmans Publishing Company, 1978. Contains the marvelous essay "On the Reading of Old Books." A Christian history teacher only needs to read *everything* Lewis wrote.

———*Mere Christianity*. New York: The MacMillan Company, 1958. Vital part of the theological toolbox of the teacher. For wisdom, graceful prose, and power, unsurpassed.

———*Surprised by Joy: The Shape of My Early Life*. New York: Harcourt Brace and Company, 1955. This is Lewis's spiritual autobiography. It is a great account of classical education, the impact of books, friends, and experiences upon our lives, and of the spiritual journey Lewis took from atheism to Christianity.

———*The Weight of Glory and Other Addresses* New York: Touchstone, 1996. Every Lewis essay collection is a set of gems. The essay, "Learning in Wartime," is a special gem.

Leyburn, James G., *The Scotch-Irish: A Social History*. Chapel Hill: The University of North Carolina Press, 1962. This is the recognized central history of the ethnic group that so dominated America's founding era and every era since then.

Loveland, Anne C., *Southern Evangelicals and the Social Order, 1800-1860*. Baton Rouge: Louisiana State University Press, 1980. This book is a model of historical scholarship. Dr. Loveland marshaled a whole host of quotes and original writings of Southern evangelicals in the ante-bellum South. This is the best book I have read on Southern Christianity before the War Between the States.

Lucas, Christopher J., *Our Western Educational Heritage* New York: Macmillan Publishing Company, Inc., 1972. If prospective teachers have to take courses in the field of education, the courses should include extensive study of the history of education instead of samplings of the latest trends.

Lytle, Andrew Nelson, *A Wake for the Living* Nashville: J. S. Sanders & Company, 1992. Lytle was the last of the original twelve Southern Agrarians. He never budged an inch from the original theses of *I'll Take My Stand*. All of his writings are worthwhile. This one is his personal and family memoir and is a great sample of what has made twentieth century Southern literature and culture so enriching.

MacArthur, John F., *Ashamed of the Gospel: When the Church Becomes Like the World.* Wheaton: Crossway Books, 1993. MacArthur is one of the best popular preachers and writers in our day. He has a gift many Reformed theologians lack and that is the ability to popularize the Reformed faith to a broad and needy evangelical audience.

Machen, J. Gresham, *Christianity and Liberalism.* Grand Rapids, MI: William B. Eerdmans Publishing Company, 1923. First, this is primary source history. You cannot understand the first three decades of American history without this book. And you cannot truly evaluate twentieth century American history without a knowledge of and appreciation for Machen. Second, this is a great theological study. Theological liberalism is a monster that still haunts the landscape. That it is slowly dying is due in part to the wounds that Machen's book continues to inflict upon it.

———*Education, Christianity, and the State.* Unicoi, TN: Trinity Foundation, 2004. A collection of brilliant, often prophetic, and always timeless essays and speeches given by Machen in the 1920s and 1930s. Great insights into the educational and religious culture of Machen's time.

McCullough, David. *1776* New York: Simon & Schuster, 2005. McCullough is one of the best historians in America today. This is his account of the key year in America's founding. We won the war in time, but it was a close run matter. Even McCullough acknowledges that the issues raise the question of God's Providence.

——— *John Adams.* New York: Simon & Schuster, 2001. This best selling biography raised the often-overlooked second President up to the front row so we could better see his greatness.

McFetridge, N. S., *Calvinism in History.* Edmonton, Canada: Still Water Revival Books, 1989 reprint. A good and rousing account of the impact of Calvinism on American and European history, politics, and theology.

McGrath, Alister, *The Twilight of Atheism: The Rise and Fall of Disbelief in the Modern World.* New York: Doubleday, 2004. Great history and theology regarding atheism. Excellent coverage of key thinkers of the 19th and 20th centuries.

McNeill, John T., *The History and Character of Calvinism.* New York: Oxford University Press, 1957. A standard and enduring history of Calvinism by one who admired, but did not adhere to Reformed theology.

McWhiney, Grady, *Cracker Culture: Celtic Ways in the Old South*. Tuskaloosa: University of Alabama Press, 1988. An exaggerated, but fun thesis that looks at Southern cultural mores that originated out of the combination of Scots and Scots-Irish heritage being transplanted to the Southern frontier. Many elements of this Cracker Culture exist to this day in the South.

Maier, Paul, "Introduction" from *Eusebius—The Church History: A New Translation and Commentary* Grand Rapids: Kregel Publications, 1999. Maier's translation of Eusebius is the best version of his works around. The introduction, notes, and commentary are very useful.

Mansfield, Stephen, *More Than Dates and Dead People*. Nashville: Cumberland House Books, 2000. I always assign this book to junior high students. Frequently, their parents decide to read it also. This is the best beginning book to understand a Christian approach to history.

———*Then Darkness Fled: The Liberating Wisdom of Booker T. Washington*. Nashville: Cumberland House Publishing Company. Read this along with Washington's remarkable testimony and autobiography, *Up From Slavery*.

Marsden, George, *Fundamentalism and American Culture: The Shaping of Twentieth-Century Evangelicalism 1870-1925*. New York: Oxford University Press, 1980. One of the best books on the time period and events related to the Scopes Trial and Machen's struggles, written by one of the best church historians in America today.

Marshall, Peter and David Manuel, *The Light and the Glory*. Old Tappan, New Jersey: Fleming H. Revell Company, 1977. A bit fluffy at points, this history of America's origins is must reading for Christian history teachers.

Mather, Cotton. *The Great Works of Christ in America*. Edinburgh: Banner of Truth Trust, 1979. Two volumes reprinted from 1702. Mather, a great American Puritan preacher and writer, was one of our earliest and wordiest historians. A better model for his presuppositions of history than for his style of writing.

May, Henry F., *The Enlightenment in America*. New York: Oxford University Press, 1976. Should be studied along with Peter Gay's long established works on the Enlightenment.

Miller, Donald E. and Lorna Touryan Miller, *Survivors: An Oral History of the Armenian Genocide* Berkeley: University of California Press, 1993. Hitler and the Nazis were not the first to attempt the total elimination of ethnic groups. The story of the persecution of the Armenian people has been vastly overlooked in the midst of a century filled with genocide.

Perry, Miller, *Errand Into the Wilderness*. New York: Harper Torchbooks, 1956. Miller was God's servant to the church. Personally Miller was not a Christian; as a historian, he did not always understand Christian theology in history; but he rediscovered the Puritans. His books are still most valuable resources.

Miller, Randall M., Harry S. Stout, and Charles Reagan Wilson, editors, *Religion and the American Civil War*. Oxford University Press, 1998. Useful collection of essays by leading scholars.

Morgan, Edmund Sears, *Visible Saints: The History of a Puritan Idea* New York: New York University Press, 1963. A great study by a senior American historian. The Puritans were really brilliant at points, but sometimes really missed the mark. Readers can profit from all of Morgan's works on colonial history.

Morris, Henry M., *The Long War Against God: The History and Impact of the Creation/Evolution Conflict*. Grand Rapids: Baker Book House, 1990. Dr. Morris was one of the great warriors for Biblical Creation. This is a useful account of the battle of two worldviews.

Morrison, Jeffrey H., *John Witherspoon and the Founding of the American Republic*. Notre Dame, IN: Notre Dame University Press, 2005. Witherspoon was the only minister to sign the Declaration of Independence. He was a vital player in the intellectual, educational, and political currents of America's beginning decades. This study focuses upon his ideas and impact on our nation's beginnings.

Morison, Samuel Eliot, "Winston Churchill: Nobel Prize Winner" from *Sailor Historian—The Best of Samuel Eliot Morison,* edited by Emily Morison Beck Boston: Houghton Mifflin, 1977. This is a collection of essays by a prolific historian whose voluminous works are all worthwhile reads and references.

Muggeridge, Malcolm, *Confessions of a Twentieth Century Pilgrim* San Francisco: Harper & Row Publishers, 1988. Muggeridge's conversion to Christianity after a life of searching for answers ranks him right up there with C. S. Lewis and Augustine in his spiritual pilgrimage.

Murray, John, *Principles of Conduct: Aspects of Biblical Ethics* Grand Rapids: William B. Eerdmans Publishing Company, seventh printing 1978. Murray, a Scotsman, graciously followed in the footsteps of John Witherspoon by crossing the ocean and lending America a brilliant mind and a godly heart. Murray was a professor at Westminster Theological Seminary and one of the best theologians of the twentieth century.

Murray, Ian, *Jonathan Edwards: A New Biography.* Edinburgh: The Banner of Truth Trust, 1987. Another Murray, another Scotsman. This one has written quite a few good histories and biographies. This wonderful and devotional biography can be paired with George Marsden's *Jonathan Edwards: A Life,* which is a more scholarly work, for a great double-barreled treatment of the best mind colonial American Calvinism produced.

Nash, Ronald H., editor, *The Philosophy of Gordon Clark: A Festschrift.* Philadelphia: The Presbyterian and Reformed Publishing Company, 1968. This is a study of a major twentieth century Calvinist thinker that includes essays by other major Calvinist writers, such as Rushdoony and Singer.

Naugle, David K., *Worldview: The History of a Concept.* Grand Rapids, MI: William B. Eerdmans Publishing Company, 2002. This is not where to begin in order to develop a Christian worldview. This is a serious study of how philosophers and thinkers, Christian and non-Christian, have developed the concept of worldview thinking. Naugle is a most gifted scholar in our age.

Neale, J. E., *The Age of Catherine de Medici.* New York: Harper Torchbooks, 1960. A short and well-written account of the Reformation in France and particularly the sad fate of the Huguenots.

Needham, N. R., *2000 Years of Christ's Power: Part One: The Age of the Early Church Fathers.* London: Grace Publications Trust, 1998.

———*2000 Years of Christ's Power: Part Two: The Middle Ages.* London: Grace Publications Trust, 2000.

———*2000 Years of Christ's Power: Part Three: Renaissance and Reformation.* London: Grace Publications Trust, 2004. Needham's books reveal his gifts as both a pastor and a professor. This is a most readable ongoing church history series.

North, Gary, *Crossed Fingers: How the Liberals Captured the Presbyterian Church.* Tyler, Texas: Institute for Christian Economics, 1996. This book rambles endlessly, thrashes about through a maze of historical events, sledgehammers theological modernists past and present, and from beginning to end highlights the significance of J. Gresham Machen and his battles for theological orthodoxy in the Presbyterian Church.

———*The War on Mel Gibson.* Powder Springs, Georgia: American Vision, 2004. North is a Calvinistic, Theonomic, Reconstructionist Christian hit man. The targets he takes out in this book deserve what they got.

North, Gary, editor, *Foundations of Christian Scholarship: Essays in the Van Til Perspective.* Vallecito, CA: Ross House Books, 1979. This book is aptly titled. Van Til's forte was Christian apologetics; that is, how Christians should defend the faith. His method focused upon a firm reliance upon the presuppositional certainty of God's Word for every situation. Hence, his Christian thought has spurred other Christians to apply his precepts to history, philosophy, education, politics, sociology, economics, and, of course, apologetics. This major study is a good introduction not just to Van Til, but also to a brilliant host of men who have built upon his thought, including North, Rushdoony, Singer, Greg Bahnsen, and John Frame.

——*The Journal of Christian Reconstruction,* Symposium on Education, edited by Gary North Volume 4, Number 1, Summer 1977. For many of us, this is where we first discovered Dorothy Sayers' essay "Lost Tools of Learning."

Olson, Lynne and Stanley Clous, *A Question of Honor: The Kosciuszko Squadron—Forgotten Heroes of World War II.* New York: Alfred A. Knopf, 2003. The fourth largest Allied air force in World War II was the Polish air force. The war started over an invasion of Poland by Germany and Russia. It ended with Russian occupation and subjugation of Poland. This is the story of true heroes whose bravery was largely betrayed and unrequited.

Orr, James, *The Christian View of God and the World.* Grand Rapids: Kregel Publications, 1989. Orr was a Scotsman and a Christian worldview thinker of the late nineteenth century.

Ozment, Steven, *When Fathers Ruled—Family Life in Reformation Europe.* Cambridge, Mass.: Harvard University Press, 1983. Ozment is a key historian on the Protestant Reformation. This book rightly shows how central the reformation of the family was to that era, and from there we can surmise its importance for now.

Packer, J. I., *A Quest for Godliness: The Puritan Vision of the Christian Life.* Wheaton: Crossway Books, 1990. Packer is one of the greatest Christian writers and thinkers of our time. His book *Knowing God* is a spiritual classic. This book is an outstanding apologetic for the theology and culture of the Puritans. Gleaning from the Puritans will be a key feature of our preparing for cultural conquest.

Pearcey, Nancy, *Total Truth: Liberating Christianity from Its Cultural Captivity.* Wheaton, IL: Crossway Books, 2004. Should be required for high school and college teachers and students. Major sections of this book deal with American revivalism and Darwinian naturalism, thus bringing history and science together. Mrs. Pearcey first learned her theology from Schaeffer.

Perks, Stephen C. Perks, *The Christian Philosophy of Education Explained* Whitby, England: Avant Books, 1992. In the long and ever growing list of useful books on Christian education, this one retains top billing. It reflects the apologetical vision of Cornelius Van Til.

Perlstein, Rick, *Before the Storm: Barry Goldwater and the Unmaking of the American Consensus* New York: Hill and Wang, 2001. The author is very liberal. His research and coverage of the political and moral culture of the early sixties is outstanding. If a Goldwater presidency would have been as badly managed as his presidential campaign, then Lyndon Johnson's election was a blessing—in disguise.

Phares, Ross, *Bible in Pocket, Gun in Hand: The Story of Frontier Religion.* Lincoln: University of Nebraska Press, 1964. This is a fun place to start reading about how Christianity took root in the ever-changing American frontier.

Phillips, Kevin, *The Cousins' Wars: Religion, Politics, and the Triumph of Anglo-America.* New York: Basic Books, 1999. Phillips took a break from his quirky political commentaries to write a really brilliant history of the English Civil War, the American War for Independence, and the American War Between the States. His coverage of the first two wars exceeds his coverage of the third. His recognition of the role of Protestant Calvinists in the first two wars, especially, makes this volume most valuable.

Posey, Walter Brownlow, *Religious Strife on the Southern Frontier.* Baton Rouge: Louisiana University Press, 1965. We religious Southerners have never quite gotten over this tendency.

Neil Postman, *Amusing Ourselves to Death: Public Discourse in the Age of Show Business.* New York: Penguin Books, 1985. Postman's examples of inanities in culture, religion, and politics are nearly all outdated. Yet, the key ideas of this book and the historical look at our educational decline keep this book on the forefront for Christian education. It can be most profitably read for history, theology, or rhetoric classes.

Powell, Phillip, *Mexico's Miguel Calderas and the Taming of America's First Frontier.* Tucson: The University of Arizona Press, 1977. A great look at a totally ignored man, Miguel Calderas, whose leadership tamed some of the most savage peoples in New Spain.

———*Tree of Hate*. Vallecito: Ross House Books, 1985. This book counters the Black Legend. The Black Legend concerns the teaching of the history of the Spanish Empire that blames Spain for every evil that ever occurred in Latin America. Both Protestants (in the past) and secularists have contributed to the Black Legend. Of course, the Spanish had their share of wickedness and depravity displayed toward their colonies, but the positive contributions must be weighed in the scale. Bottom line: Cortes's army on its march of conquest is better than a feast of human body parts at Montezuma's banquets.

Purves, Jock, *Fair Sunshine: Character Studies of the Scottish Covenanter*s. Edinburgh: the Banner of Truth Trust, 1982. Devotional, historical, and moving accounts of those hearty Scots who were steadfast for the faith during the Killing Days and other persecutions.

Richard, Carl J., *The Founders and the Classics: Greece, Rome, and the American Enlightenment* Cambridge: Harvard University Press, 1996. This book is an invaluable collection of first-hand testimonies of the Founding Generation of America to their educational background, which was drenched in classical learning. Excellent history by a Christian historian.

———*Twelve Greeks and Romans Who Changed the World*. Lanham, MD: Rowman and Littlefield Publishers, Inc., 2003. The last two world changing Romans that Richard includes are Paul and Augustine. Learning history by means of biography is often the most interesting approach. These twelve mini-biographies written in the tradition of Plutarch are delightful.

Robertson, Jr., James I., *Stonewall Jackson: The Man, The Soldier, The Legend*. New York: Macmillan Publishing USA, 1997. A thorough and well-written biography by a historian with the literary skills, the historical training, and the Southern perspective needed for a biography of Jackson.

Roosevelt, Theodore, and Henry Cabot Lodge, *Hero Tales: How Common Lives Reveal the Heroic Spirit of America*. Nashville: Cumberland House, 2000. A collection of inspiring biographies of both the better known and some of the less well-known heroes of American history. The secular world may wish to teach history without heroes, but the Christian schools cannot follow such an approach.

Rushdoony, Rousas J., *The Biblical Philosophy of History*. Nutley, N. J.: Presbyterian and Reformed Publishing Co, 1974. The title says it all.

———*The Foundations of Social Order: Studies in the Creeds and Councils of the Early Church*. Presbyterian and Reformed Publishing Company, 1972. Charles Craig, who operated Presbyterian and Reformed Publishing Company, which also published under the name the Craig Press, gave the Christian world a tremendous gift from the 1950s onward in publishing scholarly and serious Reformed Christian books in a wide range of areas. As is the case above, some of the books lack the city where they were published, some lack the date or information about which printing an edition was from, and some lacked indexes. Still, these books by such authors as Rushdoony, Singer, Clark, David Freeman, Nigel Lee, Loraine Boettner, and others educated a core group of Christian thinkers. The books lacked market appeal and were theologically heavy-weighted. Mr. Craig was certainly motivated by a love of Christian scholarship rather than mere profits.

———*Intellectual Schizophrenia: Culture, Crisis and Education*. Phillipsburg, NJ: Presbyterian and Reformed Publishing Company, 1980. This book originally appeared in 1961, long before most Christians realized there was an educational and cultural crisis.

——— *The Messianic Expectations of American Education*. Philipsburg: Presbyterian and Reformed Publishing Company, 1963. A history consisting largely of intellectual sketches of American educators.

——— *The Myth of Overpopulation* Fairfax, VA: Thoburn Press, 1975. Parts of this book may now be dated, but the overall thesis—seen in the title—still stands.

———*The Nature of the American System*. The second of Rushdoony's two brilliant and path-breaking studies of American history.

——— *The One and the Many* Fairfax, Virginia: Thoburn Press, 1971. Andrew Sandlin calls this Rushdoony's best book. As usual, Rushdoony weaves theology, philosophy, and history together with amazing insights.

———*This Independent Republic: Studies in the Nature and Meaning of American History*. Nutley, NJ: The Craig Press, 1964. Without this book, my book would never have been written.

———*World History Notes*. Vallecito: Ross House Books, 1974. The updated version is titled *A Christian Survey of World History*. I wish Rushdoony would have expanded these notes into a full world history.

Rutherford, Samuel, *Letters of Samuel Rutherford.* Edinburgh: Banner of Truth, 1984, reprint. This is the 'spiritual side' of a great and devout Scottish theologian and Reformer. The 'other side' is found in his work *Lex Rex,* which is a classic of Calvinist political philosophy.

Ryken, Leland, *Worldly Saints: The Puritans As They Really Were* Grand Rapids: Academia Books, 1986. Most of Ryken's excellent studies focus on literature and literary concepts. This book is one of the best introductions to Puritan thought and life around.

Sandlin, Andrew, editor, *A Comprehensive Faith: An International Festschrift for Rousas John Rushdoony.* San Jose, CA: Friends of Chalcedon, 1996. Wonderful collection of essays highlighting key aspects of the ministry and writings of Dr. Rushdoony.

Sandoz, Ellis, *Political Sermons of the American Founding Era, 1730-1805.* Indianapolis: Liberty Press, 1991. This collection of sermons is one of the best sources for evidence and examples of the political theology that made the American War for Independence happen in the way it did.

Schaeffer, Edith, *L'Abri.* Wheaton, IL: Crossway Books, 1992. Revised edition. This delightful book tells the story of the ministry of the Schaeffer's in Switzerland.

Schaeffer, Francis, *How Should We Then Live? The Rise and Decline of Western Thought and Culture.* Old Tappan, NJ: Fleming H. Revel Company, 1976. Reviewed in book. Indispensable. All Christian history, literature, art, music, philosophy, elementary, junior high, high school, and college teachers need to thoroughly master this book. The videos are also quite brilliant. Time has not diminished the value of Schaeffer's books for Christian thinkers. Obtain his *Collected Works.*

Schaff, Philip, *History of the Christian Church.* Grand Rapids: William B. Eerdmans Publishing Company, 1910, reprinted 1978. Written by a premier church historian who migrated to America, this affordably priced set is invaluable as a reference work and is also good inspiring reading. Its coverage, however, extends only to the Reformation.

———*The Principle of Protestantism.* Eugene, Oregon: Wipf and Stock Publishers, 2004 reprint.

Schama, Simon, *Citizens: A Chronicle of the French Revolution.* New York: Alfred A. Knopf, Inc., 1989). A more realistic version of the French fiasco.

Schlossberg, Herbert, *Idols for Destruction: Christian Faith and its Confrontation with American Society*. Nashville: Thomas Nelson Publishers, 1983. Incredibly brilliant book chocked full of great quotes. Sizes up the culture war in the 1980s.

Schmidt, Alvin J., *Under the Influence: How Christianity Transformed Civilization* Grand Rapids: Zondervan, 2001. Reviewed in this book. Now retitled as *How Christianity Changed the World*. Great for reading and reference.

Schriver, George, *Philip Schaff: Christian Scholar and Ecumenical Prophet*. Macon, Georgia: Mercer University Press, 1987.

Schweikart, Larry and Michael Allen, *A Patriot's History of the United States*. New York: Sentinel, 2004. One of several useful conservative histories of the United States.

Scott, Christina Dawson, *A Historian and His World: A Life of Christopher Dawson*. New Brunswick: Transaction Publishers, 1992. This is the only complete biography of Dawson. Written by his daughter, it is an outstanding book that aptly introduces a great historian.

Scott, Otto, *James I: The Fool as King*. Vallecito: Ross House Books, 1986 reprint. Reviewed in this book. King James I was basically a jerk.

——*The Professional: A Biography of JB Saunders* New York: Atheneum, 1976. This story of a successful oilman also chronicles the political history of twentieth century America.

—— *Robespierre: The Voice of Virtue* New York: Mason and Lipscomb Publishers, 1974. A later reprinting by a different publisher had the subtitle *The Fool as Revolutionary*. Good overview of the French Revolution.

——*The Secret Six: John Brown and the Abolitionist Movement*. New York: Times Books, 1979. Any study of the War Between the States and its causes must include this book.

Scott, Otto, R. J. Rushdoony, and others, *The Great Christian Revolution*. Vallecito: Ross House Books, 1991. The bulk of this work, which is Scott's contribution, covers the events in Europe from the late Renaissance to Restoration Era in England after Cromwell.

Shakespeare, William, *Complete Plays*. Various editions. A history teacher not well acquainted with the plays of Shakespeare? Unthinkable. A Christian teacher or minister not grounded in Shakespeare? Abominable.

Shelley, Bruce L., *Church History in Plain Language*. Dallas: Word Publishing, 1995. Short chapters with events told in story form. Most readable and yet accurate and scholarly.

Shepherd, Norman, *The Call of Grace: How Covenant Illuminates Salvation and Evangelism.* Phillipsburg: P & R Publishing, 2000. Short study by a controversial theologian.

Shirer, William, *The Rise and Fall of the Third Reich.* New York: Simon and Schuster, 1960. Shirer's still popular history grew out of his experiences as a reporter in Nazi Germany.

Simmons, Tracy Lee, *Climbing Parnassus: A New Apologia for Greek and Latin.* Wilmington, DE: ISI Books, 2002. A great and daunting challenge to climb the peaks of academic excellence that constitute classical education. By calling for reading the classics in the original languages—primarily—Simmons calls for more than most of us in this generation can accomplish.

Singer, C. Gregg, *A Theological Interpretation of American History.* Nutley: NJ: The Craig Press, 1974. Reviewed in the book. Still the best supplemental survey of theological, social, and political ideas that affected and often harmed the nation. The Christian history teacher absolutely must read this book.

———*Christian Approaches: To Philosophy, To History.* Craig Press, 1978. Two short essays, both quite good. Unfortunately, out of print.

——— *John Calvin: His Roots and Fruits.* Philadelphia, PA: The Presbyterian and Reformed Publishing Company, 1974. Cited and discussed in the book. Useful survey of Calvin's influence in a number of areas of thought and life.

——— *From Rationalism to Irrationality: The Decline of the Western Mind from the Renaissance to the Present.* Phillipsburg, NJ: Presbyterian and Reformed Publishing Company, 1979. Singer's Christian historiography is reviewed in my book. This is a useful resource or supplement for studies in Western Civilization or philosophy.

Smith, Page, editor, *Religious Origins of the American Revolution.* Missoula, Montana: Scholars Press, 1976. Wonderful collection of original source material by a most apt historian.

Smith, Ralph A., *Trinity and Reality: An Introduction to the Christian Faith.* Moscow, ID: Canon Press, 2004. Useful for theology classes, Sunday school, or worldview studies. Emphasizes that the doctrine of the Trinity applies to every aspect of Christian life. Smith, a missionary in Japan, has authored two shorter, more technical books on the Trinity; they are *Eternal Covenant: How the Trinity Shapes Covenant Theology* and *Paradox and Truth: Rethinking Van Til on the Trinity,* both published by Canon Press.

Stark, Rodney, *The Victory of Reason: How Christianity Led to Freedom, Capitalism, and Western Success.* New York: Random House, 2005. Reviewed in this book. Stark is actually a sociologist by training. He has emerged as one of the best Christian historians around in this day. A previous work of Stark's is *The Rise of Christianity: How the Obscure, Marginal Jesus Movement Became the Dominant Religious Force in the Western World in a Few Centuries* and most recently, he wrote *Cities of God: The Real Story of How Christianity Became an Urban Movement and Conquered Rome.* These books on Christian history—and their long subtitles—are published by Harper Collins.

Stauffer, Ethelbert, *Christ and the Caesars,* translated by K and R. Gregor Smith. Philadelphia: Westminster Press, 1955. A rare work, but a great study of the early church and the culture war between those who acknowledged that Christ was Lord over against those saying that Caesar was Lord.

Stohlman, Martha Lou Lemmon, *John Witherspoon: Parson, Politician, Patriot.* Philadelphia: The Westminster Press, 1976. A biographical account of the great statesman and theologian.

Stonehouse, Ned B., *J. Gresham Machen: A Biographical Memoir.* Edinburgh: The Banner of Truth Trust, 1987. Stonehouse was a friend and colleague of Machen's. This is the definitive biography of a key American theologian and culture warrior of the 1920's and 30's.

Sweet, William Warren, *Religion in Colonial America.* New York: Charles Scribner's Sons, 1942. Sweet, a Methodist, was a most able church historian. His books are worth hunting for and reading.

——*The Story of Religion in America.* New York: Harper & Row, Publishers, 1950.

Taylor, Alan, *American Colonies.* New York: Viking, 2001. Never forget that colonial history covered a long period of time and a wide swath of geography. Our covenantal and political roots are found in the colonial period.

Thompson, George T. and Elizabeth Laurel Hicks, *World History and Cultures in Christian Perspective* Pensacola: A Beka Book, 1985. It may be easy now to find fault with the A Beka history textbooks, but these works laid the foundation for many Christian schools. I still view this book as one of the best world history textbooks around. Also, George Thompson is highly admired for his brilliant history lectures.

Thornton, Bruce, *Greek Ways: How the Greeks Created Western Civilization.* San Francisco: Encounter Books, 2000. This is one of many books that have been written to survey the Greek contribution to Western Civilization.

——— *A Student's Guide to the Classics.* Wilmington, DE: ISI Books. The entire *"A Student's Guide to..."* series of the Intercollegiate Studies Institute are short, conservative, and frequently Christian oriented works providing brief academic surveys for college students. This work is a handy introduction to the Greek and Roman literature.

Tolkien, J. R. R., *The Lord of the Rings,* 3 Volumes. Boston: Houghton Mifflin Company, 1982. Second Edition. In a real sense, this is an historical epic. It not only "feels like history," but it explains the meaning of history and how God raises up heroes from unlikely sources. The movie trilogy is surpassed only by the books themselves.

Trinterud, Leonard J., *The Forming of An American Tradition.* Philadelphia: The Westminster Press, 1949. This is a study of the role of Presbyterianism in the early decades of the American experience.

Tuchman, Barbara, *A Distant Mirror: The Calamitous 14th Century* New York: Ballantine Books, 1978. Reviewed in this book. This work is long and detailed, yet it can stand alone as a history of Medieval life and culture. It was the calamities of the 14th century that were used by God to pave the way for the Reformation of the 16th century.

———*Practicing History: Selected Essays.* New York: Alfred A. Knopf, 1981. Inside look at the mind, education, research style, and beliefs of one of the best narrative historians of the twentieth century. All of Tuchman's books are worth reading.

Tuveson, Ernest Lee, *Redeemer Nation: The Idea of America's Millennial Role.* Chicago: University of Chicago Press, 1968. Postmillennialism in both religious and secular (i.e. Manifest Destiny) forms has dominated much of America's historical vision.

Twelve Southerners, *I'll Take My Stand: The South and the Agrarian Tradition.* Baton Rouge, LA: Louisiana University Press, 1991. One of the greatest books ever written. This book uses the lens of the Southern condition to defend, not the Old South, but a true and Christian civilization and culture. A great apologetic for literature and community.

Van Leewen, Arend Th., *Christianity in World History* New York: Charles Scribner's Sons, 1964. Useful, but not completely satisfying.

Van Til, Cornelius, *The Defense of the Faith.* Phillipsburg: Presbyterian and Reformed Publishing Company, 1967. Van Til was a professor of Apologetics at Westminster Theological Seminary. This work is the best introduction to his overall thought. He has many admirers and ardent followers, including Dr. R. J. Rushdoony, Dr.

Greg Bahnsen, and Dr. John Frame (all of whom authored studies of Van Til). He also had others who strongly disagreed with him. The cornerstone argument in his philosophy is that the truth of God and His Revelation in Scripture and the world around us is inescapable and unmovable. Van Til's theology demands Christian education as a response.

———— *Essays on Christian Education.* Phillipsburg: Presbyterian and Reformed Publishing, 1969. Long before people were worrying about test scores or violence and drugs, Van Til was preaching the necessity of Christian education on the basis of the Lordship of King Jesus over every subject area.

————*A Survey of Christian Epistemology.* Epistemology is the study of the nature of knowledge. Much of our conflict with secular education is over epistemology rather than "facts." Van Til's many books are calling for renewed study in order to truly ground the Christian school movement in a rock solid, i.e., Reformational, theology.

Veith, Jr., Gene Edward, *A Place to Stand: The Word of God in the Life of Martin Luther* Nashville: Cumberland House, 2005. Good introduction to the life and words of the great Protestant Reformer by an author who is faithfully following in Luther's footsteps.

———— *Postmodern Times: A Christian Guide to Contemporary Thought and Culture* Wheaton: Crosssway Books, 1994. Any book by Veith is worth having and reading. For those who read only one book on Postmodernism, this is a great one.

Vercel, Roger, *Bertrand of Brittany: A Biography of Messire Du Guesclin.* New Haven, CT: Yale University Press, 1934. Perhaps this is the only biography of Bertrand of Brittany, and it is rare.

Walker, Williston, *History of the Christian Church.* An older and still most helpful history of the Christian Church.

Warfield, Benjamin B., *Calvin and Augustine.* Phillipsburg, N.J.: The Presbyterian and Reformed Publishing Company, 1980. Warfield was the among the last of the great Calvinistic theologians of Princeton Seminary. He exemplified the scholarly depth, evangelical piety, and Reformed dogmatism that characterized Calvinism at its best.

Weaver, Richard M., *The Southern Tradition at Bay: A History of Postbellum Thought* Washington: Regnery Gateway, 1989. This book is *the* scholarly, intellectual apologetic for the cause of the Old South and the Confederacy. Weaver is also remembered for his book

———*Ideas Have Consequences* (Chicago: University of Chicago Press, 1948), which is a trenchant and brilliantly titled analysis of the debilitating philosophies of the modern world.

Webb, James, *Born Fighting: How the Scots-Irish Shaped America*. New York: Broadway Books, 2004. This is a fun, but slightly erratic history of the Scot-Irish's contribution to American life and culture. The author, a former assistant secretary of the navy under Ronald Reagan, is now a slightly erratic senator from Virginia.

Weigel, George, *The Cube and the Cathedral: Europe, America, and Politics Without God*. New York: Basic Books, 2005. Weigel wrote the authorized biography of Pope John Paul II. He is a Catholic cultural commentator in the tradition of G. K. Chesterton and Christopher Dawson.

Weikhart, Richard, *From Darwin to Hitler—Evolutionary Ethics, Eugenics, and Racism in Germany* New York: Palgrave Macmillan, 2004. Reviewed in this book. A really grim, but necessary book.

Wells, David F., *Above All Earthly Pow'rs: Christ in a Postmodern World*. Grand Rapids, MI: William B. Eerdmans Publishing Company, 2005. This book is the fourth in a series by Wells that has focused upon critiquing the theological and social culture of the West. Basically, Wells has done lots of weighing of modern evangelicalism and found much there that is wanting. His books are tremendously well thought out and scholarly while still retaining a vital evangelical love for God's truth and God's people. The previous volumes in this series are *No Place for Truth; or, Whatever Happened to Evangelical Theology?, God in the Wasteland: The Reality of Truth in a World of Fading Dreams,* and *Losing Virtue: Why the Church Must Recover Its Moral Vision*. All are published by Eerdmans.

Whitcomb, John C. and Henry M. Morris, *The Genesis Flood: The Biblical Record and Its Scientific Implications*. Phillipsburg: Presbyterian and Reformed Publishers, 1961. A theologian and a scientist teamed up and wrote a book that is still inflicting damage on the once seemingly impregnable world of Darwinism.

White, Henry Alexander, *Southern Presbyterian Leaders*. New York: Neale Publishing Company, 1911. Once a rare book, the Banner of Truth Trust has reprinted it. This is great historical writing and is reviewed and frequently footnoted in my book.

Wilkins, J. Steven, *All Things for God: The Steadfast Fidelity of Stonewall Jackson*. Nashville: Cumberland House Books, 2004. Pastor Steve Wilkins is one of the best lecturers and teachers of American history around today. His audiotape series *America, the First 350 Years* has blessed many Christian students and teachers. His biographies of Jackson and Lee are great introductions to the faith and character of the two most beloved Southern Christian generals in the War Between the States.

———*Call of Duty: The Sterling Nobility of Robert E. Lee.* Nashville: Cumberland House Books, 1996.

Wilson, Clyde N., *Carolina Cavalier: The Life and Mind of James Johnston Pettigrew* Athens, GA: The University of Georgia Press, 1990. Pettigrew led his North Carolinians on that third day at Gettyburg up that same ridge that earned Pickett the name and shame of that failed charge. North Carolinians call it Pettigrew's charge. Blame for the failure of the charge has been amply passed around to quite a few participants.

Wilson, Douglas, *My Life for Yours.* Moscow, Idaho: Canon Press, 2004. One of many edifying Wilson books on the Christian family. Wilson is the father of the modern classical Christian school movement. He rightly recognizes that the classroom can never succeed in raising youth if the family is not what it should be.

———*The Paideia of God.* Moscow, ID: Canon Press, 1999. This collection of essays highlights a number of issues classical Christian schools face, such as questions about dress and uniforms and whether or not you have to be Reformed to be classical.

———*Recovering the Lost Tools of Learning: An Approach to Distinctively Christian Education* Wheaton, Illinois: Crossway Books, 1991. This is the book to start with to understand and implement classical Christian education.

Wilson, Douglas and Ty Fisher, *Omnibus I: Biblical and Classical Civilizations* Lancaster, PA: Veritas Press, 2004. Subsequent books in this series cover the Medieval and Modern periods of history. This series contains useful essays and commentaries on historical, theological, and literary works by different authors. Great resource.

Wolters, Albert M., *Creation Regained: Biblical Basics for a Reformational Worldview,* Second Edition Grand Rapids, MI: William B. Eerdmans Publishing Company, 2005. Useful for developing and refining a Christian worldview. Wolters is a disciple of Herman Dooyeweerd.

Woods, Thomas E., Jr., *How the Catholic Church Built Western Civilization* Washington, D.C.: Regnery Publishing Company, 2005. Reviewed in this book. Woods has also written *The Politically Incorrect Guide to American History.* He may well be the American Christopher Dawson.

Wurmbrand, Richard, *Tortured for Christ* Hayfield Publishers, 1967. This first-hand testimony of a victim of Communist terror is a classic. Wurmbrand spent his life preaching the Gospel of Christ and seeking to inform a sluggish West about the evils of Communism. Along with the writings of Alexander Solzhenitsyn and others, Wurmbrand's message finally got through. His organization, The Voice of the Martyrs, still labors to inform Christians about their brethren who are being tortured for Christ throughout the world.

Yeats, W. B., *The Collected Poetry of W.B. Yeats* New York: Scribners Paperback Poetry, 1989. Yeats' poetry not only earned him acclaim and a Noble Prize for Literature, it also convinced C. S. Lewis that a modern man could reject materialism as a philosophy.

Young, Thomas Daniel. *Gentleman in a Dustcoat: A Biography of John Crowe Ransom*. Baton Rouge, LA: Louisiana State University Press, 1976. The definitive biography of Dr. John Crowe Ransom, a key leader of the Fugitive Poets, the Agrarian movement, and the New Critics.

Money cannot buy happiness, but it can buy books.

Subject Index

A

á Kempis, Thomas 49, 210
Abolitionists 158
Accelerated Christian Education 8
Adams, John
    69, 151, 167, 285, 328, 340
Africanus, Scipio 38
Agrarian 2
Alaric 60, 100, 101
Alexander the Great 30, 189
Alfred the Great 48
American War for Independence
    11, 72, 328, 342, 343, 345
Anti-Federalists 73
Aristotle 44, 189, 380
Association for Classical Christian
    Schools 64
Augustine 45, 56, 60, 104, 105,
    106, 107, 108, 109, 201

B

Backus, Isaac 305, 343
Bahnsen, Greg 9, 140, 389
Bainton, Roland 279
Bancroft, George 278, 321, 327
Barca, Hamilcar 26
Billington, James H. 168
Birzer, Bradley 72
Bismarck 19
Blumenfeld, Samuel 9
Boettner, Loraine 5, 6, 137, 258, 308
Booth, Randy 9, 45
Bradford, Ernle 33, 217, 219
Bradford, William 295
Brown, John 74, 165, 171
Bryan, William Jennings 374, 383
Buchanan, George 169, 276
Burke, Edmund 167

Bush, George 396
Bush, George W. 42

C

Caesar, Augustus 16
Cahill, Thomas
    75, 99, 109, 190, 191, 199, 203
Calhoun, John C. 152
Calvin, John 3, 15, 49, 65, 91,
    93, 127, 256, 257, 258, 263–
    265, 275, 288, 314, 342, 353
Calvinism 5, 6, 93, 157, 158, 169,
    270, 272, 281, 290, 305, 308,
    333, 341
Carthage 25
Catholic Church 91
Charles Dickens 167
Charles I 274, 297
Charles V of Spain 215
Chaucer 48, 210
Chesterton, G. K. 28, 31, 106
Chilton, David 140
Church Fathers 87, 94
Churchill, Winston
    62, 73, 113, 123, 124, 399
Clark, Gordon
    21, 106, 135, 140, 198, 392
classical Christian education
    9, 10, 43, 53, 58, 68, 81
Cleveland, Grover 73
Colonial America 55
Columbus, Christopher 111, 112, 256
Communism 5, 32
Confederate armies 62
Constantine 88, 94, 98, 100
Cornwallis 62, 337, 338, 343, 370
Cortes 74

Coulter, Ann 13, 242
Cowan, Louise 380
Creationists 238, 241
Cromwell, Oliver 274

D

Dabney, Robert L.
   21, 80, 87, 365, 372
Dante 48
Darrow, Clarence 374
Darwin, Charles 237, 239, 240
Darwinian Evolution 13, 39
Darwinians 13, 15
Darwinism
   12, 238, 241, 242, 374, 375, 376
D'Aubigne, Merle 278
Davidson, Donald 250, 351, 380
Davis, Jefferson 173
Dawson, Christopher
   5, 44, 46, 47, 106, 109, 111,
   112, 113, 114, 115, 117, 119,
   120, 179, 199, 203, 267, 283,
   308
Deism 171
DeMar, Gary 140, 316
Democrats 4
Dickens, Charles 83, 99, 167
Diet of Worms 61, 261
Dooyeweerd, Herman
   14, 15, 145, 393
Durant, Will 101, 103, 151, 390

E

Edict of Milan 21, 98
Edwards, Jonathan 232, 298, 355
Eliot, T. S.
   46, 116, 175, 250, 382, 392
Emerson, Ralph Waldo 158, 172, 233
Enlightenment 152, 168
Erasmus, Desiderius 49, 54
Eusbius of Caesarea 88
Eusebius 87, 89, 90, 94, 95, 97, 98
Evolution 12, 13

F

Fabius 33, 37
Farel, William 264
Faulkner, William 26, 66, 358, 399
Federalists 73
Fischer, David Hackett 349
Fitzgerald, F. Scott 245, 247, 248, 249
Founding Era 50
France 32
Frelinghuysen, Theodore Jacob 303
French 32
French Revolution
   152, 165, 166, 167, 168

G

Genovese, Eugene D.
   5, 113, 159, 359
Gibbon, Edward 100, 115, 231, 390
Gibson, Mel 38, 328, 396
Gildersleeve, Basil L. 55
Godawa, Brian 77
Goldwater, Barry 144, 395
Gonzales, Justo 90, 92
Gorbachev, Mikhail 63
Grant, George
   6, 77, 103, 105, 140, 371
Great Awakening 306, 307, 355
Great Depression 248, 373, 382, 384
Greco-Roman World. 23
Greek 45, 56, 82
Groote, Gerard 49, 210
Guesclin, du Bertrand 207
Gummere, Richard M. 50

H

Haeckel, Ernst 239
Hakluyt, Richard 289
Hall, David 265, 269, 276, 277, 279,
   311, 314, 339, 341
Hamilton, Alexander 232, 328
Hamilton, Edith 187, 190
Hannibal 26, 27, 28, 30, 32, 33,
   34, 35, 37, 39, 101

Subject Index

Hanson, Victor Davis
  44, 45, 197, 221, 251
Harbison, E. Harris 263, 267, 269
Hayes, Carleton J. H. 24
Hemingway, Ernest
  245, 247, 248, 249, 382
Henry, Patrick 57
Henry V 208
Henry VIII 19, 272
Herodotus 44, 54, 68, 176, 178,
  189, 195, 196, 369
Himmelfarb, Gertrude 225–233
Hitler, Adolph 19, 237, 240
Hodge, Charles 5, 307
Holocaust 15, 68
Homer
  41, 44, 50, 53, 56, 192, 194, 380
Hoover, Herbert 382
Hughes, Phillip E. 14
Huguenots
  271, 287, 288, 303, 304, 318
Hus, Jan 210

I

Intelligent Design 13, 238, 241
Islamic Terrorism 32

J

Jackson, Stonewall 79, 80
James I 73, 165, 168, 170, 274, 297
Jamestown 290, 291, 293
Jay, John 51
Jefferson, Thomas 41, 62, 69
Johnson, Lyndon 387
Johnson, Paul
  92, 164, 178, 321, 329, 341, 390
Johnson, Phillip E. 241
Jordan, James 140, 161
junior high 64, 66, 68
Justinian I 60

K

Kirk, Russell 75, 198, 395
Knox, John 105, 275, 314, 354
Kreeft, Peter 17
Kuyper, Abraham
  7, 123, 143, 145, 148, 255, 269

L

La Valette, Jean 217
L'Abri 390
Latin 4, 54, 56, 82
Latourette, Kenneth Scott 91, 312
Lee, Francis Nigel 140
Lee, Robert E. 28, 80, 172
Leithart, Peter J. 197
Lewis, C. S. 17, 23, 36, 38, 48, 56,
  76, 98, 106, 116, 245, 247,
  353, 392
Luther, Martin
  19, 49, 61, 74, 93, 256–
  258, 353, 357
Lytle, Andrew Nelson 11, 107, 323

M

MacArthur, Douglas 28
MacArthur, John 352
Machen, J. Gresham
  11, 20, 106, 128, 140, 375,
  377, 383, 385, 390, 393
Madison, James 69
Makamie, Francis 370
Malta 61, 213–223, 215
Mann, Horace 146
Mansfield, Stephen 69, 130, 372
Marsden, George 375
Marxists 5, 76
Maximus, Quintus Fabius 32
McCullough, David
  328, 346–347, 349
McNeill, John T. 297, 301, 303
Medieval
  47, 48, 49, 203, 206, 209, 259
Melancthon 49

Melville, Andrew 276
Mencken, H. L. 296
Middle Ages 46, 48, 182
Miller, Perry
 151, 155, 156, 290, 292, 316
Modernism 376
Monasteries 202
Morison, Samuel Eliot 123
Morris, Henry 241
Muggeridge, Malcolm 17
Muslims 17

N

Napoleon 28, 71
Naugle, David 20
Nazism 32
Netherlands 271, 294
New Deal 20
Nixon, Richard 388
North, Gary 140, 146, 243, 342, 384

O

O'Connor, Flannery 56
Orr, James 127
Orthodox Presbyterian Church 378
Orwell, George 76, 175

P

Palmer, B. B. 159
Pearce, Joseph 5
Pearcey, Nancy 242
Pelikan, Jaroslav 92, 99
Pendleton, Rev. William N. 81, 82
Pendleton, Sandie 79, 80, 81, 82, 83
Pendleton, William Nelson 80
Pilgrims 294–295
Plato 16, 44, 189
Polybius 26
Postman, Neil 54
Presbyterian 158, 327, 331, 334, 336, 341, 365, 370, 389
Presbyterianism 332

Presbyterians
 62, 126, 274, 287, 304, 318, 331, 337, 339, 343, 362, 367, 375, 379, 383
Princeton 51
Protestant Reformation 91, 93, 352
Protestant Reformers 8
Protestantism 91
public school 3, 41
Punic Wars 24, 25, 27
Puritan 8, 19, 73, 93, 156, 291, 292, 296, 297, 298, 299, 342

Q

Queen Elizabeth 73, 169, 273

R

Ransom, John Crowe 250, 380
Reagan, Ronald 63, 113, 222, 399
Reformation
 93, 257, 258, 260, 271, 286, 352, 354
Reformed 93
Reformed theology 5
Renaissance 15, 48, 257
Republicans 42
Revere, Paul 52
Richard, Carl J. 25, 26, 50, 198
Robespierre 73, 165, 166, 168
Roman Empire 16, 48, 98
Romans 45
Rome 24
Rookmaker, Hans 393
Roosevelt, Franklin D.
 20, 62, 75, 214, 382
Roosevelt, Theodore 322
Rush, Benjamin 43
Rushdoony, R. J.
 9, 96, 106, 136, 140, 141, 141–162, 227, 229, 277, 311, 392
Rutherford, Samuel 276

Subject Index

S

Sandlin, Andrew 149, 397
Sartre, Jean Paul 15
Sayers, Dorothy 9, 64, 67, 392
Schaeffer, Edith 392
Schaeffer, Francis
　　106, 140, 227, 230, 276, 389,
　　391, 394, 395, 397
Schaff, Philip 88, 89, 90
Schlossberg, Herbert
　　47, 89, 106, 140, 352
Schmidt, Alvin J. 175, 180
Scipio, Publius Cornelius 30, 32, 33
Scopes Trial 12, 241, 374, 383
Scots-Irish 300, 301, 302, 330,
　　331, 332, 336, 338, 363
Scott, Otto 73, 163–173
Second Great Awakening 356
Shaara, Michael 72, 77, 188
Shakespeare, Willaim
　　23, 53, 56, 65, 83, 220
Shakespeare, William 397, 399
Simmons, Tracy Lee 57
Singer, Gregg
　　106, 135, 136, 140, 154, 156,
　　157, 158, 160, 162, 177, 225,
　　227, 230, 255, 268, 311, 392
Smith, John 256, 291
Smith, Ralph 13, 15, 128
Socrates 16
Solzhenitsyn, Alexander 113, 388
Spencer, Herbert 239
Sproul, R. C. 198
St. Patrick of Ireland 61
Stalin, Joseph 19
Stark, Rodney 175, 180
Stauffer, Ethelbert 97
Stein, Gertrude 246, 252
Stuart, Mary 169
Suleiman 214, 221

T

Tacelli, Ronald 17
Tate, Allen 108
Theodora 60
Thoreau, Henry David 158
Thornton, Bruce 188, 191, 196
Thornwell, James Henley
　　53, 54, 57, 159, 366, 369
Thucydides 44, 69, 189, 369
Tocqueville, de Alexis 153
Tolkien, J. R. R.
　　38, 70, 72, 75, 76, 121, 245,
　　247, 250, 251, 252
Tolstoy 26
Transcendentalism 171
Transcendentalists 158
Trivium 45, 130
Tuchman, Barbara
　　151–154, 205, 206, 211, 235,
　　249

U

Unitarianism 158, 171

V

Van Til, Cornelius
　　5, 36, 103, 106, 125, 126, 142,
　　143, 150, 155, 160, 176, 187,
　　377, 389, 390, 393
Van Til, Henry 121
Virgil 48, 51, 187, 380
Visigoths 60, 100, 101
Voltaire 213, 231

W

Waddell, Moses 52
Walker, Williston 91
War Between the States 21, 83, 171
Warfield, Benjamin 6
Washington, George
　　61, 62, 69, 74, 75, 328,
　　345–350

Weaver, Richard S. 360
Weikart, Richard S. 15, 237, 240
Western Civilization
    16, 60, 73, 180, 181, 188, 189,
    220, 229
Westminster Confession of Faith
    12, 126, 274, 353, 364
Westminster Larger and Shorter
    Catechism 365
Westminster Larger Catechism 270
Westminster Shorter Catechism 378
Westminster Standards
    126, 169, 274, 313
Whitaker, Alexander 293
White, Henry Alexander
    52, 334, 338, 362, 371
Whitefield, George
    287, 308, 315, 355
Wilkins, J. Steven 371, 372
Wilson, Clyde N. 2, 54
Wilson, Douglas
    3, 9, 71, 197, 279, 306, 371
Wilson, Woodrow 165, 382
Witherspoon, John
    51, 151, 232, 315, 339
Wolters, Albert M. 21, 126
Woods, Jr., Thomas E. 175, 181
World War I 373, 382, 384
World War II 373, 382, 384
Wurmbrand, Richard 137
Wycliffe, John 210

Y

Yeats, William Butler 5, 100, 193
Yorktown 62